Residential Landscape Architecture

Design Process for the Private Residence

Third Edition

Norman K. Booth, ASLA
The Ohio State University

James E. Hiss, ASLA
The Ohio State University

Prentice Hall

Upper Saddle River, New Jersey 07458

Library of Congress Cataloging-in-Publication Data

Booth, Norman K.
   Residential landscape architecture : design process for the private residence / Norman
K. Booth, James E. Hiss. — 3rd ed.
     p. cm.
   ISBN 0-13-027827-0
   1. Landscape architecture.   2. Architecture, Domestic.   3. Homesites—Planning.   I. Hiss,
James E.   II. Title.

SB473 .B57 2002
712′.6—dc21

                                                         2001021431

Editor-in-Chief: Stephen Helba
Executive Editor: Debbie Yarnell
Associate Editor: Kimberly Yehle
Production Editor: Mary Jo Graham, Carlisle Publishers Services
Production Liaison: Eileen M. O'Sullivan
Director of Manufacturing and Production: Bruce Johnson
Managing Editor: Mary Carnis
Manufacturing Buyer: Cathleen Petersen
Design Director: Cheryl Asherman
Senior Design Coordinator: Miguel Ortiz
Cover Design: Blair Brown
Marketing Manager: Jimmy Stephens
Composition: Carlisle Communications, Ltd.
Printing and Binding: Courier Westford

Prentice-Hall International (UK) Limited, London
Prentice-Hall of Australia Pty. Limited, Sydney
Prentice-Hall Canada Inc., Toronto
Prentice-Hall Hispanoamericana, S.A., Mexico
Prentice-Hall of India Private Limited, New Delhi
Prentice-Hall of Japan, Inc., Tokyo
Prentice-Hall Singapore Pte. Ltd.
Editora Prentice-Hall do Brasil, Ltda., Rio de Janeiro

10 9 8 7 6 5 4 3
ISBN 0-13-027827-0

To all those who aspire to craft
quality residential landscapes

Contents

Chapter 13
Special Project Sites   385

Preface

The planning and design of a residential site is an exciting and challenging endeavor for the design professional. It is exciting because the designer works closely with the clients on a personal basis, deals with the design in a detailed and artistic manner, and typically has the opportunity to see a design that has been created on paper become a three-dimensional reality in a rather short period of time. Residential site design is challenging because it directly affects the quality of life of the people who live with the design each day. Well-executed residential site design can positively influence the quality of life by eliminating functional conflicts on the site, providing proper recreational and leisure amenities, and creating an environment that is visually and functionally pleasurable.

Yet, despite the potential significance of residential site design, it is an endeavor that is commonly done inadequately, inappropriately, and, in some cases, incorrectly. A drive or a walk along a typical suburban street reveals a host of problems and offenses to the eye. Highly manicured foundation planting, overgrown plant material, inadequately sized driveways, poorly conceived approach walks and entrances, and shapeless lawn areas are just a few common problems. The areas in the back of homes are no less guilty of poor layout and visual chaos.

There are numerous interrelated reasons for these typical problems with residential sites. The list includes a lack of homeowner appreciation for good design, traditional acceptance of outdated standards concerning site development for a residence, inappropriate maintenance techniques, and financial limitations. Also on the list is a lack of understanding and training in the fundamentals of design by some of those who plan and implement residential sites.

Many individuals who are currently designing and installing residential sites are doing so as a result of on-the-job training with little or no formal design education. Furthermore, those trained as landscape architects are more often involved with larger, more complex design projects or are generally perceived as unaffordable by the average homeowner.

Consequently, the purpose of this book is to furnish the reader with the quality fundamentals of residential site design. It is written by designers/educators and presents basic principles, concepts, and procedures for preparing site plans and associated documents for residential sites. This book is primarily intended for readers who are beginning their design careers as well as for those currently practicing residential design who wish to enhance their skills and knowledge.

Chapter 1 discusses the attributes and inadequacies of typical residential site design practices. Chapter 2 presents the overall design premise that this book is based upon, that of the "outdoor room." Chapter 3 presents and illustrates techniques for designing a residential site in an environmentally responsible manner. Chapter 4 outlines a design process used by a designer to conceive, formulate, prepare, and present design solutions for a residential site. The considerations and procedures for initially accepting a project and working with clients are discussed in Chapter 5. Chapter 6 describes the tasks of site measurement and documentation, as well as the preparation of base drawings. Chapter 7 explains the development of a site analysis and design program, while Chapter 8 illustrates the process and development of functional diagrams, which provide organizational structure for proposed designs. In Chapter 9 the thoughts and processes of preliminary design are explained along with a description of basic design principles used in this phase. Chapter 10 provides the reader with the principles of form composition for establishing a design theme, while Chapter 11 presents ideas for spatial composition. Chapter 12 discusses the process and considerations involved in preparing the master plan. Chapter 13, a new chapter, provides guidelines for designing for specialty sites: the corner site, the wooded site, the sloped site and the townhouse garden.

While other books also address the subject of residential site design, including some of the topics previously outlined, this book is unique in that it clearly illustrates and discusses the actual procedures and underlying principles used by experienced residential site designers. The chapters on functional diagrams and form composition should be especially helpful to the reader. These subjects are most critical in creating functionally and visually successful design solutions; yet they are typically the subjects given little or no attention. The development of alternative design studies, at various levels in the design, is also a unique feature of the book. In addition, information has been included to assist designers to become more sensitive to the environment. These subjects, as well as others in the book, are presented in a "how-to" manner so the reader can easily apply the concepts.

This book also approaches residential site design with the underlying thought that the site associated with a home should be conceived as a series of outdoor rooms. These outdoor rooms are the basic structure of a good design and possess functions similar to those inside. In many instances, outdoor rooms serve as both literal and figurative extensions of indoor living. This book discusses what outdoor rooms are, how they can be created, how they can be designed into a site, and how to select and compose materials to furnish them.

Residential site design is not treated in this book as cosmetic decoration applied to a site only to enhance the appearance of the house. While both house and site should be considered together, good site design is more than "horticultural makeup," strategically placed around the exterior of a home to provide a pretty setting. Similarly, this book does not consider residential site design to be "landscaping" or the simple arranging of plant materials around a house. Indeed, plant materials fulfill numerous prominent roles in design, but they are not the only, nor necessarily the most important, elements used by designers to create exterior space. This book is primarily a design book and so the reader does not find a plant list nor other specific information on the growth and characteristics of plant materials.

Some of the thoughts and principles in this book represent commonly accepted design knowledge and are used as a matter of standard practice by experienced designers. Other ideas have evolved from the classroom where we have spent over 40 combined years teaching college students, nurserymen, and landscape contractors. We have discovered a number of concepts and teaching techniques that are felt to be essential in teaching and learning residential site design. Finally, there are a number of thoughts in this book that have resulted from our own practices in the area of residential site design. We are both registered landscape architects and have designed over 100 residential sites, a variety of them winning local, state, and national design awards.

We hope that you enjoy this book as much as we enjoy designing.

Norman K. Booth
James E. Hiss

1

The Typical Residential Site

INTRODUCTION

Those who deal with the design and development of residential landscapes are concerned with three important and unique aspects of each project: (1) the client, (2) the site, and (3) the home. No two clients, no two sites, and no two homes are the same. Each client has his or her own set of attributes, desires, wishes, lifestyles, etc., that makes each client special. Likewise, each site is distinctive from the next, due to topography, views, vegetation, surrounding site conditions, and so on. In addition, each home is characteristically different due to such details as its architectural character, floor plans, decorations, furniture, and accessories.

The site surrounding a residence is a most important environment. It serves numerous utilitarian, aesthetic, and psychological functions for the residents as well as for visitors, neighbors, and passersby. As a setting for the house, the residential site is the context or surroundings within which one views the architecture of the house. As the location for outdoor living, the residential site can be thought of as an exterior extension of the functions which occur inside the home. Socializing, eating, cooking, reading, sunbathing, recreating, gardening, or simply relaxing are all activities which can take place on the residential site. In addition, the site can be considered an expression of the lifestyle and values of the residents. It can reflect their personality and attitude toward their own environment, and the site can be a refuge from the routine and pressures of daily events. The sound of birds in the trees, the fragrance of a flowering plant, or the sight of a picturesque tree can provide the mind and emotions with pleasurable thoughts and feelings.

Consequently, it is critical that the residential site be designed with the utmost care and sensitivity so it indeed fulfills its vital role in the overall residential environment. But, does the typical residential site actually meet this standard? Does it really provide a proper setting for the house, furnish pleasant outdoor spaces for living, or simply function in a desirable manner? Does the average site

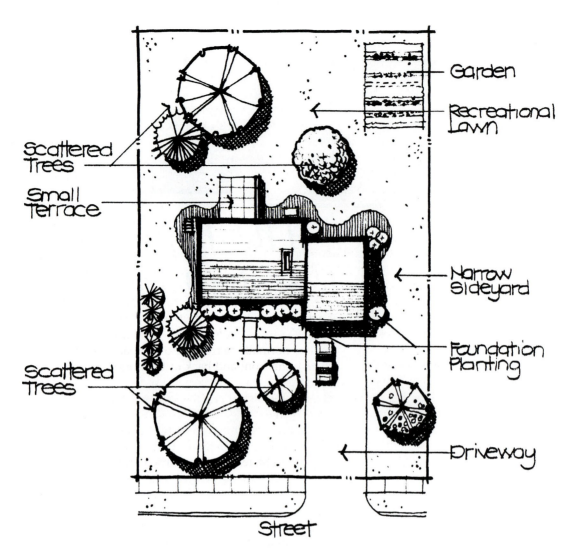

FIGURE 1-1
The typical residential site.

look attractive and provide a sense of pleasure for the eye and mind? And, does the residential site serve as a haven from daily rigors?

This chapter addresses these questions as they relate to the typical single family residential site in the United States. The first section of the chapter provides an overview of what a common residential site looks like. The second section analyzes the visual and functional qualities of front yards, back yards, and side yards of the typical residential site. The third section deals with some typical architectural styles of houses, the importance of architectural character and the need for the landscape designer to develop landscape designs that blend the house and site together. This is done to provide the foundation for making suggestions on improving the process and quality of residential site design in subsequent chapters.

THE TYPICAL RESIDENTIAL SITE

A drive or walk through almost any residential neighborhood in the United States reveals a number of commonalities among the houses and sites surrounding them. What is usually seen (Figure 1–1) is a one- or two-story house surrounded by an expanse of lawn and various plantings. Regardless of the size of the site, the house is usually placed near the middle of the site, thus creating front and back yards of similar sizes and narrow side yards.

The front yard is most often thought of as a public setting for the house. A lawn, often manicured to create a lush green carpet, occupies most of this area with a driveway situated along one side of the site. In arid areas of the country, the lawn area may be replaced with gravel or decomposed granite. The front yard is often dotted with trees, shading various parts of the yard. Typically, there is a row of plants which extends along the entire base of the house. This foundation planting often consists of only coniferous or broad-leaved evergreens which provide a year-round wall of green color. Finally, a narrow walk extends from the driveway and/or street to the front door of the house.

The back yard is the most varied area of the typical residential site. In older neighborhoods, or those found in western states of the country, the back yard is usually enclosed with walls, fences, or plantings. In these situations, the back yard is apt to be the most private area on the site. In newer neighborhoods, especially in the eastern and midwestern regions of the country, the back yard is often very open with little or no definition of where one property ends and another begins. In these conditions, there is little privacy in the back yard. On most residential sites, the back yard is a more utilitarian area than the front yard and is the location of the outdoor terrace, work space, garden, and open lawn for recreation. It is usually the location for outdoor living activities. On other sites, the back yard provides little or no use to the residents; it is just leftover outdoor space that must be maintained.

The side yards are normally narrow leftover spaces with little use except to provide access between the front and back of the house. Consequently, there are few elements occupying this space except perhaps for scattered plantings, air conditioners or heat pumps, and stored objects such as wood, trailers, and other items that do not conveniently fit in the garage or basement.

While this generalized description of the typical residential site of course does not apply to every site, it does summarize common characteristics of residential sites throughout the United States. What is particularly surprising and disturbing is that this "typical site" can be seen in all regions of the country from New England to Arizona, and from Florida to California. True, there are regional variations in use of materials (especially plant materials), construction techniques, and attitudes toward the use and style of the residential site. Still, many similarities prevail in terms of size, function, organization, and general appearance of residential sites.

Let us turn to a more critical analysis of the three major areas of the residential site: (1) front yard (often referred to as the public space), (2) back yard (commonly referred to as the private space), and (3) side yards (usually not thought of as space at all). The conditions cited in the following paragraphs are summaries of observations of single-family residential sites in the United States.

Front Yard

The front yard of most residential sites has two primary functions: (1) it is the setting or foreground for viewing the house from the street, and (2) it is the public area for arrival and entrance into the house. In terms of its function as a setting, the front yard provides the "frame" for viewing the "picture" of the house from the street. Much attention is given to arranging plant materials along the base of the house and in the yard to establish "curb appeal." That is, the front yard and house are attractive to look at from the street.

The front yard is also a public area where the main arrival and entry to the house are usually located. The residents of the house along with their relatives, friends, and other visitors use this public space as an introduction to the site.

Keeping these two functions in mind, let us look more closely at specific conditions of typical front yards.

1. Front Lawn Lacks Edges. On many residential sites, the house is placed near the middle of the lot in a manner that creates an open front lawn. The scale of this area often gives a feeling of an anonymous "no-man's land" because of its

FIGURE 1-2
Many front yards lack defined edges.

FIGURE 1-3
The driveway is a dominant visual element of many front yards.

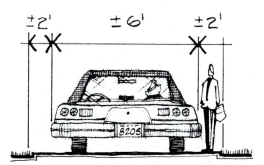

openness and undefined edges. This quality is frequently compounded when the front lawn of one site blends into the neighboring front lawn with no separation or division between the two (Figure 1–2).

2. Driveway Dominates View.   The driveway is a dominant visual element of many front yards (Figure 1–3). This extensive area of asphalt or concrete is generally not very appealing to the eye. With cars parked in the driveway, there is often little or no room for people to walk except along the narrow edge or on the lawn (Figure 1–4). This may be acceptable in good weather but can be an inconvenience in wet weather or during the winter when snow is piled along the edges of the driveway.

3. Prominence of Garage Door.   A related problem of some front yards is the prominence of the garage door. A garage door that directly faces the street and takes up a large portion of the front of the house becomes a significant visual feature of the front yard. When a driveway is lined with shrubs, the garage door is accentuated even more because a noticeable axis is formed leading the eye toward the garage door (Figure 1–5). By comparison, the front door often seems insignificant and secondary.

4. Entry Walk too Narrow.   The walk leading from the driveway to the front door is typically about three feet wide. This dimension is narrow and forces people to walk in single-file fashion (Figure 1–6).

5. Entry Walk Hidden from View.   Another problem of the entry walk is that it is not easily seen, especially where it connects to the edge of the driveway (Figure 1–7). In such cases, there is nothing to acknowledge or call attention to the location of the entry walk.

6. Entry Walk Lacks Visual Interest.   As a person proceeds along the entry walk, there is very little visual interest. A large open expanse of lawn on one side of the walk and a wall of foundation planting on the other side (Figure 1–8) usually do not provide a memorable experience. And the walk's pavement material often lacks a distinct character or appeal. It is simply a rather dull environment to walk through to get to the front door.

7. Entry Foyer too Small.   A concrete pad or stoop located at the front door serves as the outdoor foyer or arrival area. It is often so small in size that no one can stand on it while the storm or screen door is being opened without getting hit in the face or stepping away from the stoop (Figure 1–9).

8. Entry Foyer Lacks Enclosure.   The entry area or foyer often lacks an adequate sense of separation from the street and the rest of the front yard. The stoop is often exposed directly to the street or even to the neighbor's house across the

FIGURE 1–5
Shrubs lining a driveway over accentuate the view to the garage.

FIGURE 1–6
The typical 3-foot-wide entrance walk forces
people to walk single file.

FIGURE 1–7
Many entrance walks are hidden from view.

FIGURE 1–8
An open lawn and a dull foundation planting provide little visual interest from the entry walk.

street so that everyone can easily see the comings and goings of visitors (Figure 1–10). Also the entry is apt to be directly exposed to such climatic elements as hot summer sun, cold winter wind, or precipitation. All of these factors make it uncomfortable for a visitor to stand very long outside the front door.

9. Hidden Front Door. An opposite problem of some outside arrival and entry areas is that the front door is hidden from view. This most often results from overgrown plant materials screening out the view of the front door (Figure 1–11). For a first-time visitor, not knowing exactly where the front door is can be an uncomfortable and confusing feeling.

10. Foundation Planting. The use of plants in the front yard is frequently limited to foundation planting—the practice of lining the foundation of a house with a row of shrubs (Figure 1–12). These shrubs, typically evergreen for year-round green color, are often manicured to establish such geometric forms as cubes, pyramids, and spheres (or if you like, footballs, pop cans, ice cream cones, boxes, and so on) (Figure 1–13). This visual treatment of plant materials is characteristic of historic Italian and French gardens, where plants were sheared and clipped into formal shapes to reflect the strong formal character of the gardens and the architecture.

The Typical Residential Site

FIGURE 1-9
Many entrance stoops are too small, making it
awkward to open the door.

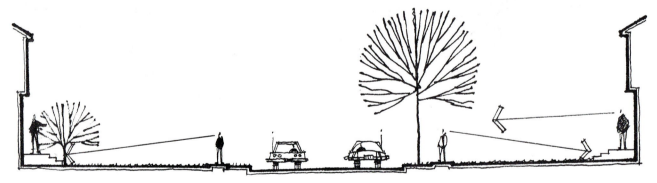

FIGURE 1-10
Many outdoor foyers lack spatial enclosure and separation from the front yard, the street, and neighbors.

Foundation planting has been used in the United States since the late 1800s to hide high foundation walls that resulted from houses constructed several feet above the ground to provide basements for gravity-air furnaces. However, most contemporary houses have little or no foundation wall exposed. Another problem of foundation planting is that it is seen more by passersby on the street than by the homeowners. Foundation planting cannot be seen from within the house unless a person is standing at the window (Figure 1–14).

11. Overgrown Foundation Planting. A major problem with many foundation plantings is that they are overgrown to the point of obstructing windows of

FIGURE 1-12
Typical "foundation planting."

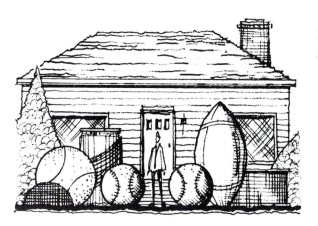

FIGURE 1-13
Foundation plants are often trimmed into precise geometric shapes resembling footballs, baseballs, etc.

FIGURE 1-14
Sometimes foundation planting cannot be seen from inside the house unless a person is standing at the window.

FIGURE 1-15
Overgrown foundation plants often hide windows and reduce the amount of sunlight entering the house.

the house and crowding adjoining entry walks. On some sites, the windows on the first floor of the house are completely covered with a mass of foliage, thus blocking out light and views to the outdoors (Figure 1–15). One reaction some homeowners have to this is to permanently close the window shades to block the view to the back of the shrubs just outside.

12. Scattered Plants in Lawn. Trees and shrubs located in the front yard are sometimes placed randomly throughout the yard so as to "fill" the lawn area (Figure 1–16). This often makes maneuvering a lawn mower like driving through an obstacle course.

13. Little Enjoyment of Front Yard. One overall characteristic of many front yards is that they lack a memorable image or style. Many front yards are bland, unexciting, and similar to the others in the neighborhood.

Most front yards are only public settings for the house and provide little opportunity for outdoor living or enjoyment by the residents. There are few places in most front yards to sit, have a cup of coffee, talk with a friend, or read a book.

The challenge is for designers to improve these conditions so that the front yard can become an attractive, useful, and inviting space on the residential site.

FIGURE 1–16
Plants are often located randomly in front yards in a manner that fills the entire yard.

Back Yard

The function of the back yard on the typical residential site is to accommodate a number of activities including (1) outdoor living and entertaining, (2) recreation, and (3) utilitarian activities such as gardening and storage. To support these activities, back yards normally contain such elements as lawn furniture, barbeque grills, sandboxes, swing sets, swimming pools, cords of firewood, air conditioners, metal storage sheds, and so on. While different and sometimes even incompatible, all these activities and elements are commonly placed in relatively close proximity to one another in the back yard. This makes the back yard the most intensely used portion of the typical residential site and also the most difficult to organize and design.

Let us take a closer look at the back yard and examine its specific qualities more critically. Following are typical conditions of the back yard:

1. Lack of Separation. The back yards in many newly developed neighborhoods are open and ill-defined areas. One yard blends into the next to form a giant green space accessible to everyone in the surrounding area (Figure 1–17). As a result, there is little sense of identity or privacy. The activity that goes on in one's back yard becomes the visual business of surrounding neighbors. This tends to discourage use of the back yard for people who enjoy privacy. With time, these same back yards generally become more enclosed by fences and plant materials to create some separation from neighboring sites.

2. Walled/Fenced Back Yards. In the western part of the United States, back yards are apt to be totally enclosed by walls or fences (Figure 1–18). Sometimes alleyways are located behind these back yards for access to garages located at the back end of the property. The result is that back yards tend to be isolated from one another with few or no views to the landscape beyond.

3. Dissimilar Visual Character. There is generally a common character to the front yards of homes in a given neighborhood owing to similar size of the homes, similar setbacks, and similar lot sizes. By comparison, the back yards in the

FIGURE 1–17
Many back yard areas blend in with each other to form an anonymous open space.

FIGURE 1–18
Some back yards, particularly in western states,
are completely enclosed by walls.

same neighborhood are apt to be very different from one another owing to variations in lifestyles, interests, personalities, and family size. When the back yards are open to each other, the overall result is visually chaotic (Figure 1–19).

4. Undersized Outdoor Living Areas. The outdoor living and entertaining space, if it exists at all, is often established by a (concrete, brick, stone, wood, etc.) terrace. One problem is that many are too small (Figure 1–20). A 12′ × 12′ area (or between 100 and 150 square feet) is common, especially in developments built since the early 1960s. While this may be enough area for several chairs, a small table, and a lounge chair, it is hardly adequate for entertaining several guests.

5. Lack of Privacy. Terraces are usually intended for relaxation and entertainment. However, they are often uncomfortable to use because they commonly lack any sense of enclosure for privacy (Figure 1–21). They are open and exposed

FIGURE 1–19
Back yards that are completely open to each other are apt to create unsightly views and visual chaos.

FIGURE 1–20
A common 12′ × 12′ outdoor living and entertaining area is too small for comfortable entertaining.

to the view of the surrounding neighbors. A person may feel as if they are on public display when sitting on the terrace.

   6. Harsh Microclimates. Another reason for the discomfort of many exterior living and entertaining spaces is that they are not located or designed with climate in mind. When located on the north side of the house, outdoor terraces are apt to be cool and damp much of the time as well as being exposed to cold winter wind (Figure 1–22). When located on the west side of a house, terraces tend to be

FIGURE 1-21
Many outdoor living and entertaining spaces lack spatial enclosure and visual separation from neighbors.

FIGURE 1-22
Some outdoor living and entertaining spaces lack consideration for sun and wind.

FIGURE 1-23
Some outdoor living and entertaining spaces are
devoid of unique character and personality.

very hot during summer afternoons, particularly when not adequately shaded. People will not use outdoor spaces where sun, wind, and precipitation have not been properly considered.

7. Lack of Appealing Character.   Like front entry walks, many exterior terraces are devoid of any personality or character. They are cold, impersonal spaces that are uninviting to use for any length of time. For many, it is a drab experience to sit on concrete slab with nothing to look at except an open expanse of lawn or the backs of the neighbors' houses (Figure 1–23).

8. Weak Relation to House Interior.   Another problem of some exterior terraces is that they have a weak relationship to the interior of the house. Elevation changes and distance tend to isolate rather than to coordinate the indoors with the outdoors (Figure 1–24). Some back doors exit onto a concrete stoop that is smaller in scale than the front-door stoop. This can create the same problem as illustrated in Figure 1–9.

9. Unsightly Storage Sheds.   Many families possess a collection of maintenance and recreational equipment such as lawn furniture, barbeque grills, lawn mowers, garden tools, wheelbarrows, children's toys, bicycles, skis, and so on. Even a typical 20′ × 25′ two-car garage has little extra space to store such things. Consequently, many homeowners erect metal or wood storage sheds in their back yards to take care of extra belongings. These sheds are usually different in style and character from the house and consequently can be eyesores.

10. Vegetable Gardens.   A vegetable garden is often stuck in one of the back corners of the yard. It is placed some distance from the nearest water source yet still close enough to the house to be seen as a brown patch of bare earth in the nongrowing season (Figure 1–25).

The real challenge of most back yards is to combine the numerous functional requirements with aesthetic considerations. The back yard doesn't have to be only an engineered organization of sitting, recreation, and gardening spaces. It can fulfill these needs while also being an attractive environment to experience.

FIGURE 1-24
A flight of steps at the door can isolate the outdoor living and entertaining space from the indoors.

FIGURE 1-25
Vegetable gardens tend to be placed in far corners of back yards where they are eyesores and remote from a water source.

Side Yards

Unlike the front yard or back yard, most side yards seem to have little use except to provide access around the side of the house. Consequently, most side yards are wasted and leftover areas (corner sites or those that do have generous space on one or both sides of the house are exceptions). They often tend to be trouble spots owing to the lack of direct access from the house and because of the narrow space that exists between the house and property line. Side yards vary in width from a very narrow 3 to 5 feet to a normal 8 to 12 feet and sometimes larger. The following list describes typical side-yard conditions:

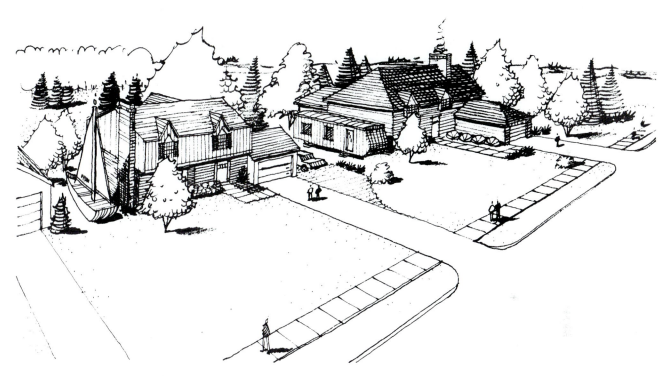

FIGURE 1–26
A driveway located in the side yard may leave little room for people to walk.

FIGURE 1–27
Side yards are sometimes used for storage of cars, trailers, boats, etc.

1. Dominated by Access.   Access through the side yard may be vehicular, pedestrian, or both. For vehicular access, a driveway usually fills the side yard, creating similar problems as a driveway along a side of the front yard (Figure 1–26). When cars are parked in a side-yard driveway, the limited space tends to feel even smaller and more cramped than the front yard.

2. Preferred Location for Storage.   Because side yards tend to be out of the main areas of activity as well as primary lines of sight, they often tend to be used for storing visually objectionable equipment and materials. Larger side yards are apt to be storage areas for cars, boats, recreation vehicles, and so on (Figure 1–27).

3. Damp and Dark Microclimate.   Some side yards tend to be dark, damp, and humid owing to their narrowness and lack of sun exposure. This is especially true of regions that receive significant rainfall.

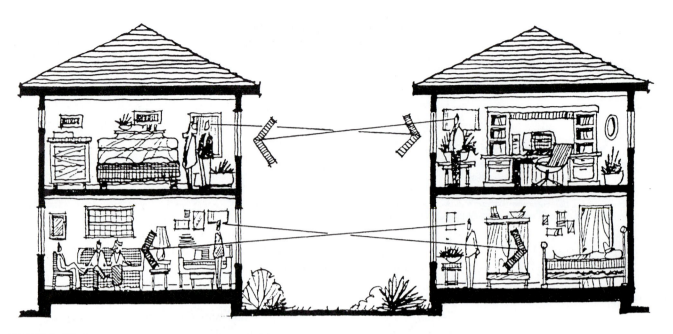

FIGURE 1–28
Narrow side yards are apt to minimize privacy between adjoining houses.

4. Wasted Space. Expansive side yards tend to be unused as activity areas owing to poor accessibility from within the house. This can amount to a sizable wasted area that still has to be maintained.

5. Views Between Houses. The narrow size of some side yards allows windows of one house to directly face the windows of the neighboring house (Figure 1–28). This diminishes privacy from these windows. To minimize this problem, most homeowners keep the curtains in these windows closed all the time. A more extreme solution, which is a common occurrence, is the construction of houses with no windows facing the side yards.

HOUSES AND HOMES

Houses come in all sorts of shapes, sizes, and character. It's not easy to drive through a neighborhood and find two houses exactly the same. While there may be some that are repeated throughout a neighborhood, it is hard to find two that look exactly alike. Each owner wants their house to be different in some way. Even if you were to look inside two houses that had the same floor plan and house character, you would undoubtedly experience two different homes. You will see different wall coverings, paint, carpet, tile, furniture, wall hangings, curtains, etc. Different people have different personalities, occupations, hobbies, preferences, monetary resources, and so on. The relationship between an owner and a house gives rise to a home, a unique place for a unique individual or family. So while there may be two or more houses that have the same layout and house character, there are no two homes that are the same.

STYLE VERSUS NO STYLE

Different people like different things. I like this, she likes that, and he likes the other thing. This is quite an easy concept to comprehend. So, when something comes in a variety of styles, colors, textures, forms, or sizes, the diversity of that something is likely to attract different people. When it comes to different styles of architecture, the same thing holds true. Different styles of architecture attract different people to those styles. Clients will have individual preferences of architectural style. Some clients may be very concerned that their house have a particular style, whether it be historical or contemporary.

There are many books on the market that deal with the styles of architecture, and some of these deal specifically with the architecture of American houses. One in particular provides an excellent way to view the variety of styles. The book is titled *American House Styles,* by John Milnes Baker, A.I.A., and was published by W. W. Norton & Company in New York. Figure 1–29 shows 15 of his illustrations that depict a two-story house with an attached garage in 15 different styles of architecture dated from 1935 to the present. Some of these styles are based upon styles from other countries. These styles also relate to specific time periods since 1935. As you can see, a house can be designed in many different ways. If you were to look carefully at each of these illustrations, you would probably find some to be more appealing than others. There may be some that you actually dislike. There is nothing wrong with that. All architecture is not for everyone. In a way, architectural style is like art; it affects people in different ways, as it should.

While these illustrations identify different styles, they don't identify all the styles of houses that we see in America. Many a house was built prior to 1935. Figure 1–30 shows three such houses. The illustration shows a house in a Greek Revival style, Victorian style, and Georgian style. These houses, just as the ones shown in the previous illustration, have quite unique and significant differences in the overall character of the architecture. It is likely that each of these styles may be preferred by some and not by others. When a landscape designer has a client with a house that has a definite style, it is strongly suggested that the designer research that style in order to become familiar with other patterns and details that are unique to that style. This will help the designer to develop landscape design that is reflective and responsive to the architectural character. This attention will help blend the house with the site.

There are many people who are not aware of the vast array of architectural styles, but are still concerned about the "overall character" of their house. It's on that character that landscape designers need to focus attention, not necessarily on the actual style. Why? All houses are not built in a recognizable style of architecture. Some houses are easily recognized as having a particular style, while others may have some character that resembles a specific style. Still others may have character taken from different styles. And some can be seen to have no evidence of any style. As stated earlier, houses come in all sorts of shapes, sizes, and character.

ARCHITECTURAL CHARACTER

While architectural style is important, when it exists, architectural character is always important. Architectural character can be viewed as the composite of physical attributes and features that together display an overall integrity. Figure 1–31 shows three different houses that do not have styles that are easily recognizable. If you were to compare these with the fifteen styles shown in Figure 1–29, you would find that each house may have certain parts that resemble another style, but not in an overall sense. There are houses that may have aspects of different styles. These are often referred to as eclectic. If you were the landscape designer for a client with one of these houses, you may not be able to find resource material that helps you become more acquainted with that particular type and character of house, and that is normal. These houses do not have to have a specific style for the designer to develop architecturally responsive landscape designs. All they need is architectural character, which each of them does possess.

FIGURE 1-29
A house can be designed to reflect one of many different styles, each with distinctive architectural character. (From *American House Styles: A Concise Guide* by John Milnes Baker. Copyright © 1994 by John Milnes Baker. Reprinted by permission of W. W. Norton & Company, Inc.)

MINIMAL TRADITIONAL 1935–1950

NEO-COLONIAL REVIVAL 1950–1970s

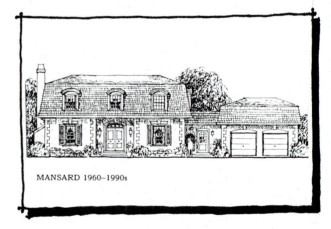

WILLIAMSBURG COLONIAL 1950–1990s

BUILDER'S CONTEMPORARY 1960–1985

MANSARD 1960–1990s

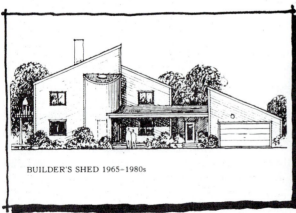

BUILDER'S SHED 1965–1980s

NEO-SHINGLE 1960–1980s

POSTMODERN 1960s–1990s

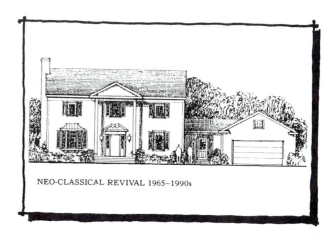

NEO-CLASSICAL REVIVAL 1965–1990s

NEO-TUDOR 1965–1990s

NEO-MEDITERRANEAN 1970–1990s

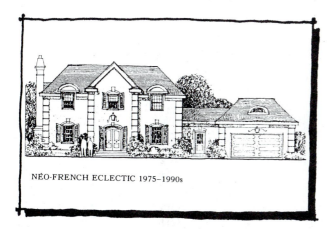

NÉO-FRENCH ECLECTIC 1975–1990s

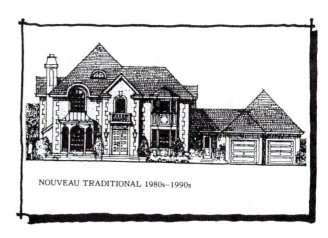

NOUVEAU TRADITIONAL 1980s–1990s

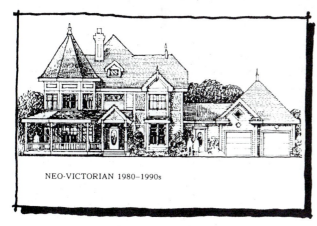

NEO-VICTORIAN 1980–1990s

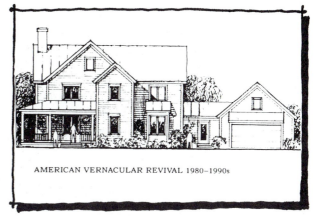

AMERICAN VERNACULAR REVIVAL 1980–1990s

The Typical Residential Site

FIGURE 1–30
Some houses have a recognizable and specific architectural style and therefore distinctive character. Design #N2979 (top), Design #N3382 (middle), and Design #N2975 (bottom) © Home Planners. Blueprints available, 800-322-6797.

Greek Revival Style

Victorian Style

Georgian Style

Landscape designers who pay attention to each house's special features will realize that new ideas for forms and patterns of proposed design elements will occur. Special features include things like materials and material patterns, proportions, roof type and slopes, window and door patterns and trim, columns, railings, dormers, cornices, and chimneys.

It is normal for people to want things similar to other people's landscapes, but they want them to fit themselves, not others. They want things to look like they belong, like the design was meant for that house and site. The uniqueness of a design

FIGURE 1–31
Some houses do not have a specific architecture style but still have distinctive character. Design #N3562 (top), Design #N3341 (middle), and Design #N3307 (bottom) © Home Planners. Blueprints available, 800-322-6797.

lies in the relationship between the existing and the proposed. What can make something special or different is focusing, with your attention on the relevant detail, on the character of the client, house, and site as a landscape design evolves and unfolds.

SUMMARY

In summary, the typical residential site has a number of good qualities as well as negative traits. On the positive side, certainly one of the notable characteristics is that most residential sites are neat and well kept. This shows much pride and care on the part of the owners. Furthermore, most residential sites are at least neutral in their overall visual quality if they are not examples of good design. The natural quality of plant materials provide a softening and unifying effect through their quantity and similarity.

Still, problems remain. As can be seen from the previous analysis of the front yard, back yard, and side yards, the site around a single-family residence doesn't always function well. Such site elements as entry walks, entry foyers, terraces, and plant materials are too small in some instances and too large in others. Plant materials frequently are used only for decoration without much thought being given to their other potential functions such as creating edges for outdoor rooms, screening wind, shading sun, or blocking views. And in most instances, plants are improperly located so that they soon outgrow the space they were originally planted. Pruning becomes a necessity simply to keep the plants "under control."

Perhaps the most significant problem of many residential sites is that they lack usefulness beyond being a setting for the house. They are not designed to create functionally logical, aesthetically pleasing, and comfortable exterior spaces. Most sites are organized in such a manner that there is no reason to go outside to enjoy the site. As mentioned earlier, the typical site lacks outdoor rooms for arrival, sitting, entertaining, eating, recreating, working, or gardening. Sure, some of these activities still take place, but under less than ideal circumstances. The premise of this book is that there is a better way to approach residential site design.

2

Outdoor Rooms

INTRODUCTION

There are numerous factors to consider in the design of a residential site. The designer must take many items into account including the clients' wants and needs, relationship between the interior (rooms, doors, windows, etc.) and the exterior, budget limitations, and the opportunities and constraints of the existing site conditions. As the designer graphically begins to put ideas on paper to create a design solution, additional considerations should address the functional relationships among the required uses, the character of the spaces to be created, and the specific sizes, shapes, colors, and textures of the materials selected for the design. However, there should be one central theme that guides all reflections about residential design: *the creation of usable space.* Creating usable outdoor space, perhaps more clearly understood as *outdoor rooms,* should be the principal way of thinking about a residential site and the basic building block for developing a design solution.

The importance of outdoor space is based on the philosophy that residential site design is a three-dimensional organization of space and not just the creation of two-dimensional patterns on the ground or the arrangement of plant materials along the base of a house. Space is the entity where we live, work, and recreate. Consequently, all the site elements that make up the outdoor environment such as plant materials, pavements, walls, fences, and other structures should be considered as the physical elements that define outdoor space. A residential designer should think of design as the creation and organization of outdoor space and should study how these other components define and influence the character and mood of space.

This chapter discusses what outdoor space is, how it is created, and how it is used. We do this by comparing and contrasting outdoor space with indoor space. In addition, guidelines are suggested for the location and design of such outdoor rooms as the arrival and entry space, entertaining space, outdoor dining space, and

25

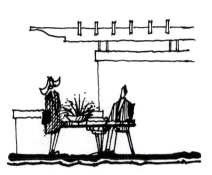

FIGURE 2–1
A successful space needs: (1) sufficient space, (2) planes of enclosure, and (3) spatial character.

recreation space. Overall, this chapter establishes the basic philosophy for residential site design that is followed throughout the remainder of the book.

OUTDOOR SPACE

What is space? When designers use the term *space* in a design context, they use it to describe any three-dimensional void or hollowness contained by the sides or edges of surrounding elements. For example, indoor space exists between the floors, walls, and ceilings of all buildings. Similarly, outdoor space can be perceived as space bound by physical elements of the environment such as the ground, shrubs, walls, fences, awnings, tree canopies, etc.

For lay people, the concept of space is often a difficult one initially to grasp because they are accustomed to describing the landscape as a collection of physical objects such as buildings, trees, shrubs, and fences rather than space itself. It takes some adjustment and training to view outdoor space as the void between those objects normally seen.

A proposed outdoor use area will function as a usable space if there is (1) sufficient space, (2) adequate privacy, (3) decoration, and (4) furnishings. The success of outdoor space can be looked at in a similar way as indoor space. We find a space to be comfortable, pleasurable, and successful if it provides sufficient room to function in, enough privacy for the function to occur, decoration, and furnishings.

Figure 2–1 illustrates three sequential steps in the development of a successful space. The basic function of a space is accommodated by the bare necessities, like a table and chairs. The basic use of the space is not dependent on anything more than this. But the space is likely to feel empty, and the users are apt to feel awkward and uncomfortable, because of the lack of spatial definition. People are used to floors, walls, and ceilings. So, by adding outdoor design elements like a patio, a fence, and an overhead arbor, the space has the opportunity to provide the user with more of what they are used to in experiencing space. But, until these three planes of enclosure have some material, pattern, and color applied to them, the space will feel like an empty model home. It is important to keep in mind that selecting materials, patterns, and colors is critical to the success of a space.

An effective means for understanding outdoor space is to think of it as a series of outdoor rooms similar to the interior rooms of a house (Figure 2–2). Each interior room has a definite sense of enclosure that is clearly defined by floor, walls, and ceiling. Similarly, there are potentially such rooms as the entry space, entertaining space, living space, dining space, and work space in the exterior environment of a residential site. Like their interior counterparts, exterior spaces are de-

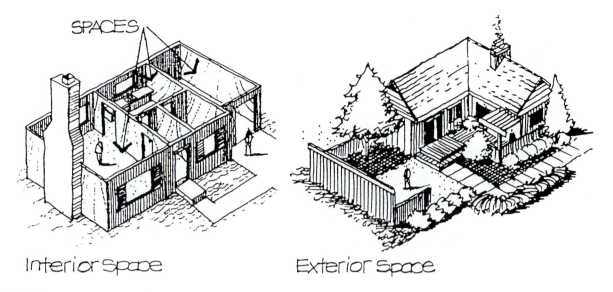

Interior Space   Exterior Space

FIGURE 2–2
Outdoor space should be thought of as being similar to indoor spaces.

Overhead Plane
Ground Plane
Vertical Plane

FIGURE 2–3
Examples of the three planes of spatial enclosure.

fined by three primary planes of enclosure: base plane, vertical plane, and overhead plane. These three exterior planes of enclosure, like the interior floors, walls, and ceilings, collectively define the edges or limits of outdoor rooms (Figure 2–3).

Base Plane

The base plane or floor of an outdoor space supports all activities and site elements in the outdoor environment. It is the plane on which people walk, run, sit, work, recreate, and play. As such, the base plane receives the most direct use and wear. Areas of a site that endure intense or concentrated use are typically covered with a hard surface such as pavement, while other areas that receive infrequent use are most often covered with a soft surface such as lawn, ground cover, or mulch.

Significantly, the base plane is the primary plane on which the designer organizes the proposed design. The organization of uses (or functions) in residential design is determined directly on the base plane. It is important to understand that good design starts with function, and functional organization begins on the base plane.

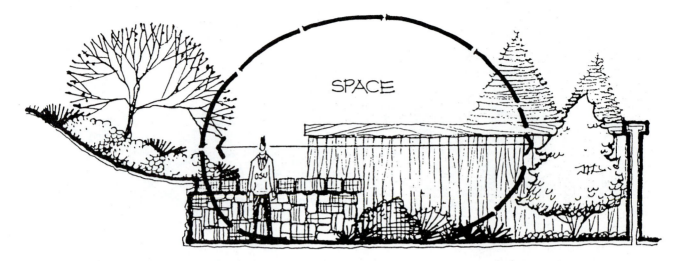

FIGURE 2-4
Vertical planes (landform, walls, fences, and plant materials) are used to provide spatial enclosure.

Vertical Plane

Vertical planes are established by such site elements as the facades of a house, walls, fences, the foliage mass of trees and shrubs, tree trunks spaced close together, and/or steeply sloped ground. The vertical planes' most prominent role in the landscape is one of enclosure (Figure 2–4). Vertical planes define the surrounding edges of a space and separate one space from another. Similarly, vertical planes directly affect views. They control how much or how little is seen from any one place in the landscape and thus influence the degree of privacy that is felt in an outdoor space. An outdoor room may be rather open with views extending outward in many directions, partially enclosed on several sides, or totally enclosed with an inward orientation (Figure 2–5). Vertical planes may be used to direct and enframe views to desirable places or screen views from unattractive features (Figure 2–6). In addition, the character of vertical planes influences the feeling of the space. Vertical planes may vary from rough to smooth, light to dark, solid to transparent, and so on. Each of these variables influence the mood of a space.

Overhead Plane

Overhead planes are created by canvas awnings, overhead trellises, arbors, pergolas, the bottom of tree canopies, or even the clouds in the sky. Overhead planes have two functions. The first is to influence the amount and quality of skylight (including sunlight) that enters into a space (Figure 2–7). Overhead planes may be completely open where maximum skylight is desired or completely solid where little or no light is needed. In between these two extremes, overhead planes may be composed of various semitransparent and translucent materials that permit filtered and diffused light to enter into an outdoor space. Very dramatic light effects can be created by an overhead arbor (with or without vines), open trees such as a honey locust or palo verde, or light colored canvas awnings. In a similar manner, a semitransparent or partially open overhead plane can cast attractive shadow patterns on the ground, adjacent walls, or fence (Figure 2–8). The second function of the overhead plane is to influence the perceived scale of a space. For instance, a low overhead plane is apt to create an intimate feeling, while a high overhead plane may establish a more uplifting or lofty setting (Figure 2–9).

In the outdoor environment, the base, vertical, and overhead planes function together to create a variety of spaces with different uses and feelings. For instance, an outdoor space may be almost completely enclosed to create a rather intimate and inward sensation (Figure 2–10). Such a space tends to have a strong sense of privacy

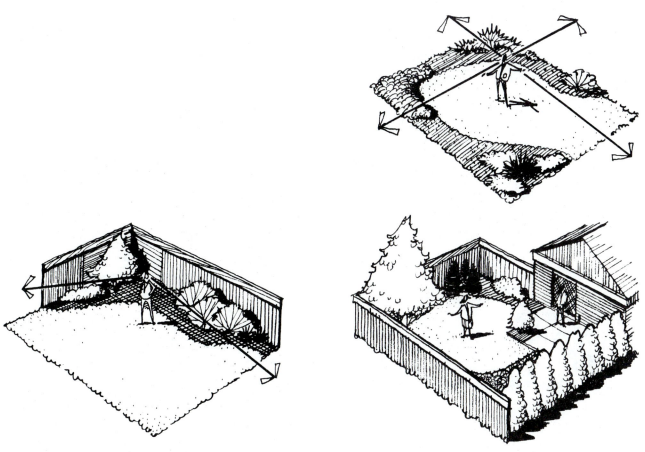

FIGURE 2–5
A space may have varying degrees of enclosure.

FIGURE 2–6
Vertical planes may enframe or screen views.

and separation from other spaces. In contrast, an outdoor space may be quite open to provide an expansive feeling and outward oriented views in many directions as well as exposure to climatic elements such as sun and wind (Figure 2–11). Ultimately, the designer must decide what type and degree of enclosure is most suitable for an outdoor space to achieve the intended use and mood.

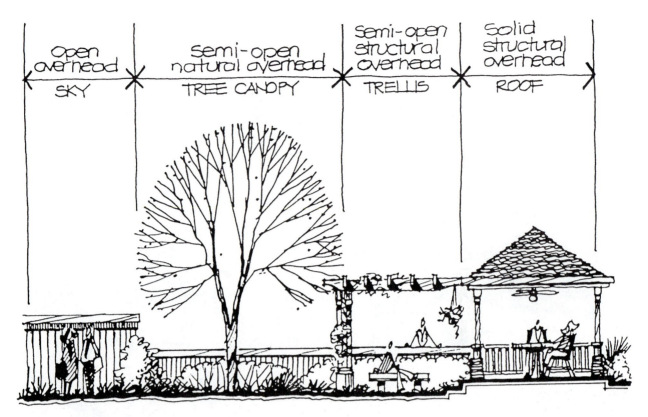

FIGURE 2-7
Overhead planes can affect the amount of natural light entering a space.

FIGURE 2-8
Overhead planes can create attractive shadow patterns.

In some ways outdoor space is similar to indoor space. Both are volumes defined by the base plane, vertical planes, and the overhead plane. Also people live, work, and play in both indoor and outdoor spaces, but there are differences that should be recognized and appreciated as well. Generally, when a person is indoors, there is little question as to where one room ends and another begins. The walls separating one room from another are typically solid and fixed in place with doors

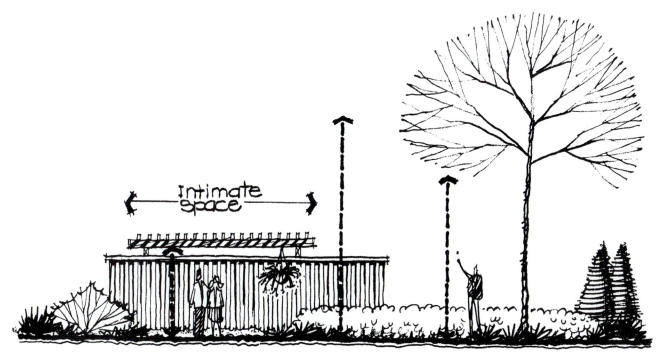

FIGURE 2-9
Varying heights of overhead planes create different feelings of enclosure.

FIGURE 2-10
An outdoor space may be completely enclosed
and isolated from its surroundings.

or other openings being the only spatial connection between them. Another characteristic of interior space is that its sense of enclosure and light does not vary much over a period of time, especially if windows are small or lacking.

By comparison, the edges of outdoor spaces are not as rigidly defined. Consequently, it is sometimes difficult to perceive where one outdoor space ends and another begins. Outdoor spaces often tend to be defined more by implication than by obvious enclosures (Figure 2–12). Plant materials, for example, don't usually provide the sharp, clear edge that the walls inside a house do unless they are pruned to form precise hedges. Many plants have a fairly open character and are amorphous in shape, thus allowing views to extend to spaces and objects beyond.

FIGURE 2–11
An outdoor space may be open and allow views
to the surrounding landscape.

FIGURE 2–12
Unlike indoor spaces, outdoor spaces tend to be more open and less defined.

In addition, the elements that define outdoor space are often arranged in an informal manner unlike the typical straight walls in a house.

Outdoor spaces change more dramatically over a period of time in comparison to their interior counterparts. Growth and seasonal variations have a tremendous influence on the space-defining abilities of plant materials. In some locations of the country, a space defined essentially by plant materials may seem very enclosed during the summer but quite open during the winter when leaves drop off. Perception of outdoor space is also influenced by variations in weather (sun, clouds, fog, rain, snow) and light. An outdoor space may seem very appealing on a warm, sunny day yet uninviting and dismal on another day. Spaces tend to feel smaller and more enclosed during the evening than during the day because of reduced viewing distance in the dark. All the possible combinations of factors make the perception of outdoor space highly variable.

OUTDOOR ROOMS ON THE RESIDENTIAL SITE

As stated earlier, a residential site can be thought of as a series of outdoor rooms or spaces. These spaces have numerous functions, some of which are similar to those found inside the house. On many residential sites, the most significant outdoor spaces include an outdoor arrival and entry space, entertaining or living space, eating or dining space, recreation space, work/storage space, and garden space. The intent of this section is to examine each of these spaces to more clearly understand their functions and to present design guidelines for their development. This is accomplished by first studying the indoor counterpart of each outdoor space in order to gain insights into how outdoor spaces might be designed.

Indoor Entry Foyer

The entry foyer is the space usually located immediately inside the front door. Its purpose is to serve as a transition space between the outdoor environment and the indoor environment. The foyer is a transition space in the sense that it acclimates a person after entering or before leaving the inside of the house. It is a place where people stand temporarily to welcome visitors or say goodbyes.

Outdoor Arrival and Entry Space

The outdoor arrival and entry space is of course the exterior complement to the interior entry foyer. In as much, it has many similarities, but a few differences as well. As discussed previously in Chapter 1, the outdoor arrival and entry space on the typical residential site lacks identity and character. While people can in fact get to the front door, an important question is: "Does this space provide a pleasant experience that says 'welcome,' or is it one that is simply tolerated until one enters the house?"

What are some design guidelines for the outdoor arrival and entry space that can assist a designer in developing a pleasant entry space to complement the residence? Of course, there are no easy answers to this question because each design project is unique with its own particular set of circumstances. Still, there are some important thoughts and suggestions with wide application to many residential sites. To start with, a well-designed outdoor arrival and entry space should fulfill a number of objectives. At the very least, it should comfortably accommodate pedestrian movement from off the site to the front door of the house in a safe and orderly fashion. The route should be obvious and easy to negotiate during the day and at night. It might also be protected from the hot afternoon sun or strong winds.

But a well-designed arrival and entry space should do more than just satisfy these utilitarian considerations. It should display an attractiveness that complements the residence as well as providing a pleasant experience for the residents and visitors. This space should give comfort and interest to visitors and may also serve as a delightful place for the residents to sit and relax. The outdoor arrival and entry space might be designed to exhibit some of the character and personality of the home and the residents, thus providing an appropriate introduction to the site, house, and residents who live there.

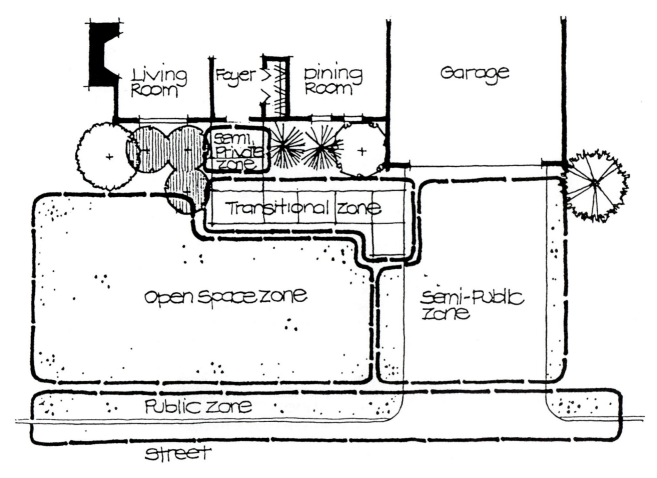

FIGURE 2-13
Zones of entry on the typical residential site.

The entire outdoor arrival and entry space can be divided into five subspaces or zones relating to arrival and entrance (Figure 2–13). A person proceeds through or by each of these zones when arriving and leaving the property. The "public" zone occurs at the curb or property lines. Whether on foot or in a vehicle, a person begins the arrival sequence the moment the curb zone or property lines are crossed. The "semi-public" zone occurs on or along the driveway. This is normally the least defined or enjoyable part of the sequence. The walk between the driveway and the outdoor entry space represents the "transitional" zone. This zone is pedestrian oriented, thus making the scale and detail of this area critical. The "semi-private" zone is the outdoor foyer. Like its interior counterpart, this space serves as a transition zone as well as a place for meeting and greeting visitors. The "open space" zone is the space that occupies the remainder of the front yard. In many instances, this zone is taken up by the front lawn and plantings. While a guest may not actually walk through the lawn, it nonetheless is a visual element.

Each of these zones contributes to the overall experience of arriving at the site and entering the home. Consequently, each should be carefully studied during the evolution of a design solution. To aid in this process, the designer should consider the following guidelines, keeping in mind that they should be applied thoughtfully to each site according to the specific circumstances.

Public Zone. This first zone can be designed to acknowledge a sense of entry into the site in a variety of ways. In one instance, the borders of the site, particularly the front edge along the sidewalk or street, may provide a sense of enclosure for the front yard through low walls, fences, or plantings (Figure 2–14). A sense of

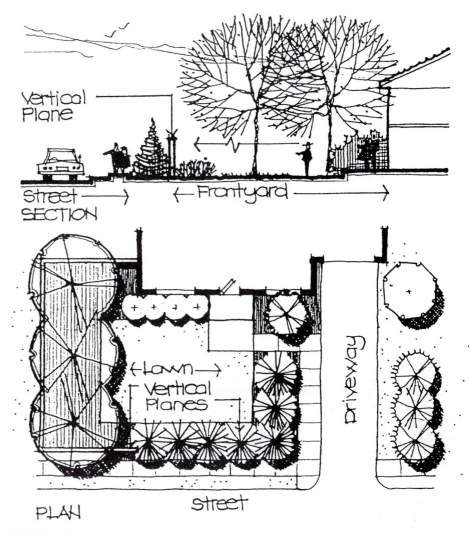

FIGURE 2–14
Vertical planes are used along the street to provide a sense of enclosure and separation from the street.

entry is felt when walking or driving through this plane of enclosure just as when a person walks through a doorway of an interior room. Another advantage of spatial enclosure along the street is that it separates the front yard from the street and establishes a greater sense of privacy. This makes the front-yard space more comfortable if used for sitting and relaxing. Some words of caution need to be made about enclosure near the street. First, the height of walls or plantings in this zone should not interfere with the ability to see in and out of the driveway, especially for drivers backing into the street (Figure 2–15). A second concern for enclosure along the street is that it should comply with local zoning ordinances. There may be restrictions on the location and height of walls, fences, and plantings in the front yard.

Semi-Public Zone.   The next zone is the driveway and the area along its sides. The major use of this zone should be to provide adequate space for the parking of cars and for moving people on foot through the space in a comfortable manner. The driveway should be wide enough to allow the desired number of cars to park comfortably, but not so large as to visually dominate the arrival area or front yard. Most cars require a 9′ × 18′ space for parking. All walls, plantings, and so on should be kept back from the edge of the driveway so as not to interfere with the opening of car doors or people walking along the edge of the driveway (Figure 2–16).

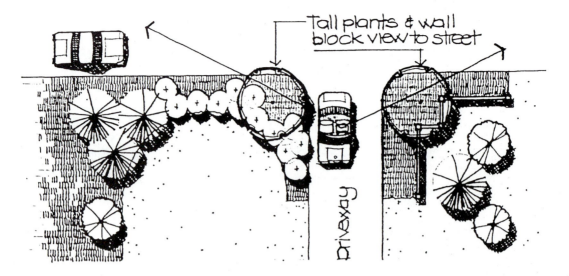

FIGURE 2–15
Tall plants and/or fences should not be placed in locations that inhibit the driver's view of the street.

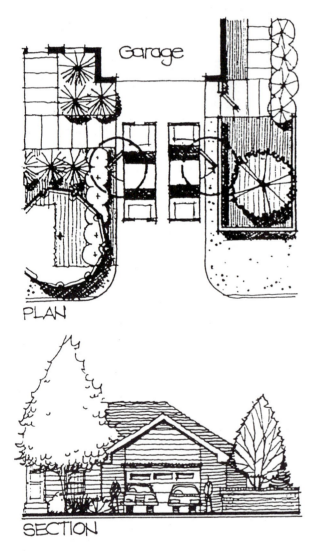

FIGURE 2–16
Plants, walls, etc. located too close to the driveway interfere with the opening of car doors and pedestrian circulation.

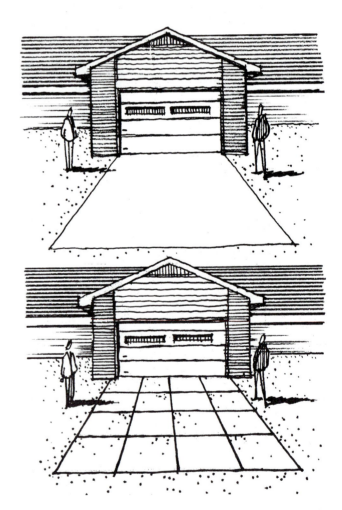

FIGURE 2–17
A simple scoring pattern can reduce the apparent size of the driveway.

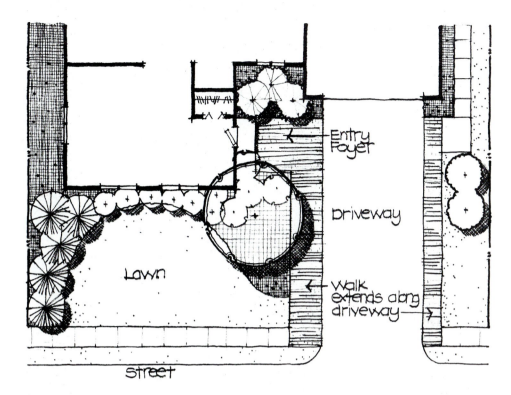

FIGURE 2–18
Walks on both sides of the driveway can provide easier access to the entry walk.

The pavement material and pattern of this zone should be given careful thought. Owing to the relatively massive size of many driveways, the pavement material can have a direct influence on the perceived scale of the driveway and its visual appeal. Simply providing a scoring pattern in the concrete reduces the apparent size of the driveway (Figure 2–17).

Adequate space should be provided along the edge of the driveway to allow people to walk along it without having to rub against parked cars, walk on wet grass or in snow piles. This can be accomplished by providing a walk that extends along one or both edges of the driveway (Figure 2–18). To identify this as a pedestrian area, the pavement should be a different material or pattern than the driveway itself. The walk surface should also be flush with the elevation of the driveway and should not contain steps or other abrupt elevation changes. Low plantings can be used to reinforce the edge of the walk or to separate it from adjoining spaces or lawn areas.

If the entry walk does not extend along the driveway's edge, there should be an obvious indication as to where the entry walk to the front door is located. This can be done by providing an expanded area of walkway or landing at an appropriate place along the edge of the driveway (Figure 2–19). In plan, this landing should ideally resemble a funnel shape to permit easy recognition and to gently guide people onto the entry walk itself. In addition, this area should be located at a place along the driveway where most cars stop to park (Figure 2–20). This allows people on one side of the car to step directly out onto the landing. Steps should not be placed right next to the driveway where they can catch someone by surprise (Figure 2–21).

The landing area can be further acknowledged by the careful placement of an accent element to attract attention such as an ornamental tree, a planting with seasonal color, light fixture, or a combination of these elements (Figure 2–22).

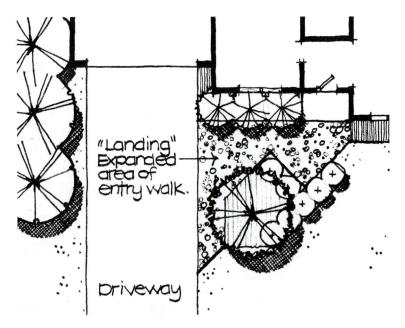

FIGURE 2–19
An expanded entry walk or "landing" provides a more welcoming approach.

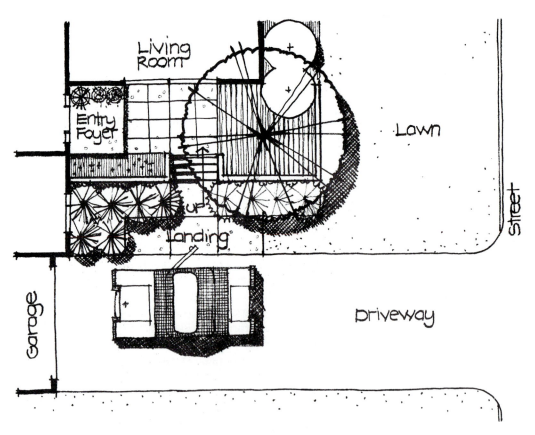

FIGURE 2–20
The "landing" should be located where a car would normally be parked in the driveway.

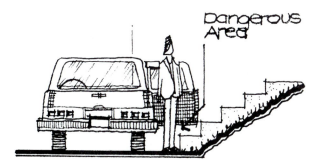

FIGURE 2–21
Avoid placing landing steps too close to the edge
of the driveway.

FIGURE 2–22
Ornamental plants, a light, etc. can accent the location of the "landing."

Transitional Zone. The next zone or subspace in the arrival sequence is the entry walk. Its primary function is to accommodate and direct movement between the landing and the outdoor foyer. In addition, it should create a pleasant and safe walking experience with a variety of views along the walk. This can be done by slightly altering the direction of the entry walk and altering views and points of interest as a person moves toward the front door (Figure 2–23). Specimen plants, seasonal flowers, sculpture, water, or other possibilities can be incorporated along the walk to enhance its character. Low walls, fences, or plant materials can be incorporated with the walk to help direct and reinforce movement (Figure 2–24). These low vertical planes will also provide a sense of enclosure so a person will feel like he or she is walking through a space rather than through an undefined open area. While the entry walk should be interesting, it should not be so indirect that it confuses or frustrates a visitor (Figure 2–25).

In terms of safety and convenience, the walk should be at least 4½ feet wide so two people can walk side by side comfortably (Figure 2–26). In addition, the walk should not exceed a slope of 5 percent. If necessary, steps can be incorporated in the entry walk to take up any grade changes.

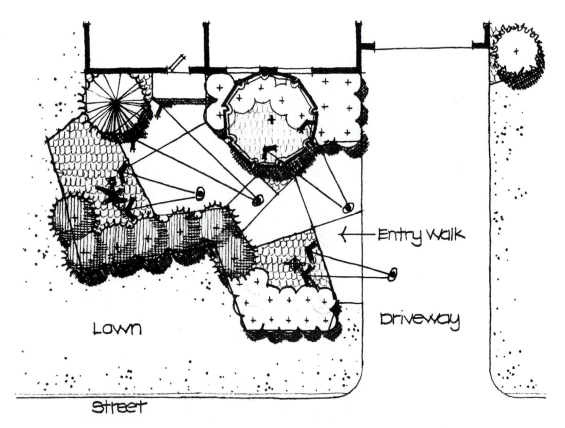

FIGURE 2-23
A "meandering" walk can provide different views as one moves toward the front door.

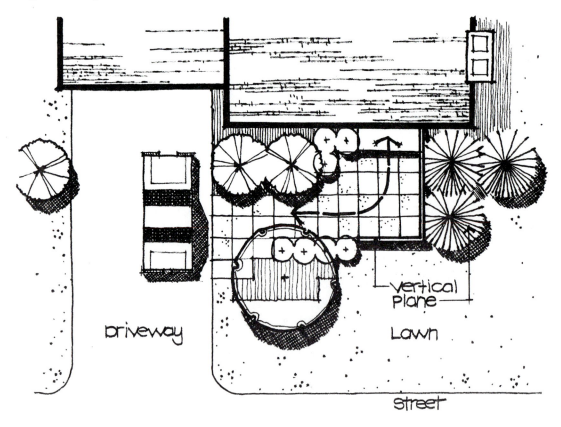

FIGURE 2-24
Low walls, fences, and plant materials can help direct movement through the space.

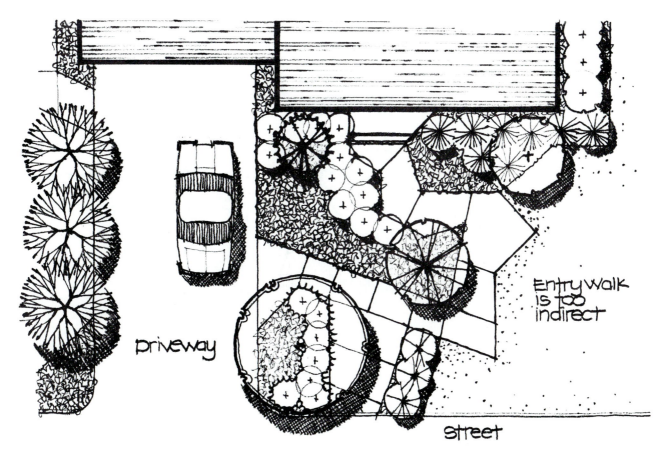

FIGURE 2–25
Avoid entry walks that are too long and indirect.

FIGURE 2–26
Minimum suggested walk width for two people.

Semi-Private Zone. The outdoor foyer is the next zone of the arrival sequence. This space should have similar functions to the interior entry foyer by acting as the culmination of the arrival sequence, providing a stopping and gathering space to serve as a transition between indoors and outdoors. To support these functions, the outdoor foyer should be larger in size than the entry walk and have approximately equal plan proportions so it feels like an arrival space. This space should be large enough to allow for a small group of people to gather outside the

FIGURE 2–27
Provide adequate space for entry in relation to the swing of the door.

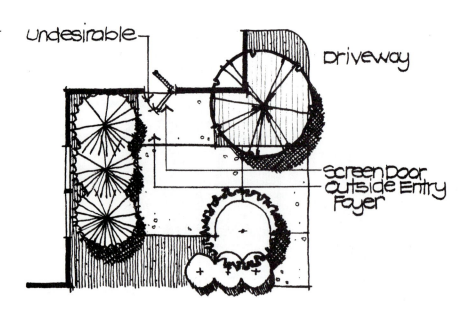

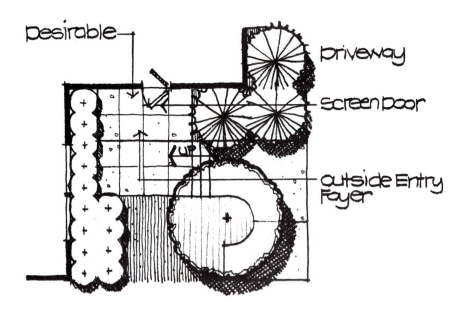

front door without being in the way of the opening and closing of the door. In addition, the outdoor foyer should be designed so the majority of its area is on the
side where the front door opens (Figure 2–27). This allows for easier entry to and
exit from the house.

To furnish an adequate sense of enclosure in the outside foyer, the designer
should give careful consideration to all three planes of enclosure. The ground
plane might be constructed of a different material or pattern than the entry walk to
suggest its distinct use as a stopping and gathering space near the front door
(Figure 2–28). Vertical planes can be utilized to control views into and out of the
outdoor foyer as well as giving a sense of separation from adjoining areas of the
front yard. As seen in Figure 2–29, the ornamental tree not only provides an accent
element, but also serves as a screen and "turning element" that directs people to-

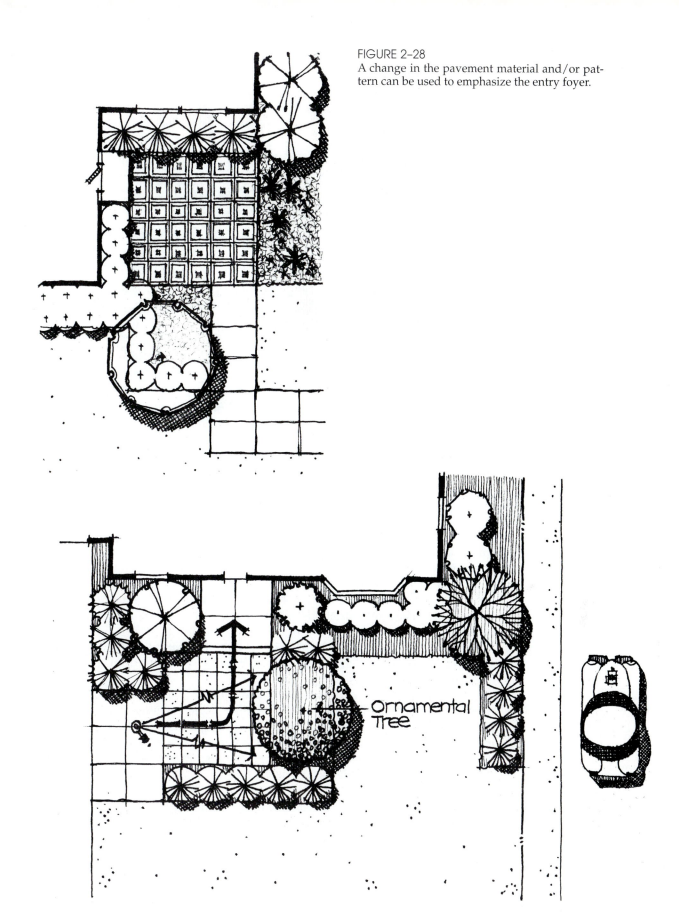

Ornamental
Tree

FIGURE 2–29
A tall element or ornamental tree provides accent, screens view, and directs movement.

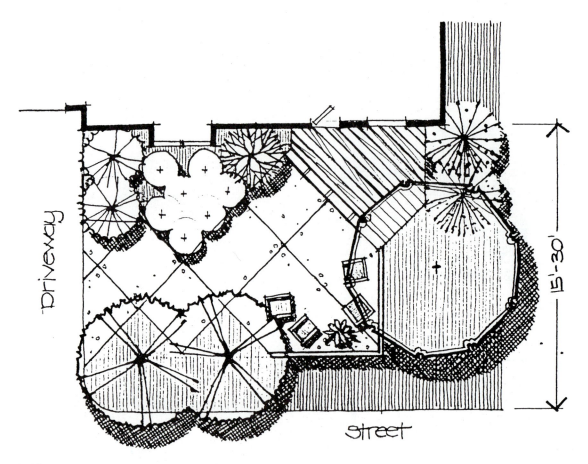

FIGURE 2–30
In small front yards, usable space and plantings may be used instead of lawn.

ward the front door. Depending on the degree of enclosure desired, the vertical planes may vary in height and transparency. In some instances, the outdoor foyer may be fairly enclosed for privacy while in other situations, carefully selected views to other areas may be established. Again, the designer should check local zoning ordinances for restrictions of height and placement of any vertical structures such as walls or fences.

The overhead plane can be used in the outdoor foyer to provide an intimate scale to the space as well as to provide protection (if it is solid) from such climatic elements as hot summer sun or precipitation.

As with the interior entrance foyer, the outdoor foyer should also say "welcome" and provide a pleasant atmosphere. Like inside the house, this can be done by furnishing the space with such things as potted plants, sculpture, or other elements that give the space a personal touch. A bench may also be placed in the outdoor foyer, for it provides a place to sit and is a gesture of friendliness and hospitality on behalf of the residents.

Open Space Zone. The last zone of the outdoor arrival and entry space is the remaining area in the front yard. Depending on the overall size of the site, this zone may vary from a small piece of ground to one that occupies many square feet. Its size will influence how this area is best used. For small sites, this zone may be used most effectively as a planting area incorporated into some of the other zones. In this situation, there may be no need for lawn. In addition, this zone may serve other uses such as an outside sitting space (Figure 2–30). Here, the sitting space is an integral part of the outside entry foyer so that the two functions work together. On sites larger yet, this last zone is often best taken up by an area of lawn, ground

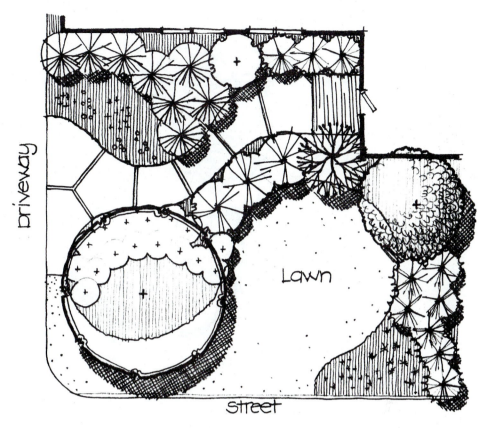

FIGURE 2–31
The entry walk may be separated from the lawn.

cover, decomposed granite, existing trees, and so on, serving as a foreground for both the house and other areas in the front yard. To what degree this area is incorporated into other zones of the front yard is a matter of circumstance and choice. The remaining yard area might be strongly separated (Figure 2–31), or may be integrated harmoniously with the other zones (Figure 2–32).

In conclusion, all the zones of the outdoor arrival and entry space can establish a friendly and welcoming atmosphere. Owing to the importance of producing this feeling, the arrival and entry space is one of the most significant outside spaces on the residential site and consequently deserves a great deal of attention on the part of the designer.

Indoor Living and Entertaining Room

One of the major rooms of the house is the living and entertaining space. Depending on the client, this space may be the living room, the family room, or great room. In any case, the entertaining space is usually semipublic in nature because it is the place where visitors can be entertained and other business conducted. In addition, the residents often spend many hours in this space. Two reasons for its frequent use are: (1) the decor and furnishings establish a comfortable and pleasant atmosphere, and (2) the space can be used for a variety of functions such as family gatherings, entertaining guests, eating, reading, listening to music, watching television, conversing, and so on. Lighting plays an important role in the utilization of the entertaining space for it can normally be altered to match the mood of the activity taking place. A corner lamp may supply just enough light for reading while the fireplace may be used to create a special mood for a cozy and intimate get-together. Or, all of the lights may be lit to provide a bright and lively atmosphere for a party or family gathering.

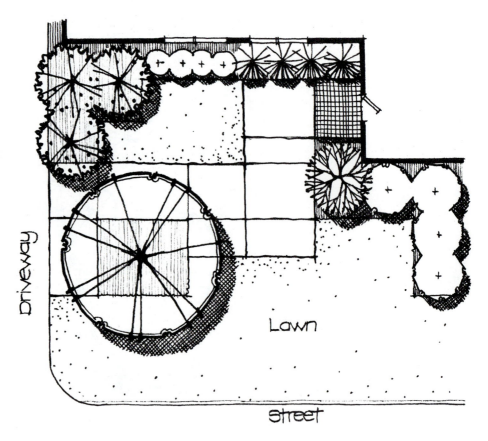

FIGURE 2–32
The entry walk may be integrated with the lawn.

One of the prime activities that occurs in this space is conversation. Consequently, the furniture usually is organized to allow conversation to happen in a comfortable and relaxing manner.

Outdoor Living and Entertaining Space

The outdoor living and entertaining space has a number of functions like those of its indoor counterpart. It should be designed to accommodate individual and small group relaxation, conversation, and interaction in relative peace and quiet, yet be flexible enough to hold larger groups of people for parties and other social gatherings.

One of the first considerations for designing the outdoor living and entertaining space is to establish the correct proportions and size so it will function properly. This space (and its subspaces) should have fairly equal plan proportions to support its use as a gathering and meeting space (Figure 2–33). Long narrow proportions should be avoided because they imply movement, like a hallway, and are difficult to arrange furniture in for conversation. The size of the space should be determined based on the anticipated numbers of people who will be using the space along with the required furniture. Information on the suggested sizes of typical spaces and elements is presented in Chapter 8. To prevent the outdoor living and entertaining space from becoming too large in scale, it can be organized as a series of smaller subspaces that each accommodate a particular function (sitting, entertaining, sunbathing, reading, and so on). This can be accomplished by varied plan configuration, differences in pavement material, and elevation changes (Figure 2–34).

The designer should also study the arrangement of furniture and other elements in the outdoor living and entertaining space so conversation, circulation,

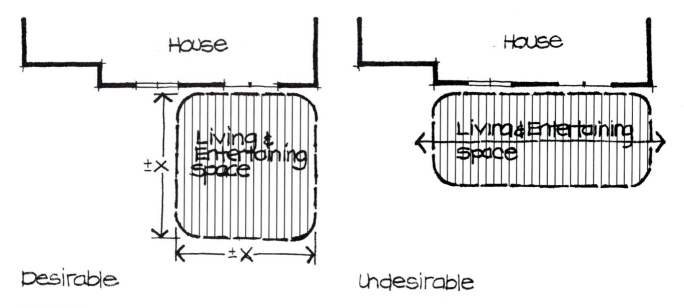

Desirable   **Undesirable**

FIGURE 2-33
The outdoor living and entertaining space should have approximately equal plan proportions.

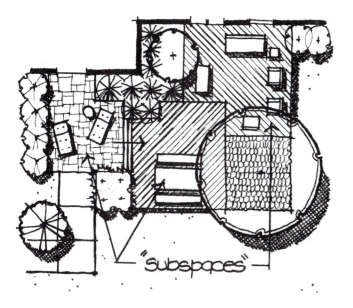

FIGURE 2-34
The outdoor living and entertaining space can be organized as a series of smaller subspaces, each with its own function.

and other activities can take place appropriately. A designer should never just create a space or become overly enamored with its shape without an idea of how the space will actually function. Too many times, a space is designed with little or no idea in mind as to where people will actually sit, what they will look at, or where they will walk through the space. Chairs, for example, should be arranged in a generally circular group so people can face each other to talk. Circulation routes also need to be anticipated so they won't cut directly through a conversation group in a disruptive manner (Figure 2–35).

Another important consideration is for the designer to establish a sense of enclosure in the outdoor entertaining space, particularly with the vertical and overhead planes. Enclosure by the vertical planes can be created with walls, fences, steep slopes of the ground, or plant materials either individually or in combination with each other. Vertical planes can also screen views of the neighbors and create privacy as well as block cold wind or hot late afternoon sun (Figure 2–36).

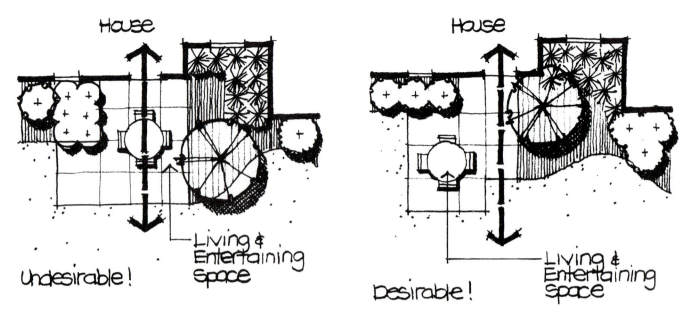

FIGURE 2–35
Circulation should pass along the edges of living and entertaining space.

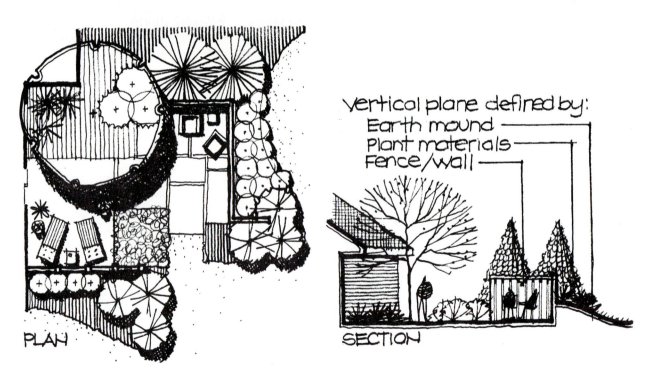

FIGURE 2–36
Vertical planes can be used to provide spatial enclosure and privacy in outdoor living and entertaining spaces.

The overhead plane can be defined with trellises, arbors, pergolas, canvas awnings, tree canopies, and so on (Figure 2–37). As in the outdoor entry foyer, the overhead plane can establish a "ceiling" and make the space seem more comfortable and intimate in scale. It is often more desirable to sit beneath an overhead plane with a partial or complete sense of cover than it is in a wide open space with a totally open feeling. The overhead plane doesn't have to cover the entire space. It may extend

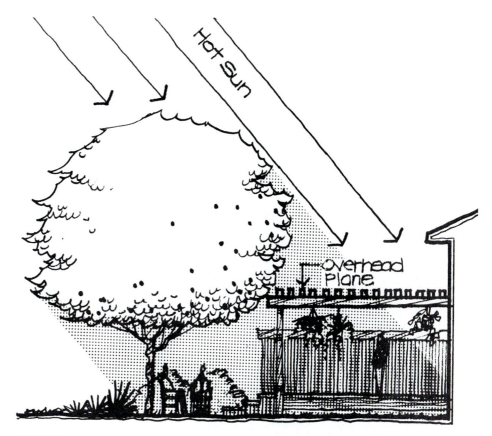

FIGURE 2–37
Overhead planes in the living and entertaining space can be defined by natural and artificial elements.

FIGURE 2–38
Living and entertaining spaces may be partially covered to create both sunny and shaded subspaces.

over only a portion of the outside living and entertaining space rather than over the entire area (Figure 2–38). This creates subspaces, some shaded and some sunny. The overhead plane can also cast dramatic shadow patterns on the ground plane and provides places to hang such things as potted plants, wind chimes, etc.

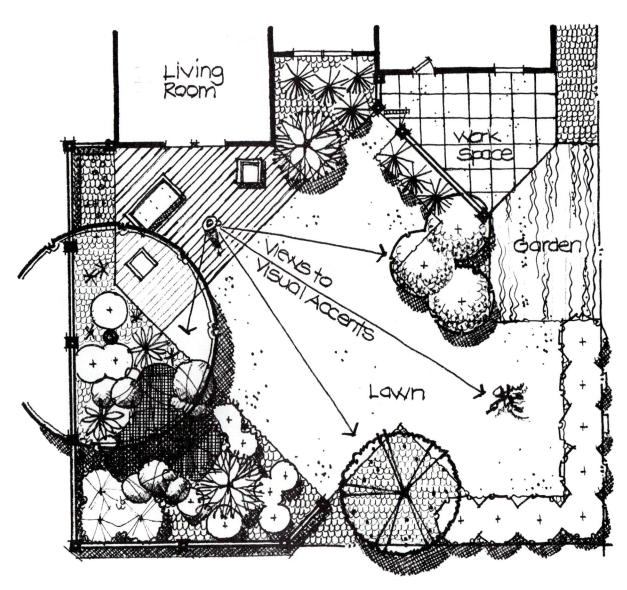

FIGURE 2–39
A variety of accents can be used to create views throughout the back yard.

While the outdoor entertaining space should have a sense of enclosure, especially for privacy, it should not feel totally walled in either. There should be adequate openings in both the vertical and overhead planes of the space to allow for some views and sunlight. At strategic points along the vertical plane, views can be directed toward special accent areas situated on or off the site. In fact, there should be a conscious effort to establish focal points at various places throughout the site to capture views (Figure 2–39). In some instances, it may be desirable to take advantage of views off the site to a golf course, lake, or distant mountain range. However, views should not be allowed to drift off the site in an unplanned manner.

The ground plane in the outdoor entertaining space should also be given considerable attention. It should be constructed with a stable and durable material that reinforces the intended character of the space. The residents and their guests are apt to spend many hours in this space, allowing them to notice the detail and craftsmanship of materials more closely than in other areas. Therefore, the texture, color, patterns, and construction detail of the materials should be visually attractive and coordinated. Potential materials and patterns are discussed more thoroughly in Chapter 12.

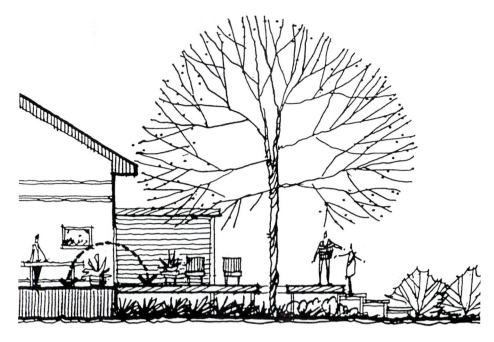

FIGURE 2-40
Indoor and outdoor spaces can be visually integrated by making the base plane the same elevation in both spaces.

FIGURE 2-41
Indoor and outdoor spaces can be visually integrated by repeating the same material on the base plane of both spaces.

Where appropriate, an attempt should be made to visually and functionally coordinate the outdoor entertaining space with the adjoining interior room(s) of the house. It is usually desirable to integrate the indoors and outdoors so they are perceived as a coordinated series of usable spaces linked together in the same overall environment. Again, the designer can work with all three planes of spatial enclosure to accomplish this. On the ground plane, one way to coordinate the indoors with the outdoors is by extending the indoor floor elevation to the outdoors by means of a wood deck (Figure 2–40). Indoor and outdoor spaces can also be visually integrated by repeating the same materials or patterns on the ground or walls. A ceiling can be extended to the outdoor living and entertaining space by means of an overhead arbor or awning (Figure 2–41).

In conclusion, the outside living and entertaining space is potentially one of the most intensely used spaces on the residential site. If designed properly, it will be the center of outdoor activity for both the family's use as well as formal and informal entertaining of guests. For this to occur, the space should be comfortable to use throughout the day and evening with similar characteristics of the indoor living and entertaining room.

Kitchen

The kitchen is normally a utilitarian room of the house. Its primary purpose is to prepare, cook, eat and store food. But the kitchen can be a place for socializing too. Have you ever noticed how many parties you have been to where people tend to congregate in and around the kitchen? But what is important to note is that all the various appliances are efficiently located around a central area for ease of working. A good kitchen typically has ample counter area for work space and for locating cooking utensils. The kitchen is normally located in the house where there is easy access to and from outdoors for transporting groceries and taking out the garbage. The kitchen is often located adjacent to the breakfast area and/or dining room so food can be conveniently transported back and forth.

Outdoor Food Preparation Space

The outdoor food preparation space can vary from a simple area of pavement where a portable grill is located to an elaborate space containing built-in appliances, counters, and storage. Regardless of the particular situation, there are several guidelines for the design of this space.

The location of the outside food preparation space is critical. It should be placed where it is convenient to the kitchen, indoor dining room, and outdoor dining space (Figure 2–42). The food preparation space needs to be relatively close to the outdoor dining space so food can be easily and quickly transported between the spaces. Ideally, circulation between these spaces should be direct, for it is very easy to trip when carrying food, plates, utensils, etc. Another consideration for the location of the outdoor food preparation space is the direction of the prevailing wind. The food preparation space should be placed so that the wind carries the smoke from the cooking fire away from the other outdoor spaces and the house (Figure 2–43).

Whether a portable grill or built-in appliances are used, there should be some counter space or a surface on which to place food and cooking utensils. This doesn't have to be elaborate, but it does make cooking a lot easier. This surface works well when it is about 36 inches above the ground (typical counter height) and 24 inches deep (typical counter depth).

Because fire in a grill or fireplace is an integral part of most outdoor food preparation spaces, it is necessary to keep its presence in mind. Branches of nearby trees should be kept some distance from the grill so that the generated heat doesn't burn any leaves above. And of course, wood surfaces should not be placed too close to the fire source.

The outdoor food preparation space should be studied carefully so that it fits into the overall design and so it works efficiently yet visually looks intentional and thought out. Too often, this space is one that is simply left to occur wherever it may without much forethought and consideration. If well planned, it can add to the overall design rather than detract from it.

Indoor Dining Room

The inside dining room, although primarily used for eating, may also serve as a location for playing games, writing, studying, and so on, due to the presence of a reasonably sized table with several chairs. The dining room is usually simple

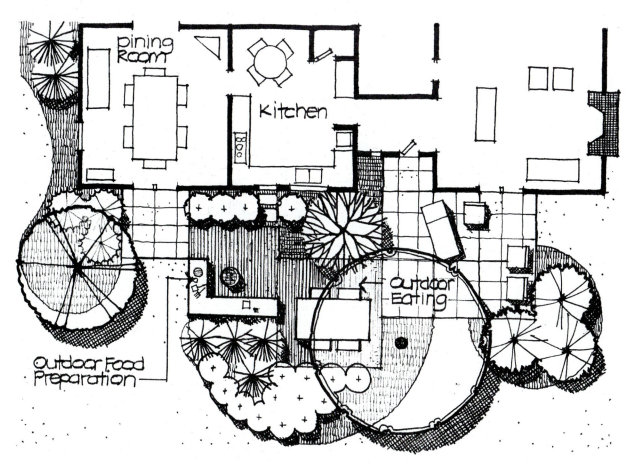

FIGURE 2–42
The outdoor food preparation space should be conveniently located near the dining room, kitchen, and outdoor eating space.

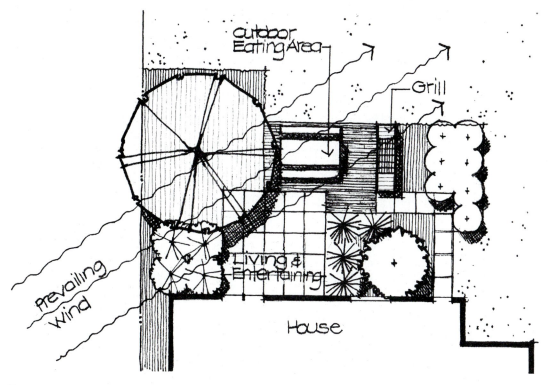

FIGURE 2–43
The grill should be located so that smoke is blown away from outdoor living and eating spaces.

FIGURE 2-44
The outdoor dining space should use all three planes of enclosure for a room-like feeling.

in organization and design. The size of many dining rooms is about 125 square feet with proportions that are equal or slightly longer than wide. More times than not, the dining room is located next to the kitchen and living room to be convenient to both. The dining room table is typically the dominant element of the dining room, with everything else in the room being secondary. The dining room does not possess the comfort and convenience of the living room and is not as utilitarian as the kitchen. However, it does combine eating, typically associated with the kitchen, with conversation, typically associated with the living room.

Outdoor Dining Space

The outdoor dining space on many residential sites is nothing more than a picnic table placed on the terrace or somewhere on the lawn. In some situations, this may be appropriate for casual eating but not for more private gatherings. In most cases, the outdoor dining space suffers from the same deficiencies as the outdoor living and entertaining space: little or no identity, spatial enclosure, privacy from neighbors, or protection from sun and wind. To address these problems, there are a number of design guidelines to consider.

As with all the other functions, the outdoor dining space should be designed as a room. Again, this means the designer should work with all three planes of outdoor space to create a sense of enclosure (Figure 2–44).

Like its indoor counterpart, the outdoor dining space should be located near the entertaining space and food preparation space for ease of access to both. In many cases, the outdoor dining space may be created as a subspace of the living and entertaining space (Figure 2–45). Again, this can be accomplished through a variation in shape, pavement material, or elevation change.

The plan proportions of the outside dining space should be equal or perhaps somewhat elongated to accommodate a picnic table. Its dimensions will vary depending on the size and number of tables and chairs that need to fit into the space.

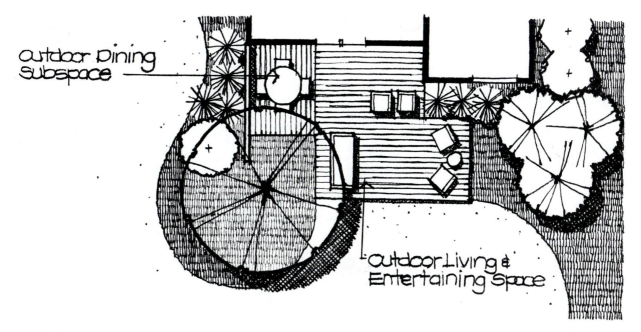

FIGURE 2–45
The outdoor dining space may be designed as a subspace of the living and entertaining space.

Other Outdoor Rooms

There are several other outdoor spaces or rooms that also deserve attention. These include the recreation space, work/storage space, and the garden space. Like the outdoor rooms already discussed, these spaces have a number of considerations that should be taken into account when designing them.

Recreation Space.   The outdoor recreation space should of course be located on flat ground, with a slight slope for adequate drainage. It should not be too close to other spaces that require peace and quiet or where delicate elements such as flowers and potted plants are located. The shape of the recreation space should be appropriately and adequately sized for the type of recreation.

Beyond the functional requirements, the recreation space should be defined as an outdoor room. It should have a feeling of spatial definition whether it is by implication or actual physical enclosure. The lawn area is often an undefined entity that takes up all of the remaining area of the site after other elements are located. The edge and shape of the lawn area should not be an afterthought or be left to chance. As discussed later, the outer shape and outline of the lawn area should be given as much study as the form of any other space on the site. The edge to the lawn area can be established by a mulch bed, ground cover, masses of shrubs and trees, walls, and fences (Figure 2–46).

Pools are a specialty item in some regions of the country while quite typical in others. In all cases, thought should be given to: (1) size of the pool desired based on the intended use (leisure, serious swimming, visual focal point), (2) adequate pedestrian circulation around the pool, (3) location of the pool in relation to the other functions on the site, (4) location of the pool's mechanical system and equipment, (5) ease of access by heavy equipment for constructing the pool, and (6) local ordinances governing fence type and height around the pool for protection of children and animals. While there may be other important factors to consider, it should be stressed that a pool is likely to be the dominant element of a design owing to its uniqueness, thus making it an extremely important element requiring extensive study.

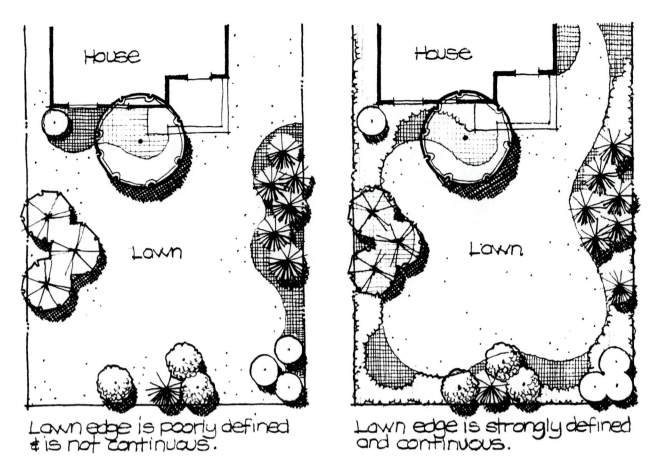

House   House

Lawn   Lawn

Lawn edge is poorly defined & is not continuous. Lawn edge is strongly defined and continuous.

FIGURE 2–46
A continuous ground-cover edge and masses of plant materials can be used in designing the recreation area.

Outdoor Work/Storage Space. The outdoor work/storage space is primarily a utilitarian room on the residential site. Its function is to store such things as firewood, garden and recreation equipment, and other items that are too large or unnecessary to keep in the house, garage, or cellar. The work/storage space is also a place where work can be done (light construction, potting plants, equipment repair, etc.). If properly designed, this space can act as an outdoor workshop. For these functions to occur, the outdoor work/storage space should be located near the garage or basement door so materials and equipment can be easily carried between them (Figure 2–47). The work/storage space should have a hard, durable, and nonslip pavement surface. A wall or fence may be needed to enclose the work/storage space for security and/or to screen it from other spaces on the site. Inside the work/storage space, a work/potting bench, shelves, and enclosed or covered storage might be provided. Much of this can be designed and built in a coordinated manner (Figure 2–48).

Garden Space. The garden space is another utilitarian area on the residential site. It exists as a work or hobby space for raising fruits, vegetables, and perennial flower beds. To function adequately, the location of the garden space is critical. It should be placed on fertile, well-drained soil on flat ground. The garden should be situated so it has adequate exposure to sunlight. If continuous sun exposure is not possible throughout the entire day, then morning and midday sun is preferred. Mid- to late-afternoon sun is the least desirable because it is the hottest and most drying. Ideally, the garden needs to be near a water source such as a well or outside water spigot. It is inconvenient if water hoses have to be stretched long

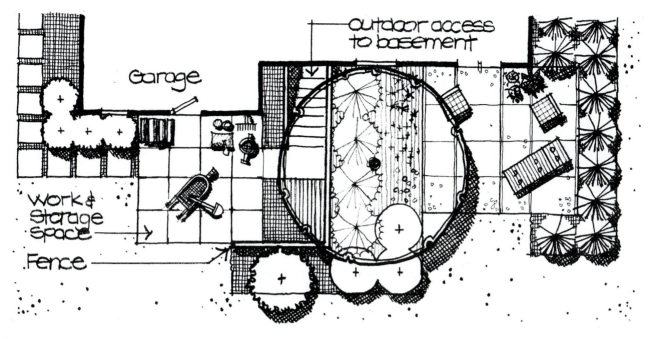

FIGURE 2-47
The work and storage space should be located near the garage and basement doors while also being separated from the living and entertaining space.

FIGURE 2-48
A work bench, potting area, and storage could be coordinated in one attractive structure.

distances to reach the garden. The garden space should also be located so it won't become an eyesore, especially during those times of the year when vegetables and other plants are not growing. It can be quite unsightly to look at a bare earthen patch in the back yard. Shrubs, fences, or walls may be utilized to provide varying degrees of screening of the garden (Figure 2–49). All of this suggests that the back corner of the property, where the garden is commonly located by default on many sites, isn't necessarily the only or best location.

A few other ideas might also be considered for a vegetable garden. One is to incorporate the planting of vegetables with other plants in the yard rather than creating a separate vegetable garden. Many vegetables do have attractive flowers and foliage texture. This concept treats vegetables like other plant materials that are used for a variety of functions such as creating the edges of space or establishing points of interest (Figure 2–50).

Another idea is to design the garden as a series of raised garden plots. This gives the garden a neat and organized appearance and makes it easier to tend the

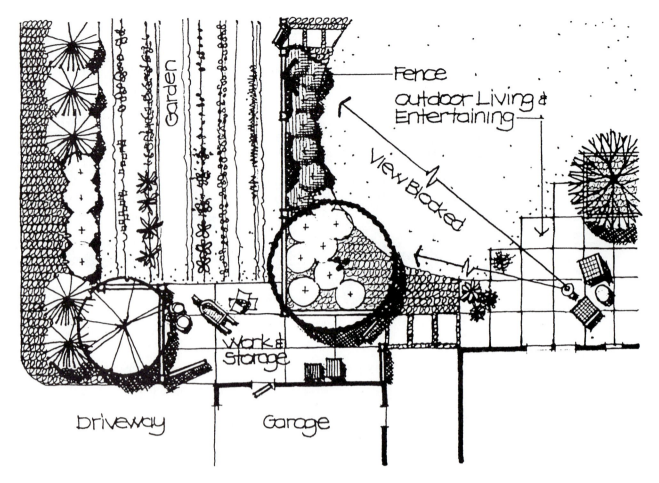

FIGURE 2-49
Plant materials and fences can be used to screen the garden.

FIGURE 2-50
Vegetables can be integrated with masses of other plant materials.

vegetables while standing. Raised plots also make it possible to prepare one's own mix of fertile soil.

SUMMARY

Outdoor rooms are the residential designer's building blocks. These are defined by the three planes of spatial enclosure that can be manipulated to create rooms of varied sizes, shapes, functions, and atmospheres. As discussed in this chapter, the most significant rooms on the residential site are the arrival and outdoor entry space, the living/entertaining space, the food preparation space, the dining space, the recreational space, the work/storage space, and the garden space. All these spaces must be designed in imaginative, yet practical ways to create exterior residential environments that enhance the quality and enjoyment of life. As you read other chapters of this book, please keep in mind that the goal of all suggestions ultimately is to create functional and pleasant outdoor rooms.

3

Environmentally Responsive Design

INTRODUCTION

Fundamental to preparing well-conceived site designs is the philosophy that each design should be respectful of and integrated with natural processes inherent in the outdoor environment. Each residential site should be "designed with nature" to sensitively blend with and use the universally present forces of nature such as precipitation, drainage, sun, wind, seasonal change, plant evolution and growth, and ecology of interdependent plant and wildlife communities. Landscape designs that work with nature rather than against it are commonly labeled "sustainable design." These type of designs are able to work with natural processes over an extended period of time with minimum input of human resources and energy.

Designs that work with nature are advantageous for a number of reasons. First, such designs save energy and money. Well-designed residential sites save on heating and cooling. It has been estimated that a site that has properly placed plant materials can save up to 30 percent in the money required to heat and cool a residence throughout the year.[1] Secondly, a properly designed site can be less expensive to maintain by using indigenous plant materials to minimize the area of lawn requiring mowing and fertilization. Thirdly, a site that is "designed with nature" also visually fits the regional context by using indigenous plant materials and local building materials found in the regional landscape.

This chapter presents a number of ideas for designing a residential site in a manner that integrates natural processes. More specifically, this chapter discusses the concept of microclimate, procedures for designing with sun and wind, and concepts for making a site more sustainable by means of proper material selection and

---

[1]Anne Simon Moffat and Marc Schiler, *Landscape Design That Saves Energy* (New York: William Morrow and Company, Inc., 1981), p. 10.

maintenance techniques. The intent is to make the residential site environmentally responsive as well as economical to manage.

SITE MICROCLIMATE

Microclimate is one aspect of the residential site to consider when making a design solution respectful of natural processes. As the name implies, "microclimate" is the small-scale climatic conditions at a particular spot or area on a site. Microclimate is the aggregation of temperature, sun exposure, wind exposure, and moisture/humidity in a relatively small area. For example, one may speak of the microclimate under a large tree as being a discrete zone on-site that has its own climatic qualities. Likewise, an open lawn area or the ground along the south side of a house each have their own particular microclimatic conditions. Thus, a residential site is composed of a variety of different microclimates.

The challenge for the residential designer is to recognize and understand these diverse microclimates so that a design can be properly matched to the existing or potential microclimatic zones on a site. Microclimates on the residential site potentially affect a number of factors. First, microclimates should be considered when deciding where to place different outdoor uses. Functions that require sun exposure should be located in the sunniest places of a site while uses that require minimum air flow should be located where they are protected from the wind. Areas that are to be frequently used by people should be carefully placed for microclimate so that they are comfortable and more enjoyably used for longer lengths of time. Microclimates also need to be considered in selecting and placing plant materials. All plant materials have their own particular climatic requirements and should be correctly matched to the microclimates that fulfill their needs. For example, plants that require cool and moist conditions should be placed in spots where they can benefit from the shade of a tree or the house.

Each site has its own microclimates that result from the particular site conditions including site orientation, house location, house orientation, house size/configuration, topography, drainage patterns, amount and location of existing plant materials, and area and location of ground materials including pavement. Even though each site is different, some broad microclimate patterns do exist on all sites. The following paragraphs discuss the characteristics and implications of generalized microclimatic zones located immediately adjacent to a two-story house based only on sun and wind. The size of these microclimate zones varies from one season to the next, but in general they extend 10 to 20 feet away from the side of the house. For the sake of discussion, it is assumed that the house sits by itself on a level, open, undeveloped site in the temperate climate zone (Figure 3–1).

South side of house:

- receives the most sun exposure throughout year
- is in shade in early morning and late evening during the summer
- is the warmest area in winter
- is protected from cold winds
- has extended outdoor use in early spring and late autumn
- has the longest growing season
- may be favorable growing plants here that are adapted to a more southerly hardiness zone

East side of house:

- is the most moderate of all zones
- receives morning sun exposure, yet benefits from afternoon shade

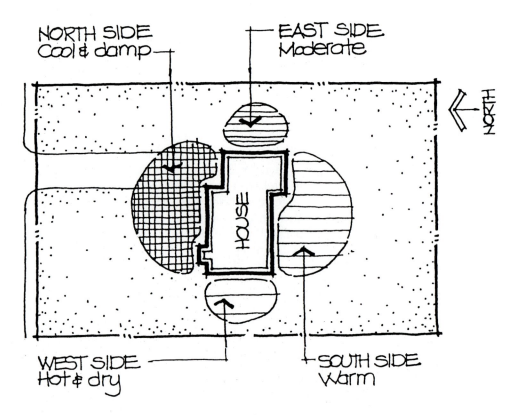

FIGURE 3-1
General microclimate zones around a house in the temperate zone.

- is protected from both prevailing and cold winds
- is a favorable location for both outdoor morning and after-noon activities
- is a good location for plant materials that require partial sun and shade

North side of house:

- is the coldest, shadiest, and dampest area throughout year
- receives no sun for most of the day throughout the year
- receives sun in early morning and late evening during the summer
- is directly exposed to cold wind
- is a good location for outdoor use during the summer; is not a good location for outdoor use the remainder of the year
- is good for plants that require shade; may require some plants that are suitable to a more northerly hardiness zone

West side of house:

- receives direct afternoon sun exposure, yet benefits from morning shade
- is exposed to both prevailing and cold winds throughout the year; is the windiest area of all
- is the hottest and driest location of all during the summer

- is not a good location for afternoon outdoor activities; must have shade provided if outdoor use is to be located here
- requires the use of plants that are heat and drought tolerant

Remainder of site located away from house:

- is a widely diverse microclimate that changes notably from one season to the next
- is an uncomfortable zone in summer due to constant exposure to sun; requires shade to be comfortably used in summer
- is an uncomfortable zone in winter due to constant exposure to wind; however, constant exposure to sun would be beneficial
- would be most enjoyable during the spring and autumn months of the year

In summary, it is clear that each side of the house has its own unique microclimate and thus deserves to be treated individually. Of course, the outlined microclimatic zones are broad generalizations and potentially vary from one site to another based on the height of the house, existing trees, topography and slope orientation, walls or fences, and ground materials. For example, a large tree located on the west side of the house can make this area much cooler and more comfortable than previously described. On the other hand, the desertlike qualities of the western side of the house can be accentuated if the ground is paved in concrete without any protection from the sun. Consequently, all the site elements and materials must be collectively considered in determining the location and characteristics of the microclimates that exist on a site.

DESIGNING WITH SUN

Sun is one factor that needs consideration to make a residential site environmentally responsible. Its presence affects air temperatures and shadow patterns, which in turn directly influence human comfort. Sun also has a direct impact on the amount of energy used for heating and cooling the house. Sun and shadow patterns also affect the ability of different plant materials to grow on the residential site.

Before being able to effectively design with sun, it is necessary to understand the movement of the sun throughout the day and at different seasons of the year. The sun's relative position in the sky is constantly changing in its plan direction as well as its angle above the horizon (Figure 3–2). In the summer season (June), the sun rises in the northeast and moves in a clockwise direction around a site until it sets in the northwest. In the temperate zone, the sun's total arch of transit is about 240 degrees between sunrise and sunset. At the same time, the angle of the sun above the horizon is constantly increasing to a zenith of about 72 degrees from the south at noon (Figure 3–3).

In the winter season (December) the sun rises in the southeast and sets in the southwest while moving through a total arc of transit of about 120 degrees in the temperate zone. At noon, the sun rises to an angle of 27 degrees above the horizon. The sun is essentially a southerly sun at a very low angle above the horizon during the winter season. Thus, the sun is less intense, restricted in its time of shining, and limited in its direction of exposure in comparison to other seasons of the year. In the solstice months of March and September, the sun's path and angle above the horizon are in between the extremes of June and December.

This information can be used to construct shadow patterns around a house on a residential site and to determine where the sunniest and shadiest zones are as well as the associated microclimates. Figures 3–4 through 3–6 illustrate the shadow patterns of a two-story house located on a level site in the temperate zone at four seasons

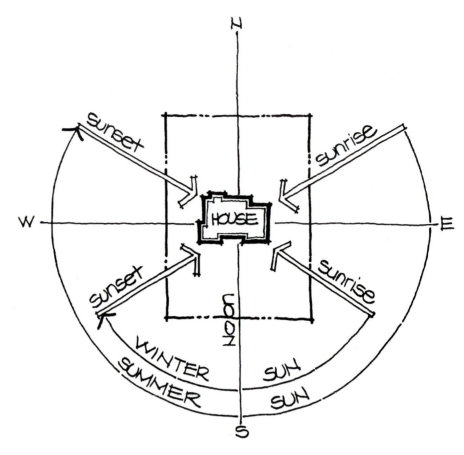

FIGURE 3–2
Plan direction of the sun at different times of the day and year.

FIGURE 3–3
Vertical angle of the sun above the horizon at noon in the winter and summer.

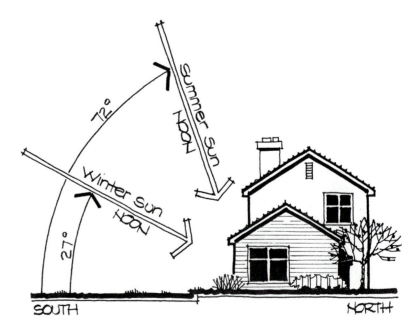

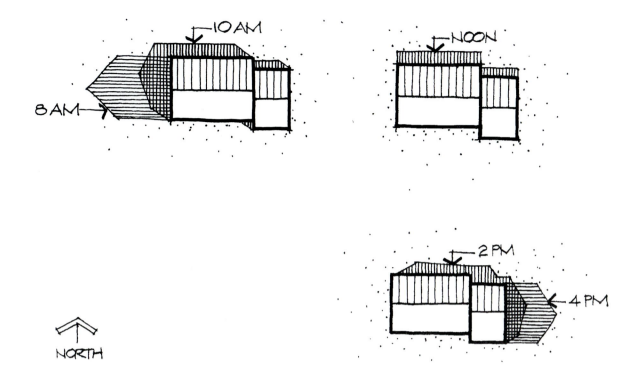

NORTH

FIGURE 3–4
Shadow patterns from a two-story house at different times of the day in June.

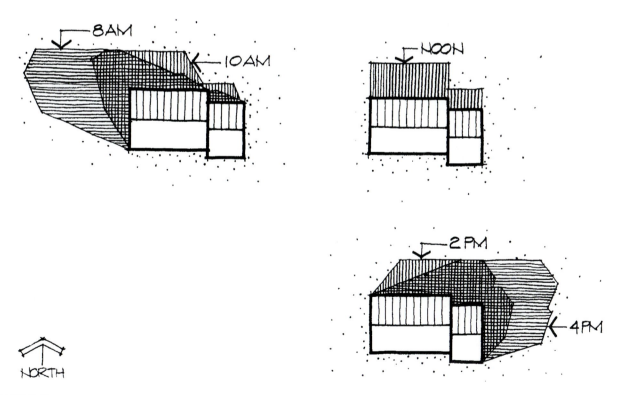

NORTH

FIGURE 3–5
Shadow patterns from a two-story house at different times of the day in March and September.

Environmentally Responsive Design

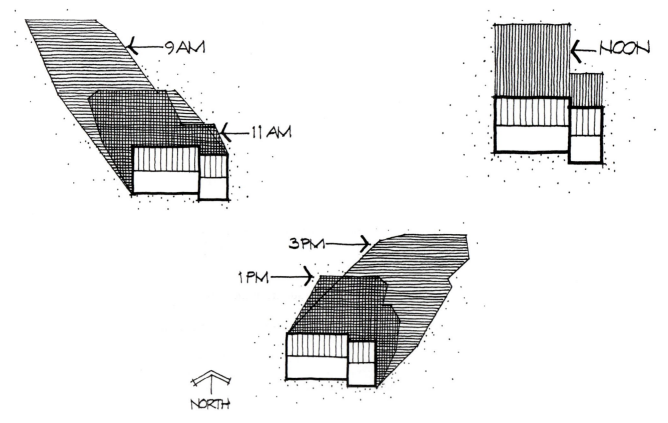

FIGURE 3-6
Shadow patterns from a two-story house at different times of the day in December.

of the year. These shadow patterns were composed by using information from sun charts that can be obtained in most public libraries or from the National Weather Service. Some general conclusions that can be drawn from these patterns are:

- all sides of the house receive sun exposure during the summer; similarly, all sides of the house experience shadow as well
- the largest areas of shadow during the summer occur on the east and west sides of the house; the north and south sides of the house experience little shadow
- only the south side of the house receives direct sun exposure in the winter; the northern side receives no sun exposure at this time of year
- the largest areas of shadow during March and September occur on the east, north, and west sides of the house
- throughout the year, the south side of the house receives the most sun exposure; the north side of the house receives the least

Similar conclusions can also be drawn for different slope orientations on a residential site. A south-facing slope, like the south side of a house, receives the most sun throughout the year and is the warmest of all during the winter season. A north-facing slope is the coolest of all, especially during the winter. The frost is apt to stay in the ground one to two weeks longer on a north-facing slope than on a south-facing slope. An east-facing slope experiences moderate temperatures while a west-facing slope is the hottest and driest of all slopes during the summer months.

Two general conclusions can be made from an understanding of the sun exposure and shadow patterns on a residential site: (1) sun protection is required for the months in late spring through the early autumn and (2) sun exposure is desirable for late autumn through early spring months of the year. These objectives are true for both outdoor spaces as well as for the house itself.

Providing Sun Protection

Sun protection is most needed for the midday and afternoon hours during the summer season when air temperatures are the hottest. Exposure to the sun during these hours increases heat generated from exposed surfaces and reduces the ability of people and animals to shed heat from their bodies. As a general guideline, people feel most comfortable in the following conditions: (1) shade, (2) no air movement, (3) air temperatures between 70 and 80° F, and (4) relative humidity between 30 and 65 percent.[2] This so-called comfort zone is exceeded when air temperatures rise above this level and/or there is direct exposure to the sun. The broad intent should be to shield the sun from the house and outdoor spaces used during the summer season, especially during the afternoon hours.

One way to accomplish this is to plan where outdoor uses should be located with respect to sun. The best location is on the east or northeast side of the house or tree mass (Figure 3–7). An area immediately to the north of the house or a tree mass is also good, though the size of this shaded area is small due to the relatively high vertical angle of the sun shining from the south in the summer. These locations are noticeably cooler and more comfortable than other potential locations on the residential site for the summer season.

Sun protection can also be created by introducing elements that cast shade on a residential site. The most common means is to strategically locate large shade trees to shield the midday and afternoon sun from the residence and outdoor spaces used during this time of day. Shade trees provide sun protection by several means. First, they block the sun's rays from striking roofs of one- and two-story buildings, exterior building walls, and ground surfaces throughout the landscape. When directly exposed to the sun, these ground surfaces convert sun rays into heat which is radiated away from the surfaces (Figure 3–8). The heat generated by exposed building roofs and walls radiates out into the nearby air as well as to the interior spaces. Similarly, exposed ground surfaces also radiate heat into adjoining air, thereby elevating the temperature. By comparison, shaded surfaces do not heat up beyond the ambient air temperature and thus do not add to the temperature of the adjoining air mass.

Secondly, shade trees provide relief from hot air temperatures through evapotranspiration, a process of giving off moisture through leaf surfaces. Moisture is taken from the ground by a plant's roots, moves through its trunk and branch structure, and ends up being released through the plant's leaf surfaces (Figure 3–9). As this moisture evaporates from the leaf surfaces, it simultaneously cools adjoining air temperatures. It has been estimated that a large shade tree can evaporate as much as 100 gallons of moisture per day, thus giving the cooling effect of five air conditioners.[3]

To provide shade, trees should primarily be located on the southwest and west sides of the house and outdoor spaces (Figure 3–10). Shade trees can be placed in other locations as well to accomplish other design objectives, such as creating spatial edges or controlling views. Still, the densest grouping of trees for shade should be placed to the southwest of areas that need shade. The best type of tree

---

[2]Victor Olgyay, *Design With Climate: Bioclimatic Approach to Architectural Regionalism* (Princeton, N.J.: Princeton University Press, 1963), pp. 17–23.

[3]Anne Simon Moffat and Marc Schiler, *Energy-Efficient and Environmental Landscaping* (South Newfane, VT: Appropriate Solutions Press, 1994), p. 9.

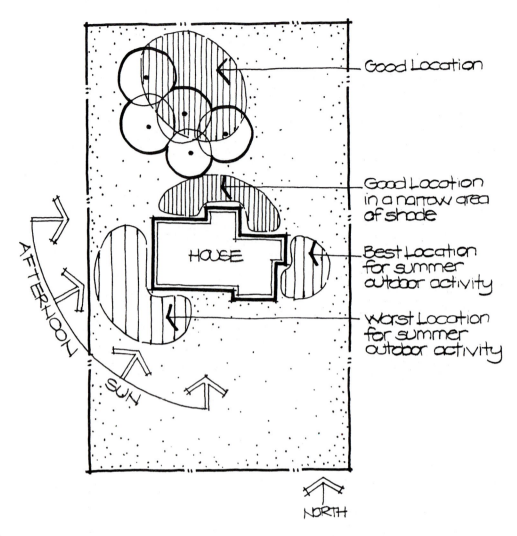

FIGURE 3-7
Locations for shaded outdoor spaces during the summer season.

for shade is one that is relatively tall, broad, and densely foliated. A broad or wide tree canopy will cast more shade than a tree that is more upright or fastigiate.

Where possible, shade trees should be located over or as close as possible to the structure or outdoor space that is to be shaded due to the high summer sun angle previously described. A 25-foot-high tree located 10 feet from the west wall of a house may shade 47 percent of the surface while the same tree placed 20 feet from the wall will only shade about 27 percent of the surface.[4] The one exception to this rule is in regions that experience severe fire hazard such as southern California. Here, trees need to be kept at least 10 feet from the residence so they cannot spread fire onto the house from the surrounding landscape. Trees planted in the next 30-foot zone away from the edge of the house should be widely spaced so they do not create the threat of crown fires.[5]

Vines and shrubs can also be used to shade the residence. Vines can be grown on exterior masonry walls of a house to shield the exterior wall surface from absorbing the sun's rays and converting them to heat as discussed earlier. A mass of shrubs

[4]Dr. James R. Fazio, editor, "How Trees Can Save Energy" *Tree City USA Bulletin #21* (Nebraska City, NE: The National Arbor Day Foundation), p. 3.

[5]Maureen Gilmer, *California Wildfire Landscaping* (Dallas, TX: Taylor Publishing Company, 1994), p. 59.

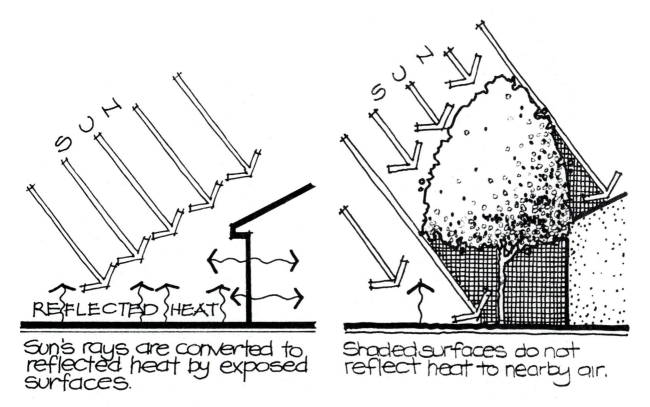

Sun's rays are converted to reflected heat by exposed surfaces.

Shaded surfaces do not reflect heat to nearby air.

FIGURE 3-8
Use of shade trees to shield roofs, exterior house walls, and the ground from the sun's rays.

FIGURE 3-9
Shade trees cool the air around them through evapotranspiration.

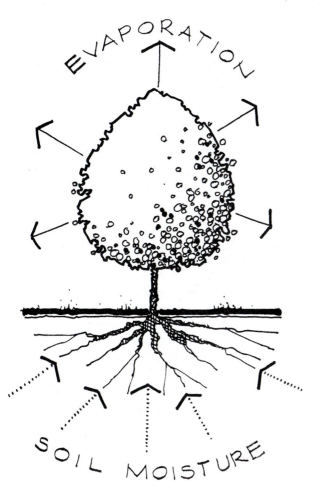

Environmentally Responsive Design

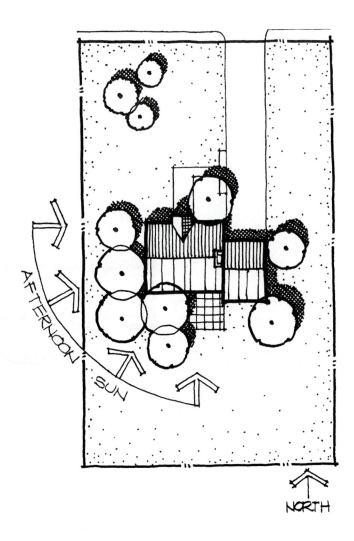

planted along an exterior wall will have a similar effect. These techniques are most effective on exterior walls that face either east or west due to the lower sun angle from these directions (Figure 3–11). Vine-covered or shrub-screened exterior walls are less useful on a southern facing wall due to the higher sun angle from this direction.

The provision of shade can have notable benefits. Houses that are shaded may have interior air temperatures up to 20° F lower and have uncomfortable internal air temperatures half the time of houses that are not shaded.[6] This translates to reducing the need for air conditioning and the associated electric bill. Similarly, an air conditioner located in the shade operates at a rate 10 percent more efficient than an air conditioner in direct sun.[7] Overall, a shaded house is simply more energy efficient than one that is not. Similarly, outdoor spaces that are shaded by large trees are cooler than those in the direct sunlight. Areas below trees may be 5 to 10° F cooler than nearby areas in direct sun. Shade makes outdoor spaces more comfortably used for longer periods of time during the summer.

Overhead structures such as arbors, awnings, and pergolas can likewise be used to provide shade for outdoor spaces used during the summer months. These structures can stand alone or be attached to the house as an architectural extension. Vines may also be grown over and through overhead structures to soften their ar-

---

[6]Anne Simon Moffat and Marc Schiler, *Landscape Design That Saves Energy* (New York: William Morrow and Company, Inc., 1981), p. 18.

[7]Dr. James R. Fazio, editor, "How Trees Can Save Energy" *Tree City USA Bulletin #21* (Nebraska City, NE: The National Arbor Day Foundation), p. 3.

MID-LATE AFTERNOON SUN

EARLY-MID MORNING SUN

Tall shrubs cast shade on west wall

Vines shade masonry wall

FIGURE 3–11
Tall shrubs and vines on walls can provide shade from the low sun angle to the east and west.

chitectural character and to provide additional shade and cooling. One advantage of awnings and structures in comparison to trees is that awnings and structures provide shade immediately after construction. By comparison, shade trees may take years to grow to a size large enough to provide effective shade.

Awnings and overhead structures are most effective in providing shade from the midday and early afternoon sun when the sun angle is high. Awnings and overhead structures are less useful for early morning and late afternoon/evening sun because of the lower angle of the sun at these times of day. Thus awnings and overhead structures are best located directly over or slightly to the south or west of outdoor spaces to be shaded (Figure 3–12).

There are a number of variables that need to be considered when designing overhead structures. One is the density and pattern of the overhead members which cast shade. Awnings or solid rooflike overhead planes provide the most shade and are most useful over outdoor spaces that are used extensively from midday through mid-afternoon. However, such solid overhead planes can create a dark space below themselves and may increase air temperatures in the space by creating a cap which holds in the heat.

It is often better to create overhead structures that are constructed with multiple individual members spaced apart. The space between the individual members allows for heat to rise and escape through the overhead plane, thus helping to keep the space cooler. The size and spacing of the individual members has a direct effect on the amount of shade cast. Large and/or closely spaced members provide the most shade while small and/or generously spaced members cast less shade. The amount of shade desired will depend on the use of the space, regional location, and the time of day when shade is needed. The density and pattern also have a bearing on the visual shade pattern cast on the ground plane. The shadow pattern on the ground plane can itself be an attractive quality in an outdoor space.

Another consideration for creating overhead structures is the direction of the overhead members. This, too, should be based on the amount of shade required.

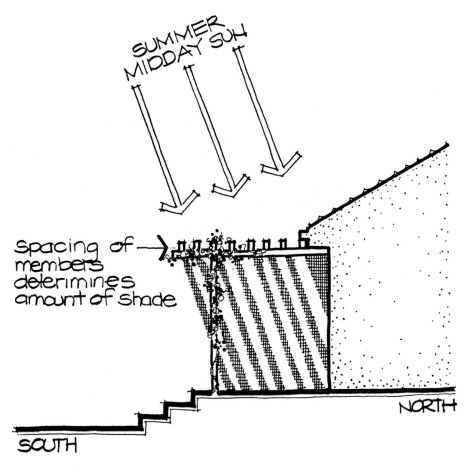

FIGURE 3–12
Overhead structures should be located over or slightly to the south of outdoor spaces for maximum shade.

Density aside, more shade will be cast by individual members that extend in a direction perpendicular to the direction of the sun (Figure 3–13). Consequently, individual members should be placed in an east-west direction to cast effective shade from a southern sun during the midday, while a north-south direction is more effective when the sun is shining from the west, as occurs from mid- to later afternoon in the summer. The angle of the individual members should also be considered. Members that are placed at right angles in relation to the sun's rays will provide more shade than members that are positioned parallel to the sun's rays.

Sun protection can also be produced by walls and fences. These vertical planes are most effective in providing shade in the early to mid-morning and from mid-afternoon to evening during the summer season. During these hours of the day, the sun angle is lower and is more directly blocked by a vertical plane instead of an overhead plane. Therefore, walls and fences are best located to the east and/or west of the spaces that are to be shaded. These same elements are also effective in casting shade onto the west wall of a house to relieve a residence from the intense heat buildup in this microclimate. As with overhead structures, there are numerous design variables available to create a wide range of shade density.

Maximizing Sun Exposure

Exposure to the sun is desirable for the late autumn through early spring months of the year. This need is greatest in northern regions and less of a requirement in southern regions of the country. During these months, exposure to sun can

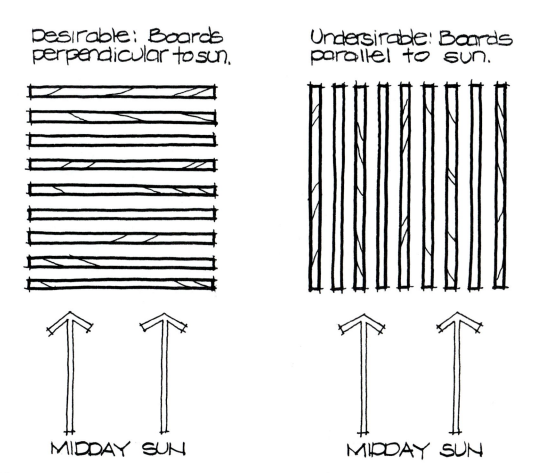

FIGURE 3–13
Individual members of an overhead structure should be located perpendicular to the direction of the midday sun.

increase air temperatures in exterior spaces and make them more enjoyably used for longer periods of time. This is especially true in the transitional months of October/November and March/April. Likewise, exposure of interior spaces to sun can increase ambient room temperatures and reduce heating costs during the winter season.

One technique for maximizing sun exposure of exterior spaces in the winter season is to locate and orient the spaces properly. As previously suggested, outdoor spaces that are used during the cool season should, where possible, be located on the south side of the house to receive full sun exposure during the day. Outdoor spaces located on the south side of a residence will also benefit from a "sun pocket" effect created by heat reflected away from the exterior house wall and the adjoining ground plane (Figure 3–14). A dark-colored pavement can accentuate this heat buildup by absorbing more sun rays and converting them into heat. Outdoor spaces intended for the cool season should not be located next to the north side of a residence.

A number of site design concepts need to be considered to maximize sun exposure. One is to use a predominance of deciduous vegetation on the south side of a house. Deciduous trees and other vegetation are able to shade the house during the summer while allowing the winter sun to pass through when leaves are absent. Even so, they also need to be carefully located and selected. Deciduous trees should be widely spaced on the southern side of the house so that as much sun exposure as possible is gained. Too many trees in this location will reduce the amount of sun that is able to strike the southern side of the house.

Environmentally Responsive Design

FIGURE 3-14
A winter "heat pocket" can be created on the
south side of the house.

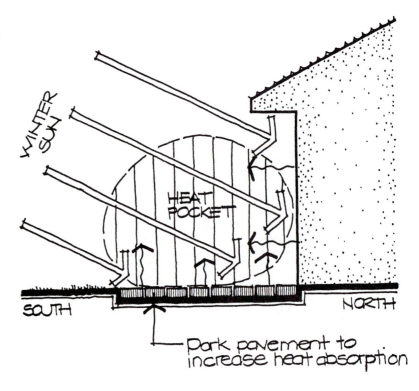

Furthermore, it is best to use trees that are limbed up and to locate them relatively close to the house (Figure 3–15). In this position, trees will provide effective shade over the house roof in the summer, but will allow the winter sun, with its lower sun angle, to shine below the tree canopy where it can directly strike the walls and windows of the house. Deciduous plants that have an open or loose branching structure are preferred for the south side of the house to minimize the number of individual branches that block the sun. Densely branched deciduous plants and most evergreen vegetation should be minimized, if used at all, on the south side of the house. Evergreen plants will, of course, completely block the sun's rays and eliminate their potential heating effect.

One other thought for intensifying sun exposure is to maximize the amount of window area on the south side of the house. When the sun's rays pass through a window, they are converted to heat energy by the surfaces they strike. This heat is retained inside the room and referred to as a "greenhouse effect." No shrubs should be planted that screen the sun from windows on the south side. When the arrangement of outdoor spaces allows, an area of pavement placed immediately adjacent to sliding glass doors or other similar expanses of windows can increase the heat gain by reflecting some sun into nearby rooms (Figure 3–16).

DESIGNING WITH WIND

Wind is another important climatic factor that needs to be considered when designing a residential site. Wind affects both human comfort and energy consumption of the house itself. Wind cools the body by increasing the amount of moisture evaporated at the skin's surface. This is desired when air temperatures exceed the comfort range of 70 to 80° F. When this occurs, wind functions like a fan to cool the body, making it feel cooler than the ambient air temperature. On the other hand, wind exposure is not desired when air temperatures drop below 70° F. Wind accentuates the perception of cold air at these temperatures and creates what is commonly called "wind chill." Similar phenomena occur for the house itself. Wind car-

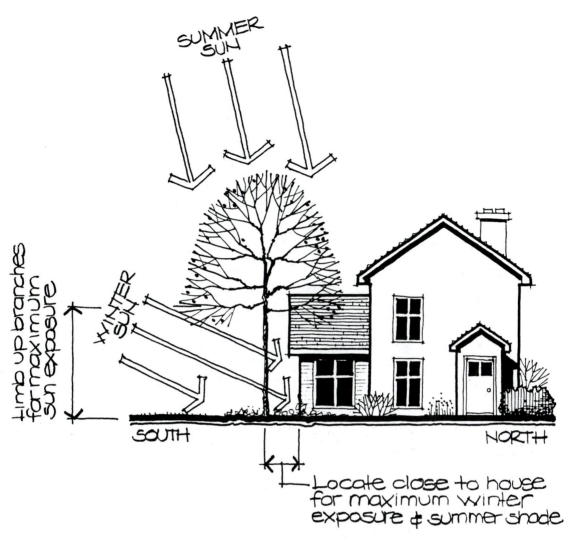

Summer Sun

Winter Sun

Limb up branches for maximum sun exposure

SOUTH

NORTH

Locate close to house for maximum winter exposure & summer shade

FIGURE 3–15
Deciduous trees should be limbed up and placed close to the residence for maximum winter sun exposure.

ries away the heat of the house and affects the amount of energy required for heating and cooling.

Unlike sun, wind is not as precisely predictable in terms of the seasons and directions from which it blows. Wind is more variable on a daily basis than sun but does hold to some generalized patterns based on season and weather fronts. In broad terms, wind blows from all compass directions throughout the year. However, wind blows most commonly from a westerly direction throughout the United States. In the summer, the prevailing wind is from the south and southwest, while during the cool season it shifts more to the west and northwest (Figure 3–17). The wind direction also responds to weather fronts. For example, wind originates mostly from the south and southwest during a warm front but shifts to the northwest following the passage of a cold front.

These general patterns are further modified by the presence of mountain ranges and large water bodies. It is best to refer to weather records kept by the National Weather Bureau to obtain more precise readings of wind direction in any given geographic setting. Additionally, wind patterns on any particular site are modified by topography, vegetation, and other buildings both on and off the site. Each individual site should be carefully examined to understand its unique wind patterns.

Environmentally Responsive Design

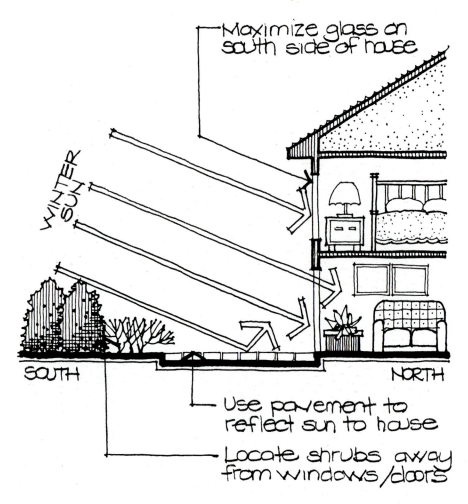

Maximize glass on south side of house

WINTER SUN

SOUTH

NORTH

Use pavement to reflect sun to house

Locate shrubs away from windows/doors

FIGURE 3–16
Rooms located on the south side of the house, with proper design, can benefit from the warming effects of winter sun.

Some broad patterns of wind are evident during the four seasons of the year for an open, level site surrounding a two-story house located in the temperate zone:

- all sides of the house are exposed to wind at some time during the course of the year
- the south, southwest, and west sides of the house receive the most constant wind on a yearly basis
- the eastern side of the house is the most protected from the wind during the year
- the south and west sides of a house are generally the most exposed to wind during the summer months and/or during a warm front
- the north and west sides of a house are most exposed to the cooling effects of winds following the passage of a cold front; this outcome is most negative during the winter season

Two overall conclusions can be drawn about designing with wind on a residential site: (1) protection is desired for winds blowing from the west and northwest and (2) exposure is advantageous for winds blowing from the south and southwest. These objectives apply for both outdoor spaces and the house itself.

FIGURE 3–17
Typical wind patterns.

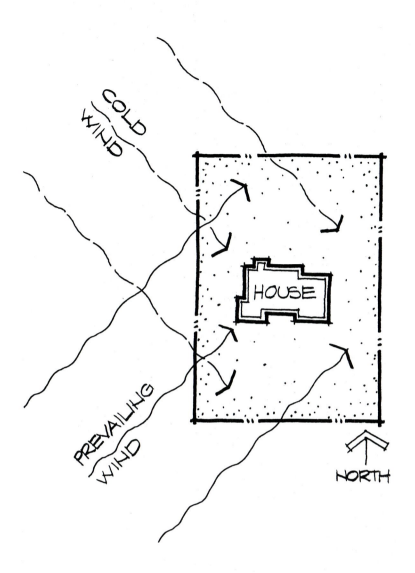

Providing Wind Protection

There are a number of means for protecting both outdoor spaces and the house from the potentially detrimental effects of wind blowing from the northwest direction. These include proper siting of outdoor uses, use of vegetation, and employment of walls/fences as wind screens. Based on the previously described zones around a house, it is best to place outdoor uses requiring wind protection on the east and/or southeast side of the house, where the house itself blocks direct exposure to the cold west and northwest wind. This location is most desirable for outdoor uses that would be used in late autumn, winter, and/or early spring.

Likewise, vegetation can be used to screen and direct wind on the residential site. The foliage mass of plants acts like a solid object in the landscape to direct the wind around and over itself, thereby creating a protected, calm zone on the side opposite from the wind. Coniferous evergreen trees and shrubs do this best because they possess relatively dense foliage present throughout the year. Closely spaced coniferous evergreen trees function as a wall to direct wind up and over their mass, creating two protected zones (Figure 3–18). The smallest zone exists on the windward side of the tree mass while the largest zone is on the "lee" side of the tree mass. Various studies have shown that the open field velocity of wind can be reduced by up to 60 percent in the leeward zone for a distance that is

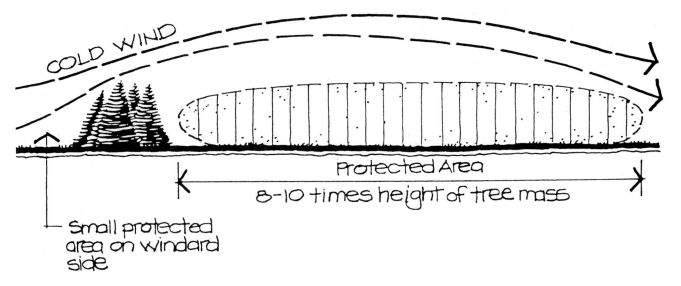

FIGURE 3–18
A mass of coniferous evergreen trees can create an area protected from cold wind.

approximately 10 to 20 times the height of the tree mass.[8] In other words, a 10-foot-high mass of evergreen trees would create a protected area extending about 100 to 200 feet from its base.

It should be noted that the most efficient screening of wind from a grouping of coniferous evergreen trees occurs when the foliage density is approximately 60 percent.[9] That is, about 60 percent of the vegetation is foliage and trunk/branch structure while the remaining 40 percent is void or open space. This condition allows some wind to penetrate through the tree mass and to uphold wind that is being pushed up and over the tree mass. When the density increases, the lack of wind through the mass permits the deflected wind to return to the ground more quickly, thus reducing the extent of the protected area.

To take advantage of their potential screening effect, coniferous trees and shrubs should be located on the west and northwest sides of the house as well as in outdoor spaces, where they can reduce the impact of the cooling northwest wind (Figure 3–19). To be effective, coniferous trees should be organized in a continuous band along the west and northwest edges of a site. Evergreen trees will not be effective if scattered in smaller groups as this will create openings allowing wind to flow through (Figure 3–20). In fact, openings in the tree mass may actually increase the wind's velocity through these areas. Proper planting of coniferous evergreen vegetation can save up to 30 percent of the heating cost for the cool season of the year.[10]

Specific site conditions such as available space, orientation of the house to the street, and direction of desirable views may not always permit coniferous evergreen vegetation to be organized around the outer northwest quadrant of a site. Thus, one alternative approach is to mass coniferous evergreen shrubs immediately along the exterior wall of the house on the west and northwest sides (Figure 3–21). This coniferous shrub planting not only screens cold wind from the house wall, but also forms a "dead air space" between the plant mass and the house wall, in effect creating an additional layer of insulation. This technique also reduces heating costs.

---

[8]Gary O. Robinette, *Plants/People/Environmental Quality* (Washington, D.C.: U.S. Department of Interior, 1972), pp. 77–78.

[9]Ibid, p. 82.

[10]Anne Simon Moffat and Marc Schiler, *Energy-Efficient and Environmental Landscaping* (South Newfane, VT: Appropriate Solutions Press, 1994), p. 75.

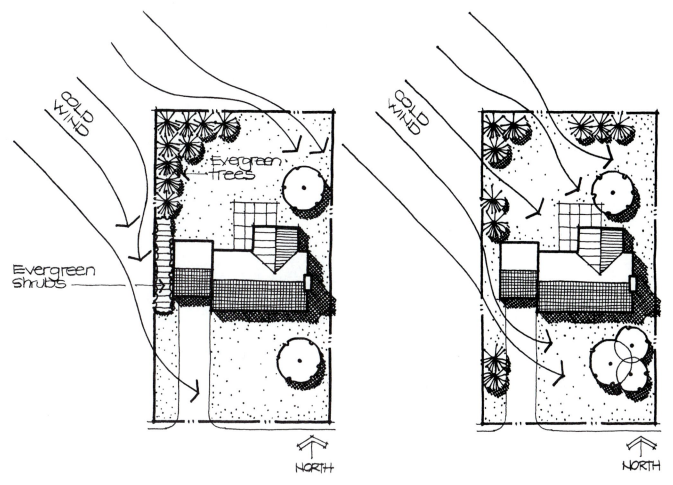

FIGURE 3-19
Coniferous evergreen trees and shrubs should be massed on the west and northwest sides of the site for cold wind protection.

FIGURE 3-20
Scattered coniferous evergreen trees will allow cold wind to easily move through the site toward the house.

One disadvantage of using coniferous vegetation to block wind is the amount of ground area needed by the plants. One option that requires less space is to screen unwanted cold wind by using walls and fences. These too can be used to lift the wind above an outdoor space or away from the west and northwest walls of the house. One potential application of this concept is to locate a wall or fence around the west and north sides of a front door entrance space on the north side of a house (Figure 3–22). Such a space is often inhospitably dark, cool, and windy due to its orientation. A carefully designed and located vertical plane can ameliorate the negative aspects of the space by blocking wind and permitting the front door to be opened and closed with a minimal amount of wind infiltration.

As with vegetation, walls and fences are more satisfactory wind screens when some wind is allowed to filter through them. A solid wall or fence acts like a dense vegetation mass by pulling the lifted wind back to the ground with eddies on the lee side (top of Figure 3–23). Therefore, walls or fences intended as wind screens should be designed with small openings, individual slats (louvers) that allow some wind to filter through, (bottom of Figure 3–23). The infiltering wind helps to uplift the wind that is moving over the top of the fence. Vertical or horizontal slats are often the best because they provide an even filtration of wind through the entire plane of the wall or fence. Horizontal slats that are angled upward will lift the wind somewhat above the space. Horizontal slats that are angled downward are not suggested because they direct the wind toward the ground where it may disturb plants or move debris and dust about the space.

Environmentally Responsive Design

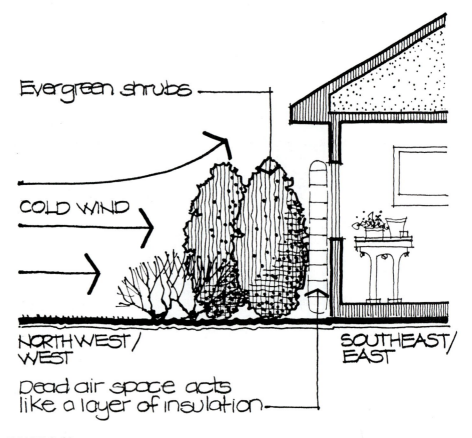

FIGURE 3-21
A mass of tall evergreen shrubs located next to the exterior house wall can protect the house from cold wind.

FIGURE 3-22
Coniferous evergreen plants and a wall/fence can protect a doorway located on the north side of the house.

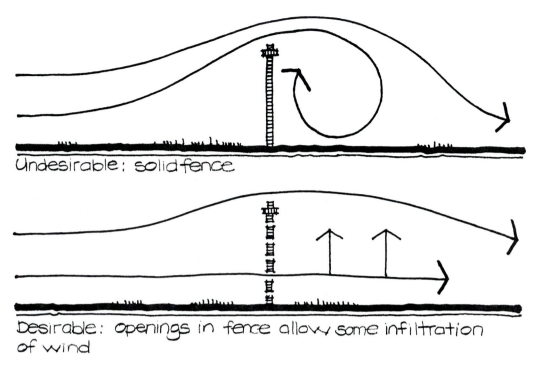

Undesirable: solid fence

Desirable: openings in fence allow some infiltration of wind

FIGURE 3-23
A fence with some openings offers maximum protection from the wind.

Several other more innovative approaches may also be taken to minimize exposure to cold wind. One is to use vertical panels of canvas that are suspended between posts or poles. This provides an opportunity for using bright color in a space while fulfilling the more utilitarian need to block wind. Tempered glass or Plexiglas panels may be desirable to use in locations where a view must be preserved while simultaneously blocking wind. An outdoor space with spectacular panoramic views and intended for cool season use is one example of a situation where a glass wall would work well.

The best method for screening wind is not necessarily achieved by either vegetation or walls/fences alone. Rather, it is frequently advantageous to combine these elements so they can form a coordinated approach to minimizing the potential negative effects of wind.

Enhancing Wind Exposure

Wind should also be thought of as a potential asset. During the warm season of the year, air movement can enhance the evaporation of moisture from people's skin and thus give the perception of cooler air temperatures. Wind can also prevent the air in outdoor spaces from becoming too stagnant. There are a number of means for capturing and taking advantage of the possible benefits of wind on a residential site.

One is to provide generous open lawn or meadow areas to the south and southwest of the house and outdoor spaces used in the warm season (Figure 3–24). Such an open area will permit the prevailing wind to move toward the house or outdoor space without obstruction. Similarly, plant materials and other elements of height should be kept low to the south and southwest sides. Areas of ground cover, low perennials, or shrubs below 2 feet will give maximum exposure to wind.

Moreover, wind exposure may be enhanced by channeling air movement. As with coniferous plants, wind is deflected in all directions around the canopy mass of a large deciduous tree; some wind is directed below the canopy where

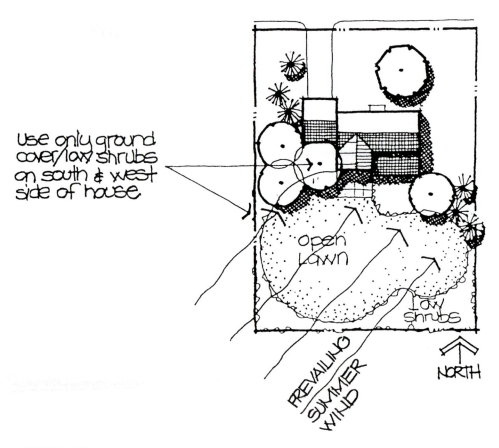

FIGURE 3–24
An open lawn area to the southwest of a house will give maximum exposure to prevailing summer wind.

wind velocity is intensified between the canopy and the ground. Increased wind speed and the shade make the space below a tree canopy feel cooler, an occurrence regularly appreciated by players who seek respite under a tree on a golf course on a hot summer day. To take advantage of this possibility on a residential site, deciduous shade trees should be located near the south or southwest of the house or outdoor space (Figure 3–25).

The plan arrangement of vegetation, walls/fences, and landform, either singularly or collectively, can likewise funnel wind toward the house or outdoor spaces. These elements can be located in a general V-shaped configuration that directs the prevailing wind to a specific area (Figure 3–26). While channeling wind, the surface material the wind is blowing over before it enters the house or outdoor space should be kept in mind. It is best to allow the wind to move across a vegetated surface such as lawn or ground because air temperatures above this type of ground material are comparatively cool. When possible, it is likewise desirable to allow wind to move over water such as a lake, pond, or even small water features such as a pool or waterfall. It is not wise to permit wind to move across a paved surface such as a parking lot or driveway because air temperatures above these areas are relatively high. These extreme temperatures are then transferred to the adjoining house or outdoor space.

Fences and walls can also enhance exposure to wind. As previously discussed, a wall or fence can be designed to direct the wind in different ways around and through an outdoor space. To assist wind exposure, a wall or fence should be designed with generous openings. An open wrought iron fence or open grid of different materials allows maximum exposure to wind while also providing enclosure by the fence. A louvered fence is frequently an excellent approach as well.

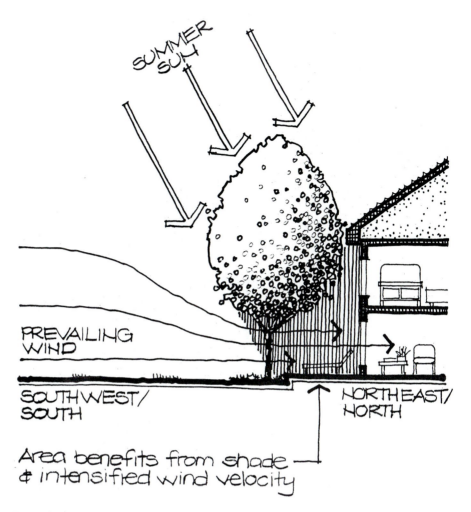

SUMMER SUN

PREVAILING WIND

SOUTHWEST/ SOUTH

NORTH EAST/ NORTH

Area benefits from shade & intensified wind velocity

FIGURE 3–25
A deciduous shade tree can channel wind and provide shade for the outdoor space and house located beneath it.

Louvers in a fence may be designed to swivel or turn so that they can be adjusted to affect the size and orientation of the openings. This allows the fence to respond to varying wind directions and velocities.

In summary, there are numerous techniques that can be implemented on the residential site for properly designing with wind. Each needs to be analyzed with respect to the existing regional and specific site conditions to determine its feasibility and potential impact. These techniques should be coordinated with considerations for sun and other requirements of the site (see last section of this chapter). Using some or all of these means for designing with wind will ultimately benefit the quality of a residential site design and its associated enjoyment of use by the homeowners.

OTHER ENVIRONMENTAL CONSIDERATIONS

There are a number of other considerations for "designing with nature" beyond those previously discussed for sun and wind. The selection of structural and plant materials, management of water, and maintenance practices all should be coordinated with natural processes when possible. This section presents how these additional objectives can be accomplished on a residential site.

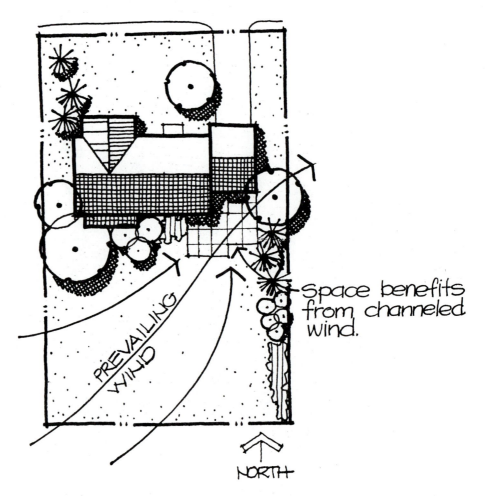

FIGURE 3–26
Plants can be arranged in a "V" shape to channel the prevailing wind toward outdoor spaces.

Material Selection and Use

Landscape materials used on a residential site have a direct effect on the compatibility of a design with natural processes and indicate sensitivity to environmental issues. Two general categories of materials should be considered: (1) plant materials (commonly referred to as "softscape") and (2) structural materials (sometimes called "hardscape," especially in reference to pavement). The following paragraphs provide pertinent concepts and solutions for designing with plant materials and structural materials to integrate a residential site with nature.

Plant Materials

Plant materials are prime design elements on the residential site. As discussed in Chapter 10, plant materials fulfill numerous valuable functions in addition to being sources of splendor and inspiration. But plant materials should also be compatible with natural processes by being properly selected and located on a residential site. This is best accomplished by using "native" plant materials, those plants that are indigenous, that is, naturally found on the site or in the surrounding region. Native plants are those that might have previously grown on the site before it was developed as well as those that presently exist in undisturbed areas of the region. Plant materials that have been "imported" from other regions or even distant countries are customarily called "exotics."

Native plant materials are recommended for a number of reasons. First, they tend to grow better over time because they have naturally acclimated to the climatic, ecological, and geological conditions of the region. They are accustomed to the seasonal cycles, temperature ranges, precipitation amounts, soil pH, soil composition, and insects prevalent in the region. Thus, native plants do not normally require special care beyond customary maintenance procedures. They do not need special watering or irrigation, soil amendments, pest control, or protection from extreme temperature. Also, they require less care, time, and energy to maintain their vigor in comparison to "exotics." Another reason for using native plant materials is that they visually fit the general landscape character of the region. They look compatible with the palette of materials and landscape quality, including topography, found throughout an area.

Native plants are generally available from several sources. First, many nurseries stock native plant materials as part of their overall inventory. Some nurseries and wholesalers even have catalogs and nursery tags which specifically identify those plants considered to be natives to the region. Other nurseries specialize only in native plants and typically carry a selection of plants not found anywhere else. The other source of native plants is in abandoned fields, hedgerows, waterways, and native forests in the region. Here, one can find a wide selection of native plants. However, accessing and transplanting plants in these natural territories is often difficult at best. Additionally, one must be careful not to remove plants from private property or ones that are rare and endangered. Removal of these types of plants is often an offense carrying a stiff fine or other penalty.

Another common "plant material" on the typical residential site is lawn. This too has a profound influence on a site's compatibility with natural processes. Lawn has come to occupy the vast majority of land area on most residential sites. In fact, it has been estimated that lawn areas across the United States collectively add up to between 25 and 30 million acres, an overall area larger than the state of Virginia.[11]

Lawn, as a design element, evolved from the historical precedent established by the English landscape gardens in the eighteenth century. During this time, the concept of garden changed from an enclosed formal space to one which was a large, informal, and open landscape. Many English landscape gardens of this time such as Stourhead, Stowe, and Petworth took on the character of a "natural" park. They were characterized by rolling topography, carefully placed clumps of tree, and broad expanses of meadow. In fact, many of these gardens looked very similar in style to modern-day golf courses. The meadow was often filled with cows, deer, and sheep, which added to the bucolic nature of the landscape while also keeping the grasses in the meadows cut to a relatively low height.

An expansive manor house was frequently strategically placed in the English landscape garden in a custom that permitted the meadow to extend almost to the base of the house. The manor house was seen as an architectural accent in an open meadow dotted with trees. This prototypical image of wealth and establishment was brought to the United States and first replicated in the southern plantations, which were similar in scale and grandeur to their English predecessors. In the nineteenth century, Andrew Jackson Downing applied this tradition to a scale more common to the typical landowners. Downing promoted a rural style of cottage and surrounding lawn and trees through his practice along the Hudson River Valley and his extensive writings. Downing's notion of a single house on a site dominated by lawn and trees has come to prevail in the American residential landscape.

Despite its prevalence, there are numerous reasons to question the extensive use of lawn. First, lawn and the grasses that compose it are only indigenous to cool, wet regions such as those found in Great Britain and the northwestern United States. Lawn does not grow well in other climatic regions without special care.

---

[11]John Skow, "Can Lawns Be Justified?" *Time* (June 3, 1991), p. 63.

Secondly, lawn is an ecological monoculture composed of one plant type. A monoculture is an artificial habitat that rarely exists in nature. Rather, almost all natural ecosystems are composed of numerous plant and animal species that are interdependent. An ecosystem composed of numerous species is healthy and sustaining because the system can usually survive if one species is harmed or lost. Not so with a lawn. Finally, the height of grass in a lawn is also unreal; most lawn grasses grow six to eight inches in height if let alone. Lawn must of course be periodically mowed at great expense of time and energy to prevent the grasses from reaching their "natural" height.

As a synthetic environment, lawn must therefore be supported by other means to maintain its health and vigor. Lawn typically requires watering, fertilization, pest control, and weeding to preserve the appearance that is usually expected of a lawn area. This requires time and the input of numerous resources, some of which are environmentally harmful. For example, the pesticides and insecticides used on many lawns are directly harmful to people, especially children, and most birds and animals. The warning tags placed around a lawn after a chemical application is one indication of this. There are numerous reports about people who have become ill, sometimes severely so, after exposure to the chemicals applied to lawns. The quantity of use is also troublesome. About 40 percent of all private lawns are treated with pesticides at a rate that is three to six times more per acre than that used by farmers.[12]

The fertilizers applied to lawns to make them grow vigorously are also potentially detrimental to the larger environment. Some of the fertilizer applied to the average lawn is carried away during a rainstorm and ends up in nearby streams and rivers. Here, the added fertilizer causes algae and other aquatic plants to dramatically grow, ultimately reducing the available oxygen for fish and other marine life. The fish and other aquatic life die, creating a biologically dead marine environment.

Lawn areas on the residential site should therefore be considered carefully due to their ecological shortcomings. Two general considerations should prevail as the designer works with lawn areas: (1) reduce the amount of lawn area and (2) maintain lawn in an environmentally responsive manner. To reduce lawn, the designer should study the need for lawn and the potential functional and aesthetic roles it plays. Lawn areas are desirable where they are used for various recreational uses including volleyball, badminton, croquet, throwing baseballs and footballs, etc. Lawn areas are also more critical when children and teenagers are present. Lawn is a useful visual element in the landscape as a smooth green carpet on the floor of an open space. The tranquillity of an open lawn encompassed by plant materials and structures is an attractive setting, somewhat reminiscent of a natural meadow surrounded by taller plants and trees. The simplicity of the lawn in contrast to the complexity of its edges is most appealing to the eye.

To reduce lawn area on the residential site, the designer should locate lawn only in carefully selected areas of the site (bottom half of Figure 3–27). The remainder of the site can be designated for other uses and/or planted with other types of vegetation. Lawn should not be used on the ground plane in shaded areas below tree canopies, on slopes over a 3:1 gradient, in small pieces here and there, or in long narrow spaces, such as along the side of house near the property line (top half of Figure 3–27). Lawn is difficult to grow and maintain in these instances. These areas are best covered with another material such as ground cover or, in some instances, pavement.

Areas where lawn is located should be designed so the lawn occupies well defined, simply shaped areas (Figure 3–28). Lawn edges that are uncomplicated and curved are the easiest to mow along. Therefore, complex edges or right angle corners should be avoided. Additionally, the lawn should be relatively free of

---

[12]Ibid.

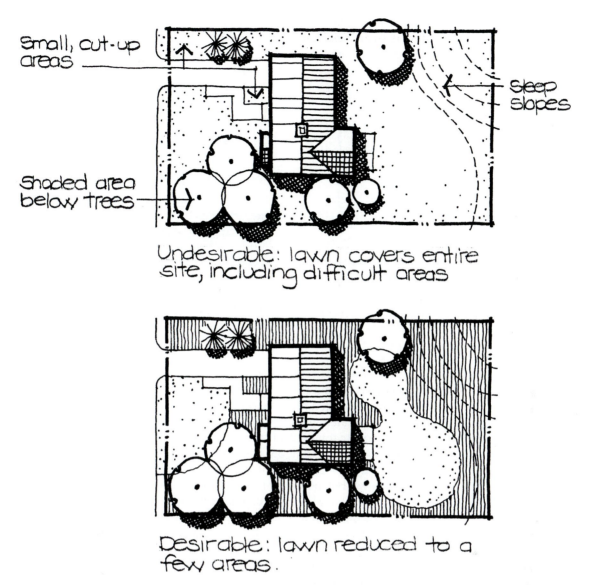

Small, cut-up areas

Shaded area below trees

Steep slopes

Undesirable: lawn covers entire site, including difficult areas

Desirable: lawn reduced to a few areas.

FIGURE 3–27
Lawn areas should be reduced in size and located only in large, open areas.

elements such as trees, light poles, boulders, and birdbaths, which act as obstacles for a lawn mower.

The lawn areas that are included on a residential site should be carefully managed. Pesticides should be used sparingly if at all. Organic fertilizers derived from manure or sewage treatment processes are preferred over readily available commercial brands because of their comparatively low phosphate and nitrogen levels. Watering should be undertaken only when necessary and then should adhere to such conservation practices as only watering in the early morning or evening when evaporation from the sun is minimal. Likewise, watering should occur long enough to saturate the ground to the full depth of the grass roots.

Structural Materials

The materials used for pavement and various site structures such as steps, walls, fences, and overhead trellises must also be selected with thought given to their environmental consequences. Generally, structural materials should be either (1) indigenous to the region or (2) composed of recycled materials. Structural

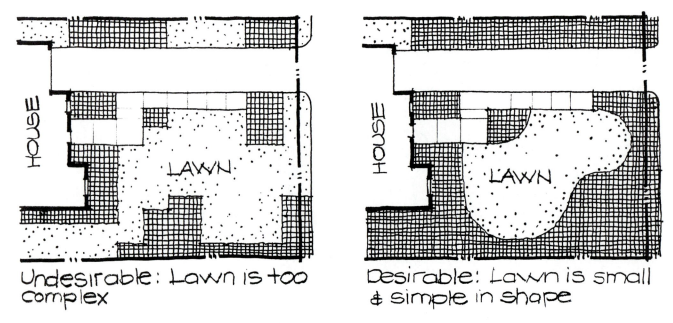

Undesirable: Lawn is too complex

Desirable: Lawn is small & simple in shape

FIGURE 3–28
Lawn areas should be simple in their shape.

materials that are native to a region are environmentally responsive for a number of reasons. First, indigenous materials visually fit the character and material palette that is prevalent in an area. The natural distribution of resources predetermines which materials are readily available and compositionally harmonious with other elements in the same location. For example, round stones and boulders are prevalent in the northeastern United States and are appropriately used for walls or other structures intended to recount the rugged regional quality. However, this same material is compositionally incompatible in Florida where such stones are alien to the native landscape. Similarly, Pennsylvania bluestone makes a good pavement material in the eastern United States, but is incongruous in California. The landscape designer is advised to carefully study the regional landscape and its natural resources as the principal source of visually compatible structural materials.

Indigenous structural materials are also recommended because they require minimal transportation costs. Transportation costs in turn are a reflection of energy costs necessary to move goods from one location to another. Consequently, it makes sense from an environmental standpoint to use materials that require the least expenditure of energy. Additionally, indigenous structural materials are advocated because their use typically supports the local economy of a region: local workers who manufacture indigenous materials are supported in their livelihood while their earnings are often spent in support of other businesses in an area.

In selecting structural materials, the landscape designer needs to be cautious about using materials that come from special environments, such as old-growth forests, rain forests, or other fragile or shrinking environments. Similarly, wood that is lumbered from redwood or cedar forests in the western United States should be carefully considered in terms of the environmental consequences in these unique habitats.

Another environmentally responsive source of structural materials is recycled materials. More and more manufacturers are making landscape elements like benches, fences, signs, and pavements from recycled materials. Many of these are made from recycled plastics or rubber and offer potentially long life spans. Also recycled glass has been experimented with as pavement material with interesting visual consequences. Brick or stone that is found in old city streets or from demolished buildings often make exciting and unique additions to the landscape. Where

Chapter 3   Environmentally Responsive Design

NO! Too much pavement. YES! Pavement minimized.

FIGURE 3–29
Pavement areas should be minimized to reduce surface runoff.

feasible and compatible with the overall design, these materials should be given serious thought because their use means that natural or primary material sources are preserved or, at the very least, used at a slower rate.

Water Management

One other consideration for establishing an environmentally responsive residential landscape is water management. This requires that (1) surface water drainage be properly planned and (2) conservation practices for water use be applied. A general objective for surface water drainage should be to retain as much water as feasible on site so that it does not contribute to downstream flooding and erosion. A common problem of many urban and suburban areas is that the prevalence of pavement and rooftops causes more runoff to occur from the landscape in comparison to natural watershed dominated by vegetation. The consequence is that streams and rivers that drain through developed landscapes typically experience flooding and erosion due to the increased quantity and rate of runoff. This can be very destructive for a region.

A number of techniques can be employed to reduce surface runoff from a residential site. First, the quantity of paved surfaces should be reduced as much as possible. Driveways, walks, patios, pool decks, etc., should be sized to minimum standards without sacrificing principles of good compositional design and needs for proper functioning. Paved areas that receive infrequent use or are inconsequential to the overall design should be reduced or eliminated (Figure 3–29).

Another approach to reducing surface runoff is to maximize the use of pervious pavement surfaces. Pervious pavements are those that have some gaps in the pavement material that permit surface water to seep through to the underlying ground (Figure 3–30). Sand, gravel, and brick or stone on a sand base are examples of pervious pavements. These pavements reduce the quantity of runoff and allow water to drain into the ground where it can contribute to plant growth by recharging the water available in the soil itself. Impervious pavements such as concrete and asphalt should be minimized because they function as a solid barrier that seals the ground surface to water seeping into the soil.

Overall surface runoff from a residential site can also be reduced by draining it toward lawn and planting areas where it can more readily enter the ground (Figure 3–31). This requires less use of drain inlets in paved areas and benefits lawn

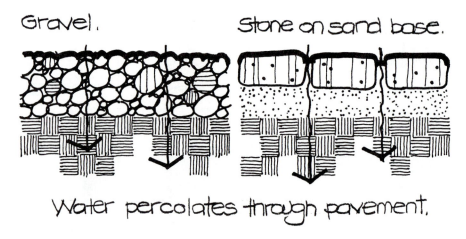

Gravel.   Stone on sand base.

Water percolates through pavement.

FIGURE 3–30
Pervious pavements allow the water to percolate to the subsurface.

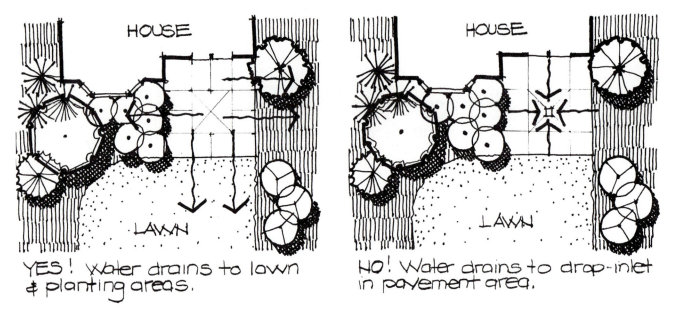

HOUSE

LAWN

YES! Water drains to lawn & planting areas.

HOUSE

LAWN

NO! Water drains to drop-inlet in pavement area.

FIGURE 3–31
Surface water from pavement should be drained toward lawn and planting areas.

and plants with an additional water source, a critical need in dry seasons of the year. Drop inlets that connect to a municipal storm sewer system are less desirable because the water that flows into them contributes to downstream flooding and erosion as previously described. A variation on this concept for roof areas is to drain gutter downspouts into "green" areas. Downspouts can also be connected to underground perforated pipes, allowing the water to directly seep into the ground (Figure 3–32).

A different consideration for water management is to design the residential site to minimize water usage. This concept is sometimes referred to as "xeriscape" and is most commonly used in arid regions, though it has applications in all areas that experience periodic droughts. A xeriscape is a site that uses minimal water, especially in the irrigation or watering of lawns and planting areas. The previously discussed concepts for reducing lawn area also coincide with the intent to minimize lawn for the least use of water. One other central technique for reducing the reliance on water is to select plants that are drought tolerant and/or require little

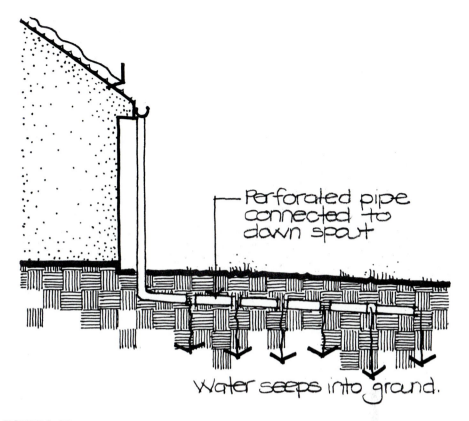

FIGURE 3-32
Water from downspouts can be directed to perforated pipes below ground to recharge groundwater.

water for survival. Numerous native plants exist in arid regions and should be used whenever possible to establish a xeriscape. In the temperate zone, there are also plants like ornamental grasses or some perennials that can be grown with small amounts of water. Sometimes it is advantageous to organize lawn and plants in different zones. One zone may be for lawn and other plants that need more water while another zone on the site can be for minimal water usage. This also helps to establish varying areas of the site with their own distinct visual character.

SUMMARY

It should be evident that there are numerous concepts that can be employed for making a residential site responsive to nature and natural processes. This is desirable because of both the environmental consequences as well as the potential economic and functional benefits, as outlined throughout the chapter. It is the responsibility of the landscape designer to be a good steward of the land and to do everything possible to design intelligently based on concepts that are one with the environment and not at odds with it. Residential sites collectively cover a significant portion of the landscape. Designers of this special setting play an important role in making sure the design process is carried out with the utmost care and with sensitivity to the broader and ever present natural processes. Good residential site design IS environmentally responsive.

4

Design Process

INTRODUCTION

As suggested in Chapter 2, the residential site should be thought of as a series of outdoor rooms where people arrive, socialize, entertain, relax, recreate, eat, and work. These rooms are the basic framework of a well-designed residential site. To create these outdoor rooms, the landscape designer should utilize a sequence of problem-solving steps usually referred to as a *design process*. A design process, in one form or another, should be followed each time a designer engages in a new project because it aids in the organization of information and thoughts as well as helps in the creation of a suitable design solution for the given circumstances. This chapter identifies the importance of designing with a process and outlines the various steps involved. Later chapters explain many of these steps in greater detail.

DESIGN PROCESS

"What is a process?" A process may be defined as "a series of steps, actions, or operations used in making something or bringing about a desired result: a manufacturing process." Similarly, it is "a series of actions, changes, etc. by which something passes from one condition to another: a lake in the process of drying up."* It can be seen that our world is filled with numerous processes. Natural processes include the development of a mountain range over centuries of time, the formation of a valley by means of erosion, photosynthesis, and the evolution of a butterfly from a caterpillar. Artificial processes include the manufacturing of a car, the sequence of events for formulating and passing a piece of legislation,

---

The American Heritage Desk Dictionary (Boston: Houghton Mifflin Company, 1981), p. 754.

FIGURE 4–1
A design process can help organize thoughts and events.

the construction of a building, and the diagnosis of a medical ailment. Again, all these processes involve a series of steps or events that lead to a change or product.

A design process is similar. It can be defined as a sequence of problem-solving and creative steps used by the designer to develop an appropriate design solution for a given client and site. The designer uses this process from the beginning to the end of a design project as an organizational framework.

A design process is critical for three reasons. First, the design process helps to organize information and thoughts. It allows the designer to obtain the right information at the right time and to use it in making decisions (Figure 4–1). Second, the design process provides an orderly approach to solving problems at appropriate times that leads the designer to develop an appropriate solution for the unique needs of the client and the particular conditions of the site. And thirdly, the design process helps the designer to explain reasons for the design solution to the clients. A designer who uses a process typically has an easier time explaining the end results.

For the lay person, the idea of a design process may seem somewhat complex. In fact, creating designs is not simple because design solutions just don't happen by magic or fall out of thin air (many people wish they did!). On the other hand, everyone uses decision-making processes similar to the design process without realizing it to solve problems or plan events on a day-to-day basis. Such activities as getting dressed in the morning, buying a new car, cooking a meal, looking for a new place to live, or writing a paper all involve a series of steps that one must go through to solve the problem or complete the task at hand. These steps usually include an analysis of the situation, defining the problem, developing ideas for solving the problem, selecting the best alternative, and then implementing this idea. As can be seen, we all use numerous processes in our lives. What is being suggested here is that the designer use a sequence of steps in creating a design solution for a residential site.

In residential site design, a logical design process includes the following major phases:

- research and preparation
- design

- construction documentation
- implementation
- maintenance
- evaluation

In one form or another, each of these phases is essential in the realization of quality residential site designs. While the focus of this book is on the research and preparation phase and the design phase of the process, an overview of all phases of the process is necessary.

RESEARCH AND PREPARATION

During the research and preparation phase, the designer is "getting ready." Necessary information required later as background information in the design phase is collected and evaluated during research and preparation. This phase includes the following steps:

- meeting the clients
- signing the contract
- base map preparation
- site inventory and analysis
- design program

Meeting the Clients

The design process for a residential site design project commonly begins with a meeting between the clients and designer. It is a time when both parties can get to know each other and discuss the prospect of preparing a design for the site. At this meeting, the clients typically convey information about their needs, desires, problems, and budget. The designer may ask a number of questions to learn important information about the clients. In turn, the designer describes the types of services that can be offered, the process used to prepare a design, and general costs for the design work. A detailed outline of this first meeting with the clients is found in Chapter 5.

Signing the Contract

If the two parties are in agreement, the designer prepares, signs, and submits to the client a written "Proposal for Design Services" that clearly specifies the scope, schedule, and costs for intended design services. This is sent to the clients a few days after the meeting. If the clients agree with the proposal, they sign and return the proposal to the designer. At this time, the Proposal for Design Services becomes a legal contract for design services to begin. This step of the design process is discussed further in Chapter 5.

Base Map Preparation

Before any design work can begin, a base map showing existing site conditions and features of the site is needed. The clients should supply information about their site including house plans, property survey, and topographic survey. If this information is complete enough, the designer is able to draw a base map of the site at an appropriately selected scale (Figure 4–2). If this information is not readily available, the designer may need to take and record measurements of the house and site. These measurements may then be used to draw a base map. A more thorough description of site measuring and preparation of the base map is given in Chapter 6.

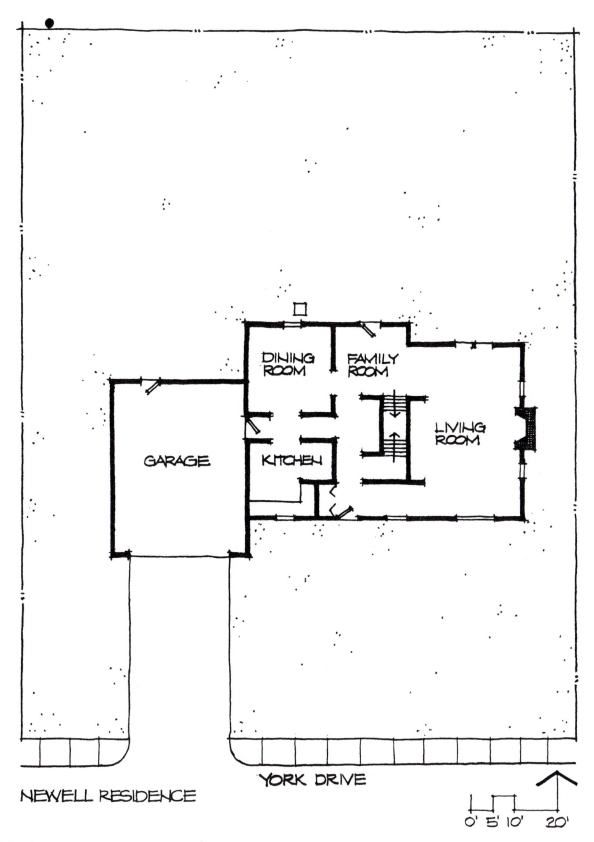

DINING ROOM

FAMILY ROOM

LIVING ROOM

GARAGE

KITCHEN

NEWELL RESIDENCE

YORK DRIVE

0' 5' 10'   20'

FIGURE 4-2
Base map.

Design Process

Site Inventory and Analysis

The designer should conduct a site inventory and analysis (sometimes called a site study). In this step, the designer first catalogues (inventories) and then evaluates (analyzes) important existing site conditions that may influence the design such as site location, character of the surrounding neighborhood, zoning ordinances, building codes, topography, drainage, soil, vegetation, climate, utilities, views, etc. (Figure 4–3). The designer should become very familiar with the site and thoroughly understand the site's character, its problems, and its potentials. The more the designer is aware of the specifics of a particular site, the more easily and appropriately decisions can be made in preparing the design. Site inventory and analysis are discussed in greater detail in Chapter 7.

Design Program

The last step of the research and preparation phase is the development of the design program. A design program can be defined as a list or outline of the elements and requirements the design solution should incorporate. The design program serves as a combined summary of the site analysis and client interview. Later in the design process, when a preliminary design has been completed, the program serves as a checklist for the designer to determine whether or not everything necessary was in fact included in the design (Figure 4–4). The design program is discussed in Chapter 7.

DESIGN

Once the research and preparation phase of the design process is completed, the designer can proceed to the design phase. In this phase, the designer studies and prepares the actual design solution based on the client interview, site analysis, and program. Typically, the design phase progresses through three major steps from the conceptual to the general to the specific. The steps of the design phase are:

- functional diagrams (conceptual)
- preliminary design (general)
- master plan (specific)

Functional Diagrams

The first step of the design phase is the development of functional diagrams (Figure 4–5). This is often the designer's first attempt at organizing the overall arrangement of the design on paper. The designer uses freehand diagrammatic symbols to show the plan relationships of all the major spaces and elements of the design to each other, to the house, and to the site. Each space is drawn as a freehand bubble that depicts its relative size, proportion, and configuration. During this step, the designer may explore alternative organizations of the basic functional layout before selecting the best idea. This type of diagram is sometimes referred to as a concept plan. Functional diagrams are discussed in Chapter 8.

Preliminary Design

The next step of the design process, preliminary design, converts the loose freehand bubbles and diagrammatic symbols of the functional diagrams into outdoor rooms that have general shapes and character. The result is an illustrative preliminary plan that can be presented to the clients for their review. There

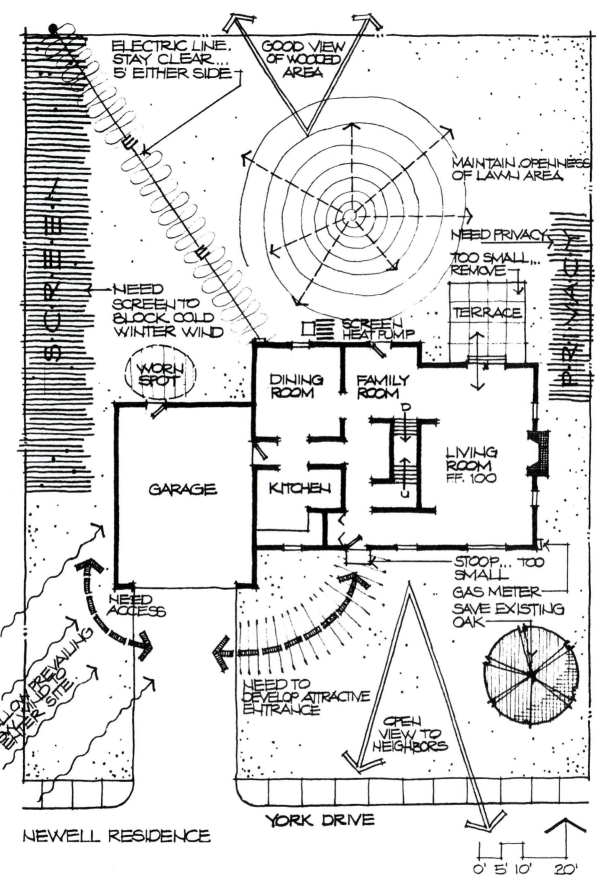

ELECTRIC LINE. STAY CLEAR... 5' EITHER SIDE

GOOD VIEW OF WOODED AREA

MAINTAIN OPENNESS OF LAWN AREA

NEED PRIVACY

TOO SMALL... REMOVE

TERRACE

NEED SCREEN TO BLOCK COLD WINTER WIND

SCREEN HEAT PUMP

WORN SPOT

DINING ROOM

FAMILY ROOM

GARAGE

KITCHEN

LIVING ROOM F.F. 100

NEED ACCESS

ALLOW PREVAILING SUMMER WIND TO ENTER SITE

NEED TO DEVELOP ATTRACTIVE ENTRANCE

STOOP... TOO SMALL

GAS METER

SAVE EXISTING OAK

OPEN VIEW TO NEIGHBORS

NEWELL RESIDENCE

YORK DRIVE

0' 5' 10'   20'

FIGURE 4–3
Site inventory and analysis.

Design Process

FIGURE 4-4
Design program.

Design Program

NEWELL RESIDENCE

1. Welcoming entrance walk
   - 4.5′ minimum
   - should provide access from both driveway and York Drive
2. Entry foyer
   - ±50–60 sq. ft.
3. Front yard lawn
   - ±400 sq. ft.
   - separate from neighbors to the east
4. Outdoor living space
   - ±300 sq. ft.
   - should have privacy from neighbors to the east
   - should be partially shaded
   - should provide good views to backyard plantings
5. Outdoor eating space
   - ±100 sq. ft.
   - should be convenient to outdoor living space and indoor kitchen
6. Back yard lawn
   - ±700 sq. ft.
   - separate from vegetable garden
7. Work and storage space
   - ±250 sq. ft.
8. Vegetable garden
   - ±400 sq. ft.
   - should be screened from rest of back yard
   - should have easy access to work and storage spaces and water
9. Wood storage
   - ±30 sq. ft.
   - provide access to back door of living room
10. Wind screen along west property line.

are three important aspects of preliminary design that are considered simultaneously to create the preliminary design. They are:

- design principles
- form composition
- spatial composition

Design Principles. Design principles are aesthetic guidelines that help the designer create a visually pleasing design solution. They aid the designer in making aesthetic judgments about the overall design layout as well as the composition of design elements, such as plant materials, walls, pavement patterns, and so forth. The three design principles covered in this text are order, unity, and rhythm. Order is the overall framework or visual structure of the design. Unity is the visual relationship among the individual elements within the design. Rhythm concerns itself with the factor of time and movement. All three of these design principles are considered together

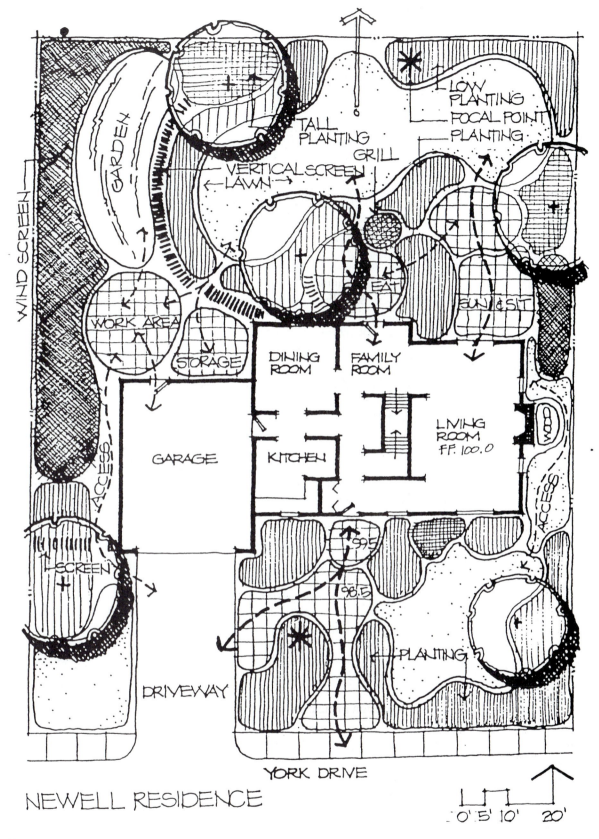

NEWELL RESIDENCE

Labels within the diagram:
WIND SCREEN, GARDEN, TALL PLANTING, VERTICAL SCREEN, LAWN, GRILL, LOW PLANTING, FOCAL POINT PLANTING, EAT, SUN & SIT, WORK AREA, STORAGE, DINING ROOM, FAMILY ROOM, LIVING ROOM F.F. 100.0, WOOD, GARAGE, KITCHEN, ACCESS, SCREEN, DRIVEWAY, 99.5, 98.5, PLANTING, YORK DRIVE, 0' 5' 10' 20'

FIGURE 4–5
Functional diagram.

when preparing the preliminary design. Chapter 9 explains each of the design principles and their application in residential site design.

Form Composition. Another key aspect of preliminary design is form composition. This step establishes specific shapes for all the spaces and elements developed in the functional diagram phase (Figure 4–6). For example, a bubble that represents an outside living space on the functional diagram is now given a definite form that may be composed of a series of specific shapes. Similarly, the edge of a lawn area is drawn with a specific line such as an attractive curve. This development of forms establishes a visual theme which furnishes an overall sense of order in the design. During form composition, the designer needs to consider the layout of the functional diagram as well as the appearance and geometry of forms. Form composition is elaborated on in Chapter 10.

Spatial Composition. To develop three-dimensional outdoor rooms, the designer utilizes grading (landform), plant materials, walls, fences, and overhead structures to define the three planes of spatial enclosure. This spatial composition must consider the height and volume relationships among the various design elements to create a design that is practical and pleasing to the eye. Spatial composition is discussed more in Chapter 11. Preliminary design concludes by drawing the preliminary plan (Figure 4–7) which is then presented to the clients for their review.

Master Plan

The master plan is a refinement or modification of the preliminary design that is drawn more precisely and with greater detail. For example, plant materials are usually drawn as generalized masses on the preliminary plan while they are shown as individual plants within masses on the master plan. Also the exact species of plant materials are likely to be specified on the master plan, whereas only general terms identify plants on the preliminary design. In addition, the form and outline of structural elements such as pavement areas, walls, and steps are apt to be drawn with more exactness in the master plan (Figure 4–8).

One key feature of the master plan is material composition. Material composition studies and develops the patterns on such structural elements as pavements, walls, and fences. While the preliminary plan often identifies the general material of a given design element, the master plan goes further to study and show more detailed pattern. Chapter 12 discusses the various characteristics and activities of the master plan in greater depth.

As stated earlier in this chapter, research/preparation and design are the two phases of the design process addressed most comprehensively in this book. However, the design process doesn't stop with these two phases. There are a number of other phases essential in completing a project in a professional manner. These other phases are outlined in the following sections.

CONSTRUCTION DOCUMENTATION

Once the master plan has been completed and accepted by the clients, there may be other necessary drawings to prepare in order to sufficiently implement the design as expressed in the master plan. These drawings are referred to as construction drawings because they illustrate and explain to the contractor how to implement the design. The various drawings that may be prepared are:

- layout plan
- grading plan
- planting plan
- construction details

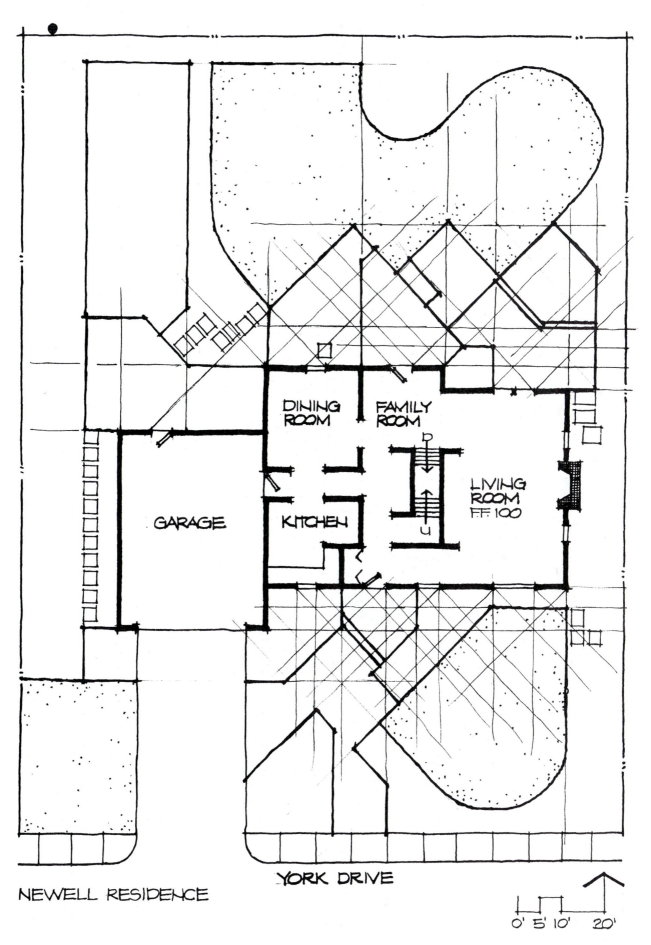

DINING ROOM

FAMILY ROOM

GARAGE

KITCHEN

LIVING ROOM
F.F. 100

NEWELL RESIDENCE

YORK DRIVE

0' 5' 10'   20'

FIGURE 4–6
Form composition study.

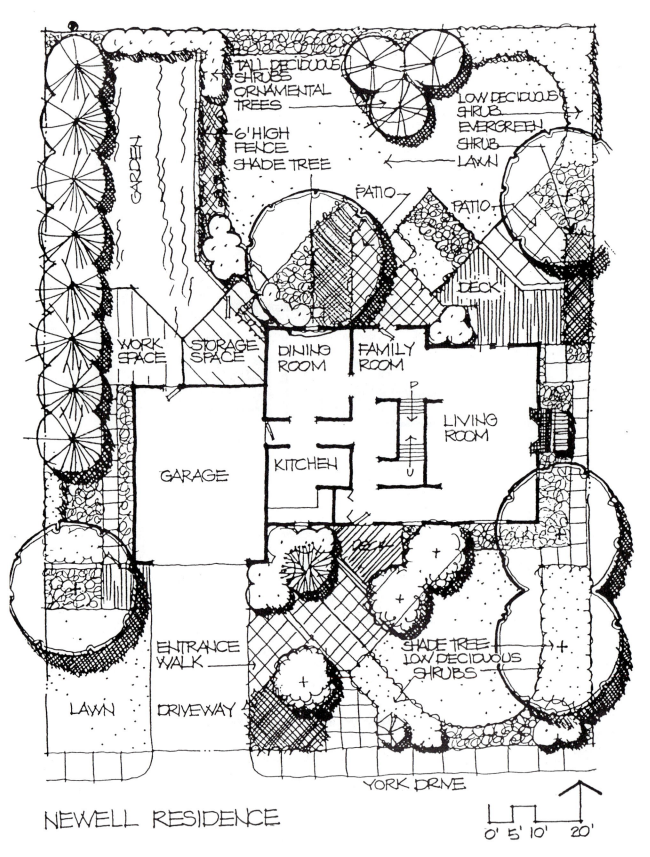

TALL DECIDUOUS
SHRUBS
ORNAMENTAL
TREES

6' HIGH
FENCE
SHADE TREE

LOW DECIDUOUS
SHRUB
EVERGREEN
SHRUB
LAWN

GARDEN

PATIO

PATIO

DECK

WORK
SPACE

STORAGE
SPACE

DINING
ROOM

FAMILY
ROOM

LIVING
ROOM

GARAGE

KITCHEN

ENTRANCE
WALK

SHADE TREE
LOW DECIDUOUS
SHRUBS

LAWN

DRIVEWAY

YORK DRIVE

0' 5' 10' 20'

NEWELL RESIDENCE

FIGURE 4-7
Preliminary plan.

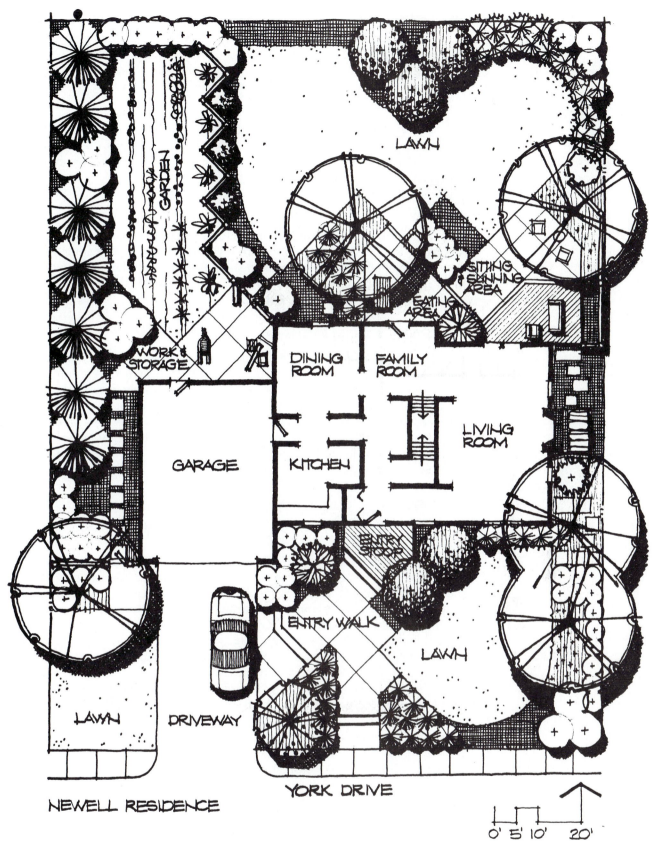

Labels within the plan:

GARDEN

LAWN

SITTING SUNNING AREA

EATING AREA

WORK & STORAGE

DINING ROOM

FAMILY ROOM

LIVING ROOM

GARAGE

KITCHEN

ENTRY WALK

LAWN

LAWN

DRIVEWAY

NEWELL RESIDENCE

YORK DRIVE

0' 5' 10' 20'

FIGURE 4–8
Master plan.

Layout Plan

The layout plan gives the horizontal dimensions of all the proposed design elements and areas of the design (Figure 4–9). The dimensions should be given in reference to fixed elements like a property line or a side of the house.

Grading Plan

The grading plan identifies the existing and proposed elevations of the ground plane. For nonpaved areas like lawns and planting beds, this is best shown with contour lines. For paved areas, proposed elevations are often communicated through the use of spot elevations (Figure 4–10).

Planting Plan

The planting plan shows the contractor what specific plants are to be planted and where they are to be located (Figure 4–11). A plant list that identifies the genus and species of all plants in the design should accompany the planting plan. The plant list normally indicates the quantity, size, condition, and other important notes about each of the specified plants.

Construction Details

Construction details often accompany the layout, grading, and planting plans. As the name suggests, construction details are drawn to communicate how specific portions of the design are to be built. For example, construction details might be drawn to show how a deck is to be built, how a fence is to be constructed, or how an area of pavement is to be installed. Sometimes several sheets or more of construction details are prepared to adequately explain how to build all the various parts of a project. A few examples of construction details are shown in Figure 4–12.

Need for Construction Drawings

The layout, grading, and planting plans along with the construction details should all be drawn in coordination with one another. When completed, these drawings inform the contractor(s) how the design is to be implemented. Whether or not these drawings are prepared for a particular project depends on the complexity and budget of the project. For example, if a design involves a simple terrace space with limited new planting and no additional structures, construction drawings are probably not needed. But where there is extensive proposed construction (decks, steps, walls, fences, trellises, and so on), planting, or regrading of the site, construction drawings are essential to ensure the design is implemented to the level of quality desired by the designer.

The type of company will also determine whether or not construction drawings are used. When a company is strictly a "design firm," these drawings are more essential than when a firm is "design/build." A typical design firm only provides design services. It does not get directly involved with implementing a project. In this type of firm, the designer should document the intentions of the design as completely as possible so that a contractor who works with another company can implement the design correctly. Typically, a contractor is selected in this situation through a bidding process. That is, the construction drawings are "let out for bid" by having a selected number of contractors submit price quotations for the implementation of the design. This type of bidding process lets the homeowner compare prices among contractors prior to selecting the one to do the work.

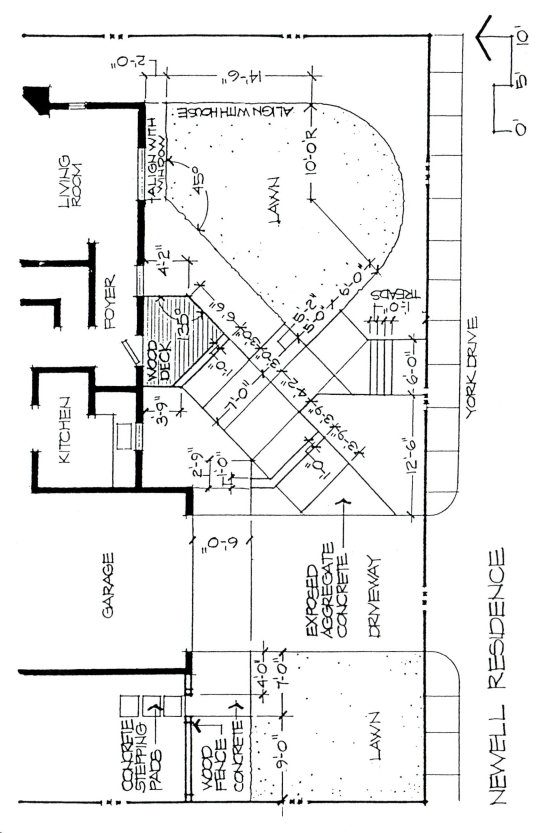

FIGURE 4–9
Layout plan.

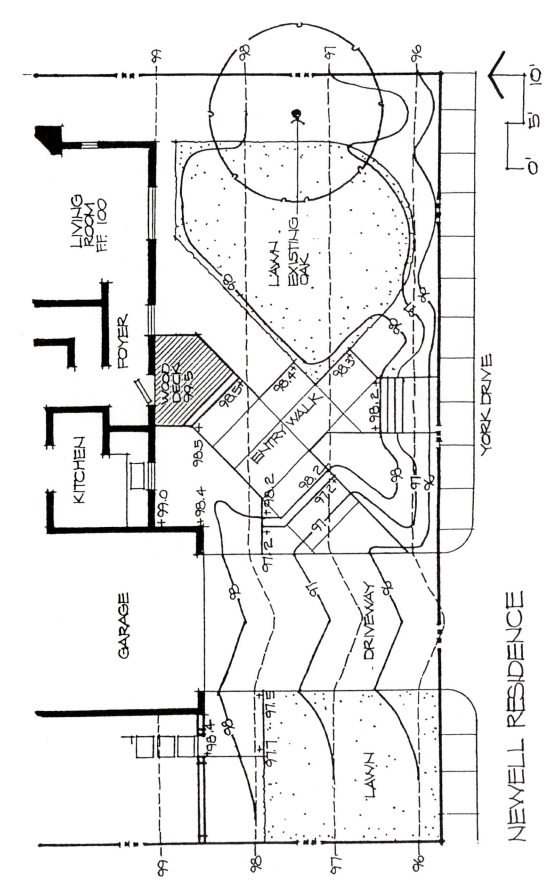

FIGURE 4-10
Grading plan.

Chapter 4   Design Process

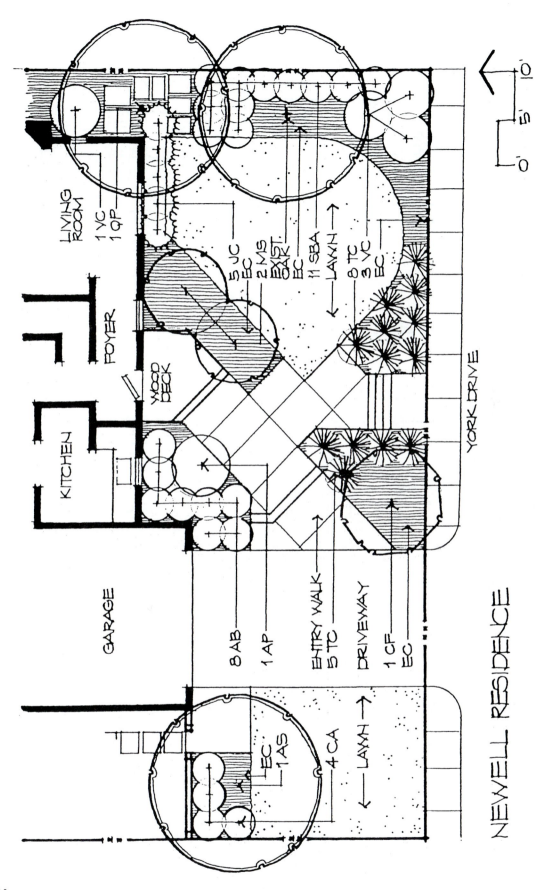

FIGURE 4-11
Planting plan.

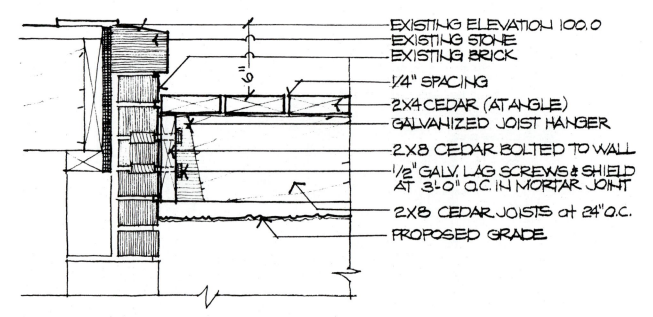

EXISTING ELEVATION 100.0
EXISTING STONE
EXISTING BRICK
1/4" SPACING
2X4 CEDAR (AT ANGLE)
GALVANIZED JOIST HANGER
2X8 CEDAR BOLTED TO WALL
1/2" GALV. LAG SCREWS & SHIELD AT 3'-0" O.C. IN MORTAR JOINT
2X8 CEDAR JOISTS at 24"O.C.
PROPOSED GRADE

SECTION: HOUSE AND DECK CONNECTION

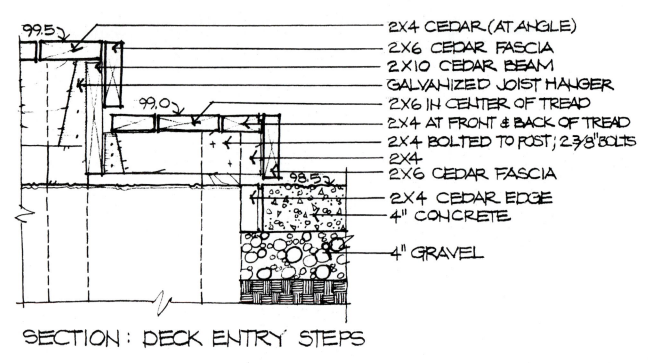

2X4 CEDAR (AT ANGLE)
2X6 CEDAR FASCIA
2X10 CEDAR BEAM
GALVANIZED JOIST HANGER
2X6 IN CENTER OF TREAD
2X4 AT FRONT & BACK OF TREAD
2X4 BOLTED TO POST; 2 3/8"BOLTS
2X4
2X6 CEDAR FASCIA
2X4 CEDAR EDGE
4" CONCRETE
4" GRAVEL

SECTION: DECK ENTRY STEPS

FIGURE 4-12
Construction details for a wood deck.

On the other hand, when working for a design/build firm, the designer usually works directly with the foreman and crew within the same firm to see that the design is properly implemented. When this is possible, construction drawings may be very simple or even unnecessary to communicate how the design is to be implemented. And there is apt to be much more supervision of the implementation by the designer in a design/build firm.

IMPLEMENTATION

Once the contractor is selected, whether by a bidding process or by direct selection, the owner should enter into a written contract with the contractor. Then, the contractor can proceed to implement the design. The two major steps within the implementation phase are:

- construction
- installation

Construction refers to the building of structural design elements like pavements, decks, walls, fences, steps, benches, railings, and trellises (the *hardscape*). *Installation,* on the other hand, refers to the planting of plant materials (the *softscape*). Some contractors specialize in the implementation of the hardscape while others specialize in the softscape. Still other contractors work with both the hardscape and the softscape.

Questions and problems typically occur during implementation that require the designer's attention. It is not unusual that something unforeseen happens or that additional information is needed to facilitate the design's implementation. The designer's role during implementation may vary depending on whether or not the designer is part of a design/build firm. As a member of a design/build firm, the designer may closely supervise the implementation of the work and be on the job site to answer questions directly and quickly. As a member of a design firm, the designer may be hired under a separate contract to periodically observe the implementation to make sure everything is going as intended. In either case, the designer should continue to keep abreast of a project after it has left the drawing board.

MAINTENANCE

In a way, the implementation of a design is just the beginning of its life and usefulness. A design should continue to serve the clients for years, assuming that it is properly maintained. Most projects don't sustain themselves in perfect condition without periodic maintenance and upkeep. Some of the typical maintenance tasks are:

- irrigating
- fertilizing
- weeding
- lawn mowing
- painting and staining
- replacing old plants or parts of structures

It has often been stated that the maintenance people, whether it be the homeowner or hired company, are the ultimate designers of a project. This is because their efforts directly affect the size, shape, and health of plant materials, the alignment of bed lines, the material and color of replaced structural elements, as well as the general appearance and cleanliness of a design over a period of years. Too often, a design deteriorates due to poor maintenance despite its good initial design qualities and proper implementation. Consequently, it is important that: (1) maintenance people be knowledgeable and well trained in all aspects of site upkeep, and (2) the designer clearly communicates the intentions of the design to the maintenance people. The designer should periodically visit the project to make sure it is being suitably maintained. If design is conceived of as being an ongoing process that includes maintenance, then the project should prove to be successful.

EVALUATION

The final phase of the design process is to evaluate the success of the design solution. This should be an ongoing procedure that, from time to time, analyzes various aspects of the implemented design. Often, the best way to evaluate is by observing the design over an extended period of time. What is learned through evaluation can be applied to subsequent designs that are created. Following are some questions that can be asked periodically throughout the years.

- How does the design appear?
- How does the design function?
- What portions of the design are easy or difficult to maintain?
- Are all the plant materials doing well? Which ones are not, and why?
- How has the pavement material held up?
- Are there any problems with the wood structures?

Like maintenance, evaluation of a design project should be a continual effort. The designer should never stop looking, analyzing, judging, and questioning. From this viewpoint, the design process is a continuous, ongoing effort extending beyond the limits of a single project.

OTHER THOUGHTS

From the preceding outline, it might seem that the design process is a straightforward and logical procedure that always leads to a well-executed and successful design. However, there are a number of qualifiers that should also accompany this overview. First, the design process doesn't always occur as a well-defined sequence of steps even though it was presented that way. In actual practice, some of the steps of the process may overlap and occur simultaneously. For example, gathering information for the preparation of a base map and conducting a site analysis may occur in the same visit. In other cases, certain steps of the process are repeated before being entirely completed. For instance, once the design is begun, the designer may wish to return to the site for a closer inspection. Often a renewed look at a site during the design phase can be valuable because the designer can view the site with a more critical and questioning eye. Thus, the site analysis may be seen as recurring throughout the development of the design solution.

There is nothing wrong with doing more than one of the steps of the process simultaneously or moving back and forth between steps in the different phases. In fact, such practice is quite healthy and often necessary to create a successful design solution. To follow the design process in a completely sequential and unyielding fashion may stifle the designer's imagination. This is not to say the designer can start anywhere in the process or jump randomly from one step to another. Nevertheless, the design process should be thought of as a general outline of steps for organizing design thoughts and procedures.

Similarly, the design process may be utilized slightly differently each time a new project is undertaken. The specific circumstances of each design project such as budget, scope of work, site characteristics, and clients' needs can influence how the process is applied. For example, a particular residential site may be so small that making an exhaustive site analysis would be a waste of time. In another instance, the clients' limited budget may restrict the number of drawings done for implementation. Or the clients' program may be very simple with obvious solutions. Consequently, the designer needs to carefully evaluate each new project at the beginning to determine what is required and how (by what process) the design should be solved.

There is another factor that should be understood about the design process. It is quite possible that a person can faithfully follow and thoroughly cover each of the steps of the design process and still end up with a design that is mediocre. The success of the design process and the resulting design depends ultimately on the designer's own abilities, experiences, knowledge, insights, judgments, and creativity. If the designer is weak in any one of these areas, the quality of the resulting design will also be diminished despite the designer's best intentions. Eventually, residential site designs that are both visually and functionally successful as well as being emotionally satisfying require sensitive observation, thorough study, experience, inspiration, and subjective creativity. The design process is not a substitute for these qualities. But it does provide a framework for design talent to be utilized effectively.

The design process involves both rational and intuitive judgments and skills. Some steps in the design process (such as site inventory, site analysis, program development, and functional diagrams) require rational and logical thinking. Other steps in the design process (such as form composition, spatial composition, material composition, and incorporation of the design principles into the design require more intuitive skills and aesthetic appreciation. The designer needs a sensitivity to shapes and forms in addition to a feel for space and volume in undertaking these particular steps. While these skills and sensitivities can be talked about, their execution often depends on an internal subjectivity that defies clear and logical explanation. Thus, the design process can also be considered a structure for both the designer's objective and subjective abilities.

One other thought should be expressed about the design process. Owing to its importance in systematizing a designer's thoughts and methods, it is essential that the inexperienced designer proceed thoughtfully through all the necessary steps. Just as in learning any new skill or procedure, it is helpful to move slowly and methodically. The beginning designer should carefully record and document each step of the process as a learning experience. Consequently, the use of the design process may seem rather tedious and laborious the first number of times it is applied. But, as one becomes more accustomed to the process, many of its steps will become more intuitive and may often occur more quickly. For the experienced designer, much of the process is apt to be second nature. Having utilized the process countless times, the seasoned designer will apply the process effortlessly yet intelligently. And having worked in a particular locale for some time, many of the aspects of the design process become common knowledge and standard methods of procedure. For example, soil, climate, building codes, plant materials, and construction methods are apt to be well understood and appreciated as standard working knowledge.

SUMMARY

In summary, the design process should be considered a useful organizational tool for the designer. Despite the particulars, it should be utilized to guide a designer in seeking an appropriate design solution in a thoughtful yet creative manner. This chapter has provided a general overview of the design process. The remaining chapters more thoroughly address individual steps of the research and preparation and design phases of the process. While each step is presented as the ideal approach as a means of explanation and understanding, you must appropriately adapt it to the unique aspects of your own form of practice.

5

Meeting the Clients

INTRODUCTION

Before developing a design solution for a residential project, the designer must undertake several preparatory tasks. Each of these tasks involves gathering, organizing, and evaluating information that will serve as the foundation for the subsequent design phases. Meeting and talking to the clients is often the first task of the research and preparation phase and is addressed more thoroughly in this chapter. The other preparatory activities are related to the site itself and include: (1) obtaining measurements of the site (2) preparing a scaled base sheet and base map, (3) conducting a site inventory and analysis, and (4) writing a design program. These tasks are discussed in Chapters 6 and 7.

Meeting and talking to the clients is a critical step because it establishes the groundwork for the ensuing design phases. This step gives the designer the necessary information about the clients' wishes and requirements about the site. If undertaken properly, it also sets the overall tone for how the designer and clients will interact throughout the remainder of the design process. It is important that both parties develop trust and respect for each other through open and honest communication. This is a key ingredient in developing a design that both clients and designer can be proud of.

This chapter provides guidelines for getting the project started in a positive and constructive manner including: (1) learning about the designer, (2) initial client contact, (3) meeting the clients, and (4) developing a proposal for design services. All these topics and activities are the basis for a professional and enjoyable working relationship between the designer and the clients.

FIGURE 5-1
Example of a company brochure.

LEARNING ABOUT THE DESIGNER

There are many possible ways clients and designers initially meet. However it occurs, it typically begins by the clients first learning about the designer and basic business information regarding the designer or design firm. This process of learning must be easy and enticing enough for the potential client to follow up with a telephone call or office visit. Potential clients may learn about a design firm by a number of means. These include: (1) advertisement, (2) brochure, (3) web site, (4) job-site sign, and (5) word of mouth. Thus, the designer must use various means to communicate with potential clients in a manner that attracts them to seek design services.

Advertisements. Homeowners may learn about a design firm from advertisements placed in newspapers, local magazines, programs for musical or sporting events, or on local TV and radio. These advertisements are typically small in size or short in length so they must capture the potential clients' attention with few words and captivating images. It is essential the images or photographs in advertisements be engaging because they are apt to be the first thing seen and because they can potentially convey the feeling and style of the designer's work. When possible, it is wise to hire a professional graphic designer or production company to produce an advertisement that will reach the intended audience. An advertisement, while sometimes costly, has the potential to reach a wide audience.

Brochure. It is good practice for a design firm to have a brochure that can be mailed or handed directly to potential clients. A brochure commonly contains text and photographs about the designer's work, design philosophy, process, and fees (Figure 5–1). Here too, appearance and layout of the brochure is critical to communicate effectively and to entice the potential client. Professional input is once again suggested in creating a brochure that can effectively communicate to potential clients.

Web Site. An internet web site is becoming a business necessity in the electronic age (Figure 5–2). A web site is in essence a digital version of a brochure though it has the added advantage of being interactive and available at any time. It can permit the potential client to navigate among multiple pages with menus and click on information or photographs. Additional benefits of a web site are that it can be frequently updated and linked with other web sites allowing for more connections.

FIGURE 5-2
An internet web site is an excellent place to communicate with the public.

Job Signs. An effective way to reach potential clients is by erecting small attractive signs at active job sites. A sign can identify who designed the project that is underway, who is installing it, and the appropriate telephone numbers. Potential clients are often curious about what neighbors might be doing and who is doing the work, particularly if the work in progress is attractive as it nears completion.

Word of Mouth. Finally, one of the best means of having potential clients learn about a designer's work is from past clients or others who have worked with the designer. Perhaps the best form of advertisement is to have previous clients give positive recommendations about the designer to friends and acquaintances. Thus, it is important for the designer to complete quality work and to maintain ongoing relationships with past clients. A once-a-year holiday greeting card or an occasional mailing that highlights recently completed work can keep past clients abreast of one's professional business status and make them feel they are still valued.

Information Provided

The previous methods for communicating with the public are alternative ways of informing potential clients about the designer or design firm. These diversified forms of communication are intended to arouse potential clients' interest while also providing basic information about the designer or design firm such as: (1) available services, (2) design philosophy, (3) design process, and (4) fees. The extent to which this information is presented varies widely depending on the media used, the targeted audience, available space or time, and budget. Advertisements and job signs provide the smallest opportunity to communicate this information while brochures and web sites offer the greatest chance.

Available Services. Advertisements, brochures, web sites, etc., should inform potential clients about what services the design firm offers. There are a variety of services that are necessary for a design project to be fully realized. These include: (1) design, (2) construction (dealing with structures such as terraces, decks, fences), (3) installation (dealing with plant materials) and, (4) maintenance (dealing with the on-going care of the landscape after it has been built and installed). Potential clients should know to what extent the design firm is able to offer these various services because firms vary widely in their capabilities.

A residential design company that offers design, construction, installation, and maintenance services is generally known as a design/build firm or full-service firm. The advantage of this type of firm is that it can offer a coordinated package of services to clients and assure a smoother flow from one phase to another. Other firms provide only design services and then work with separate landscape contractors for implementation of the design. These firms typically provide excellent quality design because that is their specialization. Further, such firms are not tied to inventories of plants or other materials and thus sometimes have more freedom to explore innovative designs. Still other firms place primary emphasis on plant materials including sales, installation, and maintenance with less attention given to design and construction services. It is important to tell potential clients about a firm's expertise and professional capabilities so they know what the company can or cannot do for them.

Design Philosophy. Potential clients should also be acquainted with the designer's "design philosophy," or underlying principles and values the designer applies to design projects. Design philosophies are those concepts and feelings that pervade a designer's work. While a design philosophy may be based on almost any idea, most design philosophies express particular attitudes towards some or all of the following: (1) aesthetics or what is considered good design, (2) perceived benefits of design, (3) importance of outdoor space, (4) environmental stewardships, (5) preferred style(s), (6) preferred materials (both structural and plant materials), and (7) method of working with clients. The designer should attempt to define his/her design philosophy in a concise statement of two or three sentences. Ideally, potential clients should find designers with design philosophies that match their own set of values and attitudes towards landscape design. The entire process is much more enjoyable for everyone involved when this is the case.

Design Process. Potential clients should be aware of the design process that will be employed in creating a residential design solution. Many homeowners don't fully understand what is required to prepare a master plan for a residential site nor the various steps that are employed. It is very helpful for the designer to provide an outline of both the necessary design process steps and the relative time it takes for each. Potential clients might be exposed to the following phases of the design process: (1) site analysis, (2) design program, (3) functional diagrams, (4) preliminary design, and (5) master plan. Each step should be very briefly described in clear, common language that can be understood by anyone. Graphic examples can sometimes be used to supplement the written description.

The underlying idea is to make the potential clients aware that design is much more than the selection and arrangement of plant materials. Each design solution is a customized functional and aesthetic synthesis of the clients' needs with the site's problems and potentials, all of which is made possible through the expertise of a design professional. It is therefore important that clients understand what really constitutes the tasks involved in the design process.

Fees. Lastly, most potential clients like to have some information about what it will cost for a master plan and its implementation. This can usually be accomplished by providing a general fee based on either an hourly rate or a typical lump sum for a master plan. While most potential clients benefit from this information, some designers are skeptical about providing it because they are afraid that fee information might scare off clients or might give competing designers or firms the ability to undercut them. Both these fears are legitimate. However, the designer must inform clients about fees at some point in the process. It is usually better to let potential clients know about fees sooner rather than later before either party wastes time only to find out that the fees are not acceptable for whatever reason.

One other concern is about whether or not to charge any design fees. Some designers do not charge clients directly for a design fee if the clients sign a contract for implementation of the design. This is what is commonly referred to as a "free plan." Some free plans ought to be free because they are nothing more than a quickly sketched planting arrangement showing where particular plants are to be placed on the site. Often, these plans are drawn on a piece of company stationery with a list of plant materials and a price quotation. This type of plan is simply an estimate and should be as "free" as a plumber's estimate or an electrician's estimate.

However, there are other so-called "free plans" whose cost should in fact be billed to the clients. These are the plans that have taken substantial amounts of time to design and prepare and then are offered as "freebees" for the sake of luring the potential clients into signing a contract for the project. Even if the designer tells the homeowners that the plan is free, the time spent to prepare the design is most certainly built into the total project cost. Thus, while the clients may think they have received something for nothing, they in fact have not.

A free plan is likely to influence the clients' perception of the worth of the designer's professional advice. Professionals charge for their advice, consultation, and services. If a designer "gives away" valuable and professional design time, what does that say for the talent it took to prepare the design? Surely the time spent designing is worth more than nothing, and clients should be made aware of that and charged for that time. Any wise consumer would look at something free as being worth nothing to the one giving it away. This same wise consumer also realizes that something "free" is a clever way of enticing them to buy something more expensive.

INITIAL CONTACT BY POTENTIAL CLIENTS

If the potential clients are positively affected by an advertisement or properly informed by a brochure or web site, they are very apt to follow up by contacting the designer or firm directly. This most typically occurs by means of a telephone call or e-mail, though it sometimes takes place with a visit to the firm's office or job site (Figure 5–3). The clients make this inquiry to get more information, to have initial questions answered, and to schedule an appointment for a more serious discussion about retaining the designer or firm to develop a master plan for their site.

The designer in turn must spend whatever time is necessary to answer the potential clients' inquiry. This might include reiterating information already given to the clients by other means because hearing it explained by someone in person can sometimes prove to be more effective. The designer should respond to the potential clients' questions in a manner that is informative and reassuring. The designer might also need to ask questions of the potential clients to make sure they are properly informed and that they seem to be the type of client that is desirable to work with. If the conversation goes well, the designer should conclude by scheduling a meeting with clients at their home.

MEETING THE CLIENTS

The next step in the process is for the designer and clients to meet "face-to-face" to discuss the particulars of the clients and their site. This meeting should take place

FIGURE 5-3
Initial contact with the designer is typically made by telephone.

at the clients' home to allow the designer to see both the site and house first hand (Figure 5–4). A meeting at the clients' house gives the designer an excellent opportunity to fully understand the concerns and interests of the clients in their own setting where they are apt to feel most comfortable. It also affords the designer the best chance to obtain the necessary information to properly proceed with the subsequent design process. In some instances, it is acceptable or even necessary for this meeting to take place at the designer's office. If this occurs, the designer will need to make a trip to the clients' site at another time.

Client Information

The primary purpose of this meeting is for the designer to obtain essential information about the clients that will serve as the basis for the design solution. This information should include: (1) family facts, (2) clients' wants and wishes (initial program), (3) clients' likes and dislikes regarding their landscape, (4) clients' lifestyle and characteristics, and (5) clients' observations about their house and site.

In addition, the meeting gives the clients and designer an opportunity to discuss the design process and design fees as they relate directly to the particular project. The meeting presents both parties with a chance to ask questions and to air whatever concerns they might have about the overall process. This meeting also allows the designer to see the site in person and to make initial judgments about it. Many times, the designer will need to return at a later time for a more in-depth study of the site (see Chapter 7). The ultimate purpose of this meeting is for the clients and designer to reach a professional agreement for working together on the design of the clients' site.

Family Facts. The designer should obtain basic data about the clients including the following:

- family members and ages
- occupation(s) of adults
- interests of family members, particularly as they relate to outdoor activities
- type and number of pets along with their use of the site

FIGURE 5–4
The initial meeting gives the designer a chance to
see the site and house in person.

Clients' Wants and Wishes. The designer needs to determine what the clients envision for their site in order to translate this into a "design program." To do this, the designer should attempt to have the clients identify their wishes by means of both general descriptions of what they foresee as well as specific spaces or use areas they want included. The general descriptions or "goals" tend to describe the feeling or atmosphere that the clients want and may be phrased in statements such as:

> "We want the front yard to be a place of inspiration and provide an attractive setting for our visitors."
>
> "We envision a garden as a haven from the busy world where birds and other wildlife will visit."
>
> "I foresee an environment where both family and friends can gather in a relaxing atmosphere."

The designer can use this information to help establish the style and character of the design. In addition, the designer should ask the clients to identify specific spaces or outdoor use areas that want to be included in the design. These wishes might be stated like:

> "We would like a hot-tub for four people in a fairly private place."
>
> "I want to have about 12 apple trees near the back of property."
>
> "I want to have a multilevel deck instead of one main level."
>
> "We need an extra parking space near the detached garage."
>
> "We want a new area for entertaining, a large lawn area for children's play, and a quiet sitting space near the tree in the back yard."

The designer will use this type of information to create the design program (see Chapter 7).

Clients' Likes and Dislikes. The designer should find out what the clients like and dislike with regard to landscape design. While there may be some overlap with wants and wishes, this discussion typically relates to defining the clients' preferences with regards to design style, aesthetic taste, materials (both structural and plant materials), and special elements or features. The intent is to begin to define the aesthetics and palette of materials of the landscape design. The designer might inquire about each of these topics to stimulate response from the clients. The

FIGURE 5–5
Some client likes and dislikes may be subjective and need clarification.

designer should also keep in mind it is just as useful to know what the clients do not want. In some instances, clients have only vague notions of what they want, but are able to clearly state what they don't want.

Statements about likes and dislikes might be similar to the following:

"I would like something that is unique to me, but still looks like it belongs."

"We don't want anything that stands out; we are a fairly conservative family."

"I see the same types of fences on so many different homes. I want something that blends with the house."

"If we could just have something rather simple, but different from others, we would be very satisfied."

Some comments regarding likes and dislikes are specific and are often relatively easy to incorporate into a design program. Other remarks about likes and dislikes may be more general and open to interpretation (Figure 5–5). Comments that include words like "special," "unique," "different," or "conservative" are subjective and reflect the clients' thoughts about their proposed project as they envision it.

How should a designer interpret these types of subjective statements?

How does a designer transform comments like those stated previously into meaningful and usable design information?

How does one incorporate these interpretations into the proposed design solution?

Carefully, very carefully! The word "special" to a lay person can mean something different to an experienced designer. The words "unique" and "different" to one person may mean something else to another. It is important to seek additional information in order to clarify subjective comments. The following questions are examples that can be asked to gain more objective information.

Original statement:

"I would like something that is unique to me, but still looks like it belongs."

Clarification questions:

"Can you define *uniquely* more specifically?"

"Do you want the design to reflect special things that you prefer, like materials, patterns, or colors?"

Original statement:

"We don't want anything that stands out; we are a fairly conservative family."

Clarification questions:

"Can you give some examples of things that stand out to you?"

"Can you elaborate on the word conservative?"

Original statement:

"I see the same types of fences on so many different homes. I want something that blends with the house."

Clarification questions:

"Can you describe the sameness that you refer to in these other places?"

"What does the word blend mean to you?"

Original statement:

"If we could have something rather simple, but different from others, we would be very satisfied."

Clarification questions:

"Can you talk about or show us examples of what simple means to you?"

"What do you mean by different? Different than what? Are there things that you really don't like and therefore want yours to be different?"

These are just some examples. It is very important to have a better and more thorough understanding of what the client thinks and says. Questions alone may not always be enough. For a designer to get a "better picture" of what the client is thinking, it often takes "actual pictures" to stimulate additional comments. We have found that many subjective comments made by clients tend to relate to their concern for the design character or appearance of elements in the proposed design.

Clients' Lifestyle and Interests. Additionally, the designer should try to determine the clients' lifestyle. That is, how do the clients currently use their house and site and how might this change with an improved landscape? The designer might ask questions such as these:

How will you use the site around your house?

How much do you entertain and for whom?

How large are your social events?

Will you cook or eat outside? If so how often?

Do you have any outdoor hobbies?

Do you like to garden?

What recreational activities do you enjoy outdoors?

FIGURE 5-6
The designer should encourage the clients to express their appreciation for their favorite interior architectural features.

Clients' Site Observations. The designer should ask the clients to define what they think are the assets and problems of the site. Even though the designer should still conduct a thorough site analysis (see Chapter 7), it is very helpful for the designer to get the clients insight as well. In fact, the clients are quite likely to know more about the site than anyone else because they have lived with and observed the site through the year in different conditions. Some site conditions may only be apparent to someone who has observed the site over a period of time. The designer should take advantage of this unique insight and use the clients' observations.

Clients' Architectural Observations. Finally, it is very helpful for the designer to seek the clients' insight about their house and its architectural style. Like the site, the clients' thoughts and observations about their house can provide valuable information that might provide ideas for developing the site master plan.

First, the designer should ask the clients whether or not there are any "interior" features that are of special interest. For instance, Figure 5–6 shows a section through several rooms of a house. In this particular house, the clients like three special things. They are: (1) the archway and trim detail in the room on the left, (2) the angled roof and window pattern in the great room, and (3) the white stucco finish on many walls of the house. This information should be well documented, for it can be used later when materials, patterns, and trim details are studied.

In addition to getting comments from the clients concerning the interior of the house, it is also important to get their remarks as they relate to the exterior architectural character. They will likely point out particular aspects of their house that influenced them to select it. As you can see from Figure 5–7, different people will like different aspects of the architecture. Some are partial to roofs and windows, others to specific materials and colors, while others are attracted to special features like porches and chimneys. In any case, documenting their likes and dislikes relating to the exterior character is as crucial as documenting their comments concerning the interior.

It is helpful to discuss the architectural character while you are walking around the exterior grounds (Figure 5–8). Being able to discuss ideas, as you point to certain architectural features, can be very beneficial. In addition, it is more effective to speak about landscape design possibilities while you are outdoors. For instance, it would be very easy to understand the following statement made by the designer as it relates to the house in Figure 5–8. "Since you have both identified the arched window as your favorite form, it is easy to conceive that form being used in the major patio area, in the pool area, or in the arched entry way into the garden from the side yard. The patterns in the upper window may provide an opportunity to use some irregular cut stone in the design to establish the same kind of contrast."

FIGURE 5–7
Different people like different houses for a host of varied reasons. Design #N2855 (top), Design #N3461 (middle), and Design #N3452 (Bottom). © Home Planners. Blueprints available, 800-322-6797.

Discussing ideas as you look at the architecture is very helpful. Again, make sure that comments made regarding any specific aspect of the architectural character, whether inside or outside, are thoroughly documented.

Methods of Inquiry

It should be apparent there is much for the designer to learn about the clients, their site, and their house. Thus, the designer needs to be well prepared for this first

FIGURE 5–8
Designers should encourage clients to express their appreciation for their favorite exterior architectural features. Design #N3409 (top). © Home Planners. Blueprints available, 800-322-6797.

meeting with the clients. The designer should go to this meeting with a clear agenda of items that must be covered. If necessary, a set of notes can be organized before the meeting to remind the designer of key topics that must be addressed.

The designer must also be able to accurately record the information and insights provided by the clients during the meeting. This can be done by careful note taking or with a tape recorder. The advantage of the latter is that it frees the designer from the burden of writing everything down and allows the designer to more fully participate in the discussion. Taping the conversation is also apt to be more accurate and allows the designer to replay it as many times as necessary to understand what was said. The taped information can be converted to notes some time following the meeting.

There are a number of possible ways for the designer to obtain the necessary information about the clients during their meeting. Each designer should consider these different methods of inquiry and determine which one (or ones) works best in any given situation. What might be appropriate for one designer or situation may not be suitable for another designer or set of circumstances. Ultimately, a designer should be able to use a number of these techniques to learn about clients.

Verbal Discussion.   Probably the most common method for gaining information about the clients is through verbal discussion. This is a personable approach

FIGURE 5-9
Sample questionnaire.

CLIENT QUESTIONAIRE

The purpose of this questionnaire is to obtain information that will be helpful in preparing a design for your residential site. All information you provide will be held in strict confidence and will aid in creating a design that fits the special needs of your family and conditions of your site. Please feel free to make additional comments or notes wherever you think it would be helpful. Thank you in advance for your cooperation.

I.   Family Characteristics. Please list the names of all family members and identify each person's age, place of employment or school, and hobbies, especially as they relate to the outdoors.

_____
_____
_____
_____
_____
_____

II. Existing Site Conditions.
    A. Front-yard Problems. Please list the current problems in the front yard which you think should be minimized or overcome in the design.
       1. Visual. _____
          _____
       2. Functional. _____
          _____

    B. Back-yard Problems. Please list the current problems in the back yard which you think should be minimized or overcome in the design.
       1. Visual. _____
          _____
       2. Functional. _____
          _____

    C. Front-yard Potentials. Please list all the positive elements and qualities of the front yard which should be retained or enhanced in the design.
       1. Visual. _____
          _____
       2. Functional. _____
          _____

    D. Back-yard Potentials. Please list all the positive elements and qualities of the back yard which should be retained or enhanced in the design.
       1. Visual. _____
          _____
       2. Functional. _____
          _____

that engages all parties and allows the clients to fully express themselves. The designer may permit the clients to talk freely or might direct the conversation with a series of questions. The clients should be given adequate time to respond to questions, though the designer may wish to interject from time to time to clarify points or ask other questions. In the end, the designer must be sure that the clients have discussed everything they wish to about their landscape and they feel comfortable with moving ahead to the next steps of the design process.

FIGURE 5–9
Sample questionnaire. (Continued)

III. Desired Outdoor Activities. Place a check mark next to those activities in which you want to participate on your site. After each activity, please identify the season(s), average number of days per week, and time of day you would enjoy this activity.

| | Season | | | | Days per Week | Time of Day |
	W	S	S	A		
_____ Barbecuing						
_____ Eating						
_____ Sitting/Relaxing/Reading						
_____ Sitting/Talking with family						
_____ Entertaining						
_____ 4–6 guests						
_____ 6–10 guests						
_____ over 10 guests						
_____ Sunbathing						
_____ Watching birds						
_____ Gardening						
_____ Annuals						
_____ Perennials						
_____ Vegetables						
_____ Fruit trees						
_____ Woody shrubs						
_____ Recreation						
_____ Badminton						
_____ Volleyball						
_____ Croquet						
_____ Swimming						
_____ Basketball						
_____ Throwing baseball						
_____ Throwing football						
_____ Throwing frisbee						
_____ Other (please identify)						

IV. Desired Site Character. Please describe how you think your site should look (formal/informal, open/wooded, etc.)

_____

V. Materials.

A. Please list the types of materials you like most for pavements, fences, walls, etc. _____

_____

B. Please list your favorite plant materials. _____

_____

C. Please list the plant materials you do *not* want used on your site. _____

_____

VI. Budget. Please identify the budget you would be willing to spend annually on your site for the next five years.

Questionnaire. Another form of inquiry is a written questionnaire. A questionnaire is a set of prepared questions that are organized on one or two sheets of paper (Figure 5–9). A questionnaire ensures that meaningful information is asked of the clients in a clear, orderly fashion. When completed, the questionnaire gives the designer a record of information about the clients that can be referred to throughout the development of the design. A disadvantage of a questionnaire is that it is sometimes seen as being too formalized and impersonal in nature.

FIGURE 5–10
A design firm should keep a portfolio of its past
and present work.

Some designers like to send a questionnaire to the clients before the meeting to stimulate their thinking. This gives the clients time to think more thoroughly about their responses. The designer then uses the meeting to review the clients' answers to the questionnaire and to clarify questions that either party might have. Other designers like to have the clients respond to the questionnaire during the meeting as a way of directing the conversation.

Review of Pictures. One additional means for gaining critical information from the clients is to review photographs or pictures of their favorite completed landscapes. Before the meeting, the designer might ask the clients to gather pictures or photographs that represent landscape styles, outdoor spaces, materials, special features, lighting, etc., the clients like (or dislike). These pictures can be from places that the clients have visited or from various books and magazines.

Like the questionnaire, this technique engages the clients in thinking about their project before meeting with the designer. For some clients, this process is very educational because it begins to suggest different ideas that they might not have previously considered. It is also an effective method for the client to communicate what ideas or aspirations they have about the landscape. The adage that "a picture is worth a thousand words" is especially true for the client who is trying to communicate what ideas they have in mind or what kind of landscapes they find appealing. Sometimes, the designer may ask to borrow some of the photographs so they can be studied more closely during the early stages of creating the design.

Review of Designer's Portfolio. A similar method for learning about the clients' preferences is for the designer to review examples of the firm's past and present work. It is excellent business practice for a designer to keep a portfolio of work that can be used for promotional purposes, showing clients one's capabilities, and for in-house record keeping (Figure 5–10). While a portfolio can include many work examples, it is recommended that the portfolio include:

- a wide range of project types that vary in size, cost, and style
- documentation of selected projects showing pictures of the design process from before the project started to its final completion
- master plans and other types of drawings such as functional diagrams, detail enlargements, planting plans, construction details, sections, etc.

A review of a portfolio during this first meeting with the client serves several purposes. First, it gives the clients a chance to see what kind of work the designer

FIGURE 5–11
A suggested breakdown of time spent by a professional designer for a site.

```
Client visits (3 at 1.5 hr. each) ........................... 4.5 hr.
Site measuring ............................................. 1.5 hr.
Base map preparation...................................... 2.5 hr.
Site analysis .............................................. 1.5 hr.
Concept development (2 alternatives) ..................... 2.0 hr.
Preliminary plans (2 alternatives)........................ 4.0 hr.
Master plan............................................... 4.0 hr.
Total..................................................... 20 hr.
```

has completed. While the clients may be somewhat familiar with the designer at this point, the designer can nevertheless show a range of work that might expand the clients' understanding of his/her abilities. Secondly, a review of the portfolio allows the clients to comment on the designer's work and to express opinions about what things they like or dislike. As with the other techniques discussed here, this too gives the designer insight about what will or will not be satisfactory for the clients. Lastly, a review of the portfolio permits the designer to explain how a project is undertaken and some of the thinking that goes into its development.

Concluding the Meeting

As the meeting approaches an end, there are still several items that may need to be addressed. First, it may be helpful for the designer to summarize what has been heard from the clients. This can be accomplished by repeating the major points and requests made by the clients. This helps to ensure the clients' thoughts have been accurately heard. Likewise, it gives the clients a chance to correct an item if it has not been understood correctly or to add anything they might have forgotten.

At this point in the meeting, the designer may also need to review information about the firm's practice. This will be necessary if the clients have not reviewed a brochure, advertisement, etc., or not talked very long to the designer prior to the meeting. The designer may need to review design philosophy, design process, etc., to make sure the clients understand how the designer intends to proceed and on what basis.

Finally, the designer needs to discuss both the clients' budget and design fees for the project. The designer should ask whether the clients have an overall budget for the design and its implementation. This discussion may require some education of the clients if they are not familiar with typical costs for master plans or with implementation costs. The designer should also make it clear that most master plans get implemented over time, thus the overall cost of construction and installation can be spread out over a number of years.

The designer needs to explain what it will cost for the master plan. Again, the designer should not be hesitant to charge fees for the design and should not hide such costs in the charges that are made later on for materials or installation. Professional design services by a site designer should be a separate fee from the construction, installation, and maintenance contracts. Time accumulates while preparing all the phases leading up to and including a master plan. Client meetings, site measuring, base map preparation, site analysis, functional diagrams, preliminary design, and master plan design can all add up to a substantial amount of time. And that may mean a sizable design fee. There is no specific amount that one should charge, but it is typical for a residential master plan to cost between $500 and $1000. This may be viewed as inexpensive by some designers and as ludicrous to others, depending on whether they currently charge for design services. A suggested breakdown of this time is shown in Figure 5–11.

When 20 hours are invested in the development of a residential site master plan, then that time should be converted to a dollar amount. Companies may charge clients 3 times the designer's hourly pay rate to cover overhead and profit. It is quite common for a company to charge a client $50 to $100 per hour for design services.

DEVELOPING A PROPOSAL FOR DESIGN SERVICES

After the designer and clients have discussed the topics presented thus far, the clients should be asked if they are interested in entering into a contract for design services. They may or may not be able to make a decision at the end of the first meeting. If they decide to go ahead with the project, then the designer should formalize the discussion by preparing and sending the clients a "Proposal for Design Services" within a few days of their meeting so the clients can study the specifics. Often, clients feel more assured about an agreement if everything is spelled out in writing. If the clients are in agreement with the proposal, they can sign it and return a copy to the designer.

Some firms have standard forms for "Proposals for Design Services" with spaces for filling in the times, dates, costs, stipulations, and signatures. Other firms prefer to prepare more personal proposals taking into consideration the first meeting's discussions. In either case, it is recommended that the proposal include the following: (1) names and addresses, (2) scope of work, (3) drawings/products, (4) client meetings, (5) time schedule, (6) fee and payment schedule, and (7) contract acceptance.

Names and Addresses.   As in any formal letter, the proposal should include both the clients' and the designer's names and addresses. It should also include the firm's or designer's telephone number so it is easy for the clients to contact the designer if they have any questions about the proposal.

Scope of Work.   The proposal should identify specific tasks the designer intends to complete. In order to prepare a master plan, typical tasks involve completing the site measurements, base map, site analysis, design program, preliminary design alternatives, and final master plan. If there are any additional tasks required, they should be identified as well.

It is also recommended that the designer identify those things that are not part of the contract. Some homeowners assume that a master plan will contain all the information necessary to actually install and construct the entire design. Many master plans involve the construction of steps, walls, decks, fences, arbors, and so forth. The construction of these structures requires additional drawings in order to provide the contractor with necessary information to build them. Detailed construction drawings are typically not part of the "Proposal for Design Services" unless both the designer and clients agreed beforehand that it was something to be included.

Drawings.   The "Proposal for Design Services" should identify the specific drawings that will be given to the clients. On a typical project, the clients should be given copies of the preliminary designs and the master plan. In addition, the designer may wish to prepare other types of drawings such as sections and/or perspectives to supplement the plans. For each of these drawing types, the proposal should also identify its scale, what type of print or copy it will be, whether or not it will be color rendered, and what it will show. Also, the Proposal should indicate the number of copies of each drawing that will be given to the clients.

Client Meetings.   Important to the proposal is a description of the number of meetings that will take place with the clients to present various phases of the project. Typically, there are three meetings with the clients. The first meeting is the one already discussed in this chapter. The second meeting usually takes place when the designer has completed the preliminary plan(s). At this time, the designer should ask for feedback from the clients about the different design ideas. At the third meeting, the designer presents the master plan to the clients. Depending on the size of the project site and the scope of work, there may need to be more meetings, especially if the project is complex.

Time Schedule.   The proposal should identify when: (1) work on the design will begin, (2) the preliminary plans will be completed, and (3) the master plan will be completed. With regard to setting completion dates for the various phases of the design project, the designer may prefer to pinpoint completion dates by telling the clients the exact date when work will be completed. However, this is not always a good practice. There may be times when unforeseen circumstances arise causing work to be delayed. Because these situations are not predictable, identifying exact dates is not a recommended practice. Approximate due dates will usually suffice. When a phase of work is completed, the designer can then telephone the clients to set a specific date and time for a meeting.

Fee and Payment Schedule.   The "Proposal for Design Services" should outline the fees for design services. It is recommended that the total fee for design services be separated into: (1) a retainer fee, (2) a partial completion fee, and (3) a final completion fee. A retainer fee is the amount of money the clients pay prior to the beginning of any work by the designer. It is similar to "earnest money" that a person pays to reserve a specific item for later purchase. A retainer fee is common practice in design professions. The amount may vary from project to project, but may be somewhere between 10 and 20 percent of the total design fee.

The partial completion fee is the amount of money paid at the presentation of the preliminary plans. This amount may vary from 40 percent to 60 percent of the total design fee. Frequently, most of the design time is spent in this phase and thus may show a substantial dollar amount. The final payment is made at the presentation of the master plan. This amount may vary from 20 percent to 50 percent. There are some companies that collect the full design fee after completion of all the specified work. Regardless which payment system is used, be specific about "how much" needs to be paid "when."

Contract Acceptance.   Our discussion so far has concentrated on the proposal. A related document is the contract. But, there is a difference between the two. A proposal is a document that simply outlines the specific services that are to be rendered for a particular sum of money. Such a written proposal is not a legal contract. It is an offer that can be accepted or rejected by the clients. However, when both the designer and the clients sign a proposal, then the proposal becomes a legal contract. Therefore, when a proposal is submitted to the clients, the designer should sign it in order to establish it as an offer from the designer to the clients. If the clients accept the proposal, they can sign it to establish their acceptance. This signed document is then considered to be a legal contract between the designer and the clients according to the specifications in the proposal. Thus, the proposal should contain spaces for the signatures of the designer and the clients as well as the dates the signatures were made. It is recommended that the offer made in the proposal be open for acceptance for a limited amount of time such as thirty days.

Upon receiving the signed contract, the designer can then begin the work. However, no work should be undertaken before receiving the signed contract because the designer has no legal authority to do so. Furthermore, the designer may be wasting time if the clients decide not to enter into the contract.

THE DUNCAN RESIDENCE

To provide additional explanation for each of the phases of the design process presented in this text, this and following chapters describe how each phase is actually applied to a sample design project. This sample project, the Duncan residence, begins here and is followed through other steps of the design process in subsequent chapters. The project is a real one and involves ordinary clients who live in a typical single-family suburban home.

The Duncans' house is a two-story, four-bedroom home with gray-blue siding, white brick, and white wood trim (Figures 5–12 and 5–13). It is situated on a site that is a little over a quarter of an acre in size and is surrounded on the west, north, and east sides by neighboring residential properties. The site is rather flat with some scattered existing trees in both the front and back yards. A more detailed description with additional photographs of the Duncan residence is found in Chapter 7.

To begin the process, Brian and Pamela Duncan telephoned James E. Kent, landscape designer, concerning the future development of their site. During this initial telephone conversation, they expressed the desire to enhance the appearance and usefulness of their site. To accomplish this, they indicated the need for privacy, an outdoor family and entertaining space, shade, development of a front entry, and some additional planting around the site. The Duncans' needs seemed to suggest the possibility of a challenging design project, and so Mr. Kent requested to meet with them at their house. Mr. Kent explained that there was no charge for this initial visit and accepted their invitation to meet with them.

Upon arriving at the Duncan residence, Mr. Kent was introduced to Brian, Pamela, and their three children. Initially, they met in the living room where Mr. Kent encouraged the Duncan family to talk about their needs, desires, and anticipations about the site. When necessary, Mr. Kent asked the Duncans questions to clarify their thoughts or to seek more specific information about their requests. Later in the meeting, they walked through the house and around the site as Mr. Kent listened to the Duncans discuss specific concerns and requests. He kept written notes of all the family's thoughts and ideas. After this, Mr. Kent talked about the capabilities of his firm and the preferred process for working with clients. He explained the need to develop an overall master plan for the site as the best way to accomplish everything the Duncans had in mind. Although the Duncans were somewhat apprehensive at first, they realized that a master plan was a comprehensive approach to developing their site. So as not to rush the Duncans into making an immediate decision, Mr. Kent told them that he would prepare a "Proposal for Design Services." If this met with their satisfaction, they could then sign the proposal and return it to begin the design process. He thanked the Duncans for the opportunity to meet with them and expressed hope that he would be able to provide them with design services.

Upon returning to the office, Mr. Kent prepared a "Proposal for Design Services" and sent two copies to the Duncans, one for their files and one to be returned to him. The cover letter and proposal he wrote are shown in Figures 5–14 and 5–15.

FIGURE 5-12
View of the Duncan residence as seen from the street.

FIGURE 5-13
View of the north side of the Duncan residence.

FIGURE 5–14
The cover letter.

James E. Kent, Landscape Designer
DESIGN RESPONSE TWO
62047 Bedford Court, Eugene Ohio 10548
Tel: (614) 830-4900

July 26, 2001

Brian and Pamela Duncan
4140 Willow Bend Road
Eugene, Ohio 10548

Dear Mr. and Mrs. Duncan:

Thank you very much for the opportunity to have met with you this past Wednesday evening and the informative discussion we had about the improvements for your residential site. The interests and ideas you shared with me are very important for properly developing a design for your site.

In response to all the ideas that were discussed during our first meeting, I am submitting the enclosed "Proposal for Design Services" in hope that I will be able to work with you on this forthcoming adventure. Although there are some obvious site problems that must be contended with, I am confident that there are a variety of possibilities that will offer alternative ways to turn these problems into potentials as well as satisfying your specific needs and requirements.

Respectfully submitted,

James E. Kent

James E. Kent
Landscape Designer
DESIGN RESPONSE TWO

SUMMARY

The initial meeting with the clients is important because the designer acquires vital information about the clients that will be used as the foundation for the design solution. The designer seeks to understand the clients' needs, desires about their site, and their observations about both the site and the house. Because of the amount of information that is discussed, it is important that the designer accurately records the clients' ideas and is able to easily refer to them in later stages of the design process. The anticipated outcome of this meeting is that the designer and clients should come to a mutual agreement about working together on the exciting adventure of the design for the clients' site. This is formalized through the writing and signing of the "Proposal for Design Services."

FIGURE 5–15
The Duncans' "Proposal for Design Services."

PROPOSAL FOR DESIGN SERVICES
The Duncan Residence

SCOPE OF WORK.   Outlined below are the proposed tasks to be accomplished.
1. Assimilation of all program and site data received from you.
2. Actual on-site measurement and development of a base map.
3. Analysis of existing on-site and immediate off-site conditions.
4. Preparation of two alternative preliminary plans which will be presented to you at your home.
5. Further refinement of one of the alternative preliminary plans or a combination of the two to establish the final master plan.

PLEASE NOTE THAT THE SCOPE OF WORK DOES NOT INCLUDE THE FOLLOWING:
1. Detailed construction or working drawings for any site structure.
2. Actual construction or installation of the design.

DRAWINGS.   I will submit the following drawings to you according to the time schedule outlined below:
1. Two preliminary plans for the entire site. These plans will be drawn freehand at a scale of $1/8'' = 1' - 0''$. They will show the location of all proposed site elements (and existing site features that are to remain) such as walks, driveway, terrace, fences, and planting. Notes will identify pavement and fence materials, fence heights, and general type of plant materials. You will receive two copies of each of these plans.
2. One master plan, drafted at a scale of $1/8'' = 1' - 0''$ will show specific names of plant materials and other materials and patterns. You will receive two copies of this drawing.

TIME SCHEDULE.   I will begin work upon receipt of the signed contract. The preliminary plans will be completed within 15 days, at which time I will telephone you to set a specific time and date for presenting them to you. Following that meeting, and after a 10-day period for you to study the preliminary plans and get back to me with your comments, I shall begin the design of the final master plan. This plan shall be finished within 7 days. I shall again telephone you to set a time and a date for presenting the final master plan.

FEE PAYMENT AND SCHEDULE.   I propose to prepare and execute the above noted drawings and services for the lump sum of $750.00. The payment for the above services shall be as follows:
$150 submitted with the signed proposal/contract
$400 paid upon completion and presentation of preliminary plans
$150 paid upon completion and presentation of the master plan

CONTRACT ACCEPTANCE.   This offer is valid for 30 days. If this proposal is satisfactory and acceptable to you, please sign the enclosed copy and return it to me for my files.

James E. Kent   7/26/01   _____   _____

James E. Kent   Date   Pamela Duncan   Date

_____   _____

Brian Duncan   Date

DESIGN RESPONSE TWO

6

Site Measuring and Base Map Preparation

INTRODUCTION

The previous chapter addressed various guidelines for meeting the clients. As discussed, this is one of several tasks undertaken in the research and preparation phase of the design process. This step culminates when the "Proposal for Design Services" is signed by both the designer and the clients, thus formalizing the agreement between the two parties. At this point, the designer is ready to proceed with measuring the site and drawing the base sheet and base map. Other work such as site inventory, site analysis, and development of design ideas cannot occur until this step is completed. Site measuring and drawing the base map are also critical because their accuracy influences all later work that is based upon them. Doing these tasks in a thoughtful and organized manner saves many headaches later on.

To help the designer perform these tasks in a professional manner, this chapter covers: (1) terms related to this phase of work, (2) guidelines and techniques for taking and recording field measurements, and (3) procedures for drawing a base sheet and base map.

DEFINITION OF TERMS

There are a number of terms related to site measuring and drawing a base map that are widely used throughout the design professions. These terms are often used interchangeably because of their similarities even though they have slightly different definitions. These terms are: (1) *lot*, (2) *plot plan*, (3) *site plan*, (4) *base map*, and (5) *base sheet*. Each of these is a common expression used to describe the initial base plan prepared for a design project. Though similar in some ways, each is different in the specific information it includes and the particular purpose it serves.

Lot

Every single-family residence is situated on a piece of property called a *lot*. This is often called a *plat* or *plot*. To avoid confusion with a map (often called a *plat*) or a scheme or secret plan (often called a *plot*), a residential piece of property should be referred to as a *lot*. Lots range in configuration from simple to complex shapes (Figure 6–1).

Lots occur in a variety of sizes, too. Although there are no standard lot sizes, a designer is apt to encounter some rather typical sizes. They are listed below and shown in Figure 6–2 in relation to the size of one acre of land, which is 43,560 square feet, approximately 208′ × 208′.

Small lot	1/8 of an acre
Average lot	1/4 of an acre
Medium lot	1/2 of an acre
Large lot	acre or greater

All lots are bounded by *property lines* which are invisible lines defining the sides or edges of a lot. Each property line is identified by a *bearing* and a *distance*. A bearing is the horizontal direction of a property line expressed in degrees east or west of true north or south. A distance is the horizontal linear measurement of the property line (Figure 6–3). The corners of a lot are typically identified by iron pins embedded in the ground.

Plot Plan

A scaled plan drawing that shows the layout of the property lines of a residential lot is termed a *plot plan*. A plot plan typically shows the following information:

- the lot configuration defined by the property lines
- orientation of the property in relation to true north
- bearings and distances of the property lines
- right-of-ways
- sidewalks and boulevards
- legal restrictions such as setbacks and easements

A *right-of-way* is the publicly owned area of land where the street or road is placed. The average width of a right-of-way is 60 feet in a residential area though the width may vary from 30 feet to 120 feet (Figure 6–4). The edge of the right-of-way coincides with the "front" property lines of the residential lot. Right-of-ways are regulated by the local governing body such as a village, township, city, or even county. Thus, it is a good idea to check with the appropriate local government office to determine the regulations pertaining to the right-of-way.

Sidewalks are often located just inside the right-of-way (Figure 6–5). Consequently, many property lines and corners are often found near the edge of the sidewalk. Even though they are typically outside of the actual property lines, the maintenance of most sidewalks is the responsibility of the homeowners.

A *boulevard*, sometimes referred to as a *berm* or *tree lawn*, is the strip of land located between the sidewalk and the curb of the street (Figure 6–6). Although this land is also usually under the jurisdiction of the city or county, maintenance of the boulevard is again commonly the responsibility of the homeowner.

A *setback* is the minimum distance that any portion of a structure, such as the house or garage, must be located from a given property line. That is, structures must be "set back" or built at least a specified number of feet from the property line (Figure 6–7). There are "front-yard setbacks," "back-yard setbacks," and "side-yard setbacks." In some subdivisions, the fronts of all the houses are aligned

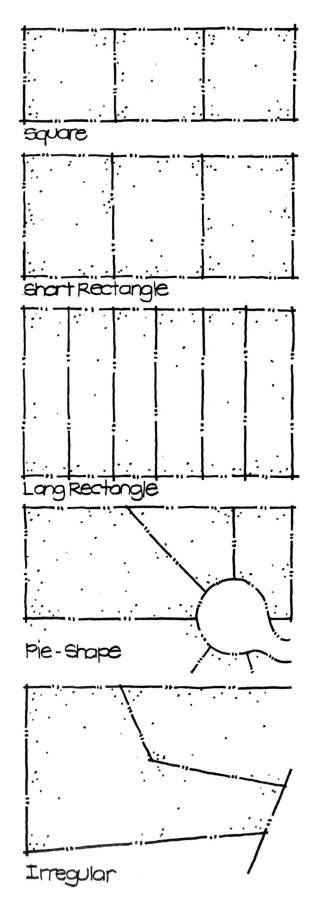

FIGURE 6-1
Typical lot configurations.

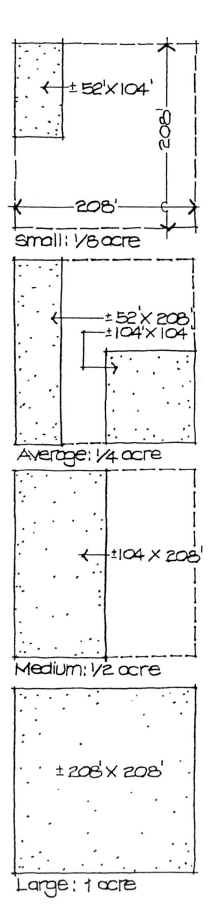

FIGURE 6-2
Typical lot sizes.

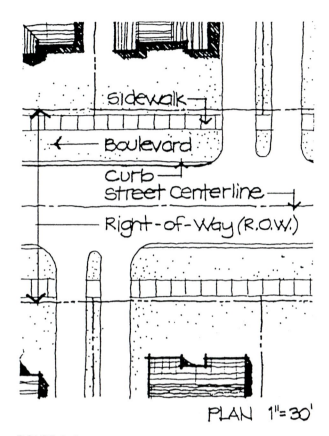

N 41° - 34' - 0" E
92.75'

S 48° - 26' - 0" E
143.00'

sidewalk
Boulevard
curb
street centerline
Right-of-Way (R.O.W.)

PLAN 1" = 30'

FIGURE 6-4
Typical right-of-way.

FIGURE 6-5
Location of sidewalk inside right-of-way.

Property Line

Corner Pin

R.O.W.

Sidewalk
Boulevard
Curb

Street

Site Measuring and Base Map Preparation

137

FIGURE 6-6
Typical boulevard.

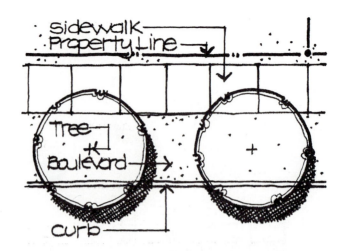

FIGURE 6-7
Sample setbacks.

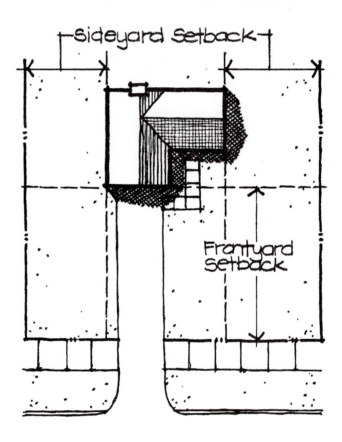

on the setback line. A landscape designer should be aware of setbacks because they influence where such structures as gazebos, pool buildings, walls, and fences can be placed.

An *easement* is a strip of land within the lot which others (often utility companies) have the right to access (Figure 6–8). In the case of utility companies, they have the right to locate utilities above or below ground within the easement. Homeowners with an easement are often restricted from building any structures or planting any sizable plant materials in this area because this would prevent access to the easement.

A typical plot plan, showing each of the preceding elements, is shown in Figure 6–9. It is usually the obligation of the clients to supply the designer with a copy of the plot plan.

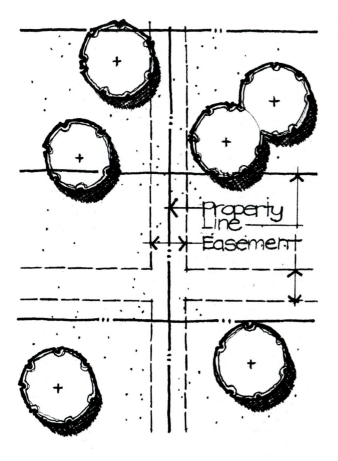

FIGURE 6-8
Sample easements.

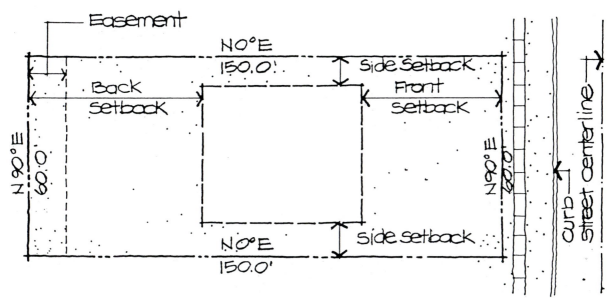

FIGURE 6-9
Typical plot plan.

Site Plan

The term *site plan* has several definitions. As used by developers or building contractors, the term *site plan* refers to a plan drawing which locates the position of the house within the lot. This site plan gives dimensions and setbacks from the property lines and corners of the site (Figure 6–10). This drawing instructs the

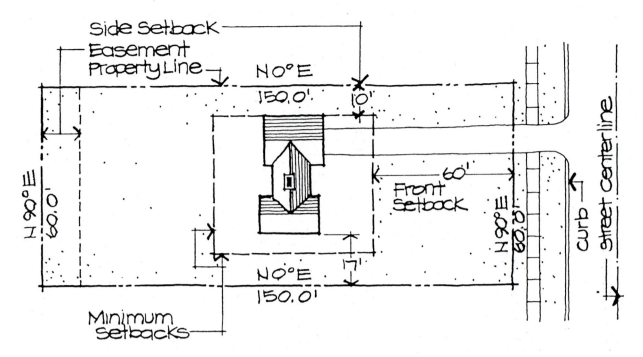

FIGURE 6-10
Typical site plan.

building contractor where to locate the new house on the site. This type of site plan may also show the location of other structures such as detached garages, gazebos, and house additions. This site plan can be viewed as a plot plan with the major structures added.

The term *site plan* is also used by landscape architects, architects, and engineers to describe the drawing which shows the proposed design or layout of a site. Used in this manner, the *site plan* can be a *preliminary design* or a *master plan*.

Base Map

A *base map* is similar to the developer's or builder's site plan, but with additional information. The base map is a plan drawing that records all existing physical site elements such as driveways, walkways, patios, decks, terraces, walls, fences, steps, utilities, plant materials, and any other visible elements (Figure 6–11). The base map is prepared by the landscape designer after all necessary measurements have been extracted from other maps or actually taken in the field.

A base map is useful for several reasons. First, it documents the existing site conditions prior to new design and construction. It can also help establish what specific elements need to be removed, replaced, replanted, or relocated later when actual construction begins. Second, the base map is used for the site inventory and analysis as discussed in Chapter 7. Both the base map and the site analysis are useful in discussions with the clients about the restrictions and potentials for the design of their site. Without an accurate recording of all existing physical site data, the designer is apt to have a difficult time relating new ideas to existing conditions and constraints.

Base Sheet

The circumstances of each new project vary. Some projects require all existing structures and plantings to remain unchanged. These become some of the physical constraints in developing a design solution. Other design projects may propose existing structures and plantings, if scarce, ineffective, or in poor condi-

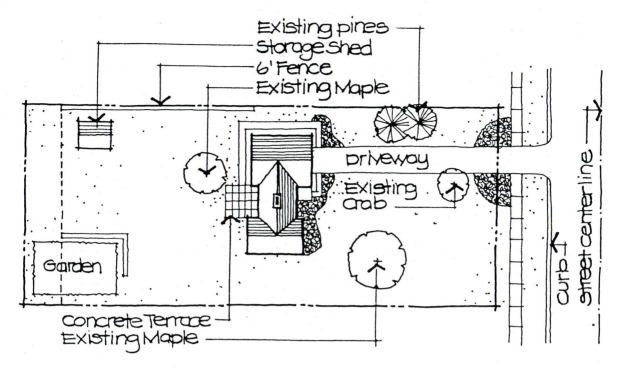

FIGURE 6-11
Typical base map (all existing conditions).

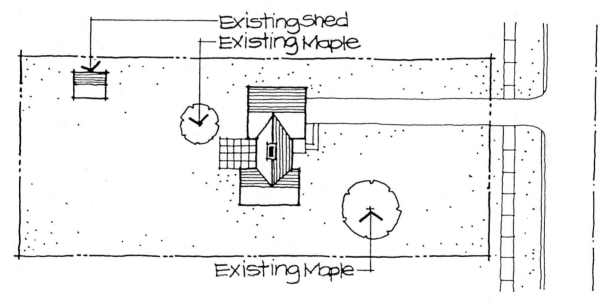

FIGURE 6-12
Typical base sheet (existing conditions that are to remain).

tion, to be partially or totally eliminated. In this situation, the designer has more freedom to alter the existing site conditions. A *base sheet* is a drawing that allows for such a situation.

A base sheet is different from a base map. A base sheet is a plan drawing that shows only those existing elements of a site that are to remain and be incorporated into the proposed design (Figure 6–12). Site elements to be removed are not drawn at all in order to give the designer more freedom and flexibility to be creative. This plan serves as the base for the designer to begin the design studies.

Both the base sheet and base map are needed to develop a design for any given site. They are usually prepared by the landscape designer or an assistant and entail the following four steps for proper completion:

- gathering all existing site data from the clients
- on-site measuring
- organizing measurements, notes, and photographs
- drawing the base sheet and map

GATHERING EXISTING SITE DATA

The owners of the site have the responsibility to supply the designer with all pertinent physical information about the site. If the homeowners are unable to locate the plot plan of their property, a copy of it may be obtained from one of several sources. The city or county engineer should have a copy of the entire subdivision plot plan which shows each individual lot within the subdivision. A record of the plot plan may also exist in the offices of the architect or home building contractor. In addition, a plot plan is often recorded in the deed or abstract of the house. The lending institution holding the mortgage on the house may have a copy in their files as well. The descriptions of most residential lots are often shown on the city or county tax and utility maps and often can be accessed on line through the Internet. If there is little or no information readily available, it is strongly recommended that the services of a registered surveyor be obtained. A surveyor's services will normally provide a drawing illustrating: (1) an accurate location of all property lines and corners, (2) the bearings and distances for each of the property lines, and (3) the location of major structures such as the house and the garage.

It is not a recommended procedure to guess or estimate the location of the property lines because they are legal boundaries of the site. Visual clues that seem to identify the location of property lines are sometimes wrong. Existing fences, for instance, are not always built on the property line. Fences are most often constructed by one of the homeowners on their own property, and not always on or immediately adjacent to the property line. Similarly, hedgerows of plant materials are usually planted by one homeowner, but not necessarily on the property line either. Where two adjacent properties meet in a grassy side yard, lawn mowers may create an identifiable line often misconstrued as a property line. Also, neighboring houses are not all similar in size and their location on their respective lots is not always the same. Therefore, the centerline of the space between the sides of the two houses cannot be assumed to be the property line. Likewise, edges of driveways cannot be assumed to be property lines. A designer should always be careful not to misinterpret what may seem to be an obvious property line. Actual location of property lines is essential.

ON-SITE MEASUREMENT SYSTEMS

After receiving all available and pertinent site information from the clients the designer may still have to locate some existing site elements. In some situations, the clients take the initiative to prepare a scaled drawing with the base map information shown. When this task is completed by the homeowners, it saves the designer time and, therefore, the clients money. However, the designer should double-check the clients' map to verify its accuracy.

Measuring Distances with a Tape Measure

For accurate measuring, a metal or cloth tape measure, preferably 100 feet long, is needed. When measuring, it is recommended that two people hold the tape; usually the designer on one end of the tape and an assistant on the other end.

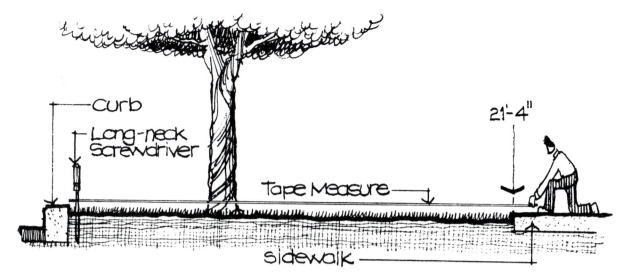

FIGURE 6–13
Use a screwdriver to secure one end of the measuring tape when measuring by yourself.

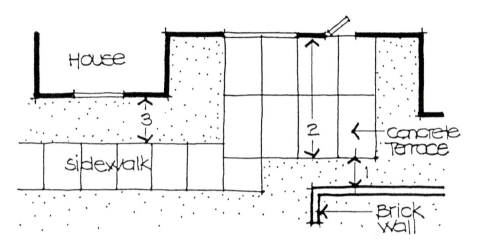

FIGURE 6–14
Direct measurement.

However, there are times when the designer may be without a measuring assistant. In such a case, it is suggested that a long-necked screwdriver be used in securing one end of the tape by inserting the neck of the screwdriver through the hook at the end of the tape and pushing it into the ground (Figure 6–13).

There are three techniques for measuring distances on a site. One needs to be acquainted with each because they will serve the designer well in most site measuring tasks.

Direct Measuring.   Direct measurement is a simple and direct measurement from the edge of one element to the edge of another. Direct measurement is the most common method of taking measurements and is used between edges that are parallel to each other. Figure 6–14 illustrates the use of direct measurement to: (1) locate the edge of a sidewalk from the edge of a wall, (2) locate the edge of a concrete terrace from the back wall of the house, and (3) locate the edge of the sidewalk from the face of the house.

Baseline Measuring.   The second system of measuring is the baseline measurement system. This system aligns the tape measure along a known line, referred to

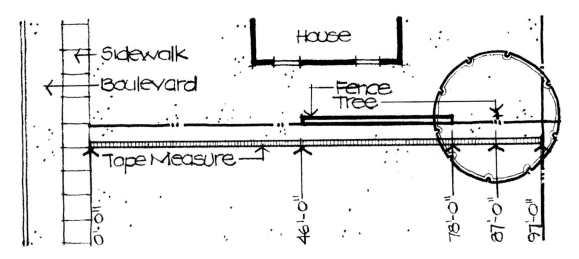

FIGURE 6–15
Baseline measurement.

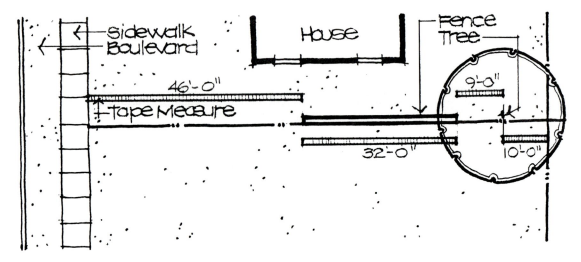

FIGURE 6–16
This type of measuring is not as efficient as baseline measurement.

as a baseline, and locates other points or edges along that baseline. Baseline measurements are best taken when there are many points that must be located along a straight edge or line. Figure 6–15 shows the tape measure stretched along the property line starting from the front edge of the sidewalk. The fence is located 46 feet from the sidewalk and extends to a distance of 78 feet from the sidewalk. The tree is then situated at 87 feet from the sidewalk. The back property corner is 97 feet from the sidewalk.

This system of measuring along a baseline from one end of the tape is more accurate and less time consuming than moving the tape and measuring each point in relation to the point before or after it. As can be seen, four separate measurements could have been taken along the property line (Figure 6–16), but this wastes time and increases the chance for mistakes. It is recommended that the tape measure be moved as few times as possible to minimize mistakes and wasted time.

The baseline method of measuring is strongly suggested when measuring the location of doors and windows of the house. Figure 6–17 illustrates the tape measure stretched along the side of the house. Each door and window jamb (side) is located a specific distance from one end of the house where the front end of the tape measure is placed. Each time a different side or wall of the house is measured, a

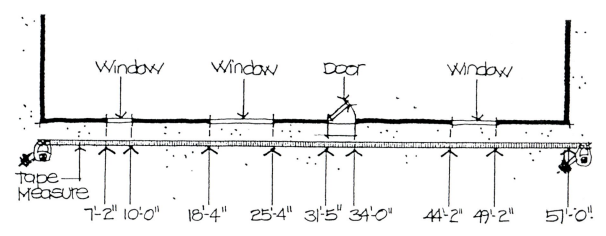

FIGURE 6–17
Baseline measurement should be used to locate doors and windows.

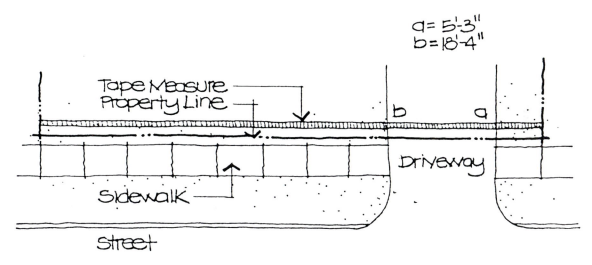

FIGURE 6–18
Example of locating the driveway at the property line.

new baseline is used. Another example of baseline measuring is to locate where the edges of the driveway cross the property line (Figure 6–18).

Triangulation Measuring. The third system of measuring is the triangulation method which is used to locate a point in relation to two other known points. For instance, assume there is a tree on a site which needs to be accurately located (Figure 6–19). This can be done by using two corners of the house (Point A and Point E) as reference points. Simply measure and record the distance from each of these corners of the house to the center of the tree. Later when drawing the base map, each of the same corners of the house serves as the center of a circle with the radius being the distance to the tree. When the circles are drafted on the base map, they will intersect at the center point of the tree. This method of locating specific points is beneficial in locating other individual elements such as poles, lights, utility boxes, etc.

Triangulation is also a good method to use when lines or elements are not parallel to each other. Figure 6–20 shows a row of trees, not parallel to the house, that must be located. Both the southernmost tree and the northernmost tree in this example are first independently located using the triangulation method. Then the other five trees are found using the baseline method by stretching the tape measure from the southernmost tree to the northernmost tree.

Site Measuring and Base Map Preparation

FIGURE 6–19
Triangulation measurement.

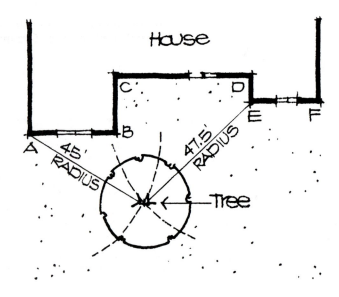

FIGURE 6–20
Triangulation and baseline measurements.

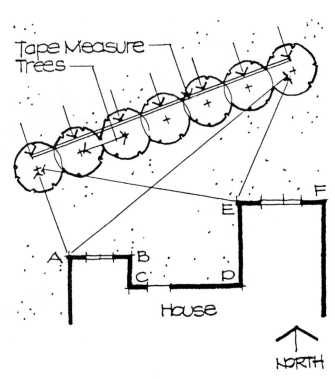

RECORDING SITE MEASUREMENTS

In addition to the process of taking measurements, one must also record the measurements in an organized and legible fashion. There are three major reasons why site measurement notes should be organized. The first reason is that the person who records the field measurements may not be the same one who draws the base map in the office. Therefore, the field measurement notes must be easily understood by anyone in the office who is given the responsibility for drawing the base map and base sheet. The second reason is that the base map and base sheet may not be able to be drafted until several days or even weeks after measuring the site. When the measurement notes are reviewed later in time, they should still be easily understood. The third reason for clearly organizing field measurement notes is to diminish the need to return to the site because a measurement was either totally forgotten or it was recorded in an illegible manner. Organized and legible notes save time and money.

To record measurements, it is suggested that a sturdy clipboard with graph paper be used. Measurements should be recorded in pencil, since there are times when mistakes are made. The use of a pen or marker is not recommended.

Locating the House on the Lot

One of the first pieces of information that is needed is the location of the house on the site. The Duncan residence, first introduced at the end of Chapter 5, will be used to show how this should be done. First, sketch the general configuration of the lot on a 8-1/2" × 11" piece of graph paper fastened to a clipboard. Whether or not the exact shape of the site is known, at least sketch a shape that corresponds to what is seen and with the correct number of property corners. Next, give each property corner a numerical notation, like Roman numerals (Figure 6–21). Then, measure each of the property lines from corner to corner. As measurements are taken, record them on the same sheet as the sketch of the lot. The property for the Duncan residence is a rectangular shape measuring 80′ −0″ × 150′ −0″. The property corners are identified by iron pipes embedded a few inches below the surface of the ground.

The next procedure is to take measurements of the house itself. The first step is to sketch the configuration of the house within the lot previously drawn on the graph paper. As can be seen from the photographs in Figures 5–12 and 5–13 from the previous chapter, the house configuration can be estimated easily. It is not necessary to draw in the doors and windows during this step; draw only the walls. Make sure that all house walls are shown in their correct direction. Next, label each major corner of the house with a capital letter of the alphabet (Figure 6–22). The fireplace located on the east wall between corners D and E is not labeled because the fireplace corners are not major house corners.

Triangulation measurements can be taken to accurately locate the house in relation to the property corners. After selecting a side of the house, measure from one of its end corners to two different nearby property corners. For instance, measurements were taken from Pt. G on the house to property corners Pt. III and Pt. IV and noted on the sketch (Figure 6–23). Likewise, measurements were taken from Pt. J on the house to property corners Pt. III and Pt. IV. These measurements located the two front corners of the house in relation to the front property line. With two house corners located, the entire house is accurately positioned on the lot.

In a similar fashion, the back side of the house can be located in relation to the back property line by measuring from house corners Pt. A and Pt. D to property corners Pt. I and Pt. II. Any two corner points of the house can be used with any two nearby and easily measured property corners. It is not necessary to measure from every corner of the house to every property corner.

Locating Walls, Doors, and Windows of the House

Now that the house has been located correctly in relation to the property corners, it is time to measure the walls of the house including the location of the doors and windows. On a second sheet of 8-1/2" × 11" graph paper attached to the clipboard, again sketch the configuration of the house. This sketch of the house should be drawn larger than the previous sketch because the property lines do not need to be shown.

There are a few guidelines to help establish a relatively proportional sketch plan of the house.

Step 1: First, sketch the overall plan configuration of the house's outside walls. This can be done by walking around the house and noting the number of corners and configuration of the layout (Figure 6–24).

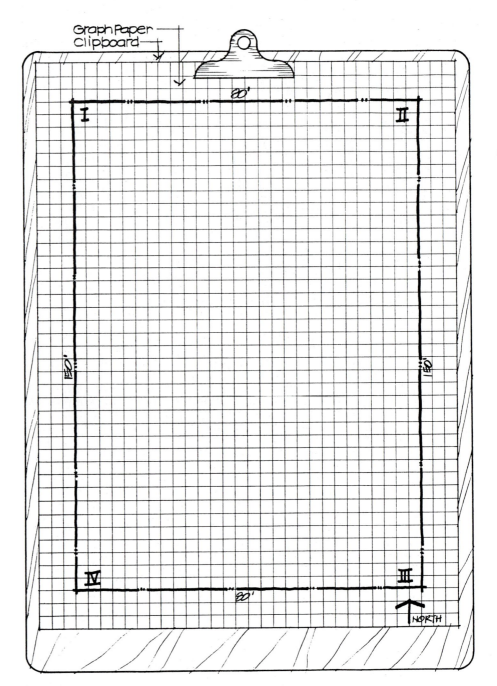

FIGURE 6-21
Use Roman numerals to note property corners.

Step 2: Next, estimate the location of all the doors and windows of the house on the sketch plan drawn in Step 1. This can be done by erasing portions of the walls drawn in Step 1 and penciling in the doors and windows. In later phases of the design process, it will be important to know where the major access points into the house are, which way the doors swing, and where the major and minor views out of the house occur. It is helpful to identify doors with one notation and windows with another notation. Doors can be noted as D1, D2, and so on, while the windows can be identified as W1, W2, and so on (Figure 6–25).

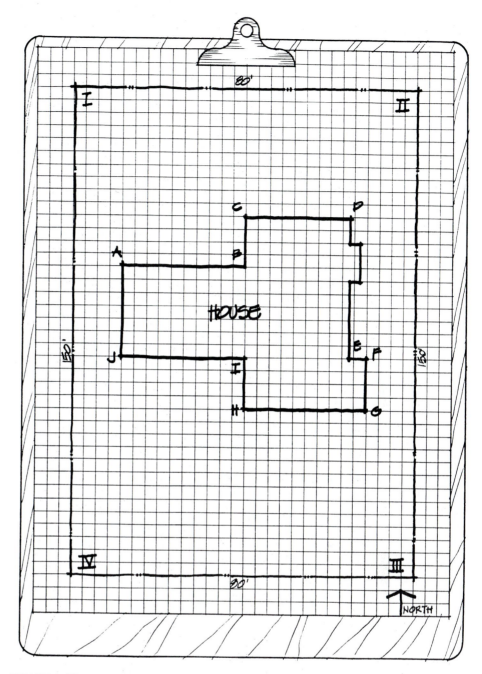

FIGURE 6-22
Use capital letters to note house corners.

Step 3: There should be two jambs (sides) for each door and window sketched in the plan. Each jamb should receive a specific notation for purposes of measuring. Starting with Pt. A and proceeding in the direction of Pt. B, number each of the jambs consecutively starting with 1 (Figure 6–26). Since there are three openings in wall AB, jambs are numbered 1 through 6. Then, starting at Pt. B and proceeding in the direction of Pt. C, number each of the jambs in a similar manner again starting with 1. Continue this system all the way around the house until all of the jambs have a notation. As you can see, even though some numbers

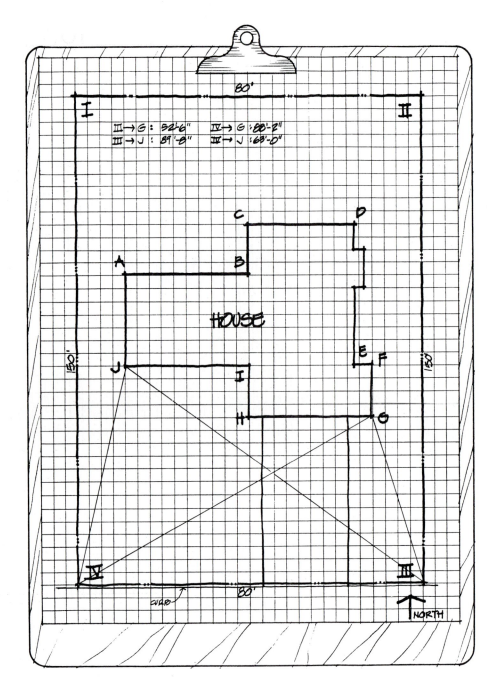

FIGURE 6–23
Triangulation measurement should be used to locate two house corners in relation to the property corners.

are repeated on each side of the house, each jamb has a specific notation. For instance, A1B refers to one jamb while B1C and C1D refer to other jambs on other sides of the house.

Step 4: Using the baseline method of measuring along each wall, locate the door and window jambs. The tape measure is stretched along wall AB to determine the jamb locations in relation to Pt. A. Again, record all the measurements in a manner similar to Figure 6–27.

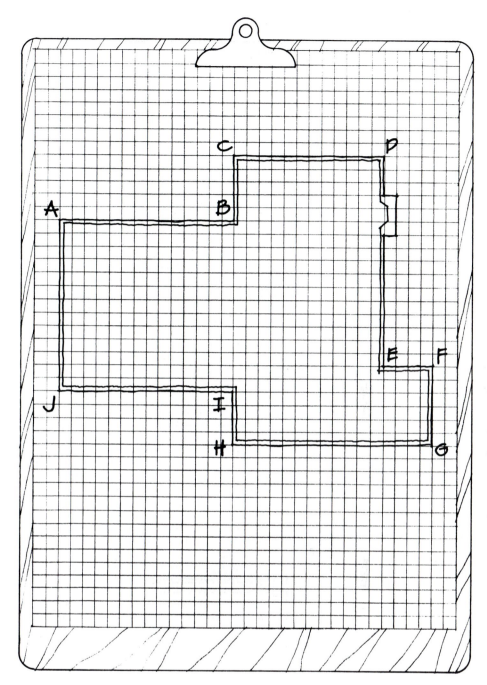

FIGURE 6-24
Estimation can be used to establish the general house plan configuration.

After the horizontal measurements of all the doors and windows have been made and tabulated, it is recommended that the heights of window sills and door thresholds above the ground be determined. As an example, W1, whose sill measures 3′ −6′ above the ground, is expressed as W1 : +3′ −6′. All the window and door sill heights are also shown in Figure 6–27.

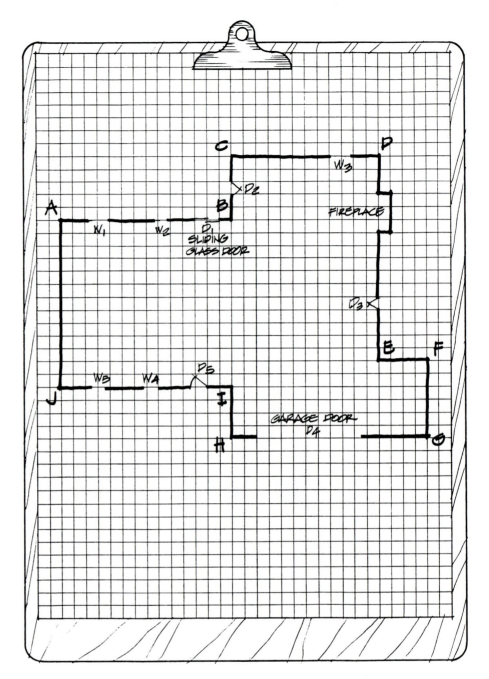

FIGURE 6–25
A method for noting doors and windows.

Locating Other Elements along the House Wall

Other important elements that are found on or along the house walls (including gas meters, electric meters, air conditioners, water spigots, downspouts, window wells (area ways), fireplace cleanouts, etc. can also be located.

The preceding elements can be sketched on the plan rather easily in relation to the doors and windows. When locating these elements on the sketch plan of the house, draw arrows pointing to their location on the house wall as shown for the Duncan residence (Figure 6–28). This will help to separate their individual location from other points or edges on the house wall. Each of these elements should re-

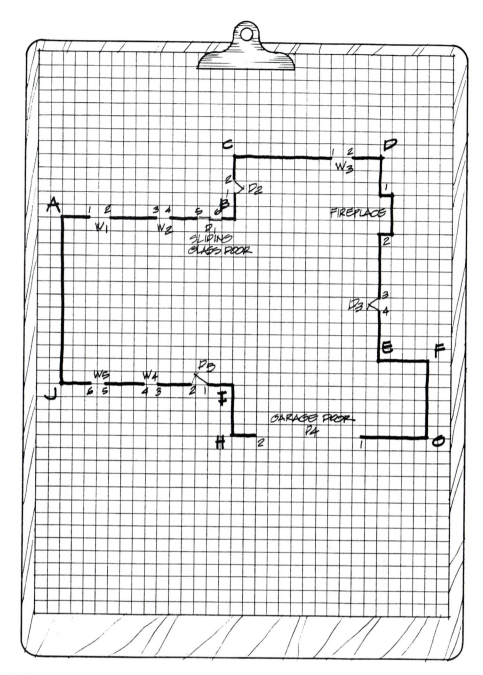

FIGURE 6–26
A method for noting the door and window jambs.

ceive an individual notation of their own. The following lists suggest abbreviations that can be used:

Gas meter	: GM	Electrical outlet	: EO
Electric meter	: EM	Cable TV hook-up	: TV
Water faucet	: WF	Dryer vent	: DV
Downspout	: DS	Flood light	: FL
Telephone hook-up	: TE		

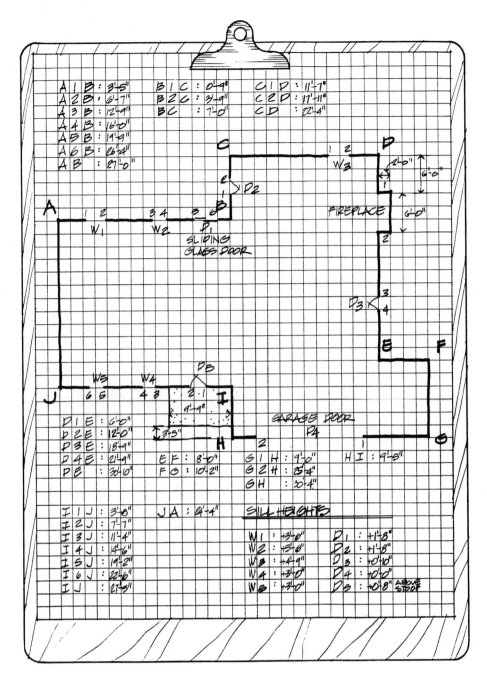

FIGURE 6-27
Door and window measurements for the Duncan residence.

When measurements of these elements are taken, they can be recorded in a similar fashion as the door and window jambs. For instance, the electric meter is located on the AB wall and is 11' −9" from A. It is also positioned 4' −0" above the ground. The heights above ground of other elements can also be recorded.

Locating Utility Lines

Above-ground Utilities. Some typical above-ground utilities are electricity, telephone, and cable television. There are five suggested measurements when recording above-ground utilities. First, if there are utility poles on or near the site, note where they are located with respect to the property corners.

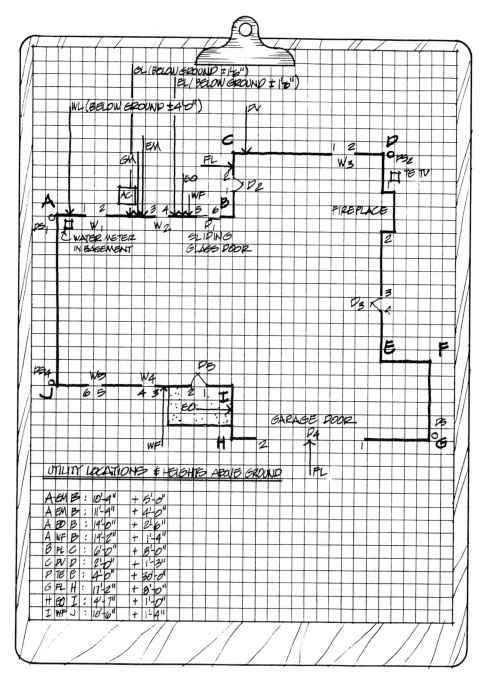

FIGURE 6-28
Utility measurements for the Duncan residence.

Second, estimate the height of the wires at the utility pole. This can be done by having an assistant stand at the base of the pole and then estimating the pole's height in relation to this person (Figure 6–29).

Third, using the baseline method of measuring, locate the point along the house where the wires attach to the house (Figure 6–30).

Fourth, estimate the height where the wires attach to the house. This can be done by utilizing the same method for estimating the height of the wires on the utility pole. Another method is to measure an individual feature or element on the house wall such as a brick or a piece of siding. Then you can count the number of bricks or pieces of siding there are between the ground and the point where the wires attach to the house.

Site Measuring and Base Map Preparation

FIGURE 6-29
Estimate height of wire connection on telephone pole.

FIGURE 6-30
Record where wires attach to the house.

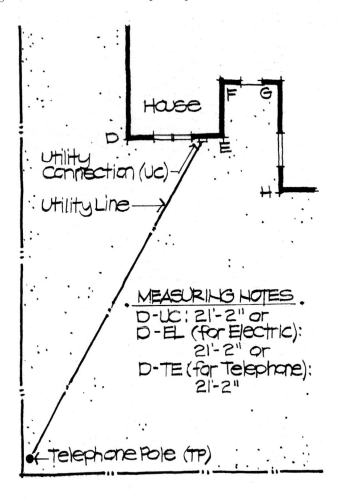

Finally, there will be a low point in the height of the wires above the ground somewhere between the utility pole and the house. Identify the height of this low point of the wires and the plan location where the low point occurs (Figure 6–31). This information is important when studying the location of proposed structures and trees.

Underground Utilities. Underground utilities are usually gas, water, and sewers. In most new neighborhoods, electricity and telephone utilities are also placed underground.

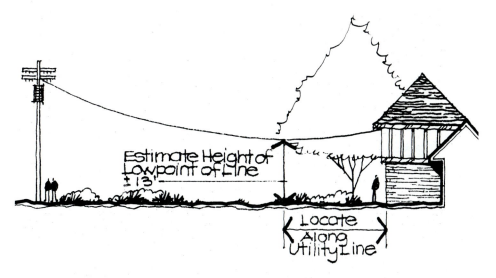

FIGURE 6-31
Locate the low point of the utility line.

When locating underground utility lines, there are four measurements that should be taken. First, similar to above-ground utilities, locate the source of underground utilities. In the case of electric or telephone lines, there may be transformers, junction boxes, or other metal containers where these utilities originate. In the case of the gas and water lines, there should be shut-off valves located at or just below the ground's surface somewhere on the site or in the street right-of-way. They usually have a cast-iron cover which identifies their location. These features can be located with the triangulation method of measuring.

Second, note the length, width, and height of the electric and telephone transformers and junction boxes.

Third, locate where the utilities enter the house. With a house that has a basement, a close inspection of the basement wall will usually reveal where this occurs. If a house doesn't have a basement, then looking carefully at the crawl space or base of wall along the first floor might indicate where the utilities enter the house.

Finally, note the depth at which the line is beneath the surface of the ground. This information is commonly obtained from the utility company. Make sure the underground location of utilities is known so they are not cut or ruptured during construction.

Locating Trees and Other Plant Materials

There are five measurements that are recommended for each tree location. First, it is important to locate the center of the tree. This can best be accomplished with the triangulation method of measuring. Because the end of the tape measure cannot be placed at the very center of the tree, the tape should be held on the side of the tree trunk on line with the tree's center (Figure 6–32).

Second, the diameter of the tree trunk can be measured by holding a tape measure near the tree (Figure 6–33).

Third, the tree canopy is measured from the ground up to the underside of the foliage. This height can be estimated by relating it to the known height of an assistant (Figure 6–34).

Fourth, the spread of the tree canopy can be estimated by noting the drip line on the ground on opposite sides of the tree, and then measuring it with the tape measure (Figure 6–35).

Finally, the total height of the tree can be estimated by relating it to the known height of an assistant as suggested earlier for the height of the telephone pole.

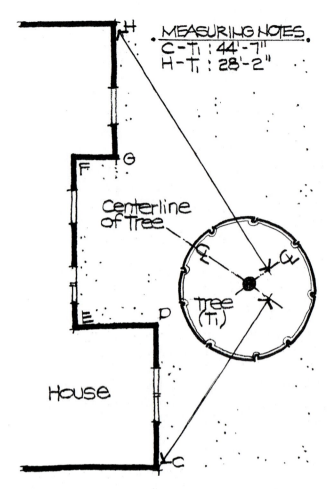

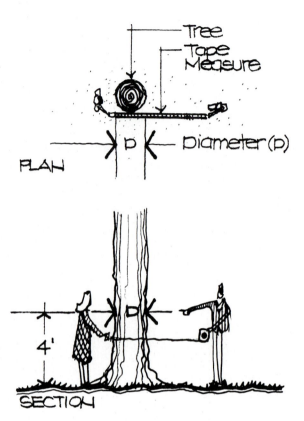

FIGURE 6-32
Example of locating a tree in relation to house corners.

FIGURE 6-33
Measuring the diameter of a tree.

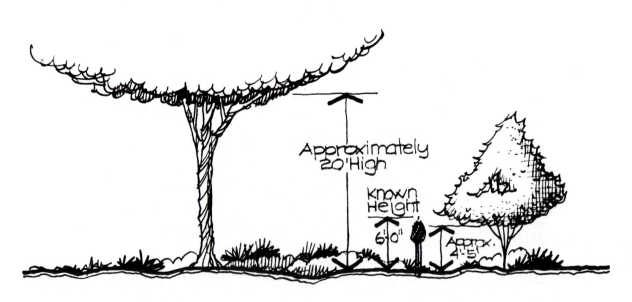

FIGURE 6-34
Use known height of a person as a reference in estimating canopy height.

FIGURE 6-35
Canopy spread is measured from drip line to drip line.

When dealing with the location of plant materials, it is suggested that each noteworthy tree, shrub, or mass of plants be identified with a special notation. For instance, the major trees that are to remain on the Duncan site are labeled T1 through T9 (Figure 6–36). Any shrub or shrub mass that is to remain can be noted as S1, S2, and so on. While trees are measured with the triangulation measuring system, plantings near the house walls can be easily located with the baseline or direct measuring system.

Photographing the Site

Photograph the site during the same visit as you take the site measurements. Color photographs in the form of prints or slides are beneficial for three reasons. First, they serve as reminders of the house and site and hopefully diminish the need to return to the site for unnecessary visits. Second, they can serve as bases for drawing sketches of proposed ideas. If slides are taken, they can be projected onto a wall and be used as a base to sketch ideas. And third, photographs can document existing conditions so as to serve as "before" pictures prior to any construction. While taking pictures on the site, it is helpful to note the location on a plan where the photographs were taken so both "during" and "after" construction photographs can be taken from the same locations. These "before and after" photographic comparisons are extremely beneficial.

PROCEDURES FOR DRAWING THE BASE SHEET AND BASE MAP

Once the site measurements have been taken and recorded, the base sheet and base map can be prepared. Since both have some elements in common, it is useful for the designer to prepare both in the same procedure. This can be done quite easily by copying techniques so that the effort of drawing one plan is applied to the other.

To draw the base sheet and base map, the designer should first draw all the existing elements of the site that are to remain unchanged and be incorporated into the design (base sheet). This of course requires a little forethought as to what the design program will include. If the designer doesn't know what existing site elements are to stay or be removed, then few or no elements should be drawn. The drawing of these elements should be done on the proper type and size of paper as discussed later in this section.

After this is completed, the drawing should be taken to a printing or copying company where it can be reproduced onto a sheet of vellum, mylar, or opaque paper. Once obtained, this should be set aside and used as the original for the base sheet. The designer's original drawing also can be taken to a copy center to have a reproducible copy made on a sheet of vellum or mylar (plastic film).

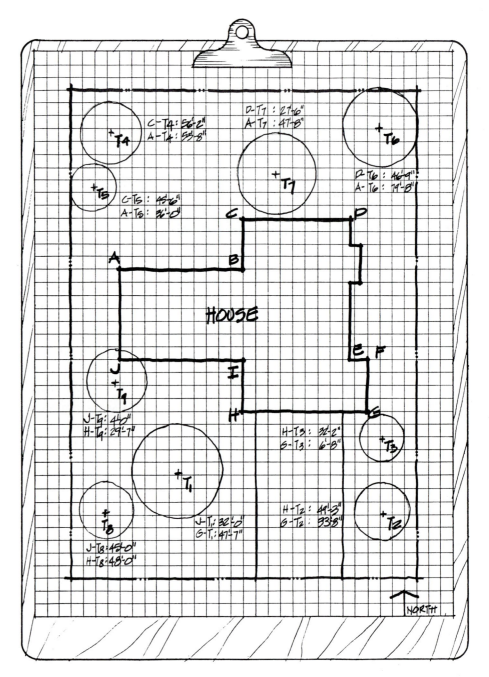

FIGURE 6–36
Tree location measurements for the Duncan residence.

The second step is to complete the base map. This is done by using the first sheet and drawing all other existing physical elements of the site. When this is complete, it is the original for the base map. This two-step process will produce two separate transparencies, each with different information; one for the base sheet and one for the base map. Once developed, the base sheet and base map will serve as sources for: (1) making a site inventory and analysis and (2) creating, studying, and developing design ideas. After the base map and base sheet have served their purpose, they should be put away in a safe, dry, flat file.

The base sheet for the Duncan residence is shown in Figure 6–37. The base map for this same residence is seen in Figure 6–38.

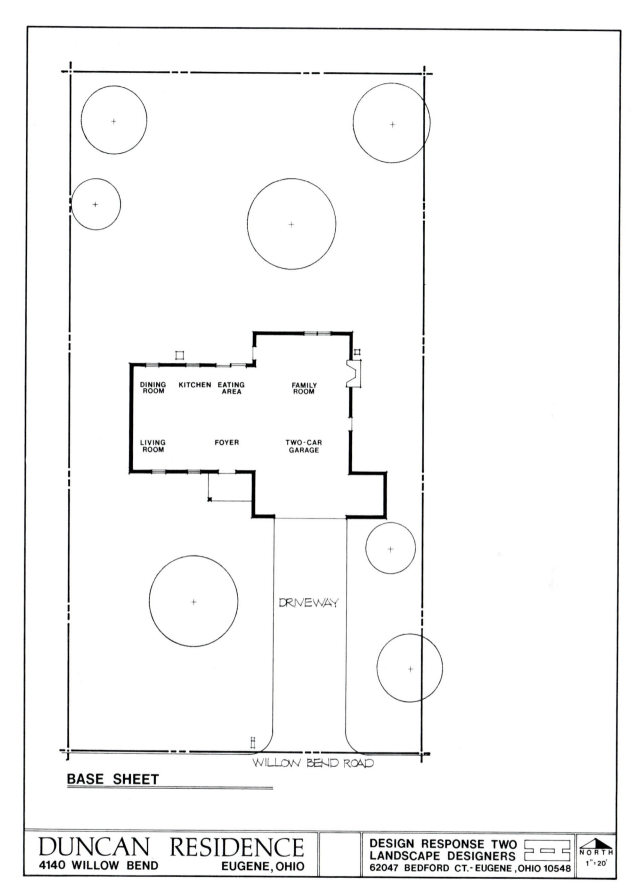

BASE SHEET

DINING ROOM KITCHEN EATING AREA FAMILY ROOM

LIVING ROOM FOYER TWO-CAR GARAGE

DRIVEWAY

WILLOW BEND ROAD

DUNCAN RESIDENCE
4140 WILLOW BEND   EUGENE, OHIO

**DESIGN RESPONSE TWO
LANDSCAPE DESIGNERS**
62047 BEDFORD CT.- EUGENE ,OHIO 10548

NORTH
1" = 20'

FIGURE 6-37
Base sheet for the Duncan residence.

Site Measuring and Base Map Preparation

161

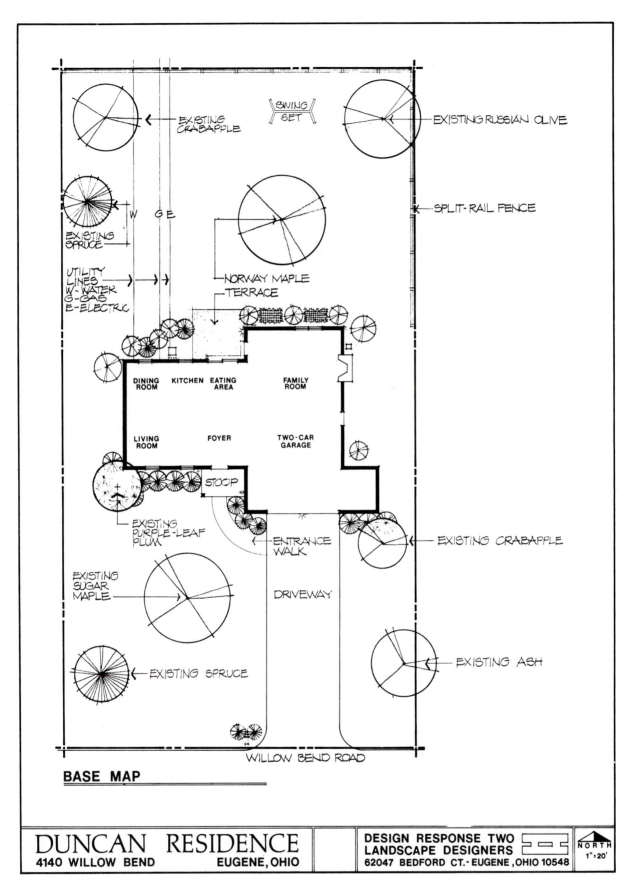

Within the figure:

EXISTING CRABAPPLE

SWING SET

EXISTING RUSSIAN OLIVE

EXISTING SPRUCE

W   G E

SPLIT-RAIL FENCE

UTILITY
LINES
W-WATER
G-GAS
E-ELECTRIC

NORWAY MAPLE
TERRACE

DINING ROOM   KITCHEN   EATING AREA   FAMILY ROOM

LIVING ROOM   FOYER   TWO-CAR GARAGE

STOOP

EXISTING PURPLE-LEAF PLUM

ENTRANCE WALK

EXISTING CRABAPPLE

EXISTING SUGAR MAPLE

DRIVEWAY

EXISTING SPRUCE

EXISTING ASH

WILLOW BEND ROAD

BASE MAP

DUNCAN   RESIDENCE
4140 WILLOW BEND   EUGENE, OHIO

**DESIGN RESPONSE TWO
LANDSCAPE DESIGNERS**
62047 BEDFORD CT.- EUGENE, OHIO 10548

NORTH
1"=20'

FIGURE 6–38
Base map for the Duncan residence.

There are several decisions that have to be made while preparing these drawings. Selection of paper type and drawing medium, drawing scale, sheet size, and sheet layout are important factors to consider in drawing the base sheet and base map.

Paper Type and Drawing Medium

The two most widely used paper types are vellum and mylar. Vellum is a semitransparent paper used primarily when pencil is the chosen medium for drawing. Typical pencil grades are HB, H, and 2H. It is not recommended to draw with ink on vellum because it is difficult to erase. Vellum is generally cheaper than mylar and slightly lighter in weight. By comparison, mylar is a thin transparent plastic film and is used when either pencil or ink is the chosen medium for drawing. When using pencil on mylar, be careful because pencil tends to smear very easily on the plastic film. Pencil smears less on vellum than on mylar because the lead of the pencil is embedded more in the texture (called *tooth*) of the vellum. Advantages of mylar are that ink can be erased rather easily from it, and it is a little more durable than vellum because it is not as susceptible to tearing or wrinkling. However, the sturdiness of both vellum and mylar enables numerous copies or prints to be made from them. One caution: refrain from using tracing paper to draw the base sheet or base map. Tracing paper is much too light and flimsy and, as a result, tears and rips easily.

Drawing Scale

There are two scales that are suggested for residential design. If the designer typically works with engineering scales, then $1'' = 10.0'$ is the recommended scale. This scale is also advantageous when measurements are frequently obtained from surveyors because they almost always work in an engineer's scale. A $75' \times 150'$ lot drawn at this scale would produce a plan measuring $7\text{-}1/2'' \times 15''$. On the other hand, if the designer normally deals with architectural scales, then $1/8'' = 1' -0''$ is the recommended scale. The $1/8'' = 1' -0''$ scale is also better to use if distances must be scaled to less than one foot. And the $1/8'' = 1' -0''$ is apt to be more easily understood by the homeowners because most people have a "ruler" on which they can read $1/8''$. The same $75' \times 150'$ lot drawn at this scale would produce a plan measuring $9\text{-}3/8'' \times 18\text{-}3/4''$. There will be times when areas of the design may need to be enlarged to study in more detail. When this situation occurs, a scale of $1/4'' = 1' -0''$ is suggested.

Sheet Size

When selecting a sheet size, the designer should keep in mind that vellum, mylar, and print paper are available in standard sizes. A typical sheet size for each of these types of paper is $24'' \times 36''$. Therefore, it is suggested that the sheet size for the base sheet and base map be $24'' \times 36''$ or a module of it. Typical sheet sizes based on this situation system are:

$24'' \times 36''$ (one full sheet)
$12'' \times 36''$ (one half sheet)
$18'' \times 24''$ (one half sheet)
$12'' \times 18''$ (one quarter sheet)

Using one of the preceding sheet sizes will enable the designer to save money when making numerous prints. One sheet of $24'' \times 36''$ print paper can be cut in half and used to make two prints of an $18'' \times 24''$ drawing. But, if the drawing measures $19'' \times 25''$, two full sheets of $24'' \times 36''$ print paper must be used.

FIGURE 6-39
Sample of a graphic scale.

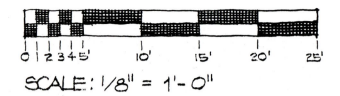

SCALE: 1/8" = 1'-0"

Sheet Layout

Every base sheet and base map, regardless of the scale or sheet size, should have a well-organized layout. To accomplish this, the designer should consider the placement of: (1) title block or sheet title information, (2) plan, (3) north arrow, (4) scale, (5) notes and/or legends, and (6) sheet border. The following paragraphs provide guidelines for organizing these items on a sheet.

Title Information. Each drawing that is produced for design and/or construction should have a title block with the following information:

A. Client/designer information
   1. Clients' names
   2. Clients' address
   3. Designer's or firm's name
   4. Designer's or firm's address
B. Drawing information. The drawing information can be located either inside or outside the title block because it relates more to the drawing itself than to the clients or designer.
   1. Sheet title
   2. Written scale and graphic scale. A graphic scale as shown in Figure 6–39 is recommended. If the drawing is ever reduced, then the graphic scale will enable the observer to understand the size and dimensions of the project. The written scale, when reduced, tends to confuse the observer.
   3. North arrow
   4. Date

The location and lettering size of this information are two important considerations when drawing the base sheet and base map. There are several typical places to position the title block on a sheet (Figure 6–40). The most common placement is the bottom right corner of the sheet. This location can be read easily by a person turning the pages of a set of several drawings. Other good locations for the title block are along the bottom or right sides of the sheet. The title block should never be placed at the left side of the sheet because this becomes difficult to read when several sheets or more are stapled together.

There should be a hierarchy of lettering sizes used in the title block. The clients' names are the most important element and should be the largest and boldest letters of all. Letters about 1/2 inch high are typical for this. The designer's name is less important and should be in smaller print, approximately 1/4 inch high. The addresses and the drawing information, although important, should be identified with the smallest lettering (although not smaller than 1/8 inch high).

Plan. The plan should be placed on the sheet so it can be easily viewed. Generally, the plan is best placed off center to allow for some "white space" or leftover area on one or more sides of the plan. This white space can be used as a location for notes, legends, or simply a blank background area (Figure 6–41).

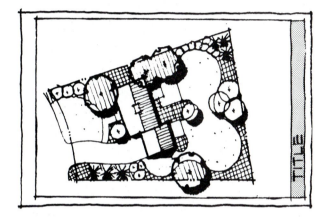

FIGURE 6-40
Possible title block locations on sheet.

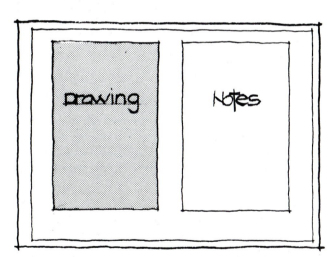

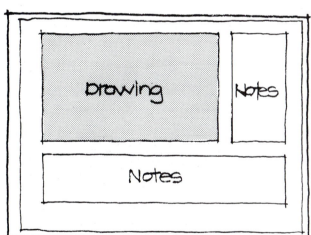

FIGURE 6-41
White space is useful for placement of notes and legends.

North Arrow and Scale. These two items should be placed inside the title block near the bottom right of the plan. It is helpful to locate the two items near each other so they can be read together.

In terms of orientation, it is standard procedure to place the plan and north arrow in such a way that north points toward the top, left side of the sheet, or somewhere

Site Measuring and Base Map Preparation

165

FIGURE 6-42
North should generally point toward the top of
the sheet.

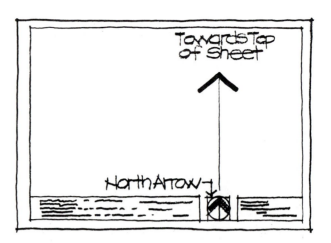

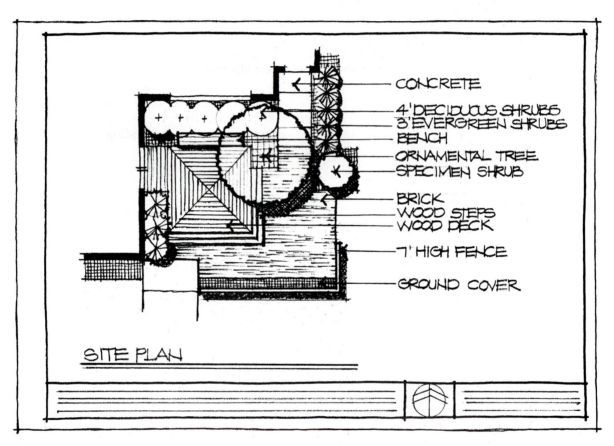

SITE PLAN

FIGURE 6-43
Notes should be organized in neat columns.

in between (Figure 6–42). An exception to this rule of thumb is when the clients are
used to viewing their property from a certain direction such as the street. In this case it
may cause the north arrow to point toward the bottom and/or right side of the sheet.

Notes and Legends.   Notes and legends are best placed in the white space
next to the plan. In the case of notes, they should be placed as close as possible to
the point or area they refer to on the plan. Lines (called leader lines) which extend
from the note to a specific point on the plan should be kept as short as possible.
Both notes and legends should be neatly lettered (1/8 inch high is ideal) and well-
organized (Figure 6–43).

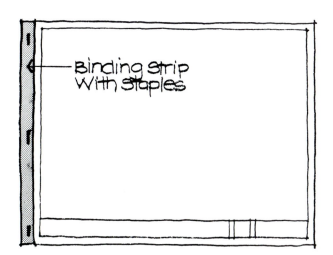

Borders. Borders, although not absolutely essential, often give an appealing touch to a sheet. Borders act like picture frames and "hold" the drawing and notes on the sheet. Borders are generally placed between 1/2 inch and 1 inch from the edge of the sheet. More space is required on the left side of a sheet if the drawing is going to be combined and stapled with others in a package. When there is more than one sheet, it is common practice to put a binding strip on the left side of a package of drawings (Figure 6–44).

SUMMARY

Measuring the site and preparing the base map and base sheet are critical steps in establishing the base information of the site. Both steps should be undertaken with the utmost care in organization and accuracy because later steps of the design process use these drawings as their starting point. We have spent much time in this chapter providing suggestions for taking site measurements and organizing field notes so this step can proceed in an orderly fashion with a minimum of mistakes. While many ideas presented here may seem unnecessary when doing a single project, you should remember that in most successful practices, several projects will be going on at the same time. Thus, it is easy to forget important facts or get several jobs confused with each other if information is not recorded accurately and legibly. A successful design practice records and organizes all base information in a professional manner so that the information can be used and referred to throughout the remainder of the design process.

7

Site and Design Program

INTRODUCTION

The site analysis and preparation of the design program are two other tasks undertaken in the research and preparation phase of the design process. The purpose of the site analysis, also referred to as site study, is to identify all the vital site conditions and determine how they might influence the eventual design solution. During the site analysis, the designer should become as familiar as possible with the site so a design solution can later be developed to suit the particular conditions of the site. The design program, which is usually prepared after the site study is completed, is the culmination of the research and preparation phase. The design program is an outline of all the elements and requirements that must be included in the design and provides the basis for the beginning of the design phase.

Before proceeding, it is necessary to have a clear understanding of the differences between the two distinct steps of the site study: (1) inventory and (2) analysis. Site inventory is the gathering of facts and information about a site. It identifies and records the location, size, material, and condition of existing site elements such as walkways, terraces, fences, utilities, and plant materials. The inventory also records other aspects of the site such as soil type, degree of slope, location of utilities, prevailing wind directions, sun and shade patterns, specific views of importance, and so forth. In other words, the site inventory is data collection.

Site analysis, on the other hand, is an evaluation of the information obtained in the site inventory. Site analysis makes judgments about this information and determines how the design solution should respond to these conditions. For instance, how should the proposed design relate to an existing patio space? How might the utility locations affect the layout of the design? How could the design respond to the sun and shade patterns? What plant materials should be retained and incorporated into the proposed design?

Generally speaking, the site inventory is relatively easy to do. The designer needs to: (1) look at the site with an open and inquisitive mind, (2) be well organized (perhaps following an outline of items that need to be identified), and (3) be accurate in recording the required information. The gathered information should be organized in a manner that is easily read and understood so it will be a helpful reference in later design phases. Much of the information can be shown on a copy of the base map (Figure 7–1). Notes and graphic symbols are used to identify and highlight necessary information. Typically, each landscape designer or firm has a particular vocabulary of symbols that has been developed through experience.

There is a variety of information to be identified and catalogued during the site inventory. Some information (such as prevailing wind direction, sun angles, soil type, and zoning regulations) is apt to be common knowledge that results from the experience of working in a given geographic area. Other information (such as surface drainage patterns, off-site views, existing vegetation, and areas of sun or shade) is unique to each new project.

Much information can be gathered during the site inventory by walking around the site and taking careful notes. This is usually done by making notes on a copy of the base map. As suggested earlier, photographs can be taken from different vantage points throughout the site. Photographs are extremely helpful tools because they assist in: (1) recording existing information (downspout locations, types and conditions of plant materials, views, and style and materials of the house), (2) providing visual reminders of what the house and site looks like as design ideas are being generated, and (3) documenting specific details of the house and site that may be useful during later phases of design (pavement patterns, fence character, architectural detail, and patterns of windows, doors, etc.). In addition, it is recommended that special attention be focused on photographing those portions and features of the house that are of major interest to the client. There should be a photograph of each side of the house, so as not to forget the changes in materials and pattern from one side to the next. It is obvious from seeing many houses that the character on one side does not always match the character on the other sides.

Close-up photographs should be taken of all those portions of the house that show detailed trim, forms, and patterns. In essence, take enough photographs that you will be able to look back at the house later in the design program and not have any questions concerning any visible portion of the house.

Information on zoning regulations and climatic data can be obtained from other sources like governmental agencies, weather bureaus, or library. Whatever the source, the designer should only collect information that is directly applicable to the project. It is of course a waste of time and money to accumulate data just for the sake of doing so. To avoid this, the designer should repeatedly ask: "Do I need this? How will I use this information? Is it important? Will this information influence how I design?" If the answer is yes, then the information should be recorded.

In addition to information about existing site conditions gathered by the designer from an on-site visit, there may be supplemental site information provided by the clients. Often, the clients have valuable site information that they have observed during the period of time they have lived in the house that may not be readily seen by the designer. For instance, the clients may have noticed where snow drifts tend to accumulate, where surface drainage flows to or accumulates after a heavy rain, where the ground dries out quickly, where the neighbor's children cut through the yard, where difficult areas to mow are, and so on. This type of site information supplied by the clients can be as valuable as that collected by the designer. Therefore, it is important for the designer to seek the clients' input about existing site conditions.

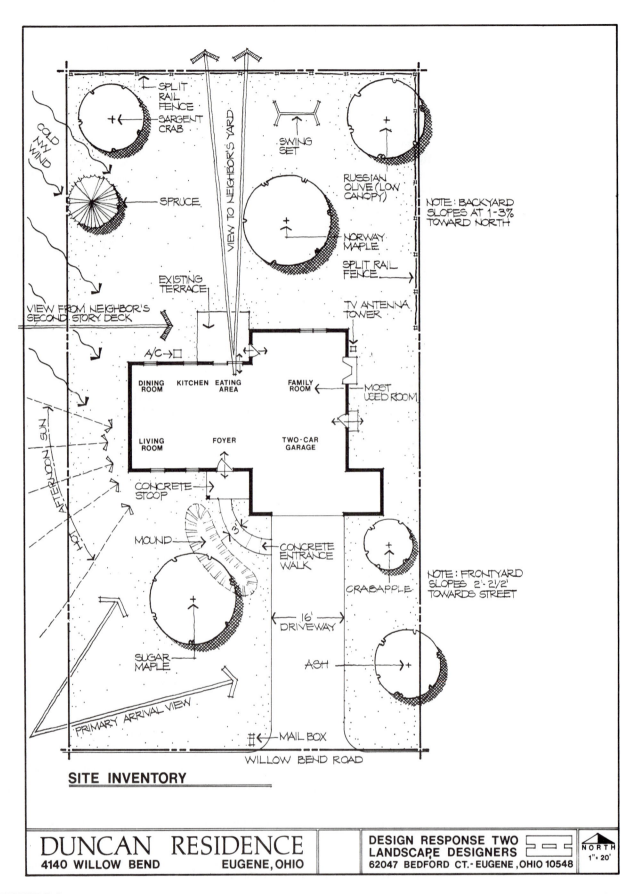

SPLIT RAIL FENCE

SARGENT CRAB

COLD NW WIND

SPRUCE

VIEW TO NEIGHBOR'S YARD

SWING SET

RUSSIAN OLIVE (LOW CANOPY)

NORWAY MAPLE

NOTE: BACKYARD SLOPES AT 1-3% TOWARD NORTH

SPLIT RAIL FENCE

EXISTING TERRACE

VIEW FROM NEIGHBOR'S SECOND STORY DECK

TV ANTENNA TOWER

A/C

DINING ROOM   KITCHEN   EATING AREA

FAMILY ROOM

MOST USED ROOM

AFTERNOON SUN

LIVING ROOM   FOYER   TWO-CAR GARAGE

CONCRETE STOOP

MOUND

CONCRETE ENTRANCE WALK

CRABAPPLE

NOTE: FRONTYARD SLOPES 2'-2½' TOWARDS STREET

16' DRIVEWAY

SUGAR MAPLE

ASH

PRIMARY ARRIVAL VIEW

MAIL BOX

WILLOW BEND ROAD

SITE INVENTORY

DUNCAN RESIDENCE
4140 WILLOW BEND   EUGENE, OHIO

DESIGN RESPONSE TWO
LANDSCAPE DESIGNERS
62047 BEDFORD CT. - EUGENE, OHIO 10548

NORTH 1" = 20'

FIGURE 7-1
Site inventory of the Duncan residence.

The following outline is a list of site conditions that may be identified during the site inventory. Some of the conditions listed may have been identified while measuring the site and do not have to be recorded again during site inventory. Also, not all the listed items need to be addressed for every project. What is needed for one project may be unnecessary for the next. So, use the outline as a helpful guide to be adapted to your own special means of practice.

A. Site location
   1. Identify surrounding land uses and their conditions.
      a. Are they residential, commercial, recreational, educational, and so forth?
      b. How well are the adjoining properties maintained?
   2. Identify the neighborhood's character.
      a. What is the style, age, and condition of the residential architecture?
      b. What is the size, type, and maturity of the vegetation?
      c. What is the character of the neighborhood?
         • Is it well established, open, wooded, ill kept, friendly, estate-like, and so on?
   3. Identify the nature of vehicular circulation in the neighborhood.
      a. What type of street is the site located on?
         • Is it a through street, one-way, two-way, cul-de-sac, and so on?
      b. What is the volume of traffic on the street?
         • Does the intensity vary during the day? If so, when?
      c. How much noise and headlight glare into the windows is produced by the traffic on the street?
      d. What is the primary direction for arriving at the site?
         • Is there more than one approach?
         • Which approach is most frequently used?
         • Where is the most common "first view" of the site located?
   4. Identify legal restrictions for new construction in the neighborhood.
      a. What additional building types and structures are allowed, especially detached buildings like garages, tool sheds, gazebos, pergolas, and so on?
      b. What are the restrictions for heights and floor areas of new structures?
      c. What are the setback requirements for structures?
      d. What building permits are required for construction?
B. Topography
   1. Identify degree of slope steepness at different areas throughout the site (slope inventory).
   2. Identify potential areas of erosion or poor drainage.
   3. Identify grade change between inside (finished floor elevation) and outside grade around the foundation of the house, especially at the doorways.
   4. Determine the ease of walking on various areas of the site (this will also identify relative steepness).
   5. Identify the elevation changes between the top and bottom of existing steps, walls, fences, and so forth.
C. Drainage
   1. Identify direction(s) of surface water drainage.
      a. Does water drain away from the house on all sides?
      b. Where does the water flow from the downspouts?

2. Determine wet spots or areas of standing water.

    a. Where are they located and for what lengths of time?

3. Identify drainage onto and away from the site.

    a. Does any off-site surface water drain onto the site? How much, when, and where?

    b. Where does the water flow to when it leaves the site?

D. Soil

  1. Identify soil characteristics (acid, alkaline, sandy, clay, gravel, fertile, and so on).

  2. Identify depth of topsoil.

  3. Identify depth of soil to bedrock.

E. Vegetation

  1. Locate and identify existing plant materials.

  2. Where appropriate, identify:

    a. plant species.

    b. size [caliper (diameter of a tree trunk 4 feet above the ground), spread, total height, and height to bottom of canopy].

    c. form.

    d. color (flower and foliage).

    e. texture.

    f. distinguishing features and characteristics.

  3. Determine the overall condition, importance, potential use, and clients' opinion of existing plant materials.

F. Microclimate

  1. Identify location of sun at sunrise and sunset at different times of the year (January, March, June, and September, for example).

  2. Identify the vertical angle of the sun above the horizon at different times of the day and seasons of the year.

  3. Determine areas of the site that are mostly sunny or mostly shady during different times of the day and seasons of the year.

  4. Determine areas exposed to and protected from the intense summer afternoon sun.

  5. Identify areas exposed to warming winter sun.

  6. Identify prevailing wind direction throughout the year.

  7. Determine site areas exposed to or protected from cooling summer breezes.

  8. Determine site areas exposed to or protected from cold winter winds.

  9. Identify depth of frost in winter months.

G. Existing house

  1. Identify house type and architectural style.

  2. Identify color and texture of facade materials.

  3. Identify location of windows and doors.

    a. For doors, identify direction of opening and frequency of use.

    b. For both doors and windows, identify elevation of bottoms (sills) and tops (heads).

  4. Identify interior room type and location.

    a. Identify which rooms are used most often.

  5. Locate basement windows and their depth below ground.

6. Locate outside elements such as downspouts, water spigots, electrical outlets, lights attached to house, electric meter, gas meter, clothes' dryer vent, air conditioners, etc.

7. Locate overhangs and note their distance beyond the face of the house and their heights above the ground.

H. Other existing structures

1. Locate and identify condition and materials of existing walks, terraces, steps, walls, fences, swimming pools, and so on.

I. Utilities

1. Locate utility lines (water, gas, electric, telephone, cable, storm sewer, septic tank, leach field, etc.).

a. Are there any easements associated with the utility lines?

b. Are there any telephone and electrical junction boxes?

c. Are there any utility shut-off valves?

2. Identify location and height of air conditioner or heat pump.

a. What direction is the intake and exhaust of the air flow?

3. Identify location of pool equipment and associated utility connections.

4. If existing, locate irrigation system.

J. Views

1. Take note of what is seen from all sides of the site looking off-site.

a. Do the views vary during different seasons?

2. Observe views from inside the house looking to the outside.

3. Experience views from off the site looking onto the site (views from the street as well as from different sides of the site).

a. Where are the best and worst views of the site?

K. Spaces and senses

1. Determine the location and extent of outdoor rooms. Identify materials of the floors, walls, and ceilings of the rooms.

2. Identify the feeling and character of these rooms (open, enclosed, light, airy, dark, gloomy, cheerful, restful, and so on).

3. Determine pleasant or disturbing sounds (singing birds, traffic noise, children playing, rustling leaves, and so on).

4. Identify fragrances and odors.

L. Existing site functions and problems

1. Identify how and when different areas of the site are currently used.

2. Determine location for such activities as daily leaving and arriving home, outside recreation, gardening, work areas, and so on.

3. Determine site maintenance problems (unkept lawn, worn lawn edges along walks, worn lawn areas due to intense use, lack of weeding, broken pavement, and so on).

4. Identify location of snow drifts in the winter.

Again, Figure 7–1 shows the site inventory for the Duncan residence. As introduced in Chapter 5, the front yard is rather open with existing trees in good condition located on both sides of the driveway. As seen in Figure 7–2, a 3-foot-wide concrete walk leads from the asphalt driveway to the front stoop with a low earth mound to its west.

The side yards of the Duncan residence are narrow and of little practical use, though the east side of the house is an eyesore due to the garbage cans and debris stored here (Figure 7–3).

FIGURE 7–2
View of the existing concrete entry walk and earth mound in front of the Duncan residence.

FIGURE 7–3
View of garbage cans and debris along the east side of the Duncan residence.

The back yard is open and free of obstacles with the exception of a Norway maple and the swing set located on the northern part of the site. A split-rail fence and plantings on the northern and eastern property lines of the back yard give it a partially enclosed feeling. Nevertheless, there are some notable off-site views. When

FIGURE 7–4
View of the neighbor's house to the west as seen from the Duncans' back yard.

FIGURE 7–5
View of the neighbor's house to the north as seen from the Duncans' back yard.

standing in the Duncan's back yard, the neighbors' houses to the west (Figure 7–4) and north (Figure 7–5) seem relatively close and are easily seen while the view to the east (Figure 7–6) is more pleasant through several neighbors' back yards. The views to the northwest (Figure 7–7) and northeast (Figure 7–8) are also attractive.

SITE ANALYSIS

As stated earlier, the site analysis is the second and more difficult phase of the site study. Whereas the site inventory merely seeks to collect and organize information about the site, the site analysis evaluates the value and importance of this information. The purpose of the site analysis is to determine the problems and potentials

FIGURE 7–6
View of the neighbors' back yards to the east as seen from the Duncans' back yard.

FIGURE 7–7
View to the northwest from the northwest corner of the Duncans' back yard.

created by the existing site conditions, so that the eventual design solution can be tailored to meet the specific conditions of the site.

During the site analysis, the designer should answer a number of questions that can aid in evaluating the collected inventory information. These include the following:

- Is this information important?
- If it is important, does it create a problem or offer a potential?
- If it creates a problem, how might it be solved?
- If it offers a potential, how might it be taken advantage of?

The designer should be aware of the differences in wording in comparison to the site inventory. Notes on the site inventory are simply statements of fact while the notes on the site analysis are words of evaluation and action. Key words found on the site analysis include should, need to, limit, allow for, make, save, take advantage of, screen, and enlarge. Here are some examples:

FIGURE 7–8
View to the northeast from the northeast corner of the Duncans' back yard.

Site Inventory	*Site Analysis*
• 3-foot-wide concrete walk	• too narrow; need to widen to 5 feet and change to a warmer material
• open view to wooded area at back of site	• maintain view by enframing it on either side
• existing terrace is 100 square feet	• should be enlarged to at least 200 square feet
• large sycamore tree is in good condition	• should be preserved; remote sitting area might be placed beneath it
• back of house and site are exposed to the hot afternoon summer sun	• back of house should be shaded by trees or other means; any outside uses in this area must also be protected from sun

Figure 7–9 shows the site analysis for the Duncan residence. Recall that a number of factors and conditions were recorded about the Duncan residence on the site inventory (Figure 7–1). Now, the site analysis evaluates this information and makes recommendations about a number of actions that should be taken into account as the design solution is developed. For example, it is suggested that the following be considered for the front yard:

1. The existing trees should be kept and integrated into the design.
2. A more welcoming front entry should be established by widening the existing walk between the driveway and the front door. The adjacent earth mound should be removed or altered as necessary.
3. The view into the front entry space (outdoor foyer) should be emphasized and coordinated with views from the hallway and living room.

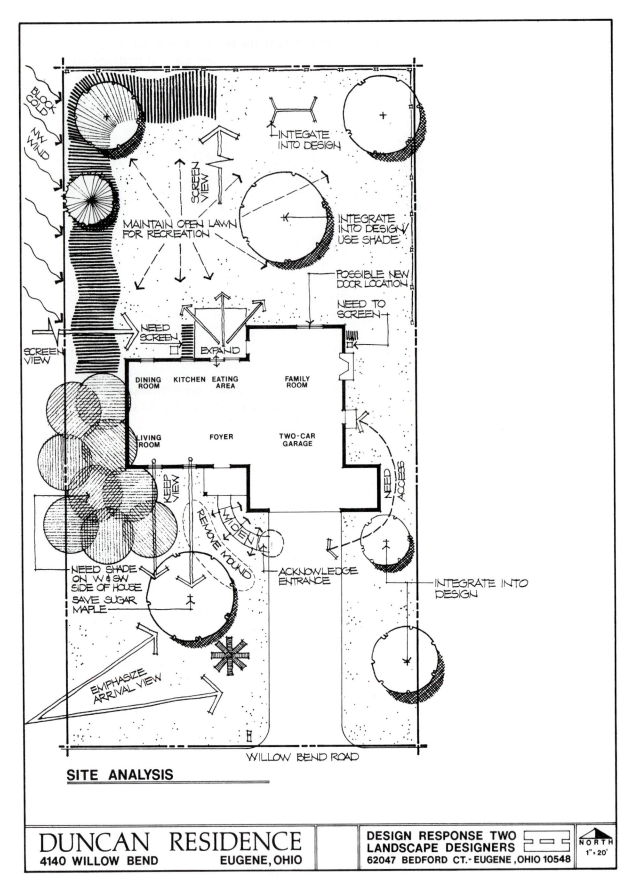

FIGURE 7–9
Site analysis of the Duncan residence.

4. Shade is needed on the southwestern and western sides of the house to provide protection from the hot summer afternoon sun while allowing the winter afternoon sun to warm these sides of the house.

5. Paved access is needed from the driveway to the east side garage door.

There are also a number of considerations for the back yard of the site. These include:

1. Screens or barriers need to be provided to establish privacy from the neighbors to the west and to block the views to the neighbors' entertaining space to the north. These same screens could serve as a wind break for the cold northwest winds during the winter.

2. An outside living/entertaining space needs to be developed with better access to the inside. Consideration should be given to the possibility of incorporating sliding glass doors in the north wall of the family room if the outdoor entertaining space is placed nearby.

3. The lawn area should be kept as open as possible for recreation. The existing Norway maple may provide shade on a nearby patio.

4. The swing set should be integrated into the back yard so as not to be an obvious eyesore.

5. The TV antenna tower should be screened to reduce its overwhelming scale.

These observations and recommendations will be taken into account when the design program is written and during the subsequent steps of the design phase. It is a good idea to continually refer to the site analysis to make sure the design is responding to its conclusion and recommendations.

There may be times when the client is interested in seeing and reviewing the site analysis. When this situation arises, it is important to provide a legible drawing for presentation and discussion purposes. Figure 7–9 is an example of that type of drawing. More often, the site analysis is not presented to the client, but is a "study of the site" for the designer's personal use for design. When this is the case, the graphic quality may be as loose and as sketchy as the designer chooses.

DESIGN PROGRAM

The final step in the research and preparation phase of the design process is the development of a design program. A program may be defined as an organizational outline of activities for an event or procedure. More specifically, a design program is a written list or outline of all the elements, spaces, and requirements that should be incorporated into the design solution. Like the program guide for a theatrical play or a sporting event, the design program lists the "cast" of elements that will "play" a role in the design solution for a particular site and clients.

A design program brings together the expressed needs and wishes of the clients with the conclusions of the site analysis. The clients' needs and the information about the existing site conditions have been gathered and recorded separately until this point in the process. Now the design program combines the findings from these earlier steps to establish an overall summary about the requirements for the design.

A design program serves three functions. First, it provides the designer with a foundation of elements that need to be incorporated into the design solution. In a way, the design program's list of required elements tells the designer: "This is what the design must include and do."

The second function of the design program is to serve as a checklist for the designer. The designer may periodically refer to the design program throughout the design process to make sure that all the elements of the program are being met. It is easy to forget about all the requirements and details without a list to refresh the designer's memory.

Finally, the design program can function as a communication tool between the designer and clients. After having prepared the design program, the designer should review it with the clients to make sure that it meets their approval. It can permit the designer to see whether or not the clients' expressed desires and needs were in fact understood correctly. It also allows the designer to suggest to the clients that other elements or requirements could be incorporated into the design solution based on the findings of the site analysis.

Like all other steps and phases of the design process, the design program should not be considered to be final by either the designer or the clients. While it should be as complete as possible when it is prepared, it should not be thought of as being absolute or beyond the possibility of change. As the development of the design solution proceeds with more and more definitive thinking, original ideas and intents may change. There is nothing wrong with this. In fact, it is quite healthy because it is evidence that the designer and clients are open-minded about tailoring a design solution to the unique conditions of the situation; they are not forcing preconceived ideas onto a site.

The following design program has been prepared for the Duncan residence. It is presented as a sample program and is by no means the only way a design program can be written or organized. This particular design program resulted from meeting and talking with the Duncan family (Chapter 5) and from the conclusions of the site analysis of the Duncan residence presented in the previous section of this chapter.

Design Program for the Duncan Residence
Prepared by James E. Kent
Landscape Designer
Design Response Two

    A. Warm and welcoming entry walk
        1. Size: minimum of 4½-5 feet wide.
        2. Material: something that will complement the house materials.
    B. Outside entrance foyer and sitting space
        1. Size: large enough for two chairs and a small table.
        2. Material: same as for entry walk, but in a different pattern to help imply a special place.
    C. Paved access from driveway to east side door of garage
        1. Size: minimum of 3 feet wide.
        2. Material: undecided.
    D. Outside entertaining space (terrace)
        1. Size: 250-300 square feet; must accommodate 8-10 people for social gatherings and informal dining.
        2. Material: possibly a raised wood deck due to the elevation change from the breakfast area to ground level.
    E. Recreational lawn area
        1. Size: as large as possible.
        2. Material: grass.
    F. Play area for swing set and additional equipment
        1. Size: 125-150 square feet.
        2. Material: sand or bark mulch.

G. Storage for one cord of wood
  1. Size: 4' × 8'.
  2. Materials: gravel or concrete.
H. Visual screen from neighbors on the west
  1. Size: unknown at this time.
  2. Materials: undecided; could be plant materials, a structure, or a combination of both.
I. Visual screen of bad view to the north of site
  1. Size: unknown at this time.
  2. Material: probably plant materials, due to available space.
J. Screen air conditioner on north side of the house
  1. Size: about 2-3 feet high.
  2. Materials: could be evergreen plant materials for year-round color or small fence structure.
K. Existing trees
  1. Should be retained.
L. Budget
  1. The Duncans realize that a master plan, when implemented, may cost more than they originally anticipated. To be realistic, they have established a 5-year budget of between $22,500 to $30,000, which is 15 to 20 percent of the cost of their $150,000 home.

SUMMARY

As can be seen from this chapter, there are a number of important tasks that must be accomplished before any actual design work can take place on paper. The information gathered during the research and preparation phase of the design process provides a foundation for subsequent phases of the process. The site inventory and site analysis identify and evaluate the existing site conditions in order to determine the critical site conditions that must be worked with or overcome in the design. The more that can be learned during this step, the easier it will be for the designer to create a design solution that is specifically tailored to the particular conditions of the site. The design program culminates the research and preparation phase by outlining all the spaces, elements, and other requirements the design solution must ultimately incorporate. The following chapters discuss and show how all the information of the research and preparation phase is used in creating a design.

8

Functional Diagrams

INTRODUCTION

After gaining an understanding of both the clients and the site, the designer possesses two general sets of information. The first set stems from meeting the clients and is a written list of elements and spaces required to satisfy the clients' needs and expectations. The second set of information is the site inventory and analysis that is recorded with written notes and graphic symbols on a copy of the base map. The written portions of these two sets of information are combined in the final step of the research and preparation phase to establish the design program.

With the research and preparation phase completed, the landscape designer is ready to start designing. To do this, an effective method is needed for combining the written design program information with the specific conditions of the site. This is done with functional diagrams. This chapter discusses what functional diagrams are, their purpose and significance in the design process, a method for preparing them, and design qualities that can be studied by using functional diagrams.

DEFINITION AND PURPOSE

Functional diagrams are freehand drawings that utilize bubbles and diagrammatic symbols to graphically depict the program elements of a design as they relate to each other and to the specific conditions of the site. While the site inventory and analysis are prepared with the aid of a base map, functional diagrams are developed utilizing the site analysis and the base sheet.

The purpose of functional diagrams is to create a broad-brushed, conceptual layout of the proposed design, based upon function. They provide the general organizational structure for a design similar to what an outline does for a written report. Functional diagrams can be considered the underlying foundation of a design. Later phases of the design process are based on these diagrams.

Functional diagrams are used to study various factors that deal with the function and general layout of the design. At this time, less thought is given to specific appearance or aesthetics which is done later in the design process.

Designers can communicate with other designers and clients concerning the overall functional organization of the site with the graphic language of functional diagrams. This graphic language allows for quick expression of ideas. It is common for designers to initially formulate a number of mental images or preconceived ideas about a design. While some of these ideas might be specific, others are more general and need to be quickly transferred to paper to allow the designer to study them. The sooner these ideas are drawn on paper, the easier it is to evaluate them. The graphic vocabulary of functional diagrams is an invaluable tool for this much needed quick expression. And because functional diagrams are freehand and general in their graphic style, they can be revised or altered rather easily. This encourages creativity by studying alternatives as one searches for an appropriate design solution.

IMPORTANCE OF FUNCTIONAL DIAGRAMS

Functional diagrams are crucial to the design process because they can: (1) establish a sound functional basis for the design solution, (2) encourage the designer to remain general about the appearance of the design, (3) encourage the designer to explore alternatives, and (4) provide opportunities for the designer to go beyond preconceived ideas.

Establishing a Sound Functional Basis

A functional diagram that has been carefully thought out will provide a proper basis for the remaining design phases. The importance of this phase cannot be overstressed. Decisions made about a design at this early stage are apt to be carried throughout the remainder of the design process. Thus, it is critical that decisions made during this step be sound ones. If they are not, they will be continually revealed in later phases of the design project. Keep in mind that the appearance of a design as reflected in form, materials, and material patterns cannot overcome functional deficiencies. A design must first and foremost have a solid functional foundation.

Staying General

One of the most common faults of inexperienced designers is the inclination to begin a design project by drawing forms and design elements in plan that are too specific (Figure 8–1). Novice designers frequently make the design look "real" as quickly as possible. For example, the edges of terraces, decks, walls, and planting beds are much too often given a highly defined form too quickly without sufficient thought toward the functions. Similarly, materials and their patterns are often drawn in too much detail without proper understanding of their location or intended function. Too much detail too soon is apt to cause the designer to overlook underlying functional relationships.

Another reason for studying a design in a general fashion before specifics are considered is the factor of time. Since changes are inevitable during the process of design, being too specific too soon will result in time-consuming changes made in later design phases. The more detailed a plan is, the more time it takes to redraw it when changes need to be made. Certainly all phases of design involve changes. But in the initial phases, general functional organization can change rather quickly and effortlessly when drawn appropriately with the graphic language of functional diagrams.

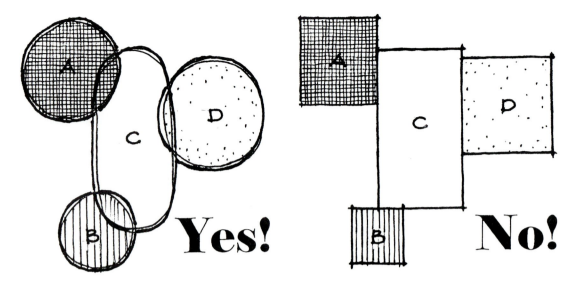

FIGURE 8–1
The spaces in a functional diagram should be drawn as freehand bubbles, not as exact forms.

Studying Alternatives

It is obvious that a designer will accumulate a substantial mental library of ideas over time as design experience is gained. The more exposure one has to designs, whether it be through photographs or actual experience, the more images one has to draw on for future reference. This mental file of ideas has tremendous value, for it enables the designer to think of different options for any given project. These options (alternatives) are very important to the growth of designers. Growth occurs when a designer tries new ideas. Studying alternatives during design phases will prove to be valuable for formulating new ideas. Functional diagrams encourage the use of alternatives because of their quick and simple graphic character.

Going Beyond Preconceived Ideas

A mental library of ideas available for future reference is developed by every designer through experience and exposure. Owing to the wealth of this stored visual information, it is common to have preconceived ideas for a design. Sometimes these preconceived ideas are so strong that a solution can be imagined quite easily. This insight can be exciting for a designer but it should be handled sensitively so it will contribute positively to a designer's growth. Too often preconceived ideas are the only ones that are considered. We are not suggesting that these insights be ignored, but keep in mind that the preconceived idea is only one idea and it is just the first one. Although the first idea may be a good one, the designer will never know if it is better than other ideas unless other ideas are explored. A designer should not accept the first idea without examining alternatives. Once this is done, a better design solution usually emerges.

FUNCTIONAL DIAGRAMS

To begin preparing a functional diagram, the designer should have a copy of the design program, site analysis, and base sheet. Each of these items will be used to develop functional diagrams. The designer should also have a roll of tracing paper and a supply of soft pencils. The use of drafting equipment (t-squares, triangles, templates, etc.) are not necessary since everything will be drawn freehand during this step.

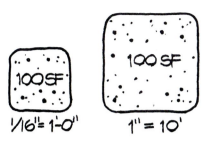
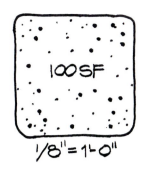

1/16"= 1'-0"   1" = 10'   1/8"= 1'-0"

FIGURE 8–2
The designer is able to visualize the size of a
space better when it is drawn at a given scale.

During functional diagrams, the designer locates all spaces and elements of the design program for the first time by using free-hand diagrammatic symbols. Each space and element listed in the design program should be located on the site when the diagram is complete.

There are a number of design factors that can be dealt with during this phase of design. They are:

1. Size
2. Location
3. Proportion
4. Configuration
5. Internal Subdivision
6. Edges
7. Circulation
8. Views
9. Focal Points
10. Elevation Change

Each of these factors is addressed individually in the following paragraphs, although each should be considered in conjunction with the others in actual practice.

Size

Before a functional diagram can be drawn, the designer should know the approximate sizes of the spaces and elements to be included in the design. In some situations, this information may already have been established in the design program. If size is unknown, the designer should consult references, which identify the size of typical functions on a residential site. Some information is illustrated in Table 8–1. The sizes indicated are common standards, nevertheless, they may be adjusted as necessary to satisfy the particular needs of any given situation.

After determining the necessary sizes, sketch each space and element of the design program on a blank sheet of paper. Each should be drawn as a freehand bubble to approximately the correct size and proportion using the same scale as the base sheet. It is sometimes difficult to comprehend the size of scaled spaces when they are described only with numbers. For example, the area "100 square feet" may not mean much by itself. But when this area is graphically expressed as a freehand bubble at a given scale, the designer is able to see more clearly how much space it actually covers in the plan (Figure 8–2).

Once the spaces and elements have been sketched at their approximate scaled sizes, the designer should have a better understanding of where certain uses should be placed on the site. For example, the designer may need to look for especially open or generous areas of the site for spaces that are particularly large. Also, the designer should have a notion of whether or not all spaces and elements of the design program will fit on the site. It may be found that certain spaces or elements

TABLE 8-1 Functional Size Requirements

1. Person standing alone: 5 sq ft
2. People standing in conversation: 8 sq ft/person
3. Sitting
   a. Single aluminum lawn chair: 2′ × 2′
   b. Single wood deck chair with cushions: 2′ − 6″ × 2′ − 6″
   c. Groups of chairs:
      Two chairs

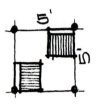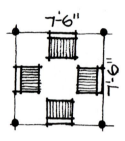

      Four chairs

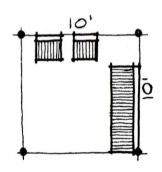

      Two chairs and couch

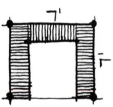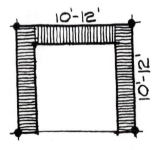

   d. Bench: seat depth: 18″
            seat length: 2′ − 6″ linear feet/person
   e. Bench arrangement for conversation
      Intimate

      Group

   f. Single aluminum lounge chair (for sitting or sun bathing): 2′ × 6′
   g. Groups of lounge chairs

Two lounge chairs

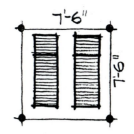

Three lounge chairs
and coffee table

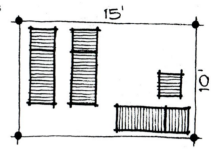

4. Eating
   a. Two people
        Chair by itself: 2′ × 2′
        Table by itself: 2′ × 2′
        Minimum area needed: 2′ − 6″ × 5′
        Preferred area:

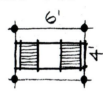

   b. Four people
        Chair by itself: 2′ × 2′
        Table by itself: 2′ − 6″ × 2′ − 6″
        Minimum area needed: 6′ × 6′
        Preferred area:

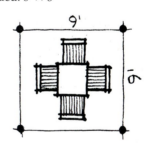

   c. Six people (picnic table)
        Bench by itself: 1′ × 5′
        Table by itself: 2′ − 6″ × 5′
        Minimum area needed: 5′ × 6′
        Preferred area:

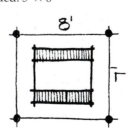

d. Eight people (picnic area)
   Bench by itself: 1' × 5'
   Table by itself: 2' – 6" × 5'
   Minimum area needed: 5' × 7' – 6"
   Preferred area:

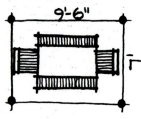

5. Cooking and food preparation
   a. Grill by itself: 2' × 2'
   b. Counter top: 2' × 4'
   c. Overall area needed: 20 sq ft

6. Recreation
   a. Badminton (doubles): 17' × 39' (playing surface)
                           20' × 44' (overall area)
   b. Croquet: 38' × 85' (playing surface)
              50' × 95' (overall area)
   c. Frisbee, baseball, football throwing: 15' × 40'
   d. Horseshoes: stakes 40' apart
                  10' × 50' (overall area)
   e. Tennis (doubles): 36' × 78' (playing surface)
                        60' × 120' (overall area)
   f. Volleyball: 30' × 60' (playing surface)
                 45' × 80' (overall area)
   g. Back-yard basketball: 25' × 25' minimum
   h. Half-court basketball: 42' × 40'
   i. Swimming
      Average-sized pool: 18' × 36' (without deck)
                          need between 24 and 36 sq ft/swimmer
      Lap pool: 10' × 60'
      Spa/Jacuzzi: 5' × 5'
   j. Sand box: 4' × 4'
   k. Swing set: 10' × 15'
7. Storage
   a. Garbage can: 2' diameter
   b. Two garbage cans: 2' × 6'
   c. Cord of wood: 4' × 4' × 8'
8. Parking
   a. single car: 9' × 18'

just don't fit. If this happens, then there needs to be a change in the design program after consulting with the clients.

Location

With a firm comprehension of the size needed for required spaces and elements, the designer is now ready to start actually drawing a functional diagram. The designer should first place a clean sheet of tracing paper on top of the site analysis. This should be done so that the observations and recommendations of the site analysis can be continually referred to during the first tries at placing the various spaces and

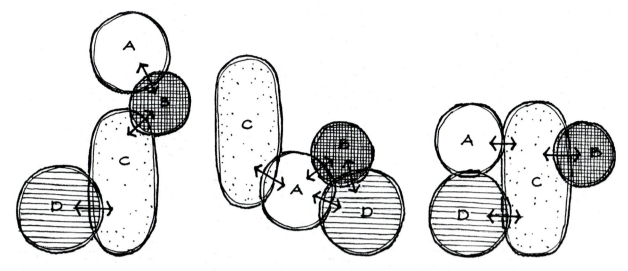

FIGURE 8–3
The designer should explore alternative functional relationships among the spaces.

elements on the site. With the site analysis serving as a base, it is more likely the designer will keep the site factors in mind while organizing the functional diagram.

The site location of each of the required spaces and elements should be based on functional relationships, available space, and existing site conditions.

Functional Relationships. Each space and element should be located on the site so that it is compatible with the functions of adjacent spaces and elements. For example, the designer might ask: Where could the living/entertaining space be placed? Could it be located near the play area? Or could it be located near the outdoor eating space? If the outdoor living/entertaining space is placed here, what might go on the west side of it? Questions should also be asked about the relationship between indoor and outdoor. For instance, where could the outside eating space be placed in relation to the kitchen?

Of course, functions that work together or depend on each other should be placed next to or near each other, while functions that are incompatible should be separated. Some decisions about the functional relationship between spaces and elements will be obvious while others need to be studied before decisions are made. The designer should try alternative relationships among the spaces (Figure 8–3). Quite frequently, new functional relationships are discovered through trial and error. The designer should not be afraid to make mistakes in this early phase of the design process. In most design professions, it is common to put ideas on paper that are not perfect or completely worked out during this conceptual phase. This is a better approach than trying to work everything out in one's head before drawing it.

Available Space. The decision as to where to place the various spaces and elements is also dependent on the availability of space. Each space and element must fit its selected location. Problems arise when a space is too large for a particular area of the site. This situation may require a reorganization of the functional diagram, a reduction of the size of the space or element, or the elimination of the space or element from the design.

Existing Site Conditions. Each space and element should be situated on the site so that it relates properly to the existing site conditions and the site analysis. For example, an outdoor living and entertaining space ideally should be located in a place that has partial shade, views of attractive site features, and has direct access to the inside of the house. The vegetable garden should be placed on well-drained

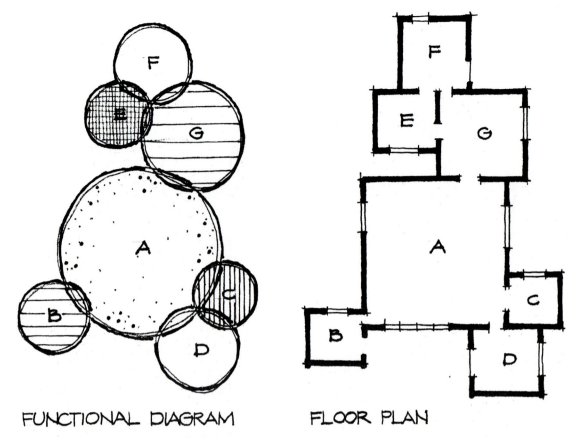

FUNCTIONAL DIAGRAM   FLOOR PLAN

FIGURE 8-4
A diagram that has all the spaces drawn as circles is like a building in which all the rooms are square.

and fertile soil, in mostly full sunlight, and near a water source. And there are different ideal site conditions for other spaces. To identify and understand these conditions more clearly, the designer may want to make a list of the ideal site conditions for each space and element that is to be located on the site.

After identifying the ideal site conditions required for each space or element, the designer can proceed to locate the spaces and elements on the site where these ideal conditions exist. This sounds simple in theory and often is in practice. However, there are times when some or all of the ideal conditions desired for a required space or element do not exist on the site. For example, there may not be a place on the site with partial shade, attractive views, and direct access for the outdoor living and entertaining space. In this situation, the designer should attempt to place the space or element where as many of the ideal conditions as possible are located without jeopardizing the site or the ability of the space to function properly. Or, the designer may propose to carefully modify the existing site so it will serve as a proper setting for the space or element. For example, shade trees or attractive features could be added to the site if these conditions do not exist for the outdoor living and entertaining space.

Proportion

Another factor that should be taken into account when drawing the functional diagram is proportion. The proportion of an outdoor space is the relative relationship between length and width. One common tendency in this step is to draw most spaces as simple circular bubbles (Figure 8-4). This type of diagram makes each outdoor space similar to a building where every room is a perfect square. Of course, this would not be appropriate.

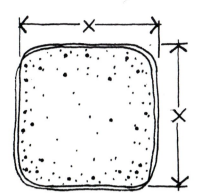

FIGURE 8-5
Length and width are approximately the same in a space with equal plan proportions.

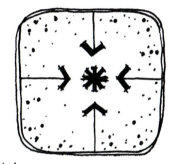

FIGURE 8-6
A space with equal plan proportions may suggest an inward orientation conducive to conversation.

DIAGRAM

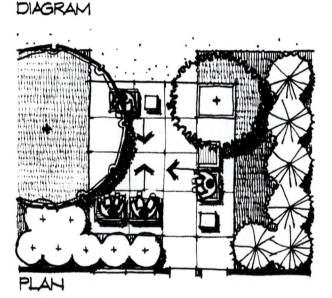

PLAN

Each outdoor room needs special consideration based on the intended use of that space. Proportions should vary as intended uses vary. Generally, spaces can have equal plan proportions or unequal plan proportions.

Equal Plan Proportions. A space that has equal plan proportions is one in which the length and width are about the same (Figure 8–5). Such a space lacks an implication of direction and therefore is well suited for collection, stopping, or gathering. A space of equal plan proportions can be inward oriented when proper enclosure exists (Figure 8–6). This type of space is often suitable for sitting and conversation among individuals in a group. The outside entry foyer where people stop and gather before entering or after leaving the house is another space where equal plan proportions are appropriate (Figure 8–7).

FIGURE 8–7
The outside entry foyer may have equal plan proportions to suggest stopping and gathering.

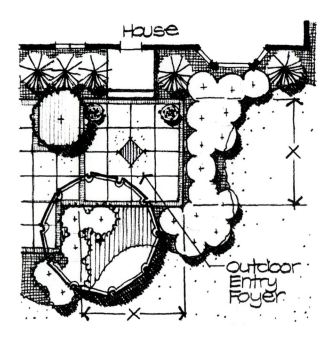

FIGURE 8–8
Length and width are not similar in a space with unequal plan proportions.

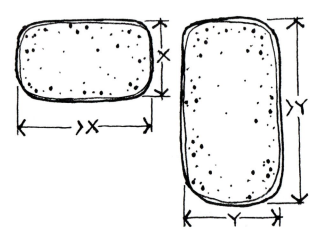

Unequal Plan Proportions.   A space with unequal proportions (Figure 8–8) is one in which length is greater than width or vice versa. Outdoor rooms with such proportions are like hallways in a building and suggest movement due to their long, narrow quality (Figure 8–9). Long enclosed spaces are also appropriate for directing views in the landscape toward their ends or terminus points (Figure 8–10). While spaces with unequal plan proportions are good for circulation, they are not suited for gathering because such activity gets in the way of movement through the space. And it is difficult to arrange furniture for conversation in long narrow spaces; such an arrangement looks similar to a subway car (the left side of Figure 8–11). It is easier for people to talk to each other when they face each other (the right side of Figure 8–11). However, long spaces are good for arrangement of furniture for looking out at other points in the landscape, such as from a porch or veranda (Figure 8–12).

Configuration

Configuration is the general shape of a space. For example, the configuration of a space may be simple, L-shaped, or complex. However, configuration does *not* refer to the specific form of a space, such as whether an area is round, square, curved, or angled. Configuration is similar to proportion in that it is concerned

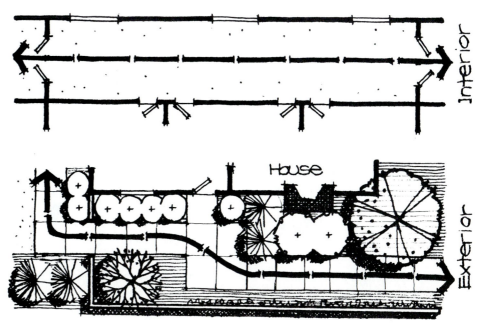

FIGURE 8-9
Spaces with unequal plan proportions are like hallways and suggest movement.

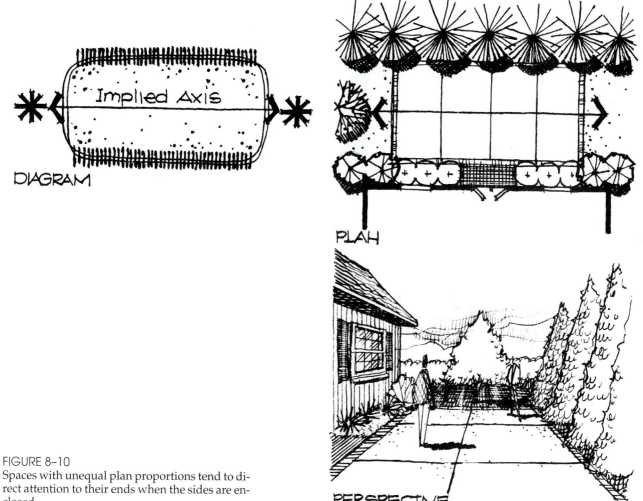

FIGURE 8-10
Spaces with unequal plan proportions tend to direct attention to their ends when the sides are enclosed.

No! Yes!

FIGURE 8–11
The plan proportions of a space influence its ability to be used for gathering and conversation.

FIGURE 8–12
Spaces with unequal plan proportions permit furniture to be arranged to direct views outward into the landscape.

with the outline of a space, although in more detail. Some basic plan configurations are described and illustrated in the following paragraphs.

Simple Configuration.   The generalized shape of a space can have a simple configuration (Figure 8–13). A space with this configuration has a strong sense of unity because the entire area can be seen easily and completely at one time from any location. A simple configuration is most suitable for gathering spaces like an eating area or an outdoor entry foyer.

"L-shaped" Configuration.   As the name implies, a space with this configuration bends around a corner (Figure 8–14) and establishes two smaller subspaces in the legs of the "L" while still maintaining a sense of connection between them. A space with an "L" configuration can offer a sense of intrigue because each subspace may not be entirely apparent as viewed from the other subspace. A feeling of mystery is created by what lies hidden around the corner (left side of Figure 8–15). The

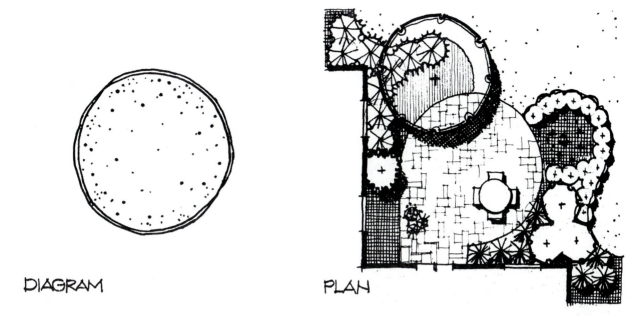

DIAGRAM   PLAN

FIGURE 8–13
A space with a simple configuration has a strong sense of unity.

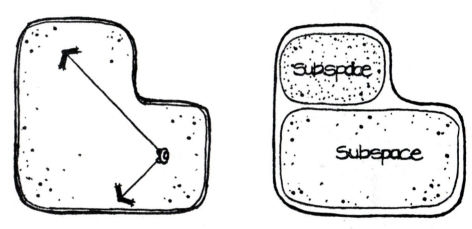

FIGURE 8–14
A space with an "L-shaped" configuration tends to divide itself into two subspaces.

inside corner is a strategic place that can be seen easily from all locations within the "L" configuration and therefore is a potential place for a focal point (right side of Figure 8–15). Examples of L-shaped spaces might include a major entertaining space with a small seating area to the side (left side of Figure 8–16), or a wood deck with an eating area and an observation area adjacent to it (right side of Figure 8–16).

Complex Configuration.   A third possible configuration for outdoor space is composed of an edge that has many variations in its alignment (Figure 8–17). These edge variations or "pushes and pulls" add variety to the space they surround. Each "push" away from the space creates a small subspace and each "pull" provides some separation between the subspaces. When this is done with an outdoor entertaining space, small pockets of space (the "pushes") for small intimate groupings are created around the perimeter of the central space (Figure 8–18). Another example of a complex configuration is a wood deck designed to provide several different and unique views into the surrounding landscape (Figure 8–19).

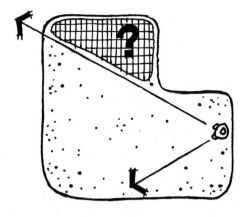 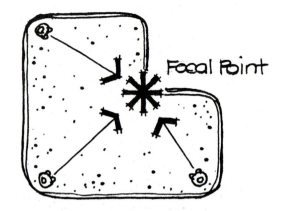

FIGURE 8–15
Characteristics of a space with an "L-shaped" configuration.

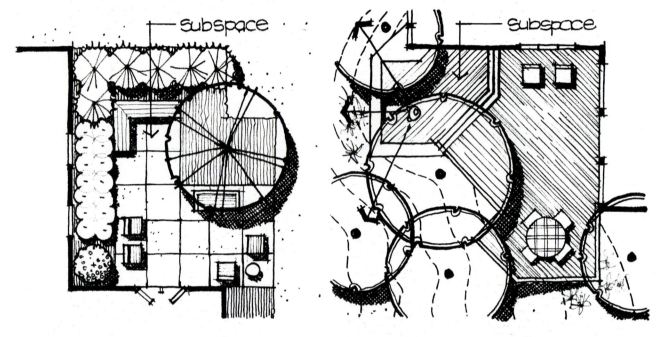

FIGURE 8–16
Spaces with an "L-shaped" configuration may have one corner function as a subspace of the other larger area.

FIGURE 8–17
A space with a complex configuration has "pushes" and "pulls" in its edge.

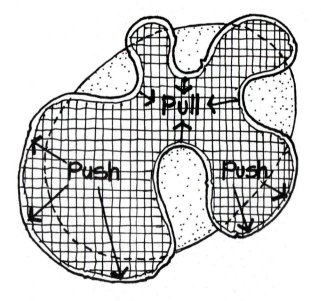

FIGURE 8–18
A complex configuration can create several small spaces around the perimeter of the central space.

Internal Subdivision

Another important consideration of the functional diagram is to address the internal organization of each space. This step gives the designer the opportunity to understand more clearly how each space is to function within itself. One example of this is provided in Figure 8–20. Here the internal organization of an outdoor living and entertaining space was subdivided into more specific use areas. A conversation space (space "A" on the diagram), quiet sitting space (space "B"), and a sunning space (space "C") were all identified within the living and entertaining space. The same consideration is given to the planting areas, which can be divided into more specific plant types according to their size and type of foliage (Figure 8–21). However, no shrubs or other small-scale plant materials are shown or studied individually until the preliminary design phase is reached.

Edges

The outside edge around a space can be established in different ways. It may be defined by a change of materials on the ground plane, slopes or changes in elevation, plant materials, walls, fences, and/or buildings. In turn, spatial edges may have a variety of characters based on the transparency of the edge. Thus, the line drawn around a bubble in the functional diagram can be elaborated to suggest transparency characteristics.

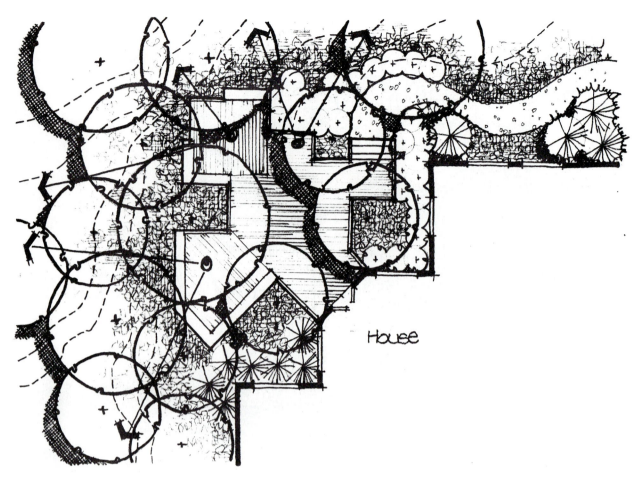

House

FIGURE 8–19
A complex configuration can provide perimeter subspaces with views directed out into the surrounding landscape.

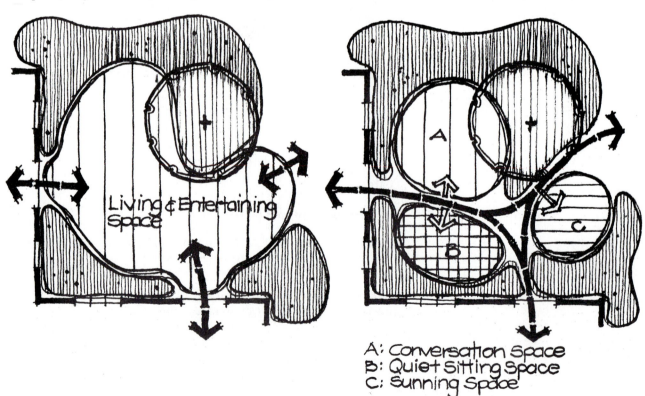

Living & Entertaining Space

A: Conversation Space
B: Quiet Sitting Space
C: Sunning Space

FIGURE 8–20
The spaces of a functional diagram can be subdivided into more specific functions.

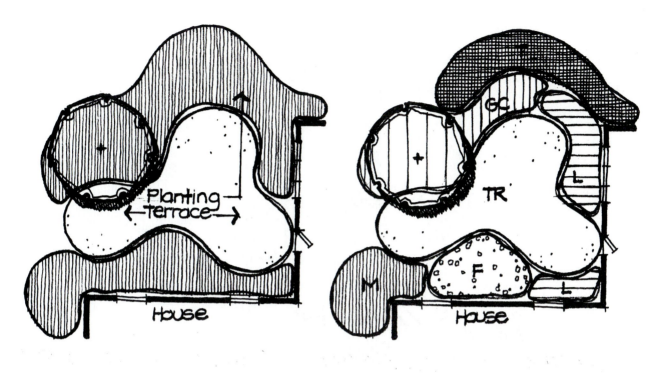

TR: Terrace   L: Low Shrubs
T: Tall Shrubs   GC: Ground Cover
M: Medium Shrubs   F: Flowers

FIGURE 8-21
The planting areas on a functional diagram can be subdivided into more specific plant types.

Solid   Semi-transparent   Transparent

FIGURE 8-22
Graphic examples of transparency.

Transparency. Transparency is the degree of opaqueness of a spatial edge, and it influences how well a person can see. Three types of transparency are: (1) solid, (2) semitransparent, and (3) transparent (Figure 8–22).

1. Solid edges are those that cannot be seen through like a stone wall, wood fence, or a dense mass of evergreen trees. This type of edge would be used where complete separation or privacy is desired.

2. Semi-transparent edges are those that can be partially seen through such as a wood lattice, louvered fence, a panel of smoked plexiglass, or a loosely foliated hedge. This type of edge provides a sense of spatial enclosure while maintaining some degree of openness.

3. Transparent edges are completely open, providing an unobstructed view into a desired area from the space. This type of edge could be created by a wall of glass or by the lack of a vertical plane.

FIGURE 8-23
Entry and exit points as well as through circulation should be shown on a functional diagram.

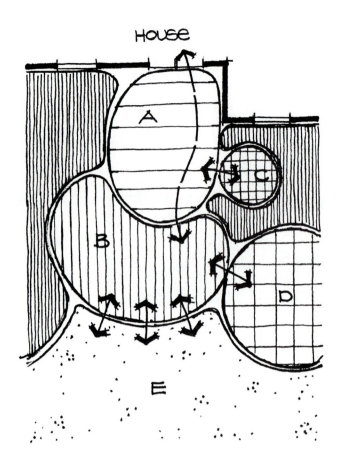

Circulation

Circulation is concerned with the access points of spaces along with a generalized pattern of movement through the spaces. The points of entry and exit can be located on the diagram by drawing simple arrows at the desired locations (Figure 8–23).
Here, the arrows indicate movement to and from the space. In addition to access, the
designer should also study and determine the most significant paths of movement
through those spaces where continuous circulation is planned. This can be designated
with simple dashed lines and arrows pointing in the direction of movement. This
should be done on the basis of the function of that space and should address only the
major routes of movement, not every possible path of movement.

In considering circulation, the designer should ask several questions. Should
the circulation occur through the middle of the space, around the outside edges of
the space, in a direct line from the entry to the exit, or casually meander throughout the space? The designer should study alternatives for circulation and decide
which is most compatible with the intended function of the space (Figure 8–24).

Not only is the location of the circulation examined, but its intensity and character are also considered. As indicated before, the graphic symbols used to represent circulation are dashed lines and arrows. The specific type of arrow drawn can
suggest, among other qualities, the intensity and character of the circulation.

Intensity. The intensity of circulation is a factor of the frequency and importance of a circulation path. Two general types of circulation intensity are primary circulation and secondary circulation.

1. Primary circulation. This type of circulation is of major importance and
   occurs with moderate to high frequency. Examples of primary circulation
   include the front entry walk between the driveway and the front door or

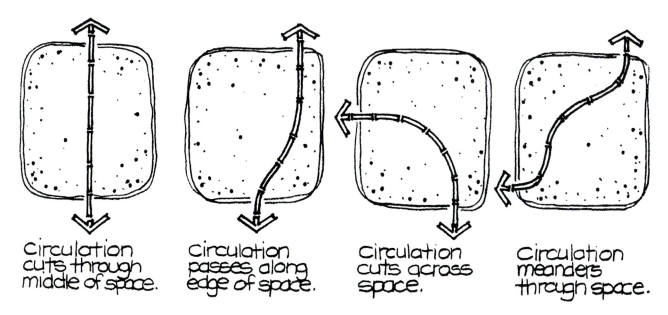

Circulation cuts through middle of space.

Circulation passes along edge of space.

Circulation cuts across space.

Circulation meanders through space.

FIGURE 8-24
Alternative ways for circulation to move through a space.

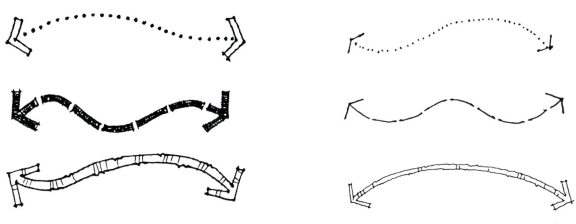

FIGURE 8-25
Graphic examples of primary circulation.

FIGURE 8-26
Graphic examples of secondary circulation.

the connection from the inside living room through the exterior living and entertainment space into the lawn area.

2. Secondary circulation. This type of circulation is of less importance and occurs with lower frequency in comparison to primary circulation. A side route around the house or a casual garden path are examples of secondary circulation. Figure 8–25 and Figure 8–26 show graphic examples of primary and secondary circulation respectively.

Views

Views are another factor that should be studied in a functional diagram. What a person sees or doesn't see from a space or a particular point within a space is important to the overall organization and experience of a design. During the development of a functional diagram, the designer concentrates on those views that are most significant to the major spaces of the design. The different types of views studied are: (1) panoramic views or vistas, (2) concentrated or focused views, and (3) blocked views.

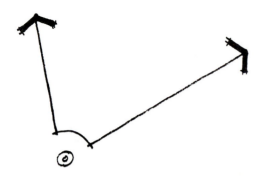
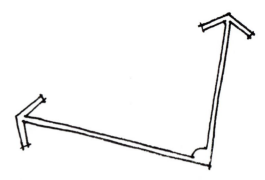

FIGURE 8–27
Graphic examples of panoramic views.

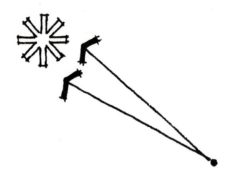

FIGURE 8–28
Graphic examples of concentrated views.

Panoramic View or Vista.   This type of view takes in a wide area and often emphasizes a view in the landscape that is some distance from the viewer. It is an encompassing view. A view to a distant mountain range, to the valley below, or out onto an adjoining golf course are a few examples. When these views extend off the site to adjoining or distant points in the landscape, they are referred to as *borrowed landscapes*. These are typically good views that a designer attempts to enframe or, at the very least, leave unobstructed so they become part of the design's visual experience. Figure 8–27 shows graphic examples of a panoramic view.

Concentrated or Focused View.   This type of view focuses on a particular point in the landscape, such as a piece of sculpture, a unique tree, or a bed of showy flowers. A concentrated view may be to a point either on or off the site. Figure 8–28 shows how a concentrated view might be shown in a functional diagram.

Blocked View.   This type of view is an undesirable view that needs to be screened. High plant materials, walls, fences, and so on can all be utilized to block unsightly views. Graphic examples for indicating blocked views are illustrated in Figure 8–29.

Focal Point

Focal points, closely associated with views, are visual accents or elements that are unique and stand out in contrast to their surroundings, such as a gnarled tree, a water feature, attractive spring flowers, a piece of sculpture, or a large tree. It is important to plan the location of focal points in functional diagrams so they can be coordinated with views. Focal points should be strategically placed to high-

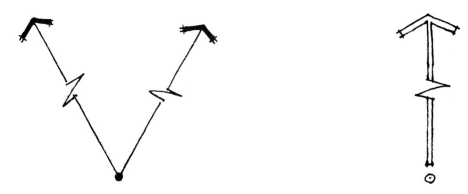

FIGURE 8-29
Graphic examples of blocked views.

FIGURE 8-30
Graphic examples of focal points.

light special points of the landscape. They should not be overused and scattered indiscriminately throughout an area as this will create a chaotic appearance requiring the eye to look at too many different accents. A few graphic examples for focal points are shown in Figure 8–30.

Elevation Changes

Elevation changes should also be studied during the development of functional diagrams. It is during this stage that the designer should start thinking about the third dimension of the ground plane. The designer might ask: "Should one have to go up from the lawn area to the outside entertaining space, or should the two spaces be at the same elevation? If there is to be a change, about how much should it be? One foot? Three feet?"

One way elevational changes between spaces can be expressed in a diagram is by means of spot grades (Figure 8–31). This method allows the designer to determine what space is higher than another and by approximately how much. Another way of indicating elevation change in the functional diagram is by lines that represent step locations along a circulation path (Figure 8–32).

As can be seen from the preceding paragraphs, there are a number of factors of design organization that need to be thought about during the functional diagram phase. It is not always easy to study all these factors together, but it is essential to do so. It is necessary to examine each of these factors in association with the others so the overall design can function in a logical, well-planned, and coordinated manner. The more study given to the organization of a design at this time in the design process, the easier the design decisions become in subsequent phases.

FUNCTIONAL DIAGRAM SUMMARY

As stated earlier, the designer should study the different design factors when preparing a functional diagram. Each of these factors influences the others and

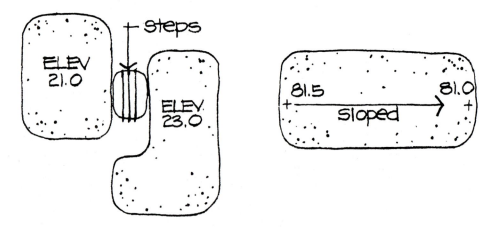

FIGURE 8–31
Elevation changes between spaces can be expressed with spot grades.

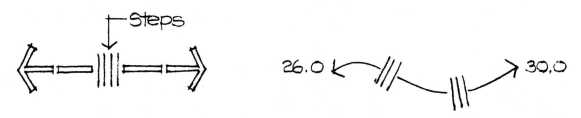

FIGURE 8–32
Lines can be used within a circulation path to graphically indicate general step locations.

should be studied in concert with one another. When the functional diagram is completed, the entire site area should be covered with bubbles and other graphic symbols representing all the necessary spaces and elements of the design (Figure 8–33). There should be no blank areas or "holes" in the layout (Figure 8–34). When this occurs, it indicates the designer has not made a decision about the use of this area of the site, and it should be determined what will occur there.

Another suggestion for this step of the design process is to remember to use alternatives. In fact, it is advisable to try two or three quickly developed alternatives for the overall site organization. Alternatives encourage the designer to be creative about organizing the site functions and to perhaps discover a better way of solving a problem than was initially apparent. With a series of alternatives, the designer is better able to pick the one alternative or combination of alternatives that is best for further elaboration in the next step of design.

FUNCTIONAL DIAGRAMS FOR THE DUNCAN RESIDENCE

To better illustrate the thought process involved in the preparation of functional diagrams, let us return to the Duncan residence. Having completed all the steps of the research and preparation phase, the designer is now ready to prepare a series of functional diagrams for the Duncan residence.

Figure 8–35 shows the first attempt to organize all the major spaces and elements for the Duncan residence in a functional diagram. The diagram shows a widened entrance walk that extends some distance along the driveway to permit better recognition of the main entrance and easy access from the driveway. The sitting space is placed adjacent to, but separate from, the entrance walk so circulation will not disturb or divide the space. Planting areas are woven in and

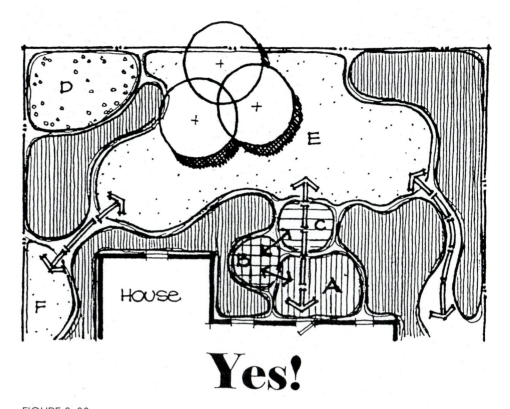

Yes!

FIGURE 8–33
The entire site area should be covered with bubbles and other symbols in a completed functional diagram.

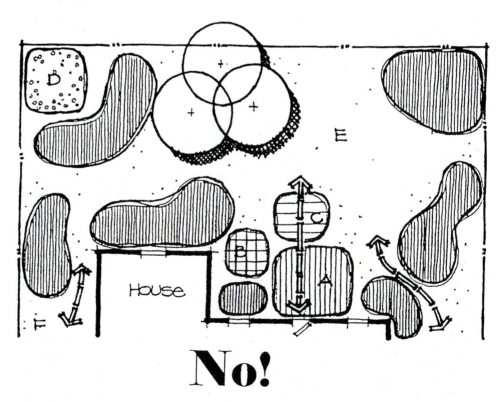

No!

FIGURE 8–34
There should be no blank areas or holes on a completed functional diagram.

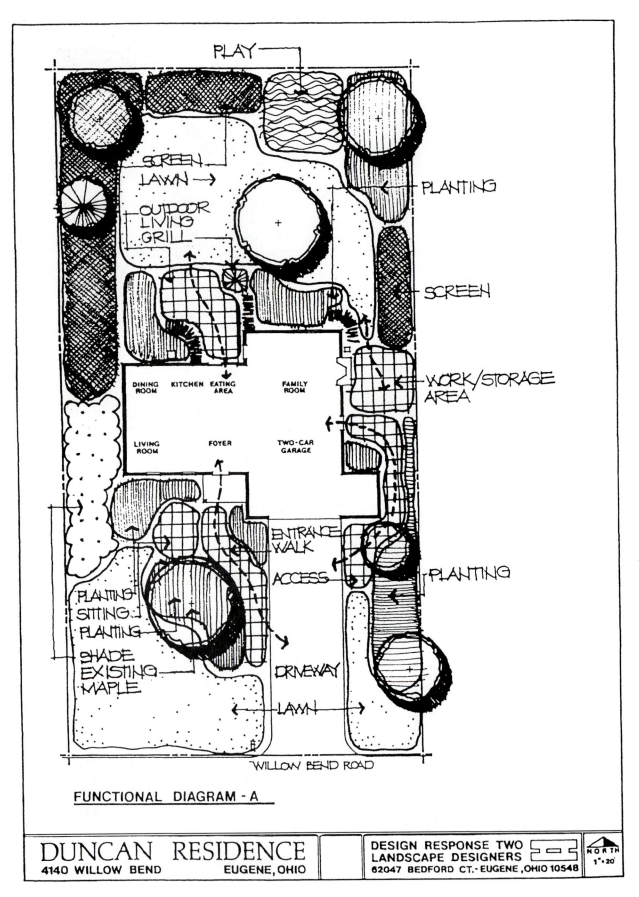

PLAY

SCREEN
LAWN →
OUTDOOR
LIVING
GRILL

PLANTING

SCREEN

WORK/STORAGE
AREA

DINING ROOM   KITCHEN   EATING AREA   FAMILY ROOM

LIVING ROOM   FOYER   TWO-CAR GARAGE

ENTRANCE WALK

ACCESS

PLANTING

PLANTING
SITTING
PLANTING
SHADE
EXISTING
MAPLE

DRIVEWAY

LAWN

WILLOW BEND ROAD

FUNCTIONAL DIAGRAM - A

DUNCAN RESIDENCE
4140 WILLOW BEND   EUGENE, OHIO

DESIGN RESPONSE TWO
LANDSCAPE DESIGNERS
62047 BEDFORD CT.- EUGENE, OHIO 10548

NORTH
1"=20'

FIGURE 8–35
Functional Diagram "A" for the Duncan residence.

around these spaces to help define them and to provide visual interest for a person walking along the entrance walk. The existing Sugar Maple is integrated with this planting.

Secondary circulation has been provided around the east side of the house for access between the driveway and the proposed work/storage space. The work/storage space is located near the side door of the garage for convenience and placement out of view from both the indoor and outdoor living spaces. The west side of the house, by contrast, is left open except for a mass of trees for afternoon shade.

In the back yard, the proposed raised terrace would function as an outdoor eating space near the family room and sitting room. The grill is located to the northeast of this space so smoke from the fire would be blown away from the space (prevailing wind is from the southwest). The outdoor living and entertaining space is placed farther from the house so it can take advantage of views into the rest of the back yard. The eating space is made more private with the suggestion of a privacy fence on the east side of the space, and the living and entertaining space is partially surrounded by plant materials for privacy.

The lawn area in the back yard has been left open and spacious to allow for recreation and games. Some screening on the west, north, and east gives privacy that is now lacking in the back yard. The play area in the northeast portion of the site has been left where it presently exists so it will be very visible for supervision from the house. The existing tree in the northeast corner is also retained and integrated with additional plantings so it will not appear as an isolated element.

Figure 8–36 shows another alternative. In this concept, the sitting space in the front has been integrated with the existing stoop, making one large space rather than two isolated ones. The entrance walk has been separated from the driveway by planting areas to cut down on the visual massiveness of the driveway's pavement. In addition, a turn-around has been proposed to make it easier to back out of the driveway. Planting occurs on both sides of the driveway near the street to soften and subtly hide the driveway. In the back yard, the outside eating and living/entertaining spaces are located so they function as outdoor extensions of the family room by converting the existing window into a sliding glass door. The play area has been moved so it will not be such an obvious element to look at. It is still located where it can be seen from the outdoor living spaces. And a narrower screen has been suggested along the northern property line so it will not take up as much area of the back yard.

Each of these alternative functional diagrams explores a different way of organizing the required spaces and elements on the site. As in most typical situations, the Duncans and the designer found some of these more appealing than others. After reviewing the two alternative diagrams, the Duncans decided they liked a combination of ideas from the different diagrams. So, the designer took the Duncans' preferences and produced one more functional diagram, Diagram "C" (Figure 8–37).

The front yard of the Duncan residence in the functional diagram has been given more study. The configuration of the entry foyer/sitting space, entrance walk, and lawn area have been modified. The entry foyer/sitting space has now been subdivided into more specific use areas and the location of the seating has been suggested. The planting areas have also been subdivided to indicate the general location of different types of plants (though no shrubs or ground cover have been shown as individual plants). In addition, study has been given to the relative ground elevation of the various spaces. This functional diagram indicates the entry foyer/sitting space is to be about one foot above the entrance walk. Views and focal points are other factors that now appear on this functional diagram. The same considerations are given to the back yard.

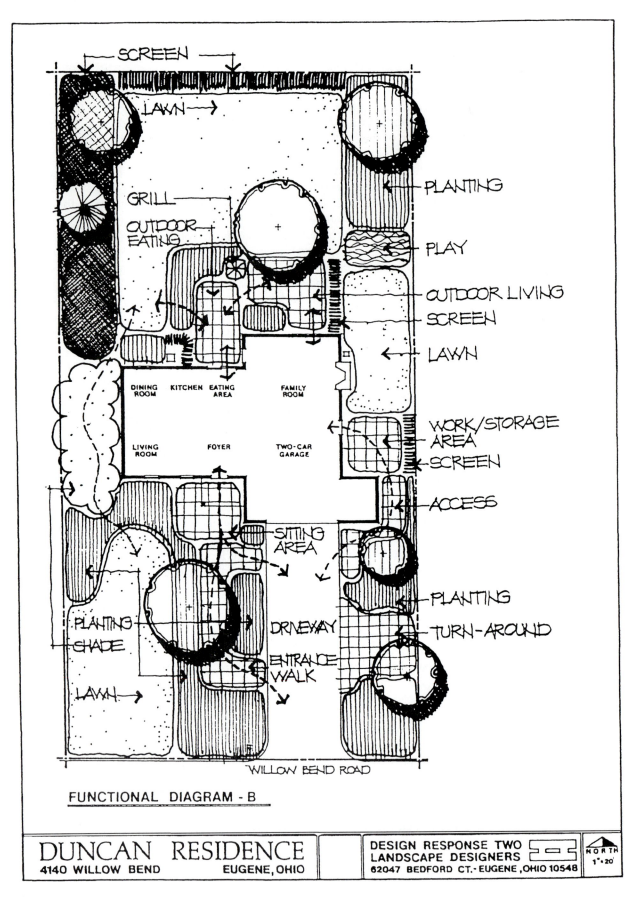

SCREEN

LAWN →

GRILL

OUTDOOR EATING

PLANTING

PLAY

OUTDOOR LIVING

SCREEN

LAWN

WORK/STORAGE AREA

SCREEN

ACCESS

DINING ROOM KITCHEN EATING AREA FAMILY ROOM

LIVING ROOM FOYER TWO-CAR GARAGE

SITTING AREA

PLANTING

TURN-AROUND

PLANTING SHADE

DRIVEWAY

ENTRANCE WALK

LAWN →

WILLOW BEND ROAD

FUNCTIONAL DIAGRAM - B

DUNCAN RESIDENCE
4140 WILLOW BEND   EUGENE, OHIO

DESIGN RESPONSE TWO
LANDSCAPE DESIGNERS
62047 BEDFORD CT.- EUGENE, OHIO 10548

NORTH
1"·20'

FIGURE 8–36
Functional Diagram "B" for the Duncan residence.

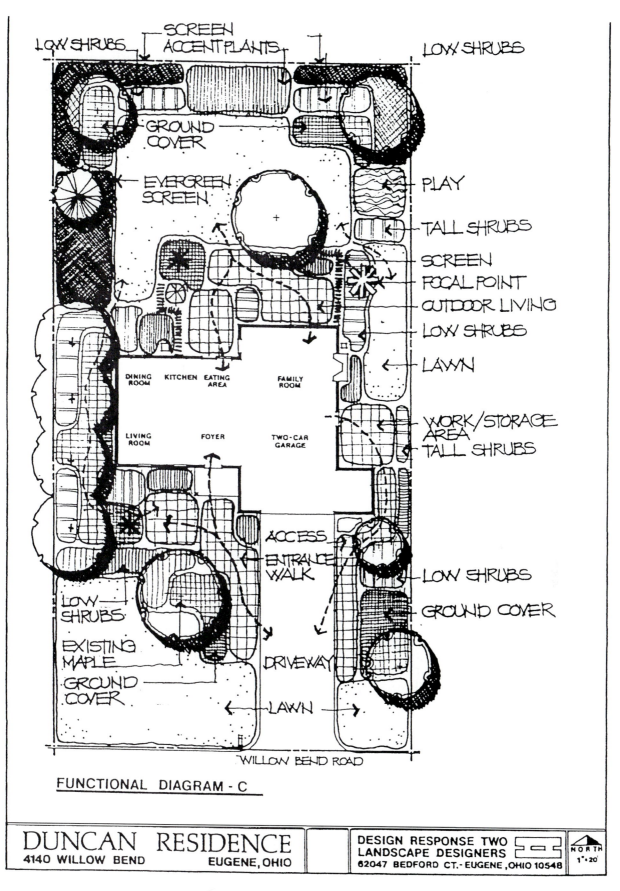

FIGURE 8-37
Functional Diagram "C" for the Duncan residence.

Functional Diagrams

SUMMARY

The entire functional diagram phase entails logical, thoughtful attention to all the qualities of the site's functional organization. During this phase, the designer is first and foremost a practical organizational planner. "What, when, where, and why?" are the major questions that need to be answered in this step. Each of these questions is addressed in a general manner without becoming overly concerned with specific details. The more thought put into functional diagrams, the easier the following steps of the design process become.

9

Preliminary Design and Design Principles

INTRODUCTION

Chapter 8 discussed how functional diagrams are utilized to establish the overall functional and spatial organization of a design during the first step of the design phase. The organization of all these factors in a functional diagram furnishes the structure and foundation for the next step of the design process: preliminary design.

Preliminary design starts with the functional diagram and ends with an illustrative site plan which may be supplemented with sections, elevations, and perspectives depicting all the elements of the design in a semirealistic graphic manner. To complete a preliminary design, the designer examines three interrelated factors. The first is careful consideration of the aesthetic organization and appearance of the design based on knowledge and application of three basic design principles: order, unity, and rhythm. These principles help the designer create a visually pleasing design solution.

The second factor, called form composition, is the study of the exact location of all two-dimensional edges and lines of the design. The designer accomplishes this by converting the approximate outline of spaces developed earlier in the functional diagrams to specific two-dimensional forms. This step begins to establish visual style or theme of the design.

The third factor examined in preliminary design is spatial composition. Spatial composition is the design's third dimension of outdoor rooms that are based on the foundation of the form composition. The designer utilizes grading (landform), planting, walls/fences, steps, overhead structures, and so on, to complete the total environment of the design during this step.

The objectives of this chapter are to: (1) discuss the definition and purpose of a preliminary design, (2) outline the process for developing a preliminary design, and (3) discuss the basic principles of design. The other important aspects of preliminary design are discussed in Chapter 10 (form composition) and Chapter 11 (spatial composition).

DEFINITION AND PURPOSE

Preliminary design is the first step of the design process in which a freehand illustrative site plan is prepared in a semirealistic graphic manner. The term *semirealistic* means that the graphic symbols combine realism with abstraction. In other words, the graphic symbols are stylized impressions of the actual elements. The plan gives the clients a view of the entire design "as seen from an airplane" with all the elements drawn to scale. (Figure 9–1).

The purposes of preliminary design are to: (1) provide the designer and clients with a comprehensive view of the entire design, (2) study the coordination of all elements of the design, (3) study the appearance and aesthetics of the design, and (4) provide the clients with an opportunity to give feedback to the designer.

Comprehensive View

One purpose of the preliminary design is to allow both the designer and the clients to study and analyze the design as a total environment. In a way, preliminary design is the first complete picture of the proposed design. While the functional diagrams also showed the entire design solution, they did so in a more general and functional manner. By comparison, the preliminary plan studies all the design elements that will make up the environment and graphically depicts them in a more exact and realistic manner.

Coordination of Elements

Another purpose of preliminary design is to study the visual relationships among the design elements. The designer considers the placement, size, form, and general material of each element in the context of other surrounding elements. For example, a wall or fence is studied in association with an adjoining pavement. Or the placement of a shade tree is coordinated with other surrounding plant materials. Each element is studied as a portion of the overall design, not as an isolated or separate piece.

Design Appearance and Aesthetics

One of the major purposes of preliminary design is to study the design appearance of the spaces and elements. The aesthetics of the entire design as well as individual elements within the design are primary concerns during preliminary design. In this step, the designer begins to make choices about size, form, and general material of all elements in the design. While decisions are not made about specific patterns of materials, the designer does select among general material types. For example, the designer might choose between stone or brick, wood or concrete, deciduous or evergreen, and so forth. The basic principles of design are also taken into account to create an overall design pleasing to the eye.

Clients' Feedback

The preliminary design can usually be understood by the clients with explanations by the designer, though some clients have difficulty understanding a plan drawing regardless of how nice it looks. In a preliminary plan, trees resemble trees, a deck seems believable because of the wood symbols, and pavement is understandable because the clients can see stone, brick, or concrete represented on the plan.

Frequently, the preliminary design is the client's first exposure to the design, and it is often their first chance to return thoughts and feelings about it to the designer. This is very critical for both the designer and the clients. The designer needs

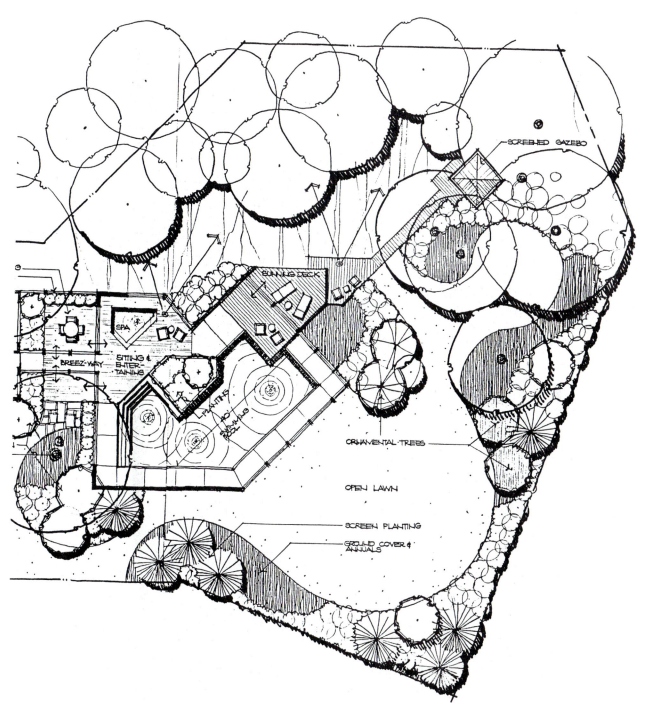

FIGURE 9-1
Sample preliminary site plan.

Labels within figure: SCREENED GAZEBO, SPA, BREEZE-WAY, SITTING & ENTER-TAINING, DINING DECK, PLANTING, SWIMMING POOL, ORNAMENTAL TREES, OPEN LAWN, SCREEN PLANTING, GROUND COVER & ANNUALS

to know how the clients feel about the design in order to understand whether or not it meets the clients' expectations. Likewise, it is important for the clients to give feedback. It is improper for the designer to possess a "take it or leave it" attitude toward the design. Ultimately, the design will be something the clients live with day in and day out and so it must be acceptable to them. They are apt to feel more positive toward a solution in which they have been involved during its creation. The clients will not only be more understanding about the design, but they will also have had a personal involvement in its growth.

The preliminary design is an intermediate solution that requires further refinement based on the reactions of the clients and/or the designer. The clients often see things within the preliminary design that need to be changed. Likewise, the designer may want to restudy portions of the design in order to improve it. It is not unusual for the designer to study a series of alternatives and refinements during preliminary design. Because all the elements are being studied in a coordinated effort, the designer may very well see things differently in comparison to earlier phases and, thus, may want to make appropriate adjustments.

PROCESS AND CONTENT

During preliminary design, the initial plan studies should be developed as tracing paper overlays on top of the best alternative functional diagram so the organization of this earlier step can be carried directly into the preliminary design. Later, as the preliminary design evolves, the functional diagram may be set aside. In some cases, the initial layout of the functional diagram may be altered during preliminary design because the designer is now looking at the design in a more complete and detailed fashion. For example, a space designated for planting may have to be enlarged to accommodate the size and number of plants that are to be placed in the area. Or the proportion and/or configuration of a space may need to be revised to make it more visually attractive. The designer seldom considers any portion or phase of the design to be sacred or outside the possibility of improvement during preliminary design.

As during the development of the functional diagrams, preliminary design ideas are drawn freehand with a soft pencil on tracing paper. Drafting equipment should be set aside because these instruments only get in the way of the quick and spontaneous thinking desirable during preliminary design. For beginners, there is often a great temptation to use drafting equipment at this point, owing to the belief that the drawing will look neater and more professional. This is generally not true. As seen in Figure 9–1, a preliminary plan drawing can be clearly legible and professional looking even when drawn freehand.

The preliminary design, as mentioned before, should graphically show all the elements of the design solution in a semirealistic manner. This graphic style is sometimes referred to as being illustrative because it attempts to illustrate the appearance of the design elements. To do this, the designer should rely on fundamental principles of drawing such as line weight variation, value contrast, use of textures to describe the appearance of materials, and the use of shadows to accentuate the third dimension in the drawing. Usually, a preliminary design plan should show the following to scale:

A. Property lines and adjoining street(s).
B. Outside walls, including doors and windows, of the house. While it is desirable to have a scaled floor plan of the interior of the house, this is not necessary. However, it is recommended to at least label where the various rooms are within the house.
C. All elements of the design drawn and illustrated with the proper symbols and textures including:
   1. pavement materials.
   2. walls, fences, steps, overhead structures, and other structures.
   3. plant materials. Trees should be drawn as individual plants while shrubs should be shown in masses.
   4. water fountains, pools, and so on.
   5. furniture, potted plants, and so on.

In addition, the preliminary design plan should identify the following with notes or a legend on the drawing:

1. Major use areas such as outside entry foyer, entertaining area, eating area, lawn, garden, and so on.
2. Materials for pavements and other structures (walls, steps, overhead trellises, etc.)
3. Plant materials by general types and sizes (deciduous shade tree, 20-foot-high coniferous evergreen tree, and 6-foot-high broad-leaved evergreen shrubs, and so on).
4. Major elevation changes on the ground plane by the use of contours and spot grades.
5. Other notes that help describe the design to the clients.
6. North arrow and scale.

DESIGN PRINCIPLES

There are a number of basic design principles that give the designer aesthetic guidance during preliminary design. Just as functional diagrams help to provide the functional organization for a residential design project, the design principles aid in establishing the visual and aesthetic organization of a design. Different sources and authorities of design theory often identify slightly different terminology and cataloguing of the various design principles. Yet they are similar in that they contend certain fundamental approaches to design contribute to a pleasing composition. This book suggests the three primary design principles are order, unity, and rhythm.

The design principles of order, unity, and rhythm are guidelines for the design composition of forms, materials, and material patterns of the spaces and elements. When the design principles are not used, the design is apt to be unpleasant to the eye (Figure 9–2). Such a design is described as being uncoordinated, chaotic, and visually disturbing. On the other hand, when the design principles are sensitively applied, the design is apt to be visually attractive (Figure 9–3).

The design principles are fundamental concepts of composition that have evolved through time and experience and are applied in a range of design fields including landscape architecture, architecture, interior design, industrial design, graphic design, and photography. The design principles are extremely useful for beginning designers because they aid in making decisions about selection and composition of forms and materials. However, these principles are not formulas. Their application does not ensure that a design solution will automatically be visually pleasing. As you have learned throughout this book, a successful design depends on numerous factors. The design principles do help make a good design more possible, and neglecting them will almost certainly result in a less than adequate design. Like other design guidelines, the design principles are not absolute rules that must always be followed. A skilled designer may in fact contradict selected design principles and still create a visually successful design.

Order

Order is defined as the "big picture" or overall framework of a design. It is the underlying visual structure of a design. In trees, order is evident in the trunk and branch structure (as seen without leaves in the winter). It is the trunk and branches that determine the overall form of the tree. The leaves merely reinforce this structure. Similarly, the skeleton of any animal also establishes order. The height, width, and shape of the animal all depend on the skeleton. In man-made objects, we see the establishment of order in buildings in the structural frame that

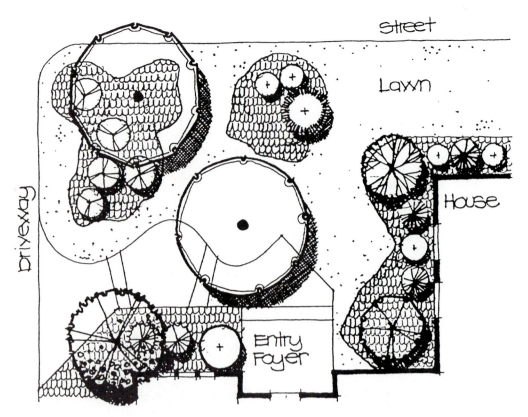

FIGURE 9–2
A residential site design is unappealing to the eye when basic design principles are not used.

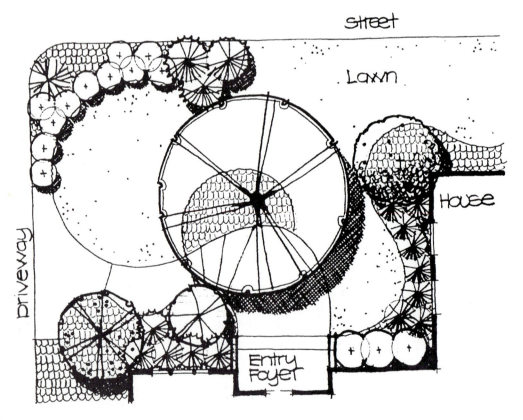

FIGURE 9–3
A residential site design is attractive and organized when basic principles of design are used.

216   Chapter 9   Preliminary Design and Design Principles

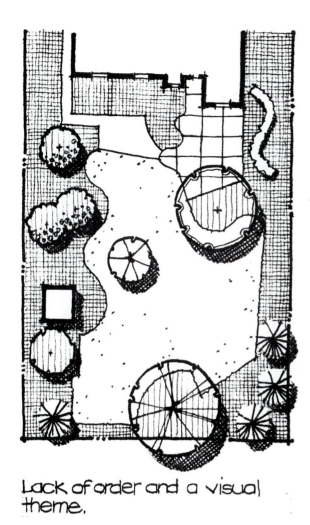

Lack of order and a visual theme.

Coordinated and consistent forms establish order and visual theme.

FIGURE 9–4
A consistent visual theme establishes order in a design.

is constructed before the walls and roof are installed. Walls, roofs, doors, windows, and other architectural elements are then added over the underlying framework.

During the preliminary design, visual order is created by establishing a coordinated composition of forms and materials. As suggested previously, form composition establishes a theme or style that in turn furnishes a strong sense of visual order. Figure 9–4 illustrates the difference between a plan that lacks a consistent theme and one that has a strong coordination of the forms. The plan on the right side of Figure 9–4 possesses a sense of order due to a consistency of forms. So as you read Chapter 10 on form composition, keep in mind that one of the underlying objectives of this step is to give a sense of visual order to a design.

Within the context of a design theme or style, there are three ways order can be established in a design composition. These include symmetry, asymmetry, and mass collection.

Symmetry.   There are two distinctly different ways of organizing the elements of a design composition to achieve order: symmetry and asymmetry. Both approaches create an overall feeling of balance in the design, but in different ways. Balance is the perception that the various portions of the design are in equilibrium with each other (Figure 9–5). In the left example, balance is lacking; too many of

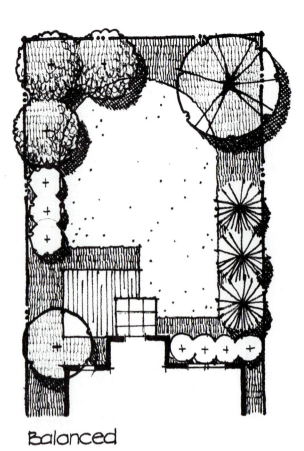

Unbalanced   Balanced

FIGURE 9–5
Balance is created when the visual weight of a design is evenly distributed.

the design's elements have been located on one side of the property, making this area seem "weighted." The other side of the site looks very "light." In the right example, the elements of the design have been placed so the visual weight is evenly distributed. Each element and area of the design balances the others.

Symmetry establishes balance in a design composition by arranging the elements of the design equally around one or more axes. Typically, what occurs on one side of the axis is repeated by mirror image on the other side of the axis (Figure 9–6). This automatically produces balance because both sides of the axis are equal. Symmetry is relatively easy to achieve. When used in a design, symmetry provides a formal character. Many historical gardens were designed on a symmetrical basis to demonstrate people's ability to control nature. Even in contemporary settings, symmetry has its place where the designer wishes to create a formal character. Any axis of a symmetrical layout also has the ability to direct views to an end point or terminus in the landscape. When done correctly, this can produce a very powerful design theme.

Asymmetry. The other primary way balance can be treated in a design composition is by asymmetry. With this approach, balance is produced more by feel than by equation as in symmetry. A good way to understand the principle of asymmetry is to think of a teeter-totter at the playground. Symmetrical balance is created when two children of the same size balance each other by sitting the same distance from the fulcrum (left side of Figure 9–7). However, when the children are not the same size, they must sit an unequal distance from the fulcrum, thus establishing asymmetrical balance (right side of Figure 9–7). Balance has been created with unequal parts by means of placement.

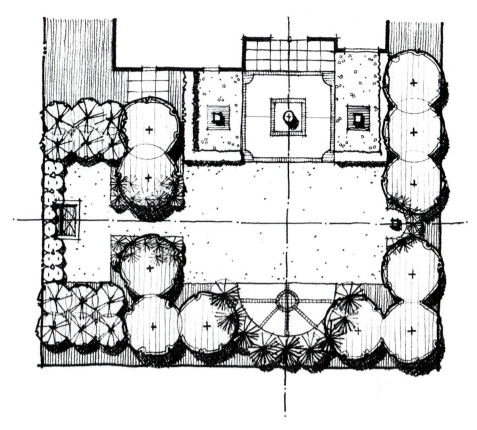

FIGURE 9–6
An example of a design that incorporates symmetrical balance around several axes.

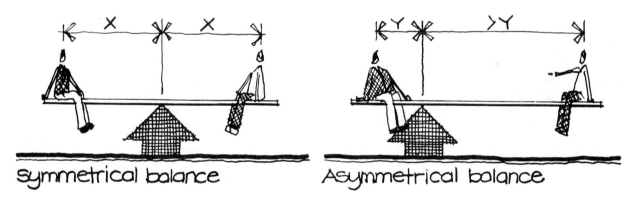

symmetrical balance   Asymmetrical balance

FIGURE 9–7
A comparison between the concepts of symmetry and asymmetry.

Compared to symmetry, a design balanced by asymmetry tends to feel more casual and informal (Figure 9–8). In addition, an asymmetrical design layout does not have only one or two major vantage points as a symmetrical design does. Instead, there are numerous points to view the design, each with a different perspective. Consequently, an asymmetrical design tends to invite movement through it to discover other areas and points of interest.

Mass Collection. Within the framework of either symmetry or asymmetry, mass collection is another method for establishing order in a design composition. Mass collection is the technique of grouping elements of a design together.

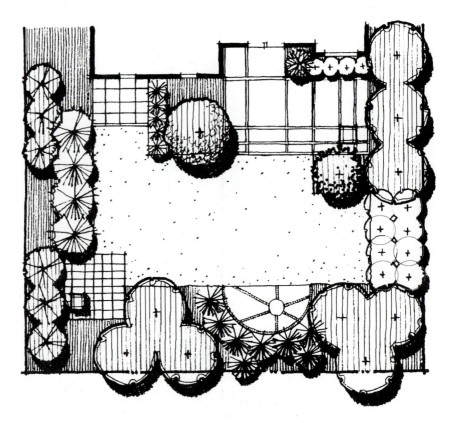

FIGURE 9–8
An example of a plan that incorporates asymmetrical balance.

Anytime the design elements are massed together in identifiable groups, a fundamental sense of order is created.

In residential site design all elements, such as pavement surfaces, walls, fences, plant materials, and so on, should also be massed together in the composition to establish order (right side of Figure 9–9). These elements should not be scattered (left side of Figure 9–9). This creates a chaotic and busy feeling in the composition. While this principle applies to all elements of a design, it has particular relevance in the arrangement of plant materials. One of the most important guidelines of planting design is to organize plant materials in masses (Figure 9–10). Additional suggestions for planting design are given in Chapter 11.

One approach to mass collection that furnishes an especially strong perception of order is to establish groups of similar elements within the masses of the composition. In planting design, plants of the same species would be grouped within the same mass (Figure 9–11).

As the designer begins to organize the layout of a design, it is important to consider how order (the overall structure) is going to be provided in the composition. It is advisable to establish a consistent theme or style along with mass collection and either symmetry or asymmetry to achieve this. The earlier the principle of order is taken into account in the design process, the better the results are apt to be.

Unity

The second principle of design that should be considered during the preliminary design is unity. Unity is the harmonious relationship among the elements of a design composition. While order establishes the overall organization of a design, unity provides an internal feeling of oneness within the design. The principle of unity influences how the size, shape, color, and texture of any element of a design will appear in the context of other elements of the design. When unity

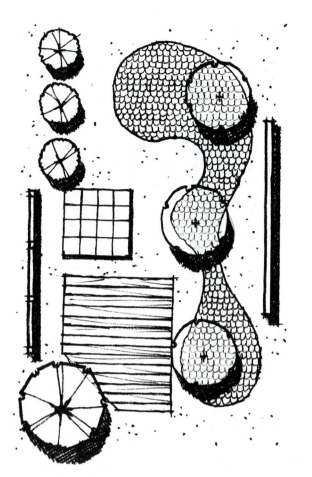

FIGURE 9-9
Order is created in the landscape when design elements are massed together.

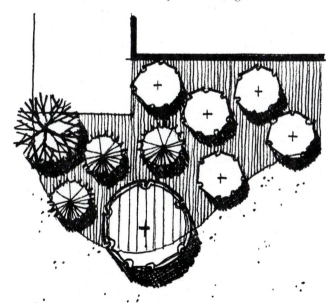

No! Plants are separated and scattered.

Yes! Plants are grouped together in masses.

FIGURE 9-10
Plant materials should be massed in groups to create order.

Preliminary Design and Design Principles

221

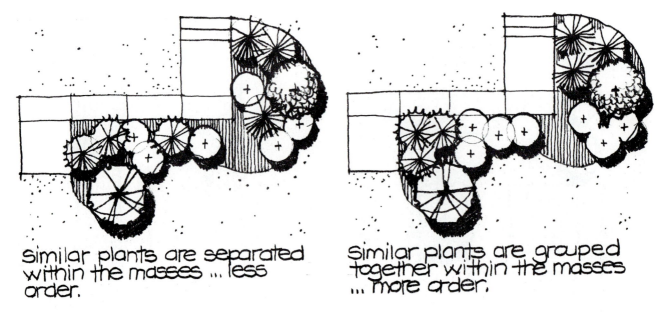

similar plants are separated within the masses ... less order.

similar plants are grouped together within the masses ... more order.

FIGURE 9-11
Similar plants should be massed together.

is achieved in a composition, all the elements of the design will feel like they were meant to go together.

In the previous section, it was described how order is established in trees, animals, and buildings. Using these same examples, unity in a tree can be seen in the similar size, shape, color, and texture of the leaves. In other words, the similarities among the leaves on a tree give it the appearance of being "one" tree. Hair and skin color are unifying elements on animals, while specific building materials and door/window types provide a sense of visual unity in a building.

Unity in landscape design is established using the principles of dominance, repetition, interconnection, and unity of three.

Dominance. Dominance is created in a design composition by making one element or a group of elements more prominent in comparison to others. The dominant element is an accent or focal point of the composition. A dominant element establishes a sense of unity in that all other elements in the composition appear subordinate or secondary to it. These other elements are visually unified by their common subordination because the differences among these secondary elements seem small in comparison to their difference with the dominant element.

Without a dominant element in a composition, the eye tends to wander restlessly throughout the composition (left side of Figure 9–12). Here, no one element or portion of the design "holds" the eye. When a focal point is introduced into this same composition, it functions like a visual magnet to pull the eye to it (right side of Figure 9–12).

An element or group of elements in a design can be made dominant by contrast in size, shape, color, and/or texture (Figure 9–13). In creating a focal point in this manner, there are several words of caution. The dominant element should have some qualities that are in common with the other elements of the composition so it feels like it is part of the composition. Furthermore, while there may be more than one accent within a design, there should not be so many as to create a chaotic situation where the eye moves continually from one accent to another without rest (Figure 9–14).

The principle of dominance can be applied to landscape design in a number of ways. One way is in the spatial organization of a design. A common fault of

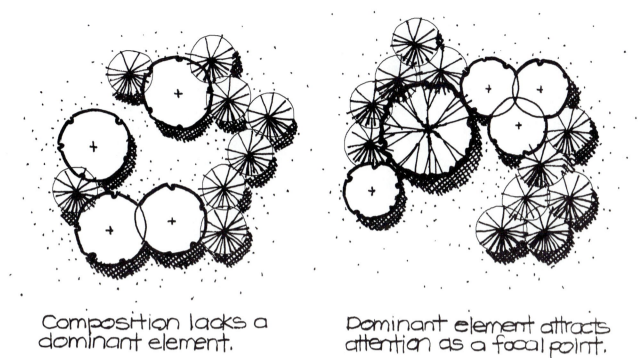

Composition lacks a
dominant element.

Dominant element attracts
attention as a focal point.

FIGURE 9–12
Dominance should be incorporated in a design composition.

many weak designs is the lack of a dominant space (left side of Figure 9–15). Without a dominant space, all the spaces seem rather equal in visual importance and function. A good landscape design typically possesses a hierarchy of spatial sizes with one or more spaces being dominant within the hierarchy. On some sites, a relatively large area of lawn establishes the dominant space (right side of Figure 9–15). On other sites, it is more appropriate for other spaces to be dominant, such as the outdoor entry foyer space (Figure 9–16) and the outdoor living and entertaining space (Figure 9–17).

Dominance can also be created on the residential site using an attractive water feature, a piece of sculpture, a prominent rock, or a spot of light at night. Each can draw the eye's attention in the landscape. In planting design, dominance can be created by shade trees, attractive plants like ornamental trees, flowering shrubs, flowers, or other unique plant forms (Figure 9–18).

Repetition. A second way unity can be created in a design composition is by repetition. Repetition is the principle of utilizing similar elements or elements with similar characteristics throughout a design composition. Figure 9–19 illustrates the extremes of no repetition and total repetition in a design. As shown on the left side, all the elements of the composition vary in size, shape, value (tone), and texture. This composition is too complex and consequently lacks unity. The right side shows all elements of the composition having similar size, shape, value, and texture. Here, there is a strong sense of visual unity owing to the commonality of all the elements.

No repetition or similarity results in a visually chaotic composition. Each element is seen as a unique item with no relationship to the other elements. On the other hand, total repetition, although providing unity, often results in monotony. The eye gets bored quickly when there is no variety. Therefore, the ideal approach is to repeat some elements throughout the design for the sake of unity while others vary for the purpose of maintaining visual interest (Figure 9–20). There should

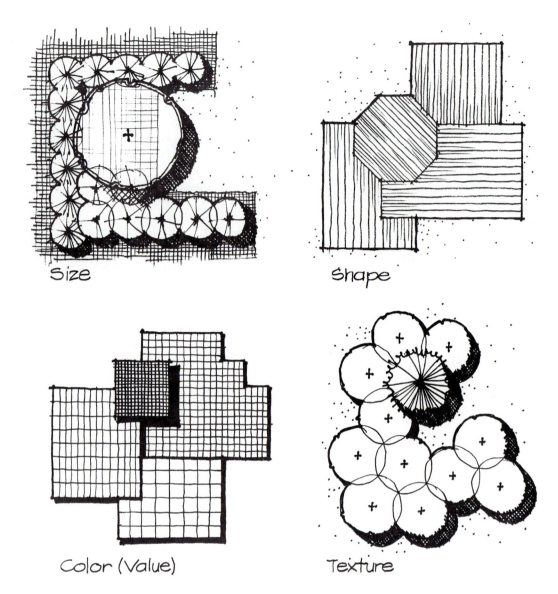

Size

Shape

Color (Value)

Texture

FIGURE 9-13
Dominance can be established by contrast of size, shape, color, and/or texture.

FIGURE 9-14
Too many competing accents in a composition create chaos.

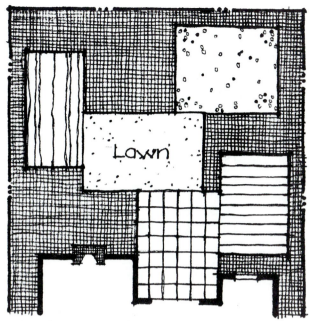

No dominant space.

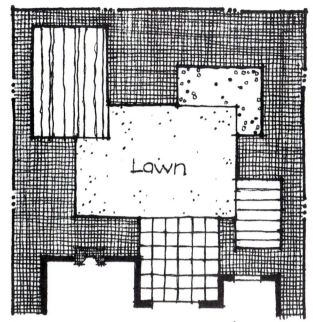

Lawn serves as a dominant space in the design.

FIGURE 9–15
One space should be dominant within a site design.

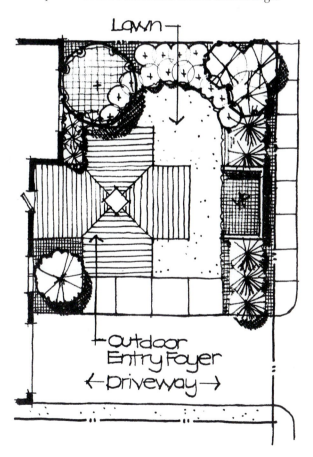

FIGURE 9–16
An example of the outdoor entry foyer serving as the dominant space.

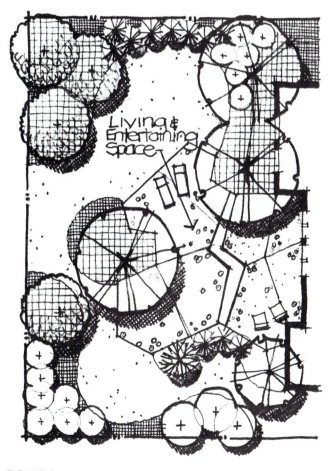

FIGURE 9–17
An example of the outdoor living and entertaining space serving as the dominant space.

Preliminary Design and Design Principles

FIGURE 9–18
An ornamental tree's unique habit of growth allows it to serve as a dominant visual element.

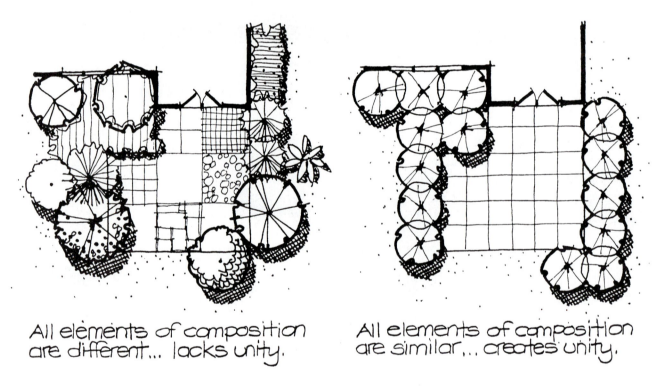

All elements of composition are different... lacks unity.

All elements of composition are similar... creates unity.

FIGURE 9–19
Unity can be created in a design composition when all the elements are similar in appearance.

be a balance between variety and repetition. Unfortunately, there is no formula for providing this balance.

The principle of repetition can be utilized in residential site design in several ways. First, the number of different elements and materials should be minimized in any area of a design. For example, only one or two pavement materials should be used in an outdoor space because too many pavement materials can be visually dis-

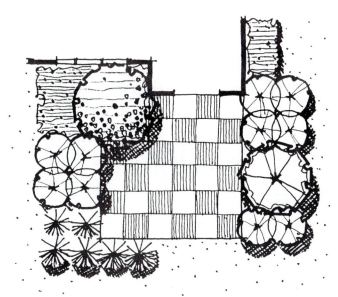

FIGURE 9–21
The repetition of brick on the house, low wall, and pavement provides visual unity.

ruptive. The designer should also limit the number of different plant materials used in any one area. A design resembling a botanical museum, containing many different types of plants, should be avoided regardless of the temptation to do otherwise.

Having limited the number of elements and materials utilized in a design, the next step should be to skillfully repeat these throughout the design. When the eye sees the same element or material placed at various locations in the design, visual recall is created. That is, the eye and mind make a connection between the two locations and mentally link them together. This, in turn, provides unity. One application of this is to use a particular material on the facade of the house and again on walls, fences, or pavement in the landscape (Figure 9–21).

Preliminary Design and Design Principles

227

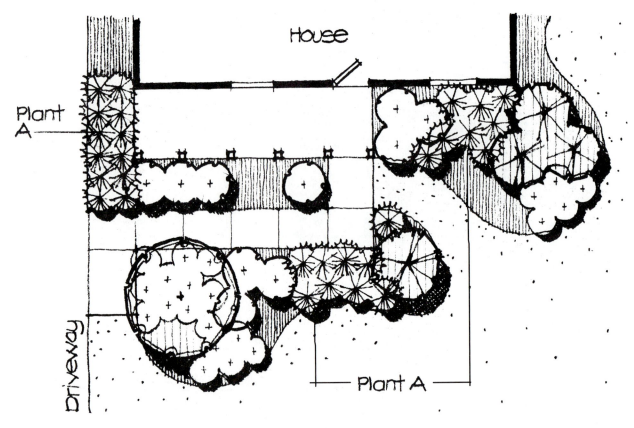

FIGURE 9-22
Selected plant materials should be repeated throughout a planting area.

A similar concept can also be applied in planting design. While only five types of plants plus ground cover have been used in Figure 9–22, they have been woven throughout the composition. Note how the low evergreen shrub material ("A") has been placed at three locations for visual recall. Also, not every plant has been repeated. Some plants appear only once in the design for variety and accent. Thus, an attempt is made to strike a balance between repetition and variety.

Interconnection. A third way unity can be established in a design composition is by interconnection. Interconnection is the principle whereby various elements or parts of the design are physically linked or tied together. When interconnection is successfully utilized, the eye can move smoothly from one element to another without interruption.

There are several ways the principle of interconnection can be applied to residential site design. On the left side of Figure 9–23, the different areas of the design are segmented. The plan lacks unity because it is fragmented into a number of isolated parts that have little or no visual relationship among each other. On the right side of Figure 9–23, the same elements of the design have been revised so that the diverse areas of the plan physically connect. The previously isolated parts of the design have now been moved together to touch each other and new elements have been introduced to connect the separated ones. The revised plan has a continuity that helps to provide unity. This desirable approach to residential site design reinforces the need to consider the entire site or design area together as one large composition rather than as a number of smaller, separated parts that are merely pieced together.

The same idea can be applied to planting design as well. The left side of Figure 9–24 shows a scattering of isolated plants in a lawn area. Again, this type of

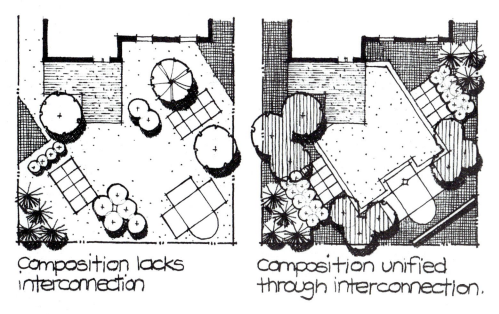

Composition lacks interconnection

Composition unified through interconnection.

FIGURE 9-23
The different spaces and elements of the site should be interconnected.

FIGURE 9-24
A ground cover bed can act as an interconnecting element in a planting composition.

arrangement lacks unity and is difficult to maintain. When these same plant materials are placed in a common ground cover or mulch bed as depicted in the right side of Figure 9–24, the eye is able to associate the plants with each other more easily owing to the visual interconnection of the bed on the ground plane.

Interconnection can be appreciated in the third dimension as well. A mass of shrubs, fence, wall, etc. can be used to physically link what otherwise would be separate elements of a landscape composition (Figure 9–25 and 9–26).

Unity of Three. The fourth means for achieving unity in a design composition is by unity of three. Whenever three similar elements are grouped together, a sense of unity is almost automatically achieved. Three of a kind, as opposed to two or four of a kind, provides a strong sense of unity. When the eye perceives an even number in a grouping, there is a tendency to divide it in half (Figure 9–27). A quantity of three is not easily split in half and therefore is seen as one group (Figure 9–28). As a general rule of thumb, it is better to use odd numbers than even numbers of elements in a single composition, although this is not a guideline to be applied

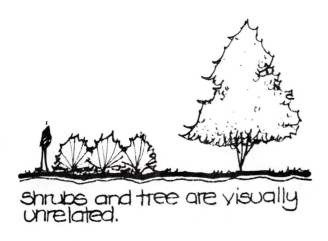

shrubs and tree are visually unrelated.

Low shrubs interconnect tree with other shrubs to create a unified composition.

FIGURE 9–25
An example of low shrubs serving as interconnecting elements.

No interconnection.

Fence and low plants establish interconnection.

FIGURE 9–26
An example of low shrubs and a fence serving as interconnecting elements.

thoughtlessly. For example, when there is a large number of plant materials in a composition, such as six, seven, eight, or more, the eye may see this as a group and not be able to detect whether there is an even or odd number. But when there are two, three, four, or five plants in a group, the eye can quickly depict even and odd amounts. However, there are some occasions when an even number of elements actually functions better than an odd number of elements, especially when there is a desire to achieve symmetry.

Rhythm

The third basic principle of design that should be utilized in preliminary design is rhythm. While order and unity deal with the overall organization of a design and the relationship of the elements within that organization, rhythm in a composition addresses the factors of time and movement. When we experience a design, whether it be a two-dimensional graphic layout or a three-dimensional spatial composition, as is the case in residential site design, we do so over a period of time. But we rarely see and experience a complete landscape design instantaneously.

We tend to view various portions of a composition in sequence, often mentally collecting them to form patterns. It is the spacing and timing of these patterns that give a design a dynamic, changing quality. This might be understood more

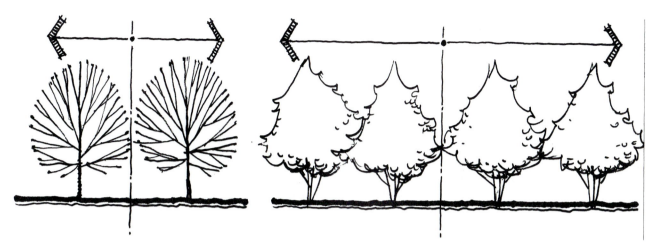

FIGURE 9–27
There is a tendency to visually split two or four elements of the same kind in a composition.

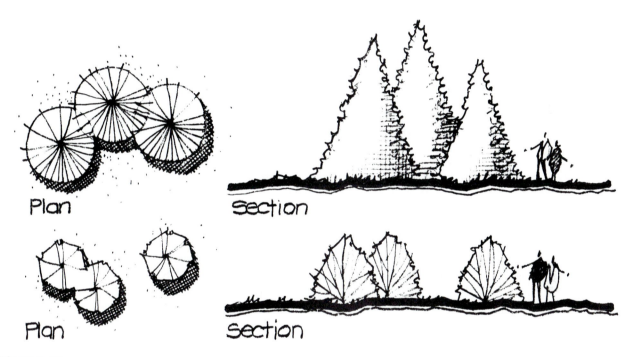

FIGURE 9–28
Groups of three similar elements in a composition have a strong sense of visual unity.

easily by thinking of rhythm in music. Here, rhythm is formed by the underlying sequence of notes, often referred to as the beat. The beat is a recognizable pattern that provides a dynamic structure to a musical piece, and it influences the timing of how we experience the music. Among numerous possibilities, it may be slow and casual or rapid and forceful.

Four ways rhythm can be created in residential site design are repetition, alternation, inversion, and gradation.

Repetition. The principle of repetition as it applies to rhythm differs slightly from the use of repetition for unity. To develop rhythm, repetition is used by repeating elements or a group of elements within a design to create an obvious sequence. For example, Figure 9–29 shows four different examples of elements repeated in linear sequences. In each, the eye moves from element to element in a

FIGURE 9–29
The repetition of elements in a sequence establishes visual rhythm.

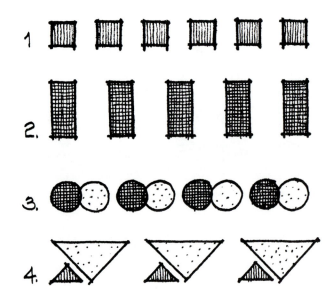

rhythmic pattern, like the beat in music. In these examples, the spacing between the elements determines the character and pace of the rhythm. In residential site design, this principle applies to such elements as pavement, fences, walls, and plant materials (Figure 9–30). Again, the spacing of elements in these examples is critical in establishing the pace of the rhythm.

Alternation.   The second type of rhythm is alternation. To create this, it is easiest to first establish a sequential pattern based on repetition. Then certain elements of the sequence are changed or altered on a regular basis (Figure 9–31). Thus, a rhythmic pattern based on alternation has more variation and sometimes more visual interest than one based only on repetition. The altered elements can furnish an aspect of surprise and relief in the sequence. As with repetition for unity, repetition for rhythm can get to be rather monotonous if it is overused. Figure 9–32 shows how alternation has been incorporated in the examples shown previously in Figure 9–30.

Inversion.   Inversion is a particular type of alternation in which selected elements are changed so their characteristics are in contrast with the initial elements of the sequence. In other words, the altered elements are inverted in comparison to the other elements. Big becomes small, wide becomes narrow, tall changes to short, and so on. Consequently, the changes that occur in this type of sequence can be dramatic and noticeable. Inversion can be incorporated in a landscape design in various ways (Figure 9–33).

Gradation.   Gradation is created by a gradual change in one or more characteristics of the repeated element of the sequence. For example, the repeated element in a rhythmic sequence may slowly increase in size (Figures 9–34 and 9–35). Or the characteristics of color, texture, and form may also vary as the sequence progresses. The change that occurs in gradation provides visual stimulation, but without causing sudden or incongruous relationships among the elements of the composition.

Pavement

Fence

Wall

Planting

As can be seen from the previous sections, the design principles of order, unity, and rhythm can have a direct influence on the visual qualities of a design. They affect the location of elements in a composition as well as the size, form, color, and texture of the elements. During preliminary design, the designer should constantly keep these principles in mind when making key decisions about the appearance of the design. Like other aids in design, design principles are only helpful guidelines that should be carefully applied. They are not recipes for design success.

DOCUMENTING PRECONCEIVED DESIGN IDEAS

As the design process proceeds into preliminary design where some realism takes effect, a designer may have some preconceived ideas for design elements and their materials, patterns, character, etc. It may help to stop and document any ideas that may exist. It is not that these ideas represent the final design decisions, but these ideas should be documented before they are forgotten.

It is good to record ideas through the development of a "character palette." Figure 9–36 shows an elevation of a house (top of figure). The drawing below it is a "character palette." It is a group of design ideas for patios, fences, and overheads that are developed based solely upon the architectural character of the house. It is developed by "pretending" that selected patterns of the architecture could be adapted to resemble landscape structures. The following chart shows

Preliminary Design and Design Principles

233

FIGURE 9–31
Alternation of size, shape, color, and/or texture can establish visual rhythm in a composition.

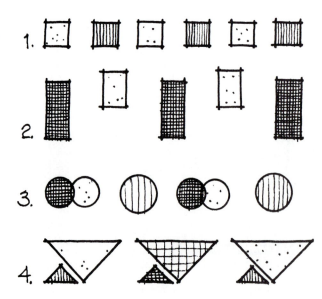

FIGURE 9–32
Alternation can be used to establish visual rhythm in different design elements.

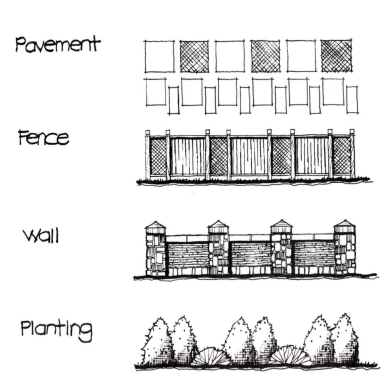

Pavement

Fence

Wall

Planting

the relationship between the design ideas in the character palette and the feature of the house each design idea was modeled after.

Design Idea	Architectureal Feature
Patio "A"	Decorative Vent over Garage Door
Patio "B"	Main Window in right Gable of House
Patio "C"	Double Gable at Left Side of House
Fence "A"	Front Porch Railing and Archway
Fence "B"	Top Left Gable with Diamond Pattern
Overhead	Front Porch Archway and Roof

Chapter 9   Preliminary Design and Design Principles

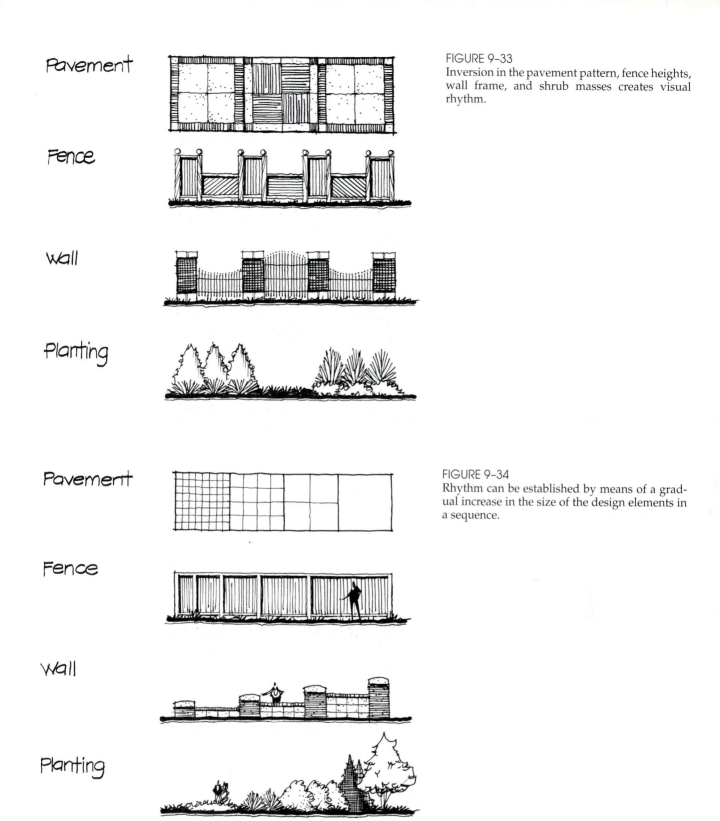

Pavement

Fence

Wall

Planting

Pavement

Fence

Wall

Planting

FIGURE 9–34
Rhythm can be established by means of a gradual increase in the size of the design elements in a sequence.

    If you were to look carefully at each of these mini-designs in the character palette, you would notice that the general pattern of each architectural feature selected was transformed into a landscape structure for the hardscape. Exact replication is not necessary. It is not important to use each and every portion or detail of the architectural feature. The emphasis is to pretend and explore ways that

Preliminary Design and Design Principles

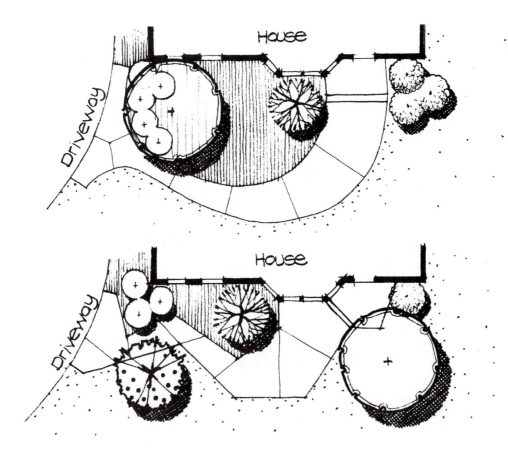

FIGURE 9-35
A gradual change in the width of a walk provides visual rhythm.

existing characteristics of the house can be blended into the character of the land-scape. It is a design effort that one can undertake to provide opportunities to enhance and enrich their exploratory techniques in developing design alternatives.

SUMMARY

Preliminary design is the most realistic and comprehensive phase to this point in the design process. It is based on all the previous steps, though it goes beyond these in scope and detail. While many of the earlier steps gathered important information and developed fundamental concepts for the design, preliminary design emphasizes the visual and emotional aspects of design. The designer's own intuition and feel for aesthetics are key in creating an exciting and pleasurable preliminary design solution. While basic design principles and other guidelines can aid the designer, ultimately the designer must also rely on a personal sense of what works and looks appropriate.

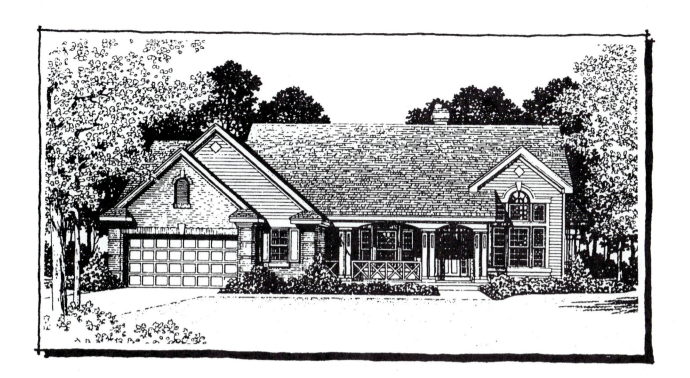

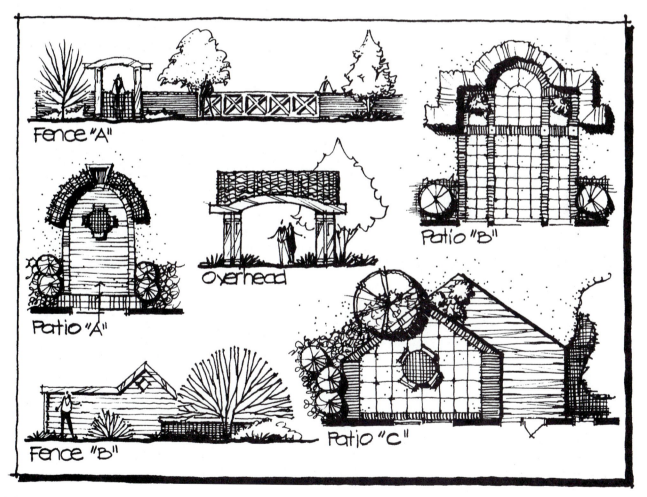

FIGURE 9–36
A "character palette" can help to record your preconceived design ideas that relate to the architectural character of the house.
Design #N3600/N3601 (top) © Home Planners, LLC Wholly owned by Hanley-Wood, LLC. Blueprints available, 800-322-6797.

Preliminary Design and Design Principles

10

Form Composition

INTRODUCTION

Chapter 9 outlined key thoughts about the preliminary design phase of the design process and made reference to two critical undertakings of preliminary design: (1) form composition and (2) spatial composition. While these two aspects are separated in this book to clarify explanation, they are usually considered and studied jointly while a design solution is being developed.

This chapter presents the purpose of form composition, fundamental principles on which form composition is based, different form compositional themes and their potential uses, the relationship of form composition to existing structures, and a process for developing form composition studies for a residential project.

DEFINITION AND PURPOSE

Form composition can be defined as the process of converting the approximate area outlines of the functional diagram to specific forms to create visual order. The general edge or outline of each space in the functional diagram is given a definite location and shape during form composition. Figure 10–1 shows the graphic difference between a functional diagram and six different form compositions for the same diagram. The spaces in all three compositions are similar in size, proportion, and function to the outlines on the functional diagram, but their edges are more precise in form and location.

Some typical examples of edges of spaces in the outdoor environment include edges between the following:

- planting bed and lawn
- terrace and lawn

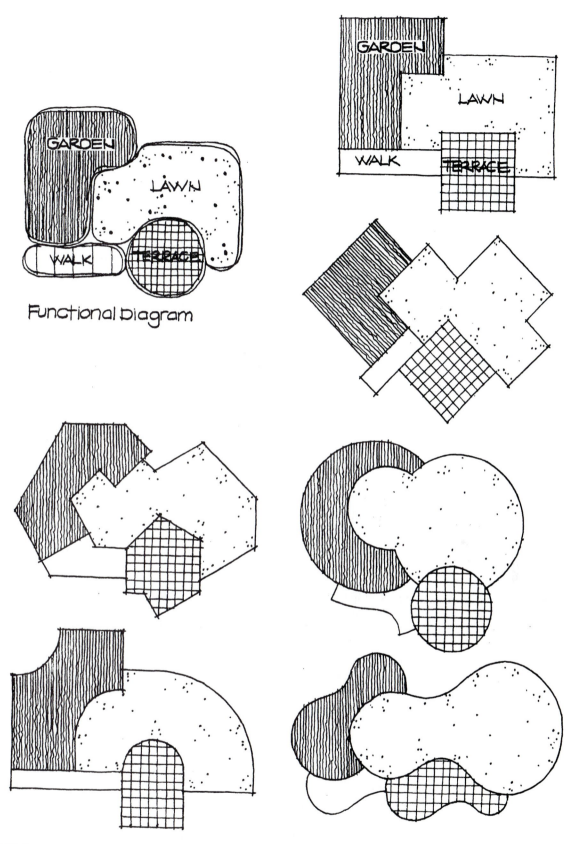

FIGURE 10-1
A graphic comparison between a functional diagram and six different form compositions.

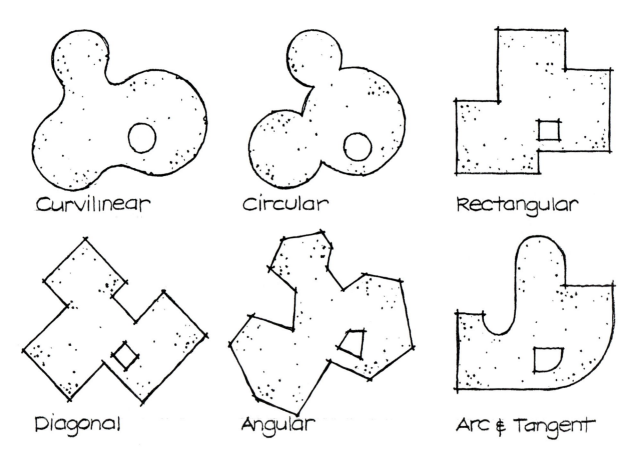

FIGURE 10-2
Potential visual themes created during form composition.

- entrance walk and planting bed
- driveway and entrance walk
- steps and adjoining pavement
- deck and terrace

In addition to establishing the exact edges of forms of a design, form composition also creates a visual theme. A visual theme provides a sense of consistency and harmony because it is created by the repetition of particular forms throughout the design. As pointed out in Chapter 9, this consistency of forms is one of the essential means for providing order in a landscape design. Particular forms may be selected based on 1) the intended style of garden design (Italian Renaissance, English, Colonial, Victorian, Japanese, California, Post Modernism, etc.), 2) a desired garden character (informal, structured, organic, passive, casual, wooded, flowing), or 3) characteristics of the site. While there are a number of potential design themes that can be created for a residential design, some of the more common themes based on geometric shapes include: (1) circular, (2) curvilinear, (3) rectangular, (4) diagonal, (5) arc and tangent, and (6) angular. These are illustrated in Figure 10-2.

While functional diagrams establish an invisible framework that is only indirectly seen or felt, a design theme provides an order that can be directly seen. The lines of the design theme establish a consistent order of forms that harmoniously relate all the elements and spaces of the design to each other (left side of Figure 10-3). Without a consistent design theme, a design is apt to break apart into a number of visually unrelated parts (right side of Figure 10-3).

Form composition establishes a two-dimensional base which serves as the foundation for the walls and ceiling of outdoor space added during spatial com-

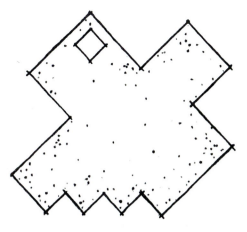

A consistent visual theme provides visual order.

An inconsistent visual theme breaks apart into unrelated parts.

FIGURE 10-3
A consistent visual theme should be used in form composition to establish order.

position. Collectively, all three of these planes of spatial enclosure can establish a distinct character or personality that is actually experienced.

Form composition is a critical step of the design process because it directly affects the aesthetics of a space. Most people are not able to determine whether or not a design works well functionally without studying or living with it for a period of time. On the other hand, people react almost immediately to the forms they see within the design. Often, a quick subjective approval or disapproval of the design is based on the visual structure created by the composition of forms.

GEOMETRY OF FORMS

Most design themes, including those described in this book, are strongly related to two fundamental geometric shapes: the circle and the square. Visually pleasing design compositions are usually based on sensitive relationships between these two shapes (or their component parts), while visually disturbing compositions fail to consider them. It is important to understand these two forms when creating a design composition because both shapes have a number of inherent geometric characteristics and components that influence their use in design.

The Circle

Among the many and varied forms we see in the world around us, the circle stands out as being unique. Due to its simplicity and completeness, the circle has often been described as the most pure or perfect form.

The circle has a number of components which are critical to its use in a design composition. These are the: (1) center, (2) circumference, (3) radii, (4) extended radii, (5) diameter, and (6) tangent (Figure 10–4). The center is, of course, the middle point of the circle. It is the place where all radii and diameters meet and/or cross each other. The circumference, or outer edge of the circle, defines the limits or edge of the circle. Radii are lines that originate at the center of the circle and extend outward to the circumference. Extended radii are similar, but extend beyond the circle's circumference. The diameter is a line that extends from one side of the circle to the

FIGURE 10-4
Component parts of the circle.

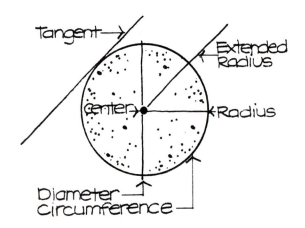

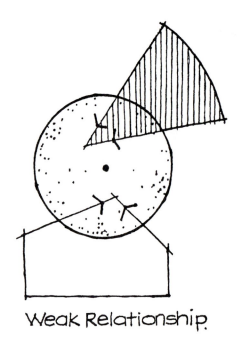

Weak Relationship

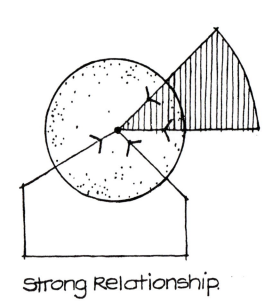

Strong Relationship

FIGURE 10-5
Lines should relate to the circle's center to create a visually strong composition.

other and passes directly through the center. A tangent is a line that touches the circumference while also establishing a right angle (90 degrees) with a radius.

Among all the circle's component parts, the center is perhaps the most important of all. First, the center is a point which inherently attracts attention. Most people can estimate the location of the center of a circle rather easily with a pencil or pen. Furthermore, the radii, extended radii, and diameters pass through the center reinforcing its position and importance. So, one of the first considerations for designing with a circle is to realize that any line that directly points to a circle's center will create a strong relationship with the circle (right side of Figure 10–5). Lines that don't point to the circle's center are apt to seem awkward or unrelated in their relationship with the circle (left side of Figure 10–5).

In a similar fashion, the manner in which lines and forms meet the circle's circumference helps determine whether or not a composition is successful. Those compositions in which lines meet the circle's circumference by utilizing an extended radius are apt to be more pleasing than those that don't (Figure 10–6). In other words, lines and edges which form a 90-degree relationship to a circle's circumference are more stable looking than compositions that lack this relationship.

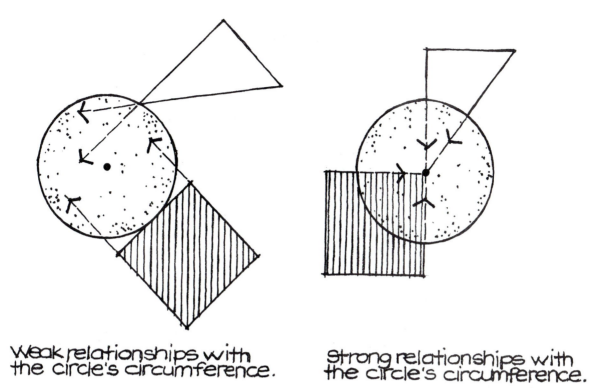

Weak relationships with the circle's circumference.

Strong relationships with the circle's circumference.

FIGURE 10-6
Lines should meet the circle's circumference at 90 degrees.

Because design involves the development of alternative ideas, it is important to realize that numerous design compositions can be generated by exploring the relationships possible among the basic components of a specific form. Each of the circle's components has the potential of becoming a form generator when combined with another component. Many design ideas are possible by utilizing two, three, four, or all five of the circle components (Figure 10–7). This type of activity can stimulate design creativity and make designing an exciting process.

Equilateral polygons can be used in developing design compositions and can be formed within a circle. The forms presented here are: (1) triangle (three sides), (2) square (four sides), (3) pentagon (five sides), (4) hexagon (six sides), and (5) octagon (eight sides).

Figures 10–8 through 10–12 illustrate how each of these polygons are formed within a circle respectively.

The Square

A square, unlike a circle, is often considered a man-made form because it is comprised of straight lines and is not found in nature. The square is also a formal form, owing to its symmetrical structure. All four sides are equal in length and the interior angles each measure 90 degrees. A square's configuration suggests an axis (a centerline) which divides the form into equal halves. There are two noticeable axes in a square which pass through its center and are parallel to the sides (Figure 10–13).

A square has four definite directions of orientation because of its clearly delineated and separate sides. Unlike a circle, the square does not face outward in all directions (Figure 10–14). These four directions create blind spots at the square's corners. This reinforces the axial nature of the square. Despite their differences, the circle and square do have one important common characteristic: Each can fit within the form of the other (Figure 10–15).

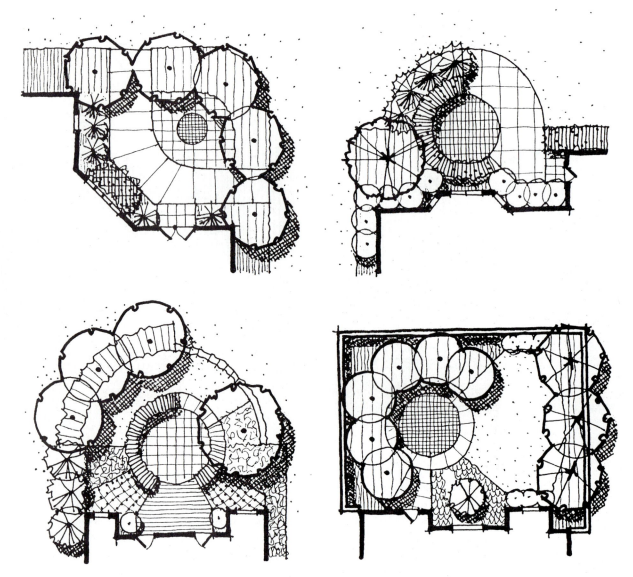

FIGURE 10–7
Various design compositions are possible when focusing on the component parts of a circle.

There are six specific components of a square that are important to form composition. They are: (1) sides, (2) extended sides, (3) axes, (4) extended axes, (5) diagonals, and (6) extended diagonals (Figure 10–16).

Experimentation and exploration with different combinations of the square's components, like with the circle's components, can lead to the development of creative design compositions (Figure 10–17).

Another idea for developing compositions with a square is to use it as a modular grid. The grid can be formed within the square by subdividing it into smaller squares of equal dimensions. For example, these smaller squares can be one-half, one-quarter, or one-third the length of the original square's sides. Once drawn, the grid can suggest an almost endless number of compositional possibilities (Figure 10–18). Diagonals can be added to the previous grids to provide different design compositions (Figure 10–19).

As has been shown, the circle and square along with their component parts are the foundation for a limitless variety of design compositions. It is important for the designer to explore these two geometric forms and their components to increase creative skills. As one engages in this type of activity, new forms are discovered which give rise to new ideas.

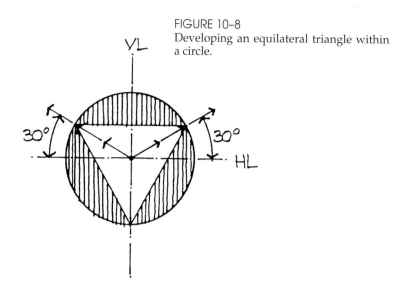

FIGURE 10-8
Developing an equilateral triangle within a circle.

Vertical Line
(VL)

Equilateral Triangle

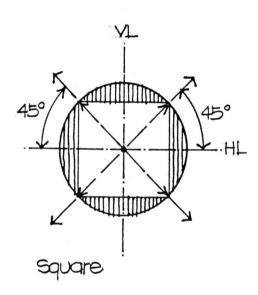

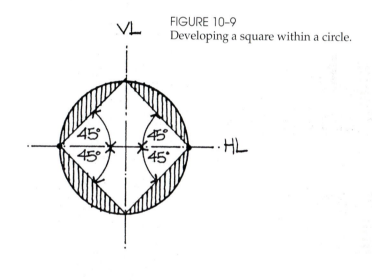

FIGURE 10-9
Developing a square within a circle.

Square

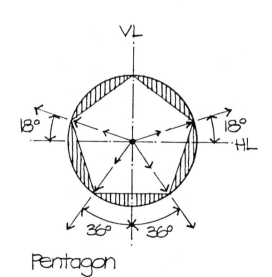

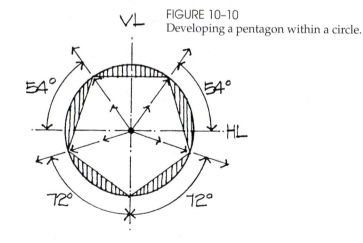

FIGURE 10-10
Developing a pentagon within a circle.

Pentagon

Form Composition

FIGURE 10–11
Developing a hexagon within a circle.

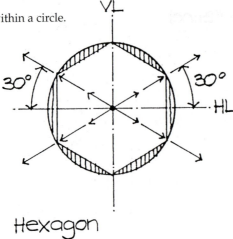
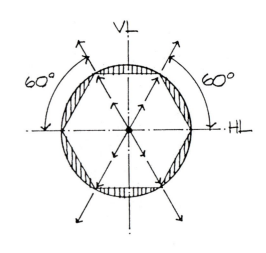

Hexagon

FIGURE 10–12
Developing an octagon within a circle.

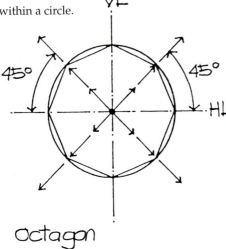
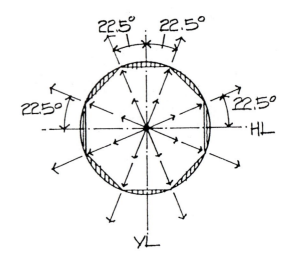

Octagon

FIGURE 10–13
The square is inherently divided by two axes
which are parallel to its sides and pass through
the center.

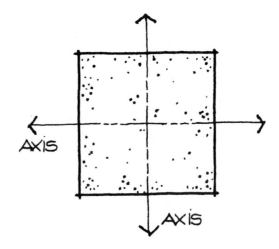

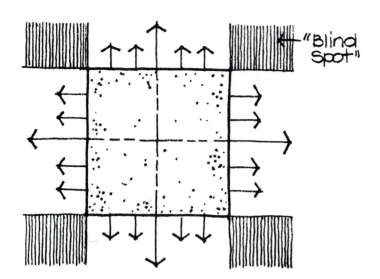

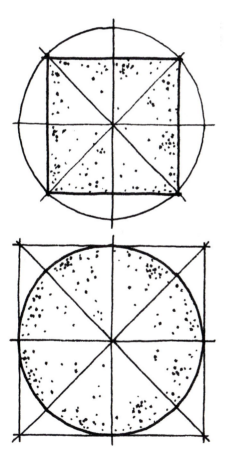

FIGURE 10-14
Unlike the circle, the square does not face outward in all directions.

FIGURE 10-15
The form of the circle and square fit within each other.

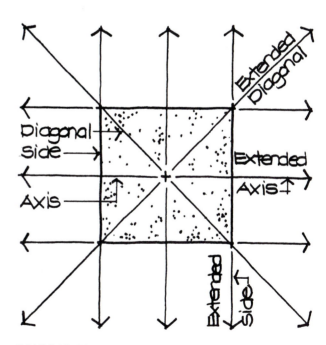

FIGURE 10-16
Component parts of the square.

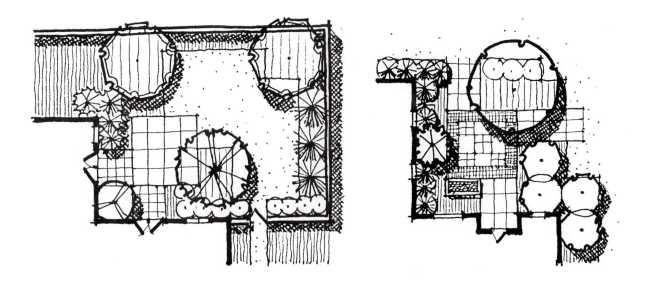

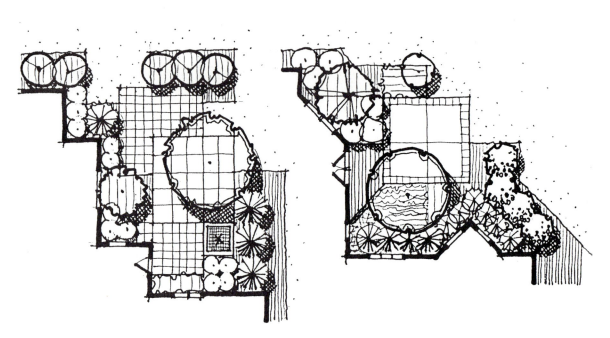

FIGURE 10–17
Various design compositions are possible when focusing on the component parts of a square.

Guidelines for Combining Forms

In creating form compositions, the designer must also consider the relationships between adjoining forms and their component parts. These relationships are referred to as form-to-form relationships.

When any two or more forms are combined, attention should be given to the relationship established among the forms' components. Figure 10–20 shows two different compositions, each consisting of the same forms. The difference between these compositions is the relative positioning of the forms within each composition. It should be obvious that composition "B" seems more organized, while composition "A" tends to suggest random placement of forms. The organization of composition "B" is based on a conscious application of four sound guidelines for

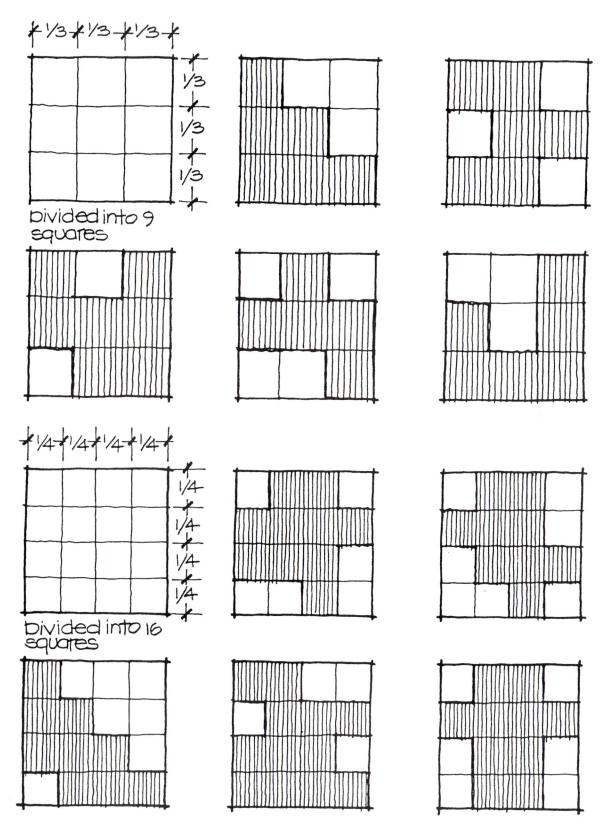

FIGURE 10–18
A modular grid can be created within a square as the basis for design compositions.

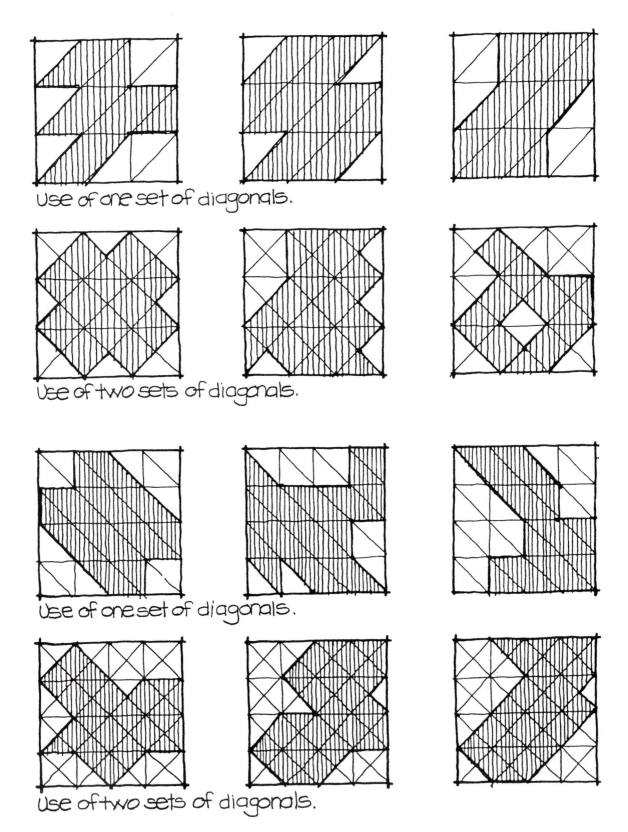

Use of one set of diagonals.

Use of two sets of diagonals.

Use of one set of diagonals.

Use of two sets of diagonals.

FIGURE 10-19
A diagonal grid can also be used to create design compositions.

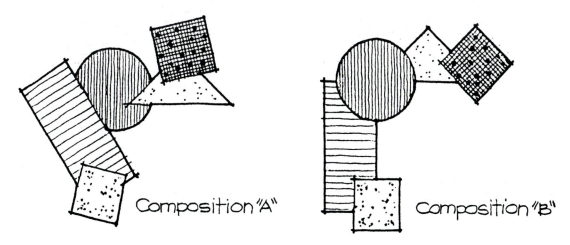

FIGURE 10–20
Form-to-form relationships are important in establishing visually attractive design compositions.

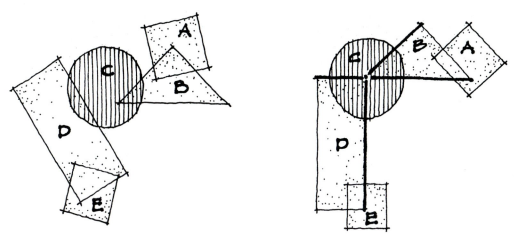

FIGURE 10–21
Component parts of adjoining forms should coincide and align with each other.

combining forms. They are 1) aligning component parts, 2) avoiding acute angles, 3) establishing form identity, and 4) form domination.

The first and foremost guideline is that the component parts of each form coincide, or be aligned, with the location of the component parts of adjoining forms. For example, notice the alignment of the various components in the composition on the right side of Figure 10–21. An extended radius of the circle (C) also serves as a side to the isosceles triangle (B) and is aligned with a side of the rectangle (D). Also, two sides of the triangle and two sides of the rectangle are extended radii of the circle. A corner of the rectangle is also the center of the square. By contrast, the internal relationship of the components on the left side of Figure 10–21 has an absence of sensitive form-to-form relationships. Here, none of the forms' components align with each other. This composition is, of course, considered to be very weak.

The second guideline for combining forms together is to avoid the creation of acute angles. An acute angle is one having less than 45 degrees. Figure 10–22 shows a variety of form compositions with acute angles. Although some of the compositions may at first seem fairly well organized and visually acceptable, some of the relationships of lines and shapes within them create disturbing acute angles. These acute angles should be avoided for the following reasons:

1. They create visually weak relationships between forms and are points of visual tension.

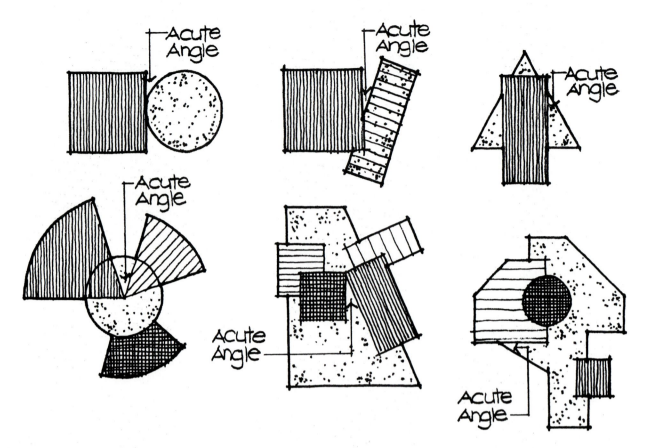

FIGURE 10-22
Acute angles should be avoided in design compositions.

FIGURE 10-23
Acute angles in pavement create areas that are subject to cracking and breaking.

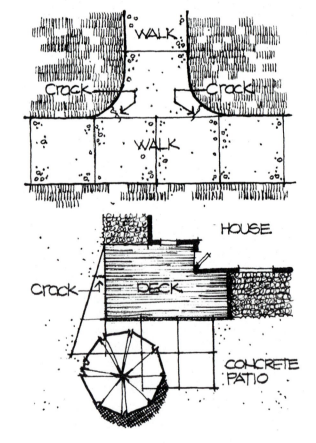

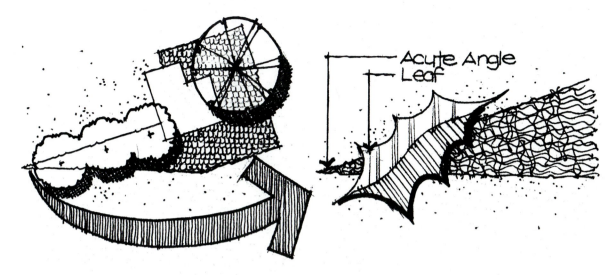

FIGURE 10-24
Acute angles in planting beds form areas that are too small to plant within.

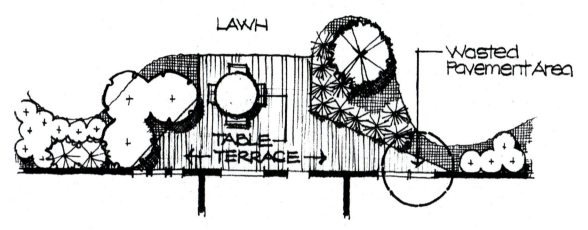

FIGURE 10-25
Acute angles within outdoor spaces create wasted areas.

2. When created within or at the edge of pavement areas, they create areas that are structurally weak and subject to breaking and cracking (Figure 10–23). The narrow angular piece of material in this area has the tendency to crack, especially in the cycle of freezing and thawing.

3. When acute angles are formed at the edge of a planting bed, they create areas where it is difficult, if not impossible, to grow shrubs or even ground cover (Figure 10–24).

4. When acute angles make up a portion of a space intended for people to use, such as an eating space or an entertainment space, they produce a wasted and useless area because of their extremely narrow dimensions (Figure 10–25).

The third guideline for combining forms is to establish form identity. Form identity refers to the ability of individual shapes within a composition to be identifiable and legible as distinct forms. For example, the circle and square shown in the composition in Figure 10–26 can be seen as identifiable shapes, with each lending some of its character to the overall composition. On the other hand, Figure 10–27 illustrates shapes within the composition which do not lend adequate visual support

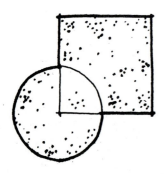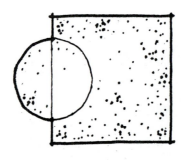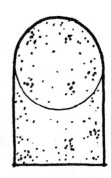

FIGURE 10–26
Examples of strong compositions where each individual form is identifiable and legible.

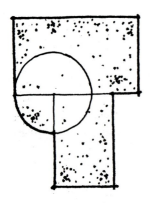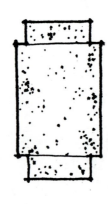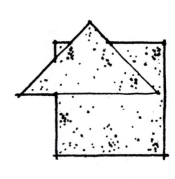

FIGURE 10–27
Examples of weak compositions where some of the individual forms are lost within the others.

to the total composition. Some of the forms are nearly "lost" inside others. When this occurs, it is best to either eliminate the lost form or increase its identity by changing its size or position.

One last guideline for combining forms is to have one form dominate in a composition. This provides greater form identity and adheres to the principle of dominance discussed in Chapter 9. A dominant form establishes a visual accent and provides a resting place for the eye (Figure 10–28).

In summary, these four guidelines for combining forms in a composition are valuable in organizing forms. While there may be some instances where these guidelines will not be suitable, in most cases they should be considered.

DESIGN THEMES

Earlier in this chapter, Figure 10–2 illustrated a variety of design themes comprised of different sets of forms and lines. These six themes provide the designer with compositional options for creating visual structure in a landscape design. Some themes are comprised of only one type of form while others include two. Rarely, however, will more than two different forms work together to create a recognizably consistent theme.

The following sections discuss characteristics of each of these themes along with their potential uses on residential design projects.

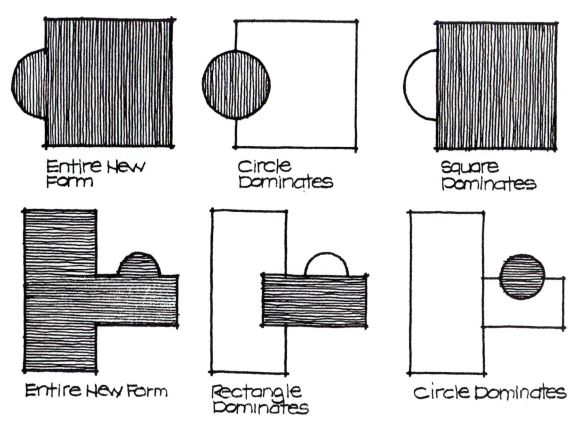

FIGURE 10-28
One form in a composition should usually dominate.

FIGURE 10-29
Two types of circular design themes.

Circular Theme

A design theme made up primarily of circles or portions of circles is called a circular theme (Figure 10–29). Two potential types of circular themes are overlapping circles and concentric circles.

Overlapping Circles. Overlapping circles create a composition with relatively "soft" edges. There are several guidelines for creating overlapping circular themes.

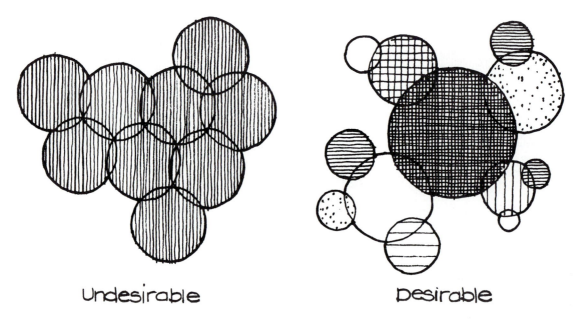

Undesirable   Desirable

FIGURE 10-30
One circle within an overlapping circular theme should dominate.

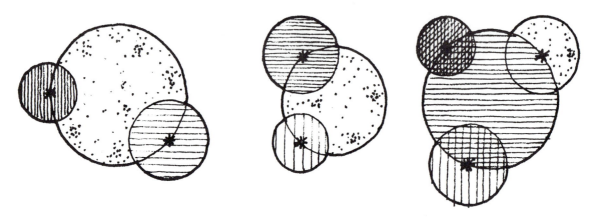

FIGURE 10-31
The circumference of each circle should pass through or near the center of adjoining circles.

First, it is desirable to use a variety of circle sizes. As suggested in Chapter 9, each composition should have a dominant space or form. Thus, one circular area of the composition should stand out as being the prominent element (Figure 10–30). Such a circular area could be used as a lawn area, a major entertaining and living space, or another important area of a design. Other spaces of the design should be smaller in size, although they should not all be the same size.

Secondly, when overlapping two circles, it is recommended that the circumference of one circle pass through or near the center of the other circle (Figure 10–31). There are two reasons for this. First, if there is too much overlap, then one circle is apt to lose its identity, being too much inside the other circle (left side of Figure 10–32). On the other hand, if there is not enough overlap between the circles, then acute angles are likely to occur (right side of Figure 10–32).

An overlapping circular theme has several qualities. First, it provides several distinct, though still related, parts. This is advantageous where there are a number of distinct functions or spaces that comprise a design. An overlapping circular theme also has many directions or feelings of orientation. Such a composition can focus on several points in the landscape (Figure 10–33).

Too much overlap among circles.

Too little overlap among circles.

Acute Angles

FIGURE 10–32
Weak circular compositions are created when there is too much or too little overlap among the circles.

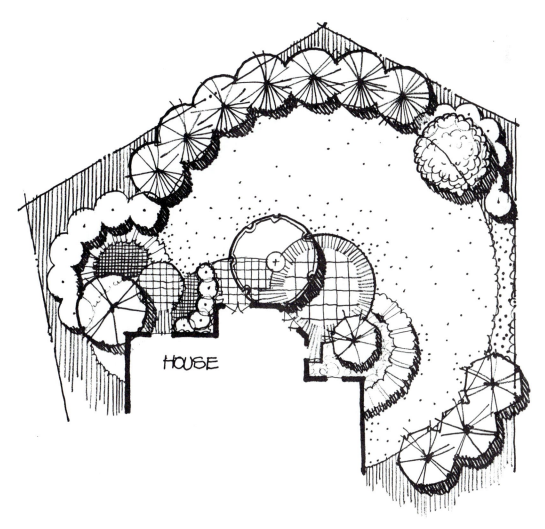

HOUSE

FIGURE 10–33
An overlapping circular theme can create several places to look out at the surrounding landscape.

Form Composition

FIGURE 10–34
Each circle in an overlapping circular theme can be treated as a separate terrace on a sloped site.

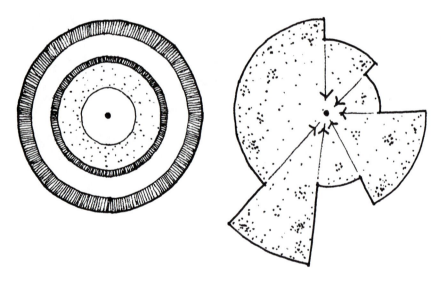

FIGURE 10–35
The center of the circle is the focus of attention in a concentric circular theme.

Because of the repetition of the circles, an overlapping circular theme is best situated on level ground or on a sloped site where each circular area is terraced at a different level into the slope (Figure 10–34). A rolling landform, on the other hand, would not be as compatible with the strong geometry of the circular forms.

Concentric Circles.   Concentric circles create a very strong composition due to the focus of attention at the center of the design where the radii and extended radii originate (Figure 10–35). It is quite difficult to deny the importance of the center in a concentric circular theme.

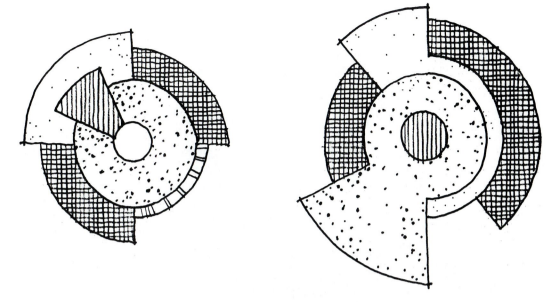

FIGURE 10–36
Interest can be created by varying the length of the radii and extended radii and/or amount of rotation.

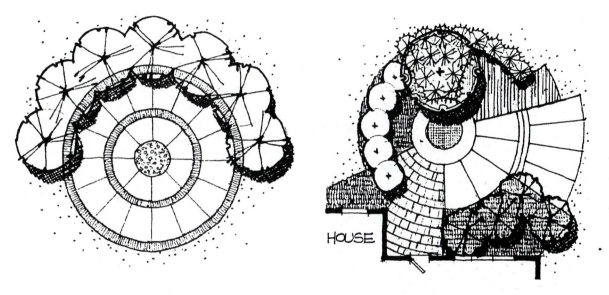

HOUSE

FIGURE 10–37
The center of the circle should be a prominent focal point created by special pavement or other element.

Compositional variety in a concentric circular theme can be created by varying the lengths and the amount of rotation of the radii and extended radii (Figure 10–36).

A concentric design theme is best used when there is an extremely important design element or space that is to be the center of attraction. The center point of a concentric circular theme should not be placed randomly on a site. It should be a significant existing or proposed feature or space which accentuates the entire composition. To acknowledge the importance of the center point, it should be a prominent focal point like a sculpture, water feature, or special pavement pattern (Figure 10–37). In addition, a concentric circular theme can be used to suggest a broad panoramic view of the surrounding landscape (Figure 10–38).

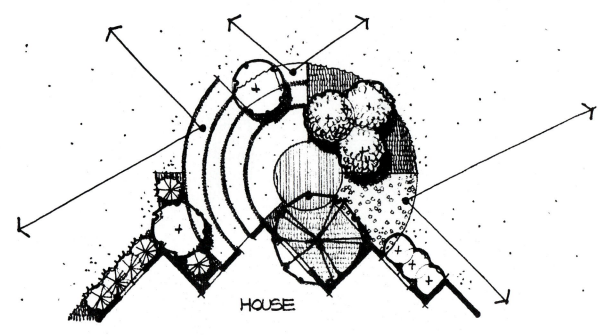

FIGURE 10–38
The outside of a concentric circular theme can provide panoramic views of the surrounding landscape.

Curvilinear Theme

A very common design theme is the curvilinear theme. The term *curvilinear* is sometimes considered to be synonymous and occasionally used interchangeably with *natural* and *freeform*. However, it is strongly suggested that the words *natural* and *freeform* not be used to replace the term *curvilinear*. A curvilinear theme is not natural. The theme is a structured system even though the soft curves inherent to this scheme resemble flowing lines seen in nature. Another reason for not using the term *natural* is to try to diminish the preconception that "everything in the land-scape should be naturally arranged." Also, by calling one theme natural infers that others are unnatural, which reflects a negative attitude. In reading this book, it is hoped that one will come to appreciate that outdoor spaces need not always be "naturally arranged" in order to be functionally and aesthetically successful. Likewise, *freeform* seems to denote something of little or no structure like a *free spirit*. Geometric structure, although very subtle, still exists in a curvilinear theme.

The curvilinear theme uses portions of different circles' and ellipses' circum-ferences for its overall form. Unlike the overlapping and concentric circle themes, the curvilinear theme relies primarily on "the soft touch" in which portions of circles and ellipses connect with each other in smooth, continuous transitions (Figure 10–39).

One guideline of the curvilinear theme is to have all intersecting curved lines meet each other at right angles (90 degrees) (Figure 10–40). This approach will elim-inate acute angles as discussed previously. For many designers, this suggestion may seem hard to accept because there usually is a tendency to have curves taper out into other lines (Figure 10–41). While this creates an apparently smooth and gradual tran-sition between lines, it also creates acute angles, and thus implementation problems.

It is also important to establish bold and generous curves in curvilinear com-positions in combination with smaller curves to give the design variety and inter-est (right side of Figure 10–42). While variety is important, it is recommended that the size and sharpness of the curves be carefully considered in relation to scale, ma-terial, and function of the composition. Too many curves with small radii will make a design look busy and sometimes erratic (left side of Figure 10–42). This type of design is also difficult to maintain.

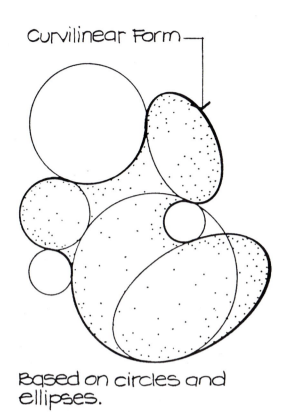

Curvilinear Form —

Based on circles and
ellipses.

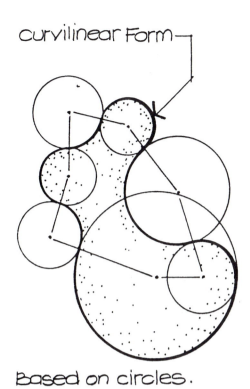

curvilinear Form —

Based on circles.

FIGURE 10-39
A curvilinear design theme has continuous flowing lines using the circumferences of nearby circles and ellipses.

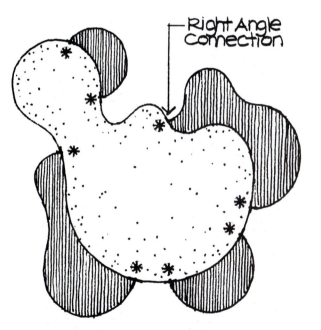

Right Angle
Connection

FIGURE 10-40
Intersecting lines in a curvilinear design theme should make a right angle.

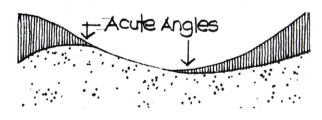

Acute Angles

FIGURE 10-41
Intersecting lines should not create acute angles in a curvilinear theme.

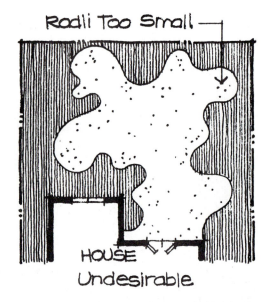
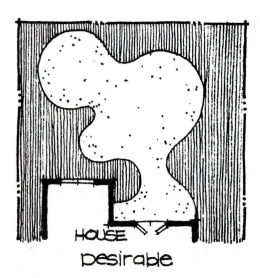

FIGURE 10–42
Curves should be strong and bold in a curvilinear theme.

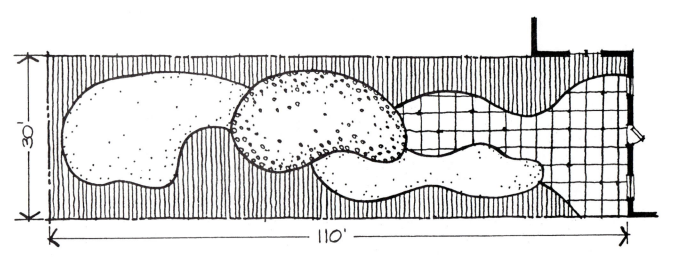

FIGURE 10–43
A curvilinear theme is not recommended for a site that is small or narrow.

The curvilinear theme has a passive, relaxing, and contemplative character. Such a design theme is suggested when there is a desire to create a composition with a serene, pastoral feeling. The flowing, sweeping lines of a curvilinear design also provide a great deal of movement for the eye. Curving edges between areas are apt to captivate the eye and lead it to another portion of the composition in a smooth fashion. There are times when curved forms are difficult to manipulate in confined areas and sometimes result in insufficient use of space for outdoor rooms (Figure 10–43).

The landform may be rolling in profile in a curvilinear theme or have an outcropping of stone as contrasting accent. Landform that is very flat can also accept a curvilinear design, but must rely extensively on using other vertical elements to accentuate a flowing character.

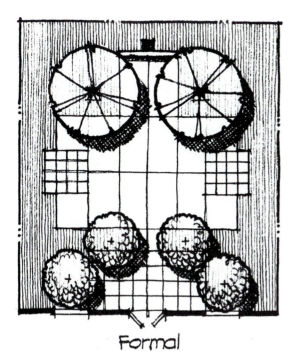
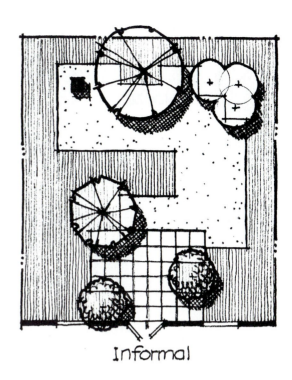

Formal   Informal

FIGURE 10-44
A rectangular theme may be either formal or informal.

Rectangular Theme

The rectangular theme is comprised of squares and rectangles that establish 90-degree relationships between all shapes and lines. This theme may be used in either a formal or informal fashion (Figure 10–44). The rectangular theme is normally oriented parallel to the sides of a house, thus complementing and reinforcing the typical rectangular layout of many houses. For some people, this type of theme may seem to be foreign to the desired pastoral outdoor environment dominated by living and changing plant materials. Although numerous straight lines in a site may take time to get used to, they are nevertheless able to structure pleasing outdoor spaces. Remember, most people live in pleasing indoor spaces consisting of rectangular forms.

When utilizing a rectangular theme in a design, consideration should be given to: (1) the variety of sizes, (2) the scale of the forms, and (3) the amount of overlap among the forms. There should be a variety of sizes of squares and/or rectangles used in a rectangular theme. This establishes visual interest and a hierarchy of spatial importance within the composition. The more important spaces of the design should have larger and bolder forms, while the less important spaces should have smaller, less prominent forms (Figure 10–45).

The scale of the forms or areas within the composition also needs thought. Too many short lines and small forms (Figure 10–46) will make a design busy, disjointed, and often difficult to maintain.

When overlapping two or more forms in a design, one guideline is to limit the overlap to one-fourth, one-third, or one-half of the dimension of the adjoining shapes (Figure 10–47). This will allow each shape to maintain its individual identity and be an adequate size and configuration for the intended use. Again, this is only a guideline and not a rule.

The rectangular theme is very appropriate to use when developing exterior spaces as extensions of indoor living spaces. This can create a strong relationship between the house and its surrounding site. A rectangular design theme is also

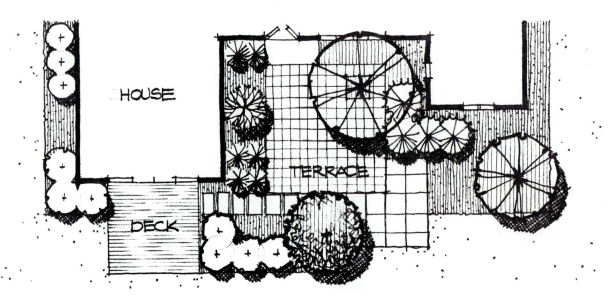

FIGURE 10-45
There should be a hierarchy of spatial size in a rectangular theme.

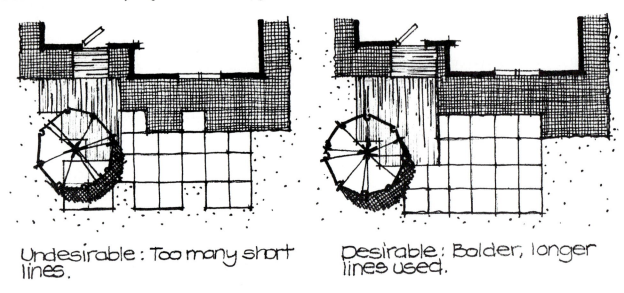

Undesirable: Too many short lines.

Desirable: Bolder, longer lines used.

FIGURE 10-46
Too many short lines in a rectangular theme will give it a busy, disjointed appearance.

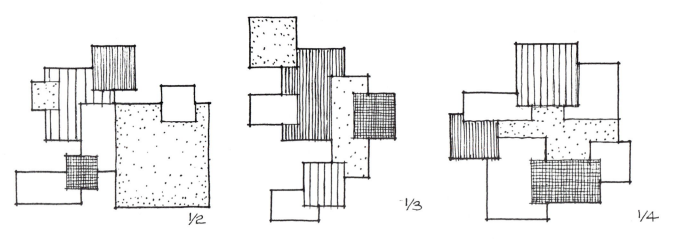

1/2

1/3

1/4

FIGURE 10-47
Thought should be given to the amount of overlap in a rectangular theme.

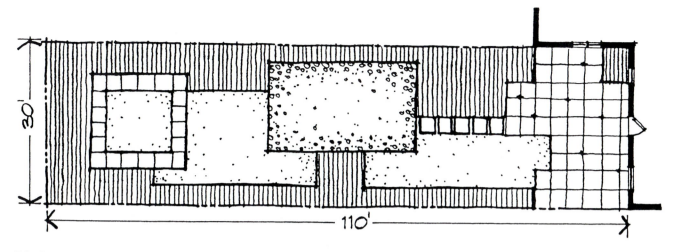

FIGURE 10-48
A rectangular theme is appropriate for sites that are small or narrow.

appropriate when the site area is narrow (Figure 10–48) because such a theme is able to make efficient use of space, unlike the curvilinear theme discussed previously (see Figure 10–43).

Some individuals feel a rectangular theme is often too boring or too formal because of the predictability of the right angles. This can happen if the third dimension is not handled appropriately. However, a well-designed rectangular theme, including one organized on a central axis, can be every bit as exciting as any other design theme if the third dimension provides proper enclosure and variety (Figure 10–49). And it should be remembered that plant materials will add natural softness and a bit of irregularity (if they are pruned in a natural fashion) to a rectangular design theme, making it more attractive in actuality than it might appear on paper.

When considering landform, a rectangular theme, like a circular theme, is best located on either level ground or on sloped ground where the different areas and forms of the design can be terraced in relation to each other.

Diagonal Theme

Two variations of the diagonal theme used on a residential site are the pure diagonal and the modified diagonal.

Pure Diagonal. The pure diagonal theme is essentially a rectangular theme turned at an angle in relation to the house (Figure 10–50). Thus, the compositional guidelines for the pure diagonal theme are similar to those for the rectangular theme. Although many angles can be selected for the relation of the diagonals to the house, it is suggested that either a 60-degree or 45-degree orientation be selected. Both of these angles are directly related to the geometry of the circle and the square and help to minimize acute angles.

When the lines of a pure diagonal theme connect to a house, there may be angular spaces created that are not totally functional. This situation can be handled in two ways. First, is to allow the angular relationships to form between the house and site (left side of Figure 10–51). This is permissible as long as the angular spaces are kept away from doors or other traveled areas or do not create awkward visual or functional relationships. Secondly, a designer may use transition lines between the house and the diagonal lines in the site (right side of Figure 10–51).

Modified Diagonal. The modified diagonal theme is a combination of the rectangular theme and the pure diagonal theme (Figure 10–52). When diagonal emphasis is preferred without the strength of the pure diagonal theme, the modified

Form Composition

265

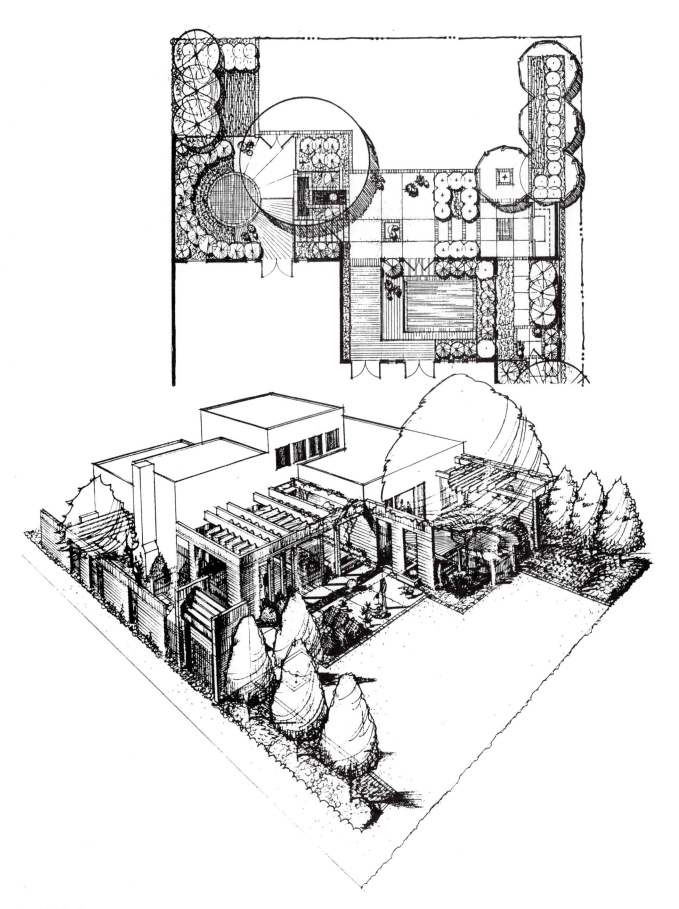

FIGURE 10-49
A rectangular theme can be enjoyable to experience if the third dimension provides variety of enclosure.

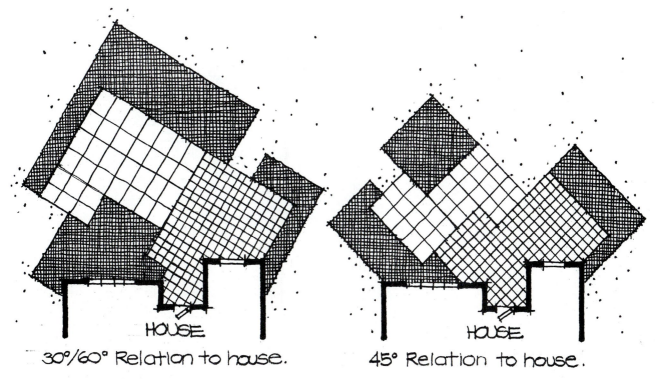

HOUSE

HOUSE

30°/60° Relation to house.

45° Relation to house.

FIGURE 10–50
Examples of pure diagonal design themes.

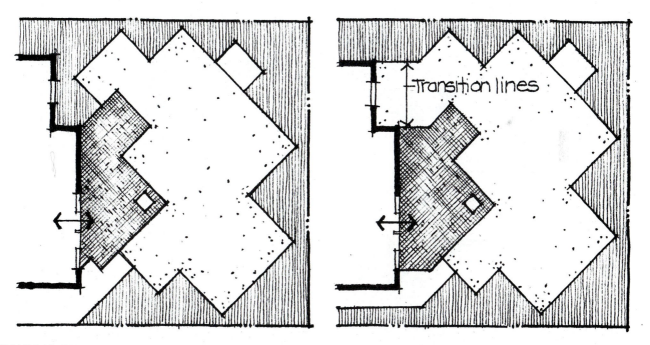

Transition lines

FIGURE 10–51
Two alternative ways to connect a diagonal design theme to the house.

diagonal theme offers a pleasant combination. This theme can easily be related compositionally to the 90-degree lines of a house yet offer boldness with the angled lines in the site.

There are several advantages and uses for both the pure diagonal theme and the modified diagonal theme. One possible use is on sites where there is a need to

FIGURE 10–52
An example of a modified diagonal design theme.

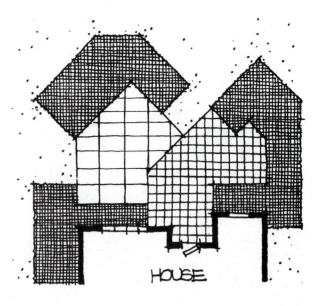

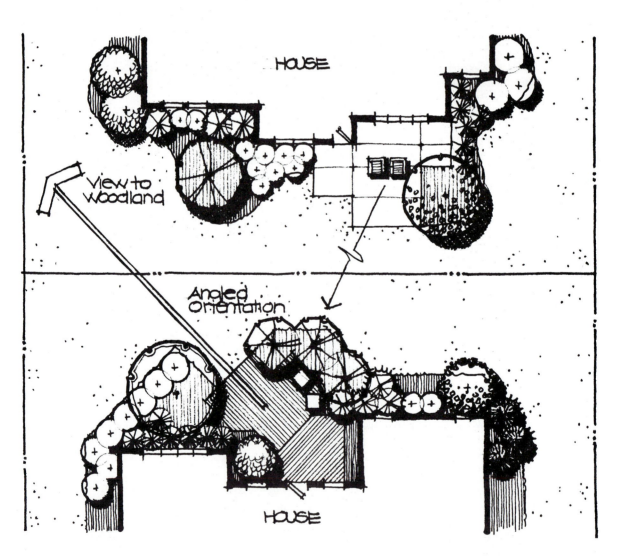

FIGURE 10–53
A diagonal design theme can establish a strong angled orientation toward a desired area in the landscape.

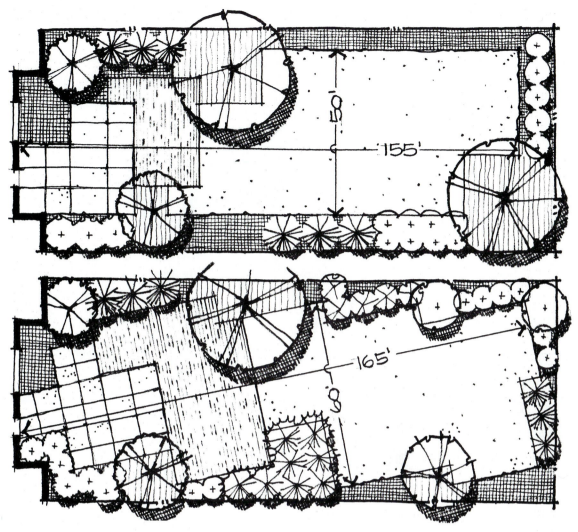

FIGURE 10–54
A diagonal design theme can make a small site seem larger by emphasizing the longest possible dimensions.

emphasize an orientation other than a direct 90-degree relationship with the house and/or property lines. With the facades of most houses in a neighborhood directly facing each other, there is often a desire to establish a different orientation that eliminates a forced view of the neighbors' houses. This is especially true when the depth of the surrounding yards is very shallow and/or the neighboring houses are rather close. An angled orientation can provide a more desirable view to some other point of interest within or off the site (Figure 10–53).

A diagonal layout is also advantageous for alleviating the perceived narrow dimensions of a small site. Diagonal lines and spaces may actually provide longer dimensions than possible with lines and spaces that have a 90-degree relationship with the site property lines (Figure 10–54). The result is that the spaces appear larger, giving the site a more spacious feeling. There may also be a desirable view, favorable orientation to the sun, or good exposure to cool summer breezes which calls for a diagonal direction. When it is suitable to emphasize a diagonal orientation, the diagonal theme offers a feasible compositional alternative for reinforcing and enhancing existing site potentials. The landform could be terraced into flat areas to reinforce the straight-line character of diagonal themes.

Form Composition

FIGURE 10-55
An example of an arc and tangent design theme.

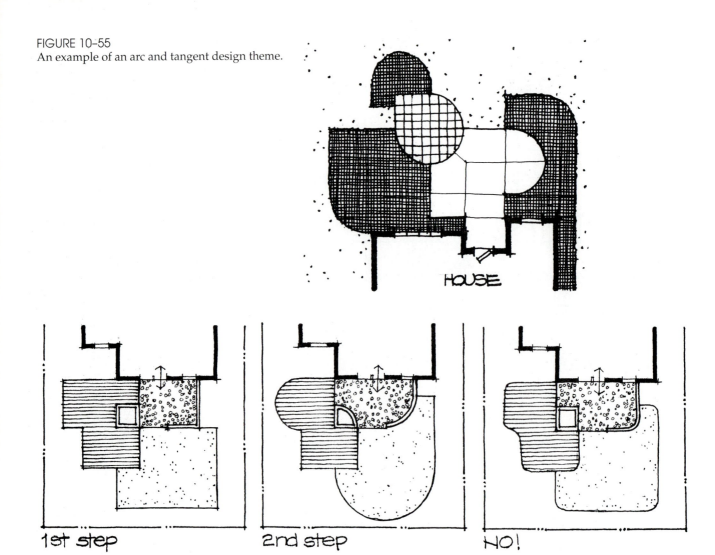

HOUSE

1st step　2nd step　NO!

FIGURE 10-56
A process for creating an arc and tangent theme.

Arc and Tangent Theme

A design theme that is derived from a combination of different themes is the arc and tangent theme (Figure 10–55). This theme combines arcs from circles of the circular theme and straight lines from the rectangular theme. The straight lines provide a feeling of structure while the curves counter this with soft, sweeping lines. Both can work well together.

Parts of the circle that can be used in the arc and tangent theme are the quarter-circle, half-circle, and three-quarter-circle. To create an arc and tangent theme, the designer might first develop the composition as a totally rectangular scheme (left side of Figure 10–56). Then selected portions of the design can be converted to selected arcs of a circle (center of Figure 10–56). The introduction of arcs is not done randomly. Rather, the designer must carefully decide which areas or lines of the composition require the use of arcs for soft corners and rounded edges. However, the designer should not merely round corners of the rectangular forms (right side of Figure 10–56). This creates a weak design with difficult corners to maintain.

Again, the designer needs to consider variety of size, scale, and overlap of forms as they relate to the arc and tangent theme. In terms of landform, sloping sites should be terraced in an arc and tangent theme owing to the structured character of many of the spaces. Rolling landform will not be very compatible with the

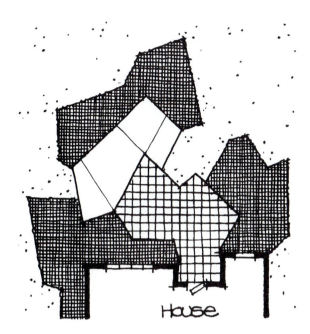

FIGURE 10-57
An example of an angular design theme.

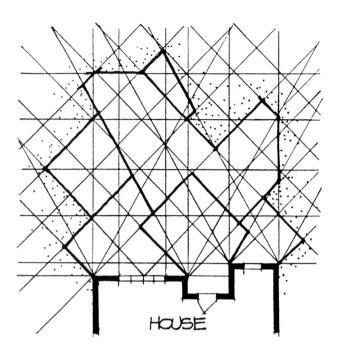

FIGURE 10-58
Guidelines should be used to form the basis of an angular design theme.

character of the strong, bold lines and arcs of the arc and tangent theme. While the plan drawing might seem appropriate in terms of form-to-form relationships, the boldness of the arcs may be lost in the actual profile of the rolling landform.

Angular Theme

The angular theme is comprised of a series of angled lines that work together to create an active and eye-catching design composition (Figure 10–57). This system of lines and forms can produce a very dynamic composition, even though it is a difficult theme to develop. At first glance, the angles drawn in Figure 10–57 may seem to be randomly drawn. But a closer examination reveals that all lines are either parallel, perpendicular, 45, or 60 degrees to the back of the house. When using this theme, it is suggested that a system of guidelines that are 0, 45, 60, and 90 degrees in relation to the face of the house be used (Figure 10–58). If a system of guidelines is not used, too many different angles are apt to be used, causing the composition to seem uncontrolled and chaotic.

There is one other suggestion when developing an angular theme. Mostly obtuse angles (angles greater than 45 degrees) should be used, while acute angles should be avoided. This will alleviate the possibility of drawing a composition, which would create problems in using and maintaining the design (Figure 10–59).

The angular design theme offers an extremely bold and dynamic design system. It has a rugged character and fits appropriately in areas that have irregular or abrupt topography with rock outcrops and boulders. For example, this theme relates well to the desert Southwest with its rugged landscape.

Theme Combinations

When designing a residential site, one design theme will probably prevail throughout the site. While the same design theme may be used in the front, sides, and back of the site, it is also possible to use one design theme in the front of the house and a different theme in the back of the house (Figure 10–60). This approach is appropriate for two reasons. First, the designer may wish to create environments

FIGURE 10-59
Acute angles and sharply pointed forms should
be avoided in an angular design theme.

HOUSE

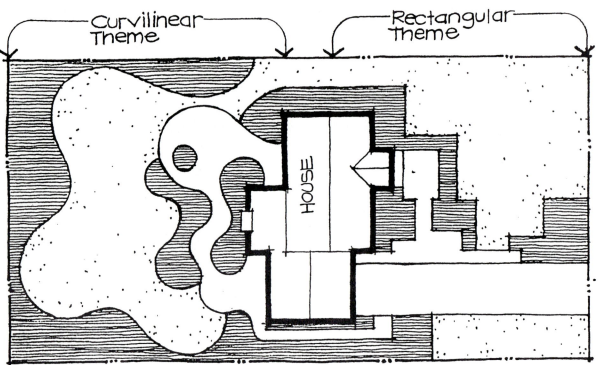

Curvilinear Theme   Rectangular Theme

HOUSE

FIGURE 10–60
The design theme used in the front yard may be different from the one used in the back yard.

of different character. For example, it may be desirable to create a formal setting for the house in the front yard while providing a casual or natural feeling in the back yard. Secondly, since a person can be in only one area of the site at one time, spaces can have different characters without clashing or conflicting with each other. However, when designing adjacent spaces with different design themes, sensible and comfortable transitions between the two should be considered.

There are times when a designer may choose to create an overall composition that combines two design themes. For instance, Figure 10–61 shows a design that incorporates a rectangular theme for the structured elements (terraces, decks, walkways, and fences), while a curvilinear theme is used for all the planting areas. The straight lines of the rectangular theme reinforce the lines of the house, while

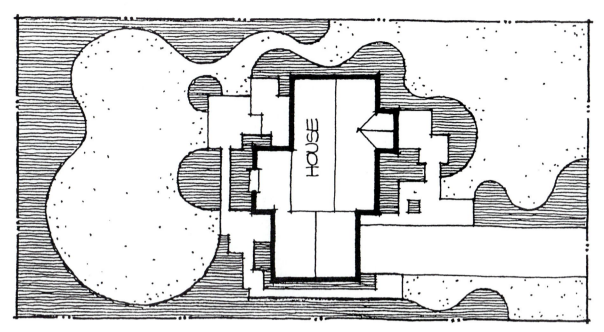

FIGURE 10–61
An example of a rectangular design theme combined with a curvilinear design theme.

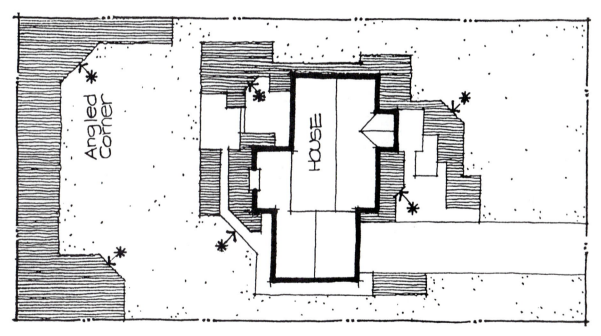

FIGURE 10–62
An example of a weak combination of a rectangular theme and a modified diagonal theme.

the curvilinear theme is associated with the softer character of plant materials. This approach works especially well when the straight lines are placed near the house and the curved lines are located away from the house, establishing a transition from structure to informality as one moves away from the house.

When two similar design themes are combined, the result is not always successful. For instance, a rectangular theme and a modified diagonal theme are so similar to each other that neither will seem to be of major importance when used together. Also, if the modified diagonal theme is used in a subordinate fashion, the design will most likely be perceived as a rectangular theme with a few corners angled in a weak manner (Figure 10–62).

Form Composition

FIGURE 10–63
A different form, such as the circle in this example, may be used as an accent in a design theme.

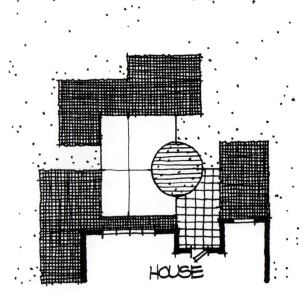

Another way to combine themes together is to add an accent form to a selected design theme. For example, Figure 10–63 illustrates a rectangular theme with a special circular feature as an accent. This accent could be a fountain or a bed of groundcover with a sculpture displayed in it. Specific shapes furnishing a strong contrast to the overall theme can add interest to a composition.

ARCHITECTURAL ATTENTION AND DESIGN THEMES

Architectural attention can be influential in selecting a design theme in the form composition phase.

There are times when a particular design theme might be selected to reflect the client's preference regarding overall design character. For instance, a client may be interested in having a very energetic design with a lot of visual action. This might lead to the use of an angular design theme, one which is usually quite different than most landscapes and can be quite visually active. In a different situation, a client might want a very conservative, casual, and soft character in their design. A curvilinear design might suit these clients well. But, many clients rely on the designer's discretion as to the proposed character of the landscape design. In these situations, it is suggested that the designer look toward the architecture for design suggestions. This can occur in a few different ways.

First, a specific design theme (rectangular, circular, angular, etc.) may be selected because it seems to be strongly related to the distinctive character of the architecture. For instance, a house with a variety of angular patterns of roofs, windows, and walls may best be suited to a diagonal or modified diagonal theme. Likewise, an arc and tangent theme may be very suitable for a house that has strong vertical and horizontal lines with circular and semi-circular archways and windows. The overall character of the house may lend itself to one particular design theme instead of others.

Secondly, when clients do not have preferred design themes, which is often the case, attention should focus on the architectural character. It is especially important to attend to those architectural features that were addressed and discussed at the client meeting, and subsequently photographed. Therefore, if the clients do not have a specific design theme they are attracted to, and the house does not have a specific style, the designer may incorporate specific architectural features into the main forms of the design. For instance, even for a house that does not have a strong style, a client may really like the character of the porch—in particular, the arches of the porch. So, the designer may choose to use the forms and patterns of the arches as strong accents within the design. In this case, the designer would select a design theme that would allow for those particular forms to be the accented areas.

Four examples are presented to illustrate how the design theme responded to certain aspects of the architecture.

Figure 10–64 shows the first example. The client, a single mother with three children, did not have any preferences concerning the proposed character of the landscape design. She stated that she was mostly a casual individual who enjoyed reading, exercising, and occasional entertaining. Since she would entertain fairly often, she wanted enough patio space to set up a few tables with chairs. In addition, she wanted a private space not only for reading and exercise, but also for entertaining an intimate group.

As you can see, the arches on the porch provide a subtle change from the strong overall rectangular pattern of the house. In response, a rectangular design theme was selected for the hardscape structures (steps, walks, patios, decks, fences, etc.). These architectural elements will have a strong relationship to the existing architecture. Then, an arc similar to the porch arches was used to accent the edge of the major gathering space. The rest of the yard was configured with a curvilinear design theme which blends with the arch character and the softness of the curves. The private space, near the dining room, is enclosed with a fence high enough to provide the requisite separation for her reading and exercising activities. The form of the patio in this space also reflects the slight arch.

Figure 10–65 illustrates another example. In this case, the clients really liked: (1) the strong angular patterns of the roof, (2) the variety of window sizes and shapes, and (3) the irregular stone pattern. In addition, they wanted to entertain larger groups of people, about 15 to 20, approximately once a month. They wanted a larger than normal patio space that would even offer the lawn as an overflow area in case they entertained a larger group. They also requested a private place for a hot tub, with a view to the river. Because they both enjoyed the water for fishing and skiing, they wanted to emphasize views up and down the river.

A modified diagonal theme was used for the major wood structures to conform with the overall character of the house. The wood deck system was used to provide easy access and views through each of the several sliding glass doors. The shape of the decks was established to emphasize access down the steps to the lower stone patio in directions of the best views to the river. Stone, similar to the stone on the front of the house, was used with a curvilinear layout to provide for a casual, welcoming connection to the lawn area and the river. A private space for the hot tub was included near the bedroom. It is separated from the entertaining space and the adjacent property with a high fence, but allows for a view of the river.

The third example is illustrated in Figure 10–66. The clients are a middle-age couple who both have top management positions in local companies. Their children are grown and married. They are champion bridge players, and often entertain 12 people once a month. Outdoor patio spaces would need to support three sets of tables and chairs. With regards to overall garden character, they prefer a formal garden design that is clean and crisp, and that responds to the architecture. In particular, they like the half-circular patterns of the windows.

As you can see, an arc and tangent design theme was selected. It not only responds to the half-circular patterns on the house, but to some of the horizontal lines of the roof. The form and pattern of the major patio space adjacent to the family room came from the arched window pattern on the front facade of the house. The two side patios, which will allow for additional table placement, are situated at an angle to reflect the strong roof pattern and to focus attention to the corners of the property where special plant masses might be established. The focal point of attention is directly out and through the central patio space into an ornamental planting

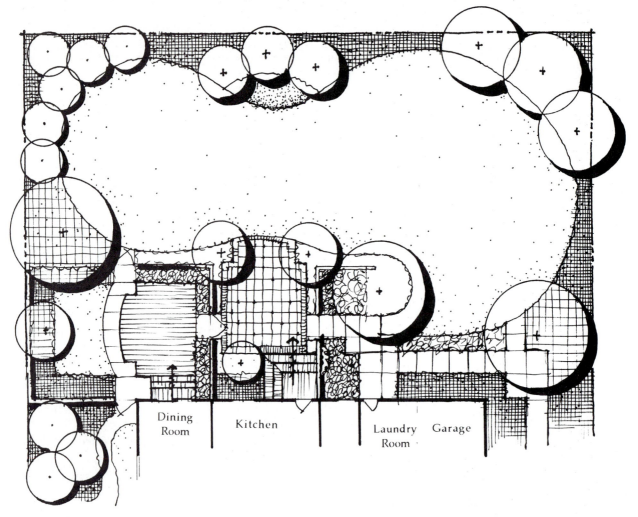

FIGURE 10–64
Form composition that uses the front porch arch as an accent in the landscape design. Design #N1956 (top) © Home Planners, LLC Wholly owned by Hanley-Wood, LLC. Blueprints available, 800-322-6797.

Dining
Room

Kitchen

Laundry   Garage
Room

FIGURE 10–65
Form composition that is modeled after the: (1) strong angles of the roof and windows, (2) wood siding, and (3) irregular stone pattern. Design #N4115 (top) © Home Planners, LLC Wholly owned by Hanley-Wood, LLC. Blueprints available, 800-322-6797.

Form Composition

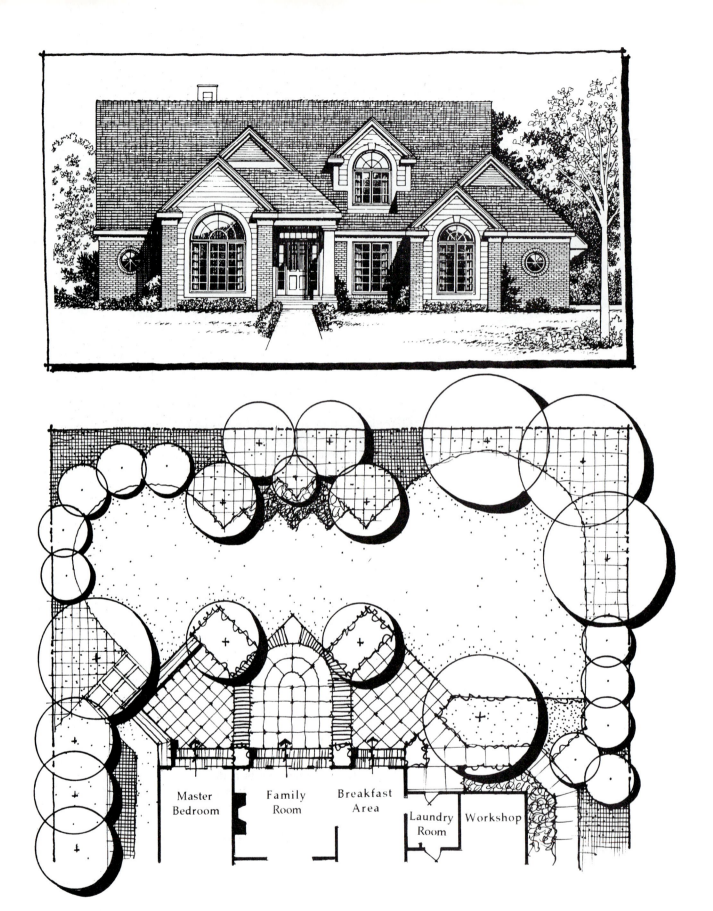

FIGURE 10–66
Form composition was designed to reflect the special character of the angled roofs and circular window patterns. Design #N3458 (top) © Home Planners, LLC Wholly owned by Hanley-Wood, LLC. Blueprints available, 800-322-6797.

area. Materials for the patios are a combination of brick and stone, both to match the same colors of the material on the house.

The fourth and final example of architectural attention in the form composition phase is illustrated in Figure 10–67. These clients are a young couple with two grade-school-aged children and two dogs. They are working parents who enjoy relaxing when they get home. They have always been partial to houses with a formal character, and really enjoy the clean white look of this one. While much of the interior decor is also quite formal, they are more interested in having a very informal garden design. For relaxation, they plan to maintain vegetable and perennial gardens. Eating outdoors is a real pleasure for them and they plan to install a permanent grill for cooking near the kitchen and breakfast areas. They entertain small groups, approximately six to eight people every other month or so. Stone is their favorite material for patio spaces since they love the low stone wall along the front edge of the property. They requested fences for retaining the dogs within the property and away from the vegetable garden.

The designer selected a curvilinear design theme that would provide for smooth, casual flowing lines. The major patio would be large enough for a table and chairs, with room for some other groupings of furniture, as well as potted plants. Stone, reflective of the front stone wall, was selected for the major patio space. The vegetable garden was placed in the back corner with a small sitting/relaxing area adjacent and beneath some shade trees. The fence is situated directly on the property line to maximize their usable space and provide a play area for the dogs. A place for the grill has been established near the indoor eating areas.

As demonstrated in these four examples, architectural character can be incorporated into a designer's thinking in the form composition phase of design. The reason there were more design decisions shown in the examples (patterns, plant materials, etc.) was to provide a better understanding of some of the other aspects that also influence a designer when selecting design themes. It is important to note that major decisions concerning design forms can be made at this form composition phase. Then, in the spatial and material composition phases of design, decisions can be made regarding the detailed forms, materials, and patterns.

FORM COMPOSITION PROCESS

Previous sections of this chapter have focused on the design themes that can be used on a residential site and some of the basic geometric principles on which these themes are based. Yet, the process for selecting and developing form composition studies for a residential site is more complex than just drawing attractive forms. The process should involve a simultaneous consideration of: (1) geometry of form, (2) desired feeling or character of the design, (3) relationship to existing structures, and (4) relationship to the functional diagram. A good form composition is a sensitive blending of all these factors.

To begin the process of form composition, the designer starts with a functional diagram. Next, the designer selects a design theme or combination of themes. This decision should be based on: (1) desired character and/or style of the design (that is, formal or informal, relaxing or stimulating, contemporary or historic, and so on), (2) appropriateness to the architectural style of the house, (3) appropriateness to the existing site conditions, and (4) preference of the clients.

Once a design theme is chosen, the designer is ready to start the process of developing a series of form studies. The two critical steps in this process are 1) relating the proposed design forms to the existing structures and 2) relating the proposed design forms to the functional diagram. While two steps should take place at the same time, they will be discussed separately in the following paragraphs.

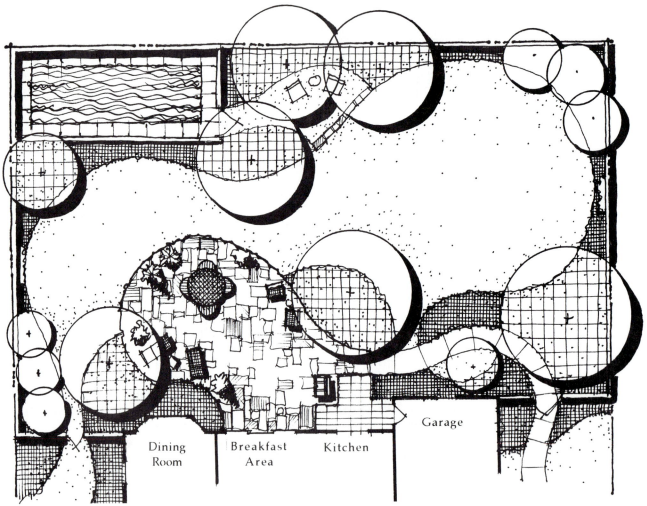

Dining
Room

Breakfast
Area

Kitchen

Garage

FIGURE 10–67
Form composition that reflects the clients' desire for a casual, informal, and soft garden design. Design #N2659 (top) © Home Planners, LLC Wholly owned by Hanley-Wood, LLC. Blueprints available, 800-322-6797.

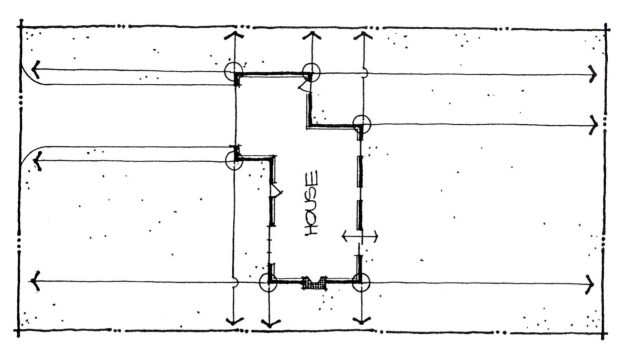

FIGURE 10–68
Outside walls and corners are of primary importance in form composition.

Relationship of Form Composition to Existing Structures. With few exceptions, almost all residential site designs are developed in association with either existing or proposed structures, such as the house, garage, storage shed, gazebo, walks, terraces, walls etc. Existing structures should influence where lines and edges of spaces are located on the site so they blend in with the proposed design and the final result is a visually coordinated and unified residential environment. When done appropriately, it may be difficult to distinguish between what was originally existing on the site and what was added.

This objective can be accomplished by relating the edges of new forms with the edges of existing elements or structures. To do this, the designer should first obtain a copy or print of the base sheet which shows existing structures to be retained. On this copy of the base sheet, the designer should identify the prominent points and edges of the existing structures. For an existing house, there is a hierarchy of points and edges that should be considered:

1. Primary importance: outside walls and corners of the house (Figure 10–68).
2. Secondary importance: edges of elements on outside walls that touch the ground surface such as edges of doors or lines created by material changes (between brick and siding, for example) (Figure 10–69).
3. Tertiary importance: edges of elements on outside walls that do not touch the ground surface, such as windows that are above the ground (Figure 10–70).

The next step is to draw lines on the base sheet from these prominent points and edges into the immediately surrounding area of the site (Figure 10–71). A color pen or pencil is suggested so that the lines are easily distinguished from other lines on the base sheet. These three sets of lines are referred to as *lines of force* because they guide or force a connection between existing and proposed compositional forms. The lines of primary importance have been drawn darker for emphasis. In addition, other lines have been drawn to create an overall grid system. These other lines were drawn perpendicular to the original set of lines of force at a selected interval. For instance, the distance X between lines A and B has been repeated away

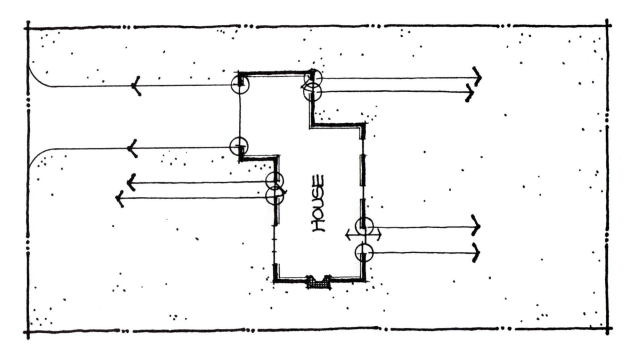

FIGURE 10–69
Edges of doors and material changes are of secondary importance in form composition.

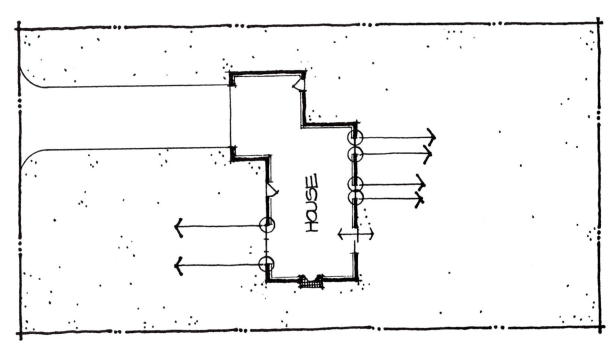

FIGURE 10–70
Edges of windows are of tertiary importance in form composition.

from the house to establish the location of lines C and D. In the back yard, the distance Y has been used to space the lines of force, with some lines such as G and H being a distance $1/2$ Y apart. There are no rules that govern the spacing of these additional lines.

After the lines of force and grid system have been drawn on the base sheet, the designer should overlay a sheet of tracing paper on top of the base sheet. A form composition study can be prepared on the tracing paper in coordination with

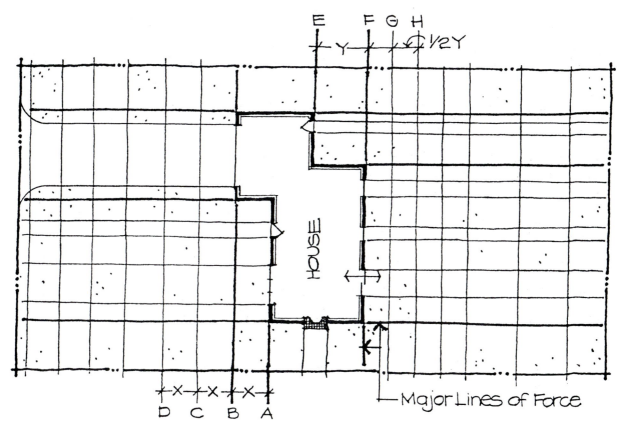

FIGURE 10–71
Lines of force are extended into the site away from prominent points of the house.

1) the lines of force and grid system beneath, and 2) in relation to the functional diagram (explained in the next section). An example of a form composition study that has been created based on the lines of force without having it relate to a specific functional diagram is shown in Figure 10–72. Several things should be apparent from this example. First, a rectangular theme can easily be developed using a 90-degree grid system. Secondly, the grid is used as the foundation for the form composition over the entire site, not just near the house. Yet, at several places, like the front entry and the back terrace, the edges of the forms have been located between the lines of force. The designer should not feel obligated to draw all the edges of forms only where there are lines of force.

The designer does not always have to use a grid system that has a 90-degree relation to the house. As seen in Figure 10–73, lines of force can be extended away from the house in any direction. In this example, the lines of force and grid system were drawn on a 45-degree angle in relation to the important points and edges of the house. Then, other lines based on a repetitive distance were added to formulate the grid. Following this, the diagonal form composition theme was drawn in response to the grid system.

Grid systems can also be used to aid in creating other design themes. One possibility is to combine the 90-degree and 45-degree grid systems to develop a modified diagonal design theme. The 90-degree or 45-degree grid system can be used as the basis for an arc and tangent theme. The grid system is most useful for rectangular, diagonal, angular, or arc and tangent design themes, since they incorporate straight lines. The lines of force and grid system have limited use for the circular and curvilinear design themes (Figure 10–74). These latter schemes might relate to a particular point or edge of an existing structure, but on the whole they are difficult to correlate to a grid system. Consequently, the grid system, except for

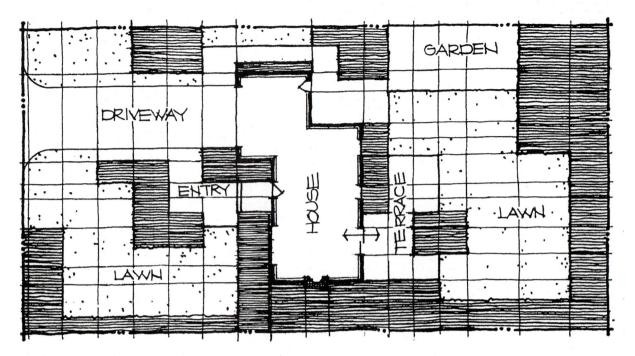

FIGURE 10–72
An example of a rectangular design theme based on the underlying grid system.

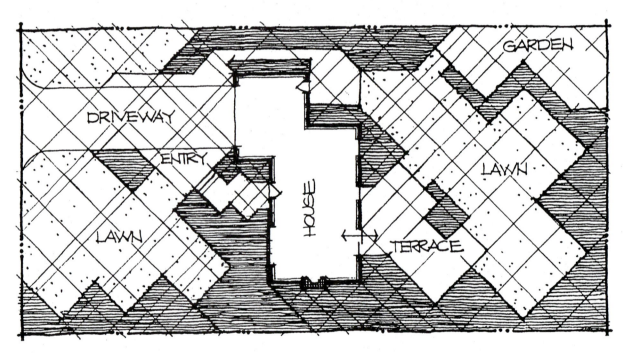

FIGURE 10–73
An example of a 45-degree diagonal design theme based on the underlying diagonal grid system.

perhaps the primary lines of force, can be dispensed with while developing the circular and curvilinear design themes.

What is important in the circular and curvilinear design themes is how the lines and edges in the site connect with the sides of the house and other straight edges. Every possible attempt should be made to avoid acute angles or other awkward visual relationships in the transition areas between new forms and existing structures. In Figure 10–74, most of the circular arcs meet the house at 90 degrees.

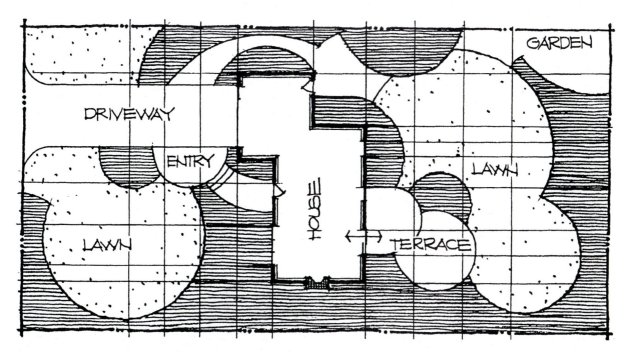

FIGURE 10–74
A grid system has limited use in developing circular or curvilinear design themes.

When there is not enough room for an arc to meet at a 90 degree angle, (left of the driveway), then the connection should be greater or equal to a 45 degree angle. Remember, avoid acute angles.

There are several points that need to be kept in mind while drawing the grid system for the form composition. First, this grid system is drawn to provide guidelines or clues for locating the edges of the new forms in the design. When the edges of the new forms are aligned with the points and lines of the grid system, the new forms will have a stronger visual relationship to the points and edges of the house. The result is a coordinated integration of house and site. Yet, there is nothing wrong if some of the design's points and edges do not align with the exact lines of the grid system. The grid system developed through the use of the lines of force is only a helpful tool and not an absolute necessity for the location of all new forms. The grid system is by no means a magic formula ensuring success.

The lines of force and grid system are most important for aligning the forms of the design near the house or other structures and are much less significant farther away from structures. The visual association between the site and any structure is greatest immediately around the structure. In this area, it can be readily seen whether or not the edge of a form in the site aligns with the corner of the house or edge of a door. But as distance increases away from a structure, it becomes more difficult to notice and appreciate any coordinated alignment between the structure and site.

Since the lines of force and grid system are only hints or clues, there is no absolute right or wrong way to establish them on the site. Given the same site and a handful of different designers, each would be very apt to place a slightly different grid system on the site. Although the primary lines of force would probably be the same, the other lines might vary substantially from one designer to the next. A suggestion is to locate only as many lines in the grid as will eventually prove useful. Too few are apt not to suggest anything to the designer, while too many may be too confusing.

Relationship of Form Composition to the Functional Diagram. In addition to relating to existing structures on the site, the new forms of the design should also relate to the selected functional diagram completed in the previous step. This

Form Composition

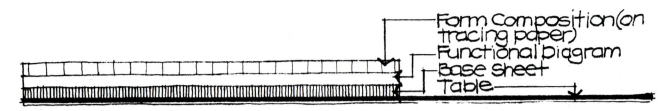

FIGURE 10–75
A system of overlays should be used for developing the form composition in relation to the functional diagram.

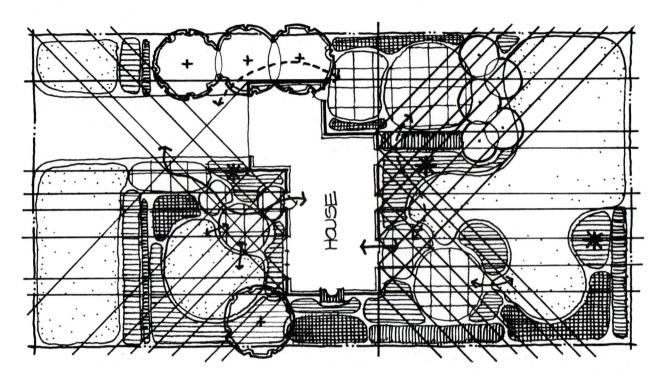

FIGURE 10–76
An example of the functional diagram overlaid on top of the grid system on the base sheet.

functional diagram or concept plan also serves as the foundation for the development of the form composition. Remember, the objective of the form composition phase is to convert the generalized or rough outlines of the functional diagram to specific edges.

The procedure for developing the form composition studies in relation to the functional diagram begins by placing the functional diagram over the base sheet which has the lines of force and grid system drawn on it. Next, a clean sheet of tracing paper, on which the first form composition study will be developed, is overlaid on top of the diagram (Figure 10–75). This permits the designer to see through the tracing paper to the functional diagram and grid system and use them as references (Figure 10–76).

Using the functional diagram and lines of force as bases, the designer next begins to convert the outlines of the bubbles in the diagram to specific edges using one of the design themes. An attempt should be made to relate the new design forms to both the functional diagram and the lines of force and grid system that are on the base sheet. The form composition can be thought of as a careful and coordinated marriage of the lines of force and the functional diagram. This process is not easy because there is much to consider. And the result may not exactly reflect either the lines of force or the functional diagram. Figure 10–77 shows a modified diagonal

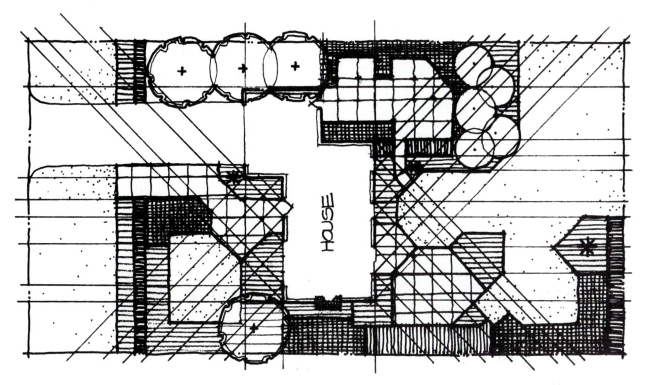

FIGURE 10–77
An example of a design theme which relates to both the functional diagram and the grid system.

form composition, using some of the lines of the grid system but also adding others. At the same time, the edges of the form composition approximate the outline of the functional diagram underneath, though again there are some variations.

In relating the new design forms to the functional diagram, the designer does not literally trace the diagram's bubbles. Instead, the diagram may be thought of as providing hints or approximate guidelines where the edges of the form composition may be positioned. Thus, where necessary, the designer should take the liberty of slightly altering the position of the edges to relate to the lines of force and to establish pleasing form relationships. But the overall size, proportion, and configuration stay generally the same as originally drawn on the functional diagram.

The first attempt at this will no doubt be rather rough, with a number of flaws. Another sheet of tracing paper can then be overlaid on the first sheet so that the first form composition study can be refined. Several attempts and refinements on tracing paper may be needed before the designer is satisfied with the results. And again, the development of alternatives is highly encouraged. The first and obvious solution may not be the best, a fact the designer may not see until the solution is compared and tested with alternatives (Figure 10–78). This overlay process should continue until the form composition is attractive as well as practical.

Now perhaps, the significance of functional diagrams discussed in Chapter 8 can be better appreciated. A sound functional diagram will result in a form composition that also possesses a solid functional basis. Unfortunately, weaknesses of the functional diagrams are also apt to be continued. So again, it is critical that the designer take the necessary time to adequately study the functional diagrams to prevent organizational flaws from becoming a problem in later phases of the design process.

When developing form composition studies in coordination with the functional diagram, it is quite possible that the designer may formulate a new idea for the design's organization that is better than the original functional diagram. When this occurs, and it will, the designer should feel free to build on the better idea. The

Form Composition

287

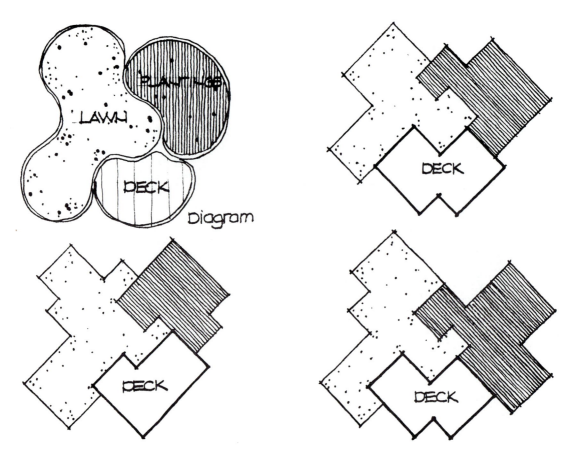

FIGURE 10–78
Examples of alternatives based upon the same functional diagram and the same design theme.

designer may go back to the functional diagram stage to make improvements and then return to the form composition phase.

FORM COMPOSITION FOR THE DUNCAN RESIDENCE

At the end of Chapter 8, a final functional diagram was developed for the Duncan residence. This diagram resulted after previously exploring different ideas by means of three alternative functional diagrams. It can now be used as the base for drawing a few alternative form composition studies for the Duncan residence.

The first alternative is a rectangular design theme (Figure 10–79). Note how this composition relates to both the functional diagram that preceded it and the lines of force. For example, notice how certain edges of the eating area and living area relate to edges of the house, doors, and windows.

The second alternative is a combination of a rectangular theme and an arc and tangent theme (Figure 10–80). The rectangular forms are used for most of the hard surfaces while arcs are used for the softer edges of the lawn and planting beds. This also makes good use of the site's limited area and provides a good blend of structure and casualness in meeting the preferences of the Duncans.

The third alternative, Figure 10–81, combines a modified diagonal theme with a curvilinear theme. Structured diagonal forms are used for structures (walks, steps, fences, etc.) while softer, sweeping forms are used for the lawn edges and planting beds. The diagonal orientation of the eating and living areas in the back yard direct views from these spaces toward the planting areas along the site's boundaries while the flowing curves furnish motion for the eye.

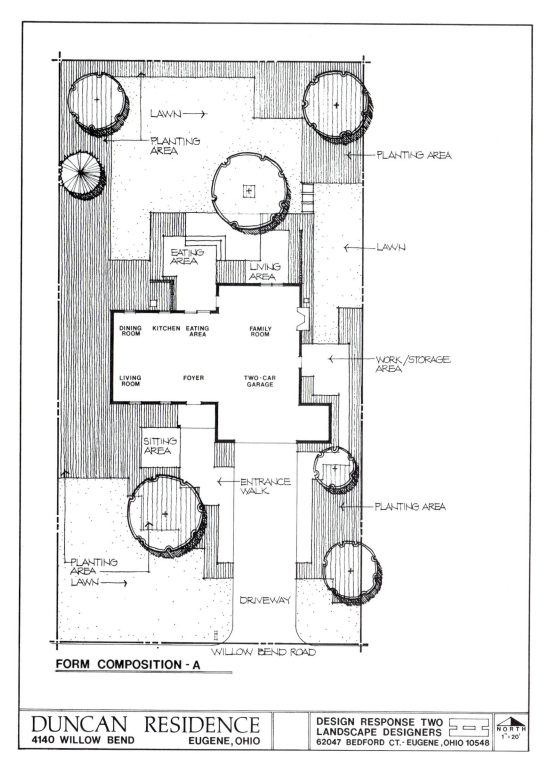

Within the figure:

LAWN →

PLANTING AREA

PLANTING AREA

LAWN ←

EATING AREA

LIVING AREA

DINING ROOM	KITCHEN	EATING AREA	FAMILY ROOM

WORK/STORAGE AREA

LIVING ROOM	FOYER	TWO-CAR GARAGE

SITTING AREA

ENTRANCE WALK

PLANTING AREA

PLANTING AREA
LAWN →

DRIVEWAY

WILLOW BEND ROAD

FORM COMPOSITION - A

DUNCAN RESIDENCE
4140 WILLOW BEND   EUGENE, OHIO

DESIGN RESPONSE TWO
LANDSCAPE DESIGNERS
62047 BEDFORD CT.- EUGENE, OHIO 10548

NORTH
1" = 20'

FIGURE 10–79
A rectangular design theme for the Duncan residence.

SUMMARY

The selection and composition of forms is just one of the steps of preliminary design, yet a vital one because it builds on the functional diagrams that preceded it and, in turn, provides the foundation for three-dimensional study during preliminary design. Form compositions that are pleasing to the eye yet practical to build and maintain are based on principles of geometric relationships among forms, a direct correlation to the functional diagrams, a respect for existing structures and

Form Composition   **289**

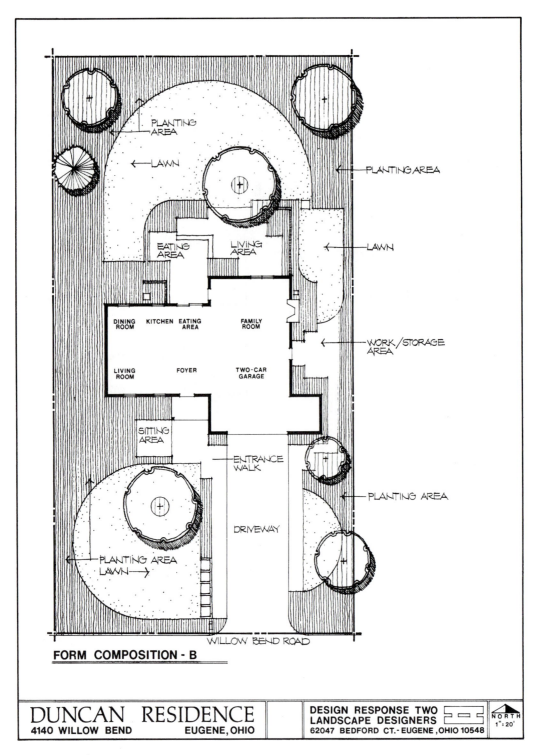

FORM COMPOSITION - B

PLANTING AREA
LAWN
PLANTING AREA
LAWN
WORK/STORAGE AREA
PLANTING AREA
EATING AREA
LIVING AREA
DINING ROOM   KITCHEN   EATING AREA   FAMILY ROOM
LIVING ROOM   FOYER   TWO-CAR GARAGE
SITTING AREA
ENTRANCE WALK
PLANTING AREA
LAWN
DRIVEWAY
WILLOW BEND ROAD

DUNCAN RESIDENCE
4140 WILLOW BEND   EUGENE, OHIO

DESIGN RESPONSE TWO
LANDSCAPE DESIGNERS
62047 BEDFORD CT.- EUGENE ,OHIO 10548

NORTH
1":20'

FIGURE 10–80
A combination of rectangular and arc/tangent design themes for the Duncan residence.

conditions of the site, the desired character of the design, and the wishes of the clients. The development of attractive two-dimensional forms on the base plane is a first step in preliminary design and not an end in itself. Form composition must extend into the third dimension of the site and be further expressed in the use of such elements as landform, walls/fences, and plant materials. Form composition provides a beginning point for the next step of spatial composition.

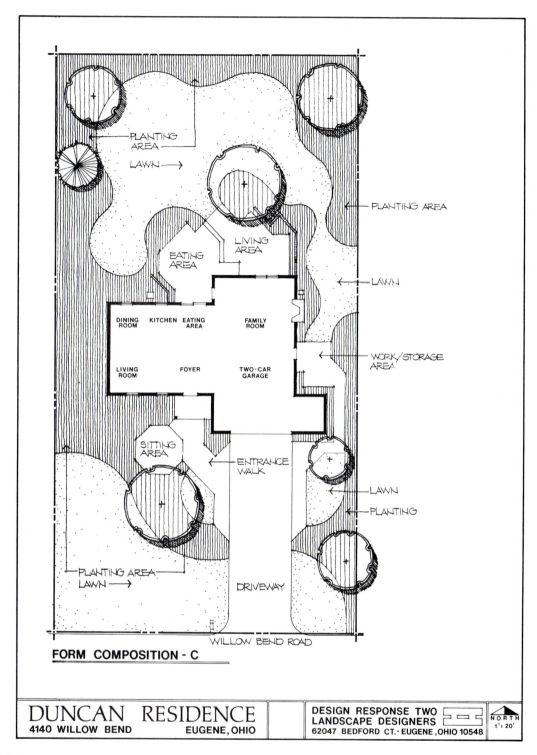

Labels within the figure:

PLANTING AREA

LAWN →

PLANTING AREA

EATING AREA

LIVING AREA

LAWN ←

WORK/STORAGE AREA

DINING ROOM — KITCHEN — EATING AREA — FAMILY ROOM

LIVING ROOM — FOYER — TWO-CAR GARAGE

SITTING AREA

ENTRANCE WALK

LAWN ←

PLANTING ←

PLANTING AREA

LAWN →

DRIVEWAY

WILLOW BEND ROAD

FORM COMPOSITION - C

DUNCAN RESIDENCE
4140 WILLOW BEND   EUGENE, OHIO

DESIGN RESPONSE TWO
LANDSCAPE DESIGNERS
62047 BEDFORD CT.- EUGENE, OHIO 10548

NORTH
1" = 20'

FIGURE 10–81
A combination of diagonal and curvilinear design themes for the Duncan residence.

11

Spatial Composition

INTRODUCTION

Chapter 10 discusses the various aspects of form composition, the first step of the preliminary design phase. When completed, form composition provides the basic structure and visible skeleton on which the remainder of the design will be built.

An essential point to realize about form composition is that it is only the beginning step of preliminary design and by itself does not create a complete residential site design. Form composition is essentially only a two-dimensional study of the design and does not fully consider the desired total spatial experience of the outdoor environment. The next step in preliminary design, spatial composition, proceeds beyond the two-dimensional form composition to establish the spatial shell or envelope of a residential site design. Spatial composition builds on the form composition's framework by adding the third dimension very much like the walls and ceilings of indoor rooms build on the underlying floor plan of a house. It considers how the overall space is formed and develops ideas for vertical and overhead planes of enclosures. As indicated before, spatial composition usually occurs simultaneously with form composition. However, the two steps are being separated here for the sake of explanation.

This chapter discusses the different aspects of spatial composition including preliminary grading, planting design, use of vertical planes such as fences and walls, and the use of overhead structures in residential site design.

PRELIMINARY GRADING DESIGN

Spatial composition in residential site design should start with the ground plane. There are several reasons for this. First, the three-dimensional design of the ground can and should be done in close association with form composition. A second rea-

292

son is that the ground plane is the foundation for every other design element such as plant materials, pavement, walls, fences, and overhead structures. Thus, the elevation of the ground has a direct influence on the function and appearance of other elements. And finally, the ground plane is the surface on which we walk, run, sit, drive, and so on. It receives the most direct use and wear in the outdoor environment. Thus, its three-dimensional composition is critical.

The term *grading* is commonly used to refer to the manipulation of the ground's third dimension and is defined as shaping or molding the ground's surface for both functional and aesthetic purposes. Grading involves physical movement of soil from one area of the site to another. When earth is added to an area, it is called *fill*. When earth is removed or excavated from an area, it is called *cut*. Generally, there is an attempt to balance the quantity of cut and fill on a given project to eliminate the need for transporting earth to or from the site.

Two general purposes for grading on a residential site are necessity and aesthetics. For necessity, grading is undertaken to properly drain surface water and to accommodate circulation or other uses on the site. For aesthetics, grading is done to create space, screen or direct views, and provide visual interest. Grading for necessity is a utilitarian and engineering process, while grading for enhancement is an aesthetic and artistic endeavor. Both types of grading should be undertaken together so that all grading is both functional and appealing to the eye. Each specific purpose for grading is discussed more in the following sections.

Drainage

One utilitarian purpose for grading is to provide proper drainage across the ground's surface. There are a number of places on the residential site where special effort should be taken to correctly drain surface water.

1. Surface water should be drained away from the house and other structures on the site to reduce problems. There are several general existing slope conditions the designer may encounter on residential sites (Figure 11–1). In the first condition where the ground slopes naturally away from the house, the designer should maintain the slope so water continues to drain away from the house. This situation typically requires little or no regrading of the existing site. In the second situation where the house is located on level ground, the surface must be regraded to slope gradually away from the house. It is usually recommended that the ground's surface be sloped away from the house or other structures at a rate of 1 percent to 10 percent (Figure 11–2).

A slope of 1 percent is approximately equal to 1/8-inch vertical elevation change for every 1 horizontal foot across the surface (Figure 11–3). Another way to understand this is by applying the formula for percent of slope:

$$\text{Rise divided by run} = \text{percent of slope}$$

Rise is the vertical elevation change of the slope and *run* is the horizontal distance across the slope (Figure 11–4). Therefore, a slope of 1 percent rises or falls 1 foot for every 100 horizontal feet (1 divided by 100 = .01 or 1 percent). A slope of 10 percent rises or falls at a rate of 10 feet for every 100 horizontal feet or 1 foot for every 10 horizontal feet.

The third situation for existing slope conditions is where the house is located on a sloped site (bottom of Figure 11–1). Here it will be necessary to create a swale or shallow valleylike landform on the uphill side to collect surface drainage and direct it around the house.

2. Water should be drained as quickly as possible from paved walks and driveways so they can be used safely during and immediately after a rainstorm. It is also desirable to prevent water from accumulating during the winter season in northern climates because wet areas are apt to become covered with ice, causing a real safety problem. It is also important to drain surface runoff from paved outdoor

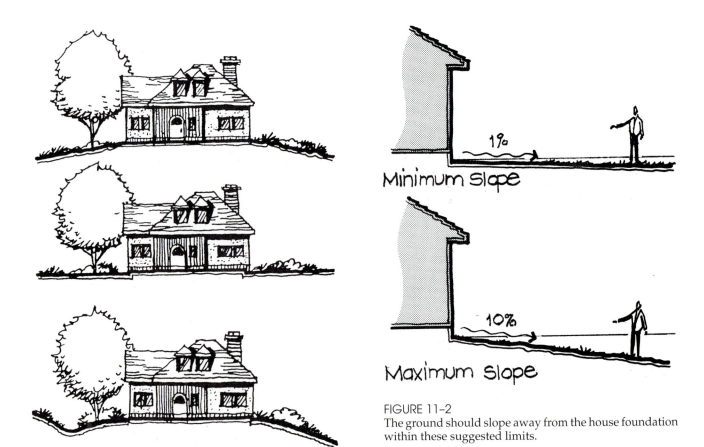

FIGURE 11-1
General types of existing slope conditions found on residential sites.

FIGURE 11-2
The ground should slope away from the house foundation within these suggested limits.

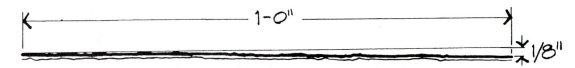

FIGURE 11-3
An example of a slope of 1 percent.

use areas like the outdoor living and entertaining space so they can be used as soon as possible after it rains. Pools of standing water on any paved surface reduce its safety and usefulness. For adequate drainage, paved surfaces of concrete or asphalt should have a minimum slope of 1 percent. Exposed aggregate concrete, brick, stone, or other rough pavement materials should have a minimum slope of 1.5 percent (a 1-1/2-foot vertical change for every 100 horizontal feet). At the other extreme, paved surfaces in outdoor spaces where people stand or sit for any length of time should not exceed a maximum of 3 percent. A paved surface that is steeper than 3 percent is perceived as having a definite slope and gives a space an uncomfortable or unstable feeling. Paved walks should not exceed a slope of 5 percent and driveways and parking areas should not be steeper than 8 percent.

3. Water should be properly drained from lawn surfaces to prevent standing water or soggy, wet areas. For positive drainage, it is recommended that lawn surfaces slope at 2 percent or 2 feet fall in every 100 horizontal feet (Figure 11-5). However, lawn surfaces should not exceed 25 percent (a 1-foot vertical elevation change for every 4 horizontal feet). Above this maximum, it becomes dangerous to operate a lawn mower. It should be noted that in some locations such as arid regions

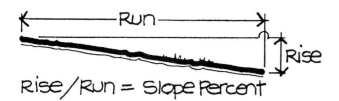

Rise/Run = Slope Percent

FIGURE 11-4
A method for determining percent of slope.

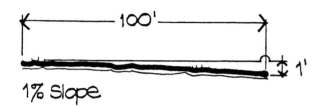

1% Slope

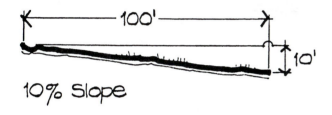

10% Slope

Preferred minimum slope for positive drainage of a lawn.

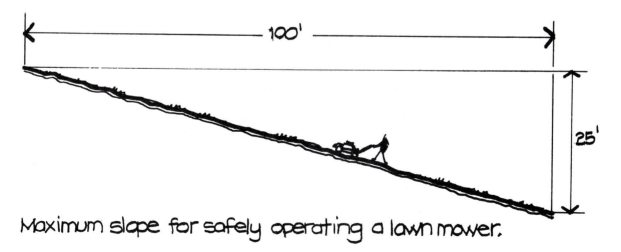

Maximum slope for safely operating a lawn mower.

FIGURE 11-5
Minimum and maximum slopes for lawns.

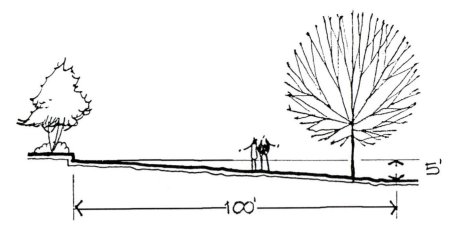

FIGURE 11–6
Maximum slopes for pedestrian walks.

or areas with problems of too much runoff from urban development, it may actually be desirable to temporarily hold water on a site during and after a storm. In this situation, lawns and planted areas may be designed to retain water until it can seep into the ground or be slowly drained away.

4. Planting beds or other vegetative surfaces should be drained to prevent damage to plant materials. For plant beds, it is recommended that the ground slope at a rate of at least 2 percent, but not more than 10 percent. A planting bed that is steeper than this is susceptible to erosion unless protected by ground cover.

Accommodating Circulation

Another purpose for grading is to accommodate circulation on sloped ground or between spaces of different ground elevations. As stated in the previous section, walks should not exceed a slope of 5 percent (or a 1-foot vertical change for every 20 horizontal feet) (Figure 11–6). This guideline is especially applicable for entry walks where comfort and safety of people are important.

Where the ground is too steep to provide a properly sloped surface, steps may be necessary to take up the elevation change between two spaces. There are a number of guidelines for the design of steps. First, they should be designed as an integral part of the overall design (Figure 11–7). Steps should not be designed as an afterthought to other aspects of the design and made to appear as an "add-on" (see the top portion of Figure 11–7). In addition, steps should have forms that are consistent with the overall design theme, and thus should be studied during form composition.

Steps also must have appropriate dimensions. Both the *tread,* the horizontal portion of the step on which the foot is placed, and the *riser,* the vertical portion of the step (Figure 11–8), must have the correct depth and height to be safe and feel comfortable. A guideline that is commonly used to establish the tread and riser dimensions is the following formula:

Twice the riser height plus the tread depth should equal 26″ or $2R + T = 26″$

Several examples in Figure 11–9 demonstrate how the formula can be applied. If the riser (R) is to be 6 inches high, then the formula is used to determine the proper tread depth (T) as follows:

Step 1 $2(6″) + T = 26″$
Step 2 $12″ + T = 26″$
Step 3 $T = 26″ - 12″ = 14″$

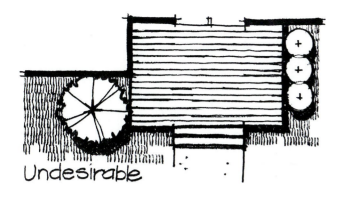

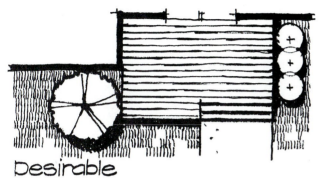

Undesirable

Desirable

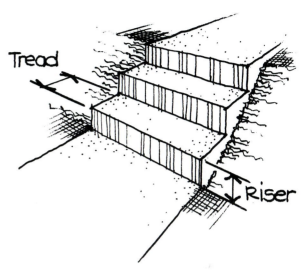

Tread

Riser

FIGURE 11–7
Steps should be designed as integral parts of the overall design composition.

FIGURE 11–8
An example of step risers and treads.

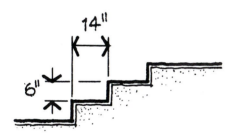

14"

6"

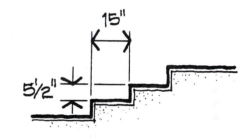

15"

5½"

FIGURE 11–9
Examples of ideal riser/tread relationships.

Or if each tread (T) is to be 15 inches, the riser height (R) is found as follows:

Step 1 $2R + 15'' = 26''$
Step 2 $2R = 26'' - 15'' = 11''$
Step 3 $R = 5.5''$

As can be seen from this formula, the dimensions of the treads and risers in a flight of outdoor steps are interdependently related. As the dimension of one becomes greater, the other becomes smaller. Once dimensions are established for a given set of steps, they should not be varied (Figure 11–10). That is, all the risers should be the same height and all the treads should be the same depth within the flight of steps. If these dimensions vary, they are apt to catch people by surprise and cause them to trip or fall.

There are several limitations on minimum and maximum dimensions for risers and treads (Figure 11–11). Each tread should be at least 12 inches deep. A tread that is smaller than this is too shallow for the average foot. The height of each riser

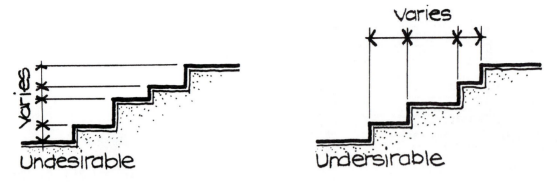

FIGURE 11–10
The dimensions for risers and treads should not vary in a flight of steps.

FIGURE 11–11
Minimum and maximum dimensions for risers
and treads.

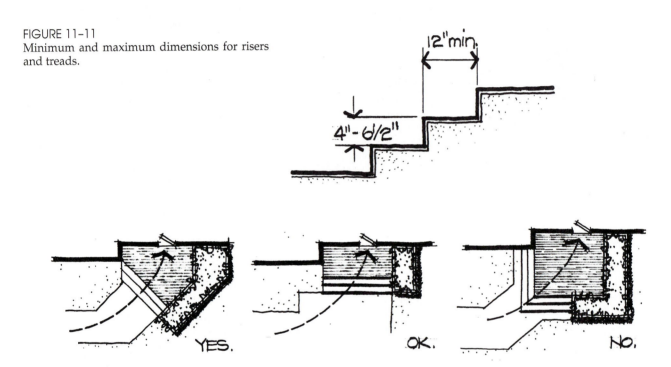

FIGURE 11–12
Steps should be oriented 90 degrees to the direction of movement.

should be at least 4 inches but no more than 6-1/2 inches. Below 4 inches, the height becomes insignificant and is not easily seen in the outdoors. This short dimension also creates the need for too many risers in a set of steps. Above 6-1/2 inches, the height of a riser becomes difficult for elderly people, children, and others with walking disabilities to negotiate.

Steps function best when they are oriented 90 degrees or at a right angle to the prime direction of movement (Figure 11–12). It is easier to walk up a flight of steps "head-on." The designer should avoid placing steps so that people have to walk up or down them across a sharp corner (right side of Figure 11–12). This is awkward and frequently dangerous.

Steps are often the best way to get people from one elevation to another. However, they do have one major problem: they cannot be negotiated by wheeled vehicles such as wheelchairs. Steps act like barriers in the landscape to free movement. Consequently, there is sometimes a need to provide ramps on a residential site to allow wheelchairs and other wheeled vehicles to move without limitation.

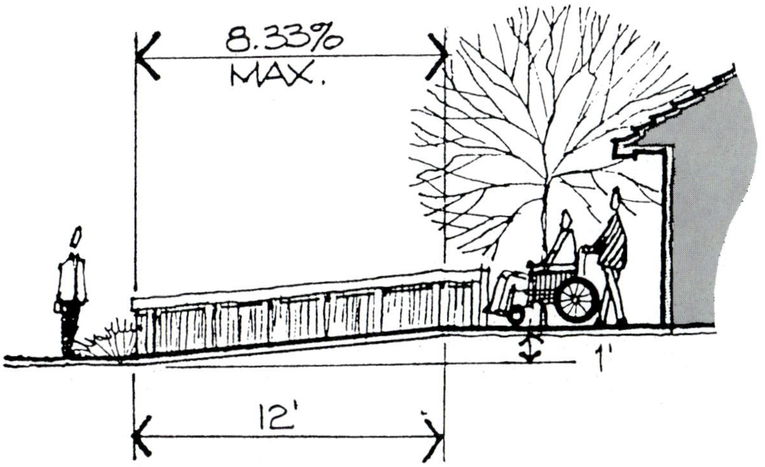

FIGURE 11–13
Maximum gradient for a handicap ramp.

There are a number of challenges in designing ramps. First, they need to be located and designed along with every other element in the design so that they appear as an integral element. Too often, ramps are added as an afterthought. When this happens, ramps usually look poorly related and out of place. Second, ramps need to conform to proper dimensions. The slope or gradient along the ramp should not exceed 8.33 percent (Figure 11–13). The slope should not rise more than 1 vertical foot for every 12 horizontal feet along the ramp. The result of this is that most ramps take up a large horizontal distance on a site, especially when compared to steps. For example, to accommodate 2 feet of elevation change between two levels, a ramp needs to extend 24 horizontal feet. This is extensive compared to only a few feet needed for a set of steps for the same elevation change. One last dimensional guideline is that ramps should be at least 5 feet wide.

Creating Space

There are several aesthetic purposes for grading on a residential site. First, grading can define edges between spaces and partially enclose space in the vertical plane. The first and simplest method is to provide an elevation change between two adjoining spaces (Figure 11–14). A small difference in elevation between one space and another makes each seem like a distinct place. The greater the change in elevation between spaces, the greater the feeling of spatial separation.

Grading can also be used to provide vertical planes around the outside of a space for implied enclosure. The existing ground can be excavated, built on with earth mounds to provide spatial enclosure (Figure 11–15), or both excavated and filled (Figure 11–16).

In all these situations, the higher the surrounding ground, the greater the sense of spatial enclosure. The greatest feeling of enclosure is gained when the ground fills a 45-degree cone of vision or extends above eye level (Figure 11–17). Whatever height is created, plant materials can be added to the surrounding slopes or walls of a space to accentuate the ground's height, thus giving the space an even more pronounced sense of enclosure (Figure 11–18).

Full enclosure with surrounding ground is most appropriate where a sense of privacy is desired, such as in a small sitting area or private outdoor lounging area. Often, a space requires enclosure on only one side with a more open feeling provided on another (Figure 11–19). The height of the surrounding ground can be varied to give different feelings of enclosure.

In all situations, the height of the surrounding ground should be limited by several guidelines. For slopes, the incline should not exceed a rise of 1 foot vertical change for every 2 horizontal feet; referred to as a 2:1 or 50 percent slope (Figure 11–20). Slopes steeper than this are subject to slippage and erosion.

FIGURE 11-14
A feeling of space can be created by a simple grade change between adjoining areas.

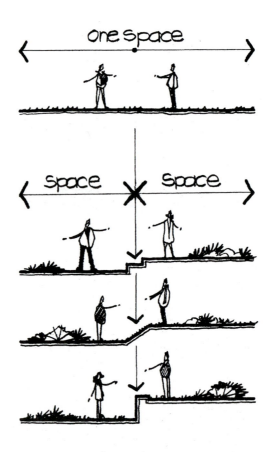

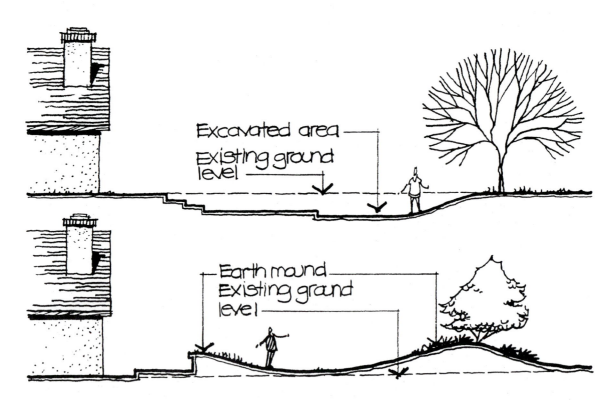

FIGURE 11-15
Vertical planes around a space can be created by excavating into the existing ground or building on it with earth mounds.

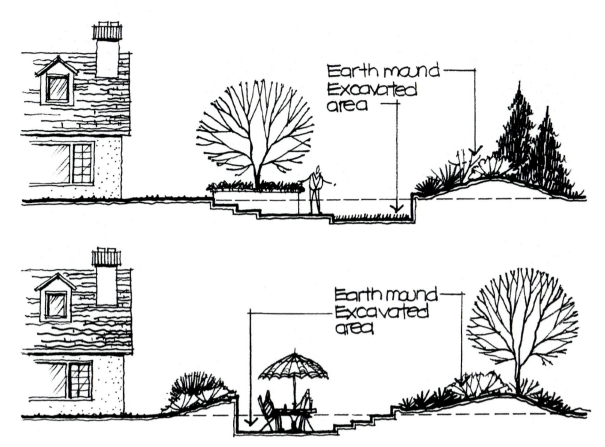

FIGURE 11–16
A combination of excavation and mounds can be used to enclose space in the vertical plane.

FIGURE 11–17
The greatest sense of enclosure occurs when surrounding ground fills a 45-degree cone of vision.

FIGURE 11–18
Plant materials can be used to accentuate the height of ground around a space.

Spatial Composition

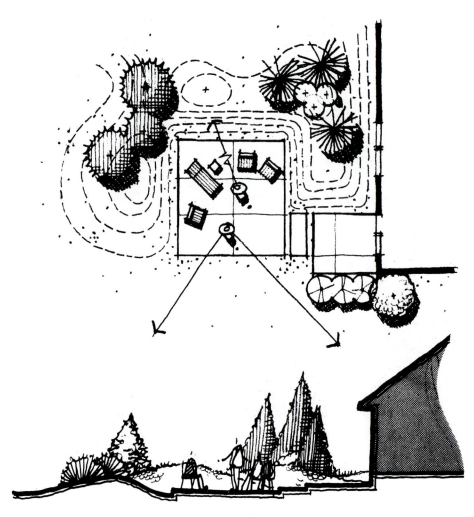

FIGURE 11-19
The location and height of ground can be varied to provide different degrees of enclosure.

FIGURE 11-20
Maximum slope steepness without erosion.

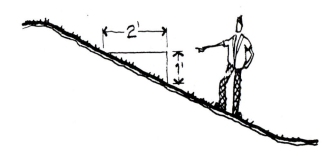

When enclosing space in the vertical plane, the designer should use slopes or low retaining walls to reinforce the style or design theme established by the form composition. For example, a curvilinear design theme should be enhanced with soft, sweeping slopes or mounds (left side of Figure 11–21). The slopes should move around the outer edge of the curves to reinforce their form in the third dimension. A rectangular design theme can be reinforced with retaining walls or rigid slopes (right side of Figure 11–21). The designer might also use a combination of slopes and retaining walls (Figure 11–22).

The character of the base plane or floor of spaces created with ground should also reinforce the intended design theme. For curvilinear design themes, the base

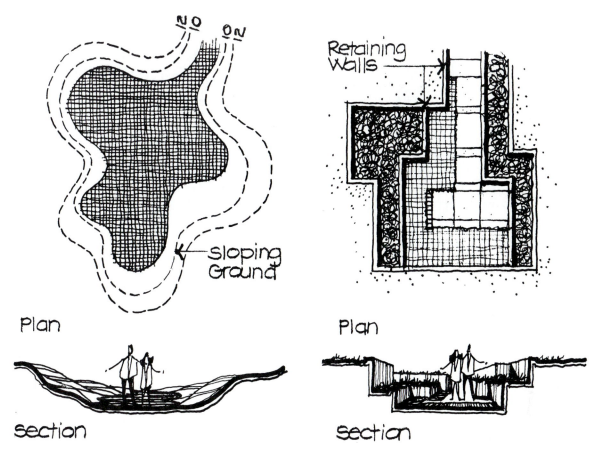

FIGURE 11-21
Slopes and retaining walls should relate to and reinforce the established design theme.

plane might be gently sloped and contoured with gradual transitions from one space to another (left side of Figure 11–23). For rectangular or other structured themes, the floor of spaces could be kept relatively level (though still providing for proper drainage) with definite grade changes (made with steps or terraces) between one level and the next (right side of Figure 11–23).

Screening and Directing Views

The second aesthetic purpose for grading is to either screen or direct views. Grading of the ground plane can elevate selected areas of the site to block undesirable views (Figure 11–24). Mounds or berms can be placed to screen views of the street, the neighbor's driveway, the adjoining back yard, and so on. One other suggestion is to make mounds or berms look as if they were part of the existing site. Earth mounds are sometimes graded with abrupt slopes that make the mounds look like unappealing bumps on the site (top half of Figure 11–25). Mounds should gradually flow into each other and the surrounding site (bottom half of Figure 11–25).

The ground plane can also be molded to direct views toward certain points in the landscape. The side slopes of a valley landform can function like blinders to block out all but the intended view (Figure 11–26).

PRELIMINARY PLANTING DESIGN

Plant materials are another element used in the spatial composition. On the residential site, plant materials are one of the most important design elements for the floor,

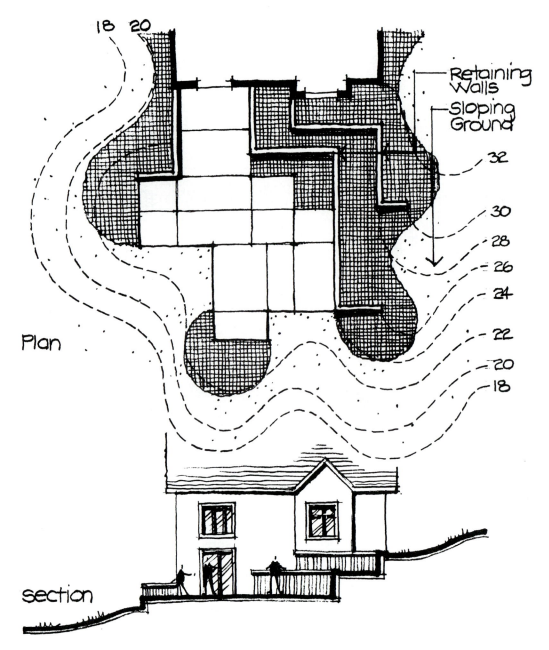

18 20

Retaining Walls

Sloping Ground

32

30

28

26

24

22

20

18

Plan

section

FIGURE 11-22
A combination of slopes and retaining walls can be carefully coordinated in terms of form composition.

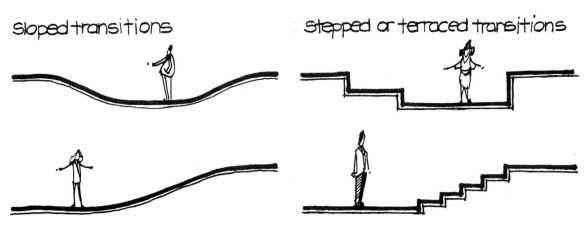

sloped transitions

stepped or terraced transitions

FIGURE 11-23
The slope of the base plane in spaces created with ground should relate to the overall design theme.

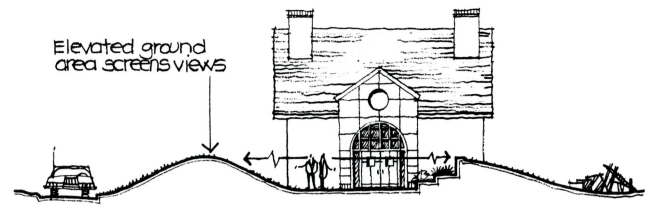

Elevated ground area screens views

FIGURE 11-24
The ground can be graded to screen undesirable views.

undesirable

Desirable

FIGURE 11-25
Earth mounds should blend smoothly with the surrounding ground.

walls, and ceiling of outdoor rooms. They are living elements and need special care in slection and placement in the landscape. They can be used by themselves or in conjunction with other elements to create outdoor rooms and reinforce the design theme.

During preliminary design, the designer takes a "broad brush" approach to the use of plant materials by deciding where plant materials should be located and what function they serve in the design. Their selection must be based on function, appearance (size, form, foliage color, flower color, foliage texture, fruit size, and color), and environmental conditions present on the site (sun exposure, wind exposure, precipitation, soil characteristics).

While plant materials can be categorized in numerous ways, one such way is by "type". They are: (1) deciduous plants, (2) coniferous evergreen plants, and (3) broad-leaved evergreen plants. Each of these types is briefly described in the following paragraphs.

FIGURE 11-26
The ground can be graded to direct views to
desirable points in the landscape.

Deciduous plant materials lose their leaves in the autumn and regain them in the spring. Because of this quality, they are often used to emphasize seasonal change and variation. In addition, many deciduous plants are distinguished by showy spring flowers and dramatic autumn foliage color. Ornamental trees such as flowering dogwoods, crab apples, and Canadian redbuds are deciduous plants that are used particularly for their appeal of seasonal change. Deciduous trees can be used for shade during the hot months of the summer while allowing exposure to the sun during the cool months of the winter.

Coniferous evergreen plants are those that have needlelike foliage. Because coniferous plants retain their foliage throughout the year, they can be used wherever a permanent mass of foliage is required. The permanence of coniferous evergreens should be used in direct association with deciduous plants so that a composition of plant materials retains some structure and green color during the times of the year when deciduous plants are without leaves. Coniferous evergreens are particularly useful for screening undesirable views or blocking cold winter winds. In addition, they can be grouped together in a mass to create a backdrop for showy deciduous plants.

Broad-leaved evergreens have leaves that resemble deciduous foliage in appearance. However, broad-leaved evergreens retain their leaves throughout the year. Broad-leaved evergreens as a group are best used in a design for their foliage texture and for their showy spring flowers. However, they should not be used only for their flowers because these last only a few weeks of the year. Broad-leaved evergreens can also be used to give a dark yet shiny leaf surface to a planting compostion.

Specific selection and the identification of plants by genus and species are usually done when the master plan is prepared.

Plant materials can function in a variety of ways on the residential site.* These functional uses can be: (1) architectural, (2) aesthetic, or (3) engineering.

Architectural Uses

Plant materials serve two primary architectural uses on the residential site by creating space and either screening or enframing views. Plant materials can func-

---

*One system for categorizing these functions was developed by Gary O. Robinette in his book, *Plants, People, and Environmental Quality* (Washington, D.C.: U.S. Department of Interior, National Park Service, 1972), p. 56.

FIGURE 11–27
Trees can be used to create walls and ceilings in outdoor spaces.

FIGURE 11–28
Tree trunks can be used to imply vertical planes in outdoor spaces.

tion as floors, walls, and ceilings to establish the spatial envelope of a residential design, just like the architectural components of a building create indoor rooms. It should be noted that the term *architectural* refers only to enclosing space and does not mean using plants in straight lines or formal layouts. Plant materials can be used architecturally in any design theme.

Creating Space. Plant materials of all sizes and types can be used to define outdoor space. However, it is best to locate trees first when creating outdoor rooms with plant materials because their size and mass establish the overall framework of the spatial composition. Trees should be placed in a design to create vertical walls and overhead ceilings of foliage (Figure 11–27). After the trees have been arranged in the design, smaller plant materials can be located to complement the spatial organization of the trees.

In the vertical plane, trees can define space by two different means. First, the trunks of trees can suggest the edges of space, particularly when they are massed or lined up (top of Figure 11–28). The tree trunks can act like the columns in a building subtly separating one room from another. Tree trunks only imply the edge of a space because views are not completely contained within the space. To create complete enclosure, smaller trees or shrubs must be used in association with the tree trunks (bottom of Figure 11–28).

The second way trees create space in the vertical plane is by means of their foliage mass. Two different levels of spatial enclosure are possible (Figure 11–29). Large trees provide walls of foliage that define the upper limits of outdoor spaces, while smaller trees create lower walls for enclosure at eye level. The residential site designer can work with these two planes to make varied degrees of spatial enclosure (Figure 11–30). Large trees are best for outdoor rooms where views below the tree canopy are desired, while smaller trees are appropriate where walls of foliage are needed at eye level. In creating vertical enclosure of outdoor space with trees, the designer should decide whether year-around or seasonal enclosure is desired. Evergreen trees should

FIGURE 11-29
The foliage mass of trees can define the vertical
plane in outdoor spaces at different levels.

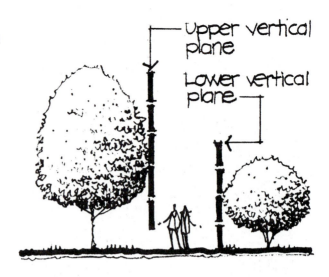

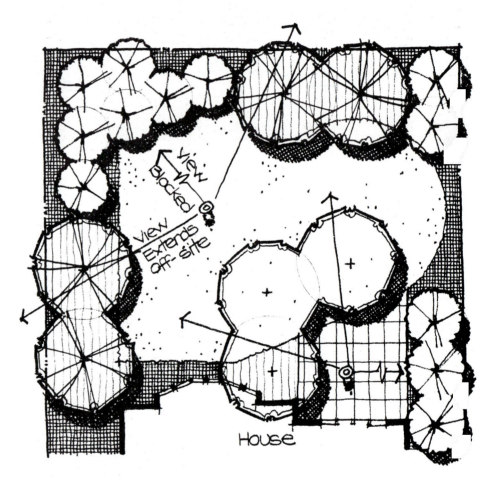

FIGURE 11-30
Different sizes of trees create varied degrees of spatial enclosure.

be used for year-around enclosure while deciduous plants can be used to enclose a
space during the late spring, summer, and early autumn months of the year.

Trees can also be used to furnish ceilings over outdoor rooms. As discussed
in Chapter 2, a vegetative ceiling can provide a sense of vertical scale in an outdoor
space, a feeling of comfort, and shade. These uses are frequently desirable where
people spend time sitting and socializing in the outdoors, such as in the outdoor

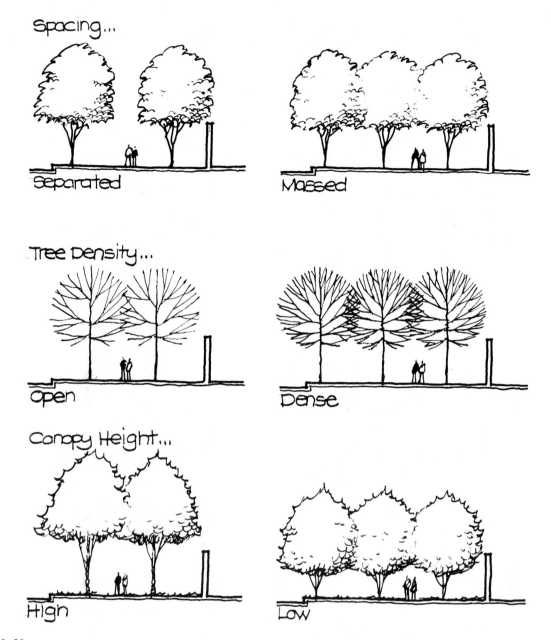

FIGURE 11–31
Different variables influence how tree canopies create the overhead plane of outdoor space.

entry foyer, the outdoor living and entertaining space, or other sitting and gathering spaces. The spacing of the trees, density of the canopy, and height of the canopy above the ground are variables that influence the degree of overhead enclosure in outdoor space (Figure 11–31).

In defining space with trees, thought should be given to coordinating their placement with the desired design theme and grading of the ground plane. Trees should reinforce the shapes in the form composition by extending the lines and forms of the ground plane upward into the third dimension. Trees should not be scattered indiscriminately in a design but should be massed together so their trunks and foliage mass reinforce the base plane patterns. Figure 11–32 shows both a bad and a good example of coordinating trees with the underlying ground plane. Trees should be placed in a structured alignment in an axial design theme and in a flowing composition in a curvilinear theme (Figure 11–33).

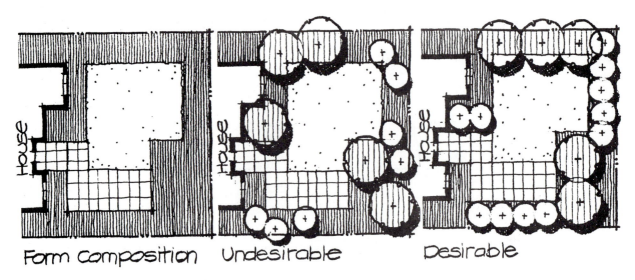

Form Composition   Undesirable   Desirable

FIGURE 11–32
The location of trees should be coordinated with the overall design theme.

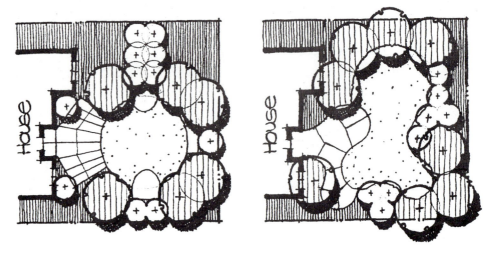

FIGURE 11–33
Different design themes and corresponding tree locations.

Outdoor space can be established with other plant materials. Tall shrubs that are 6 feet or more in height enclose space at a lower level than trees. Tall shrubs can be used by themselves to create space or in association with trees (Figure 11–34). The tall shrubs can function like walls below the ceiling of the canopy overhead.

Low shrubs, between 1 foot and 3 feet high, can also be used to indicate the limits of outdoor space much like low walls, which define a space's edges without limiting views outward to other areas of the landscape (Figure 11–35). This is desirable treatment for outdoor living and entertaining spaces or entry foyers where partial containment with views to other points in the landscape gives a sense of separation without complete enclosure. Partial containment is often a good balance between complete enclosure (with no views) and no enclosure (with unlimited views in all directions).

Ground cover, spreading plants growing to a maximum height of 1 foot, low annuals, and perennials can likewise imply the edges of space. A bed of ground cover

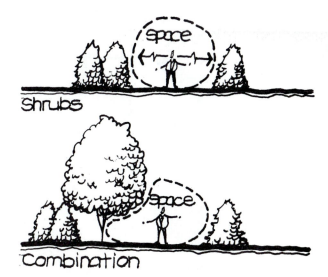

FIGURE 11–35
Low shrubs imply spatial separation without screening views between adjoining spaces.

next to an area of lawn or pavement can imply an edge to a space (Figure 11–36). The change in material and the slight height of the ground cover suggest where the outdoor room stops on the ground plane. The shape and edges of ground cover beds should be consistent with the overall design theme of the site (Figure 11–37).

Screening and Directing Views. Another architectural use of plant materials on a residential site is to screen and enframe views. In relation to other design elements, plant materials have several advantages and disadvantages for screening and directing views. In comparison to steep slopes or berms, plant materials take up less room and provide more height (Figure 11–38). Therefore, plant materials are usually better than slopes or berms for screening views on a small residential site. However, plants occupy more room than a fence or wall. Plant materials also require some time to reach mature height and may vary in their density with the season if they are deciduous. Plants also require proper conditions for growth. Walls and fences, on the other hand, give instant screening and separation.

On a residential site, plants can screen undesirable off-site views to neighboring driveways, back yards, and storage areas or to unsightly on-site elements such as an air conditioner, vegetable garden, and so on. Plants may also give a sense of privacy by screening views to the neighbor's outside living and entertaining space

Spatial Composition

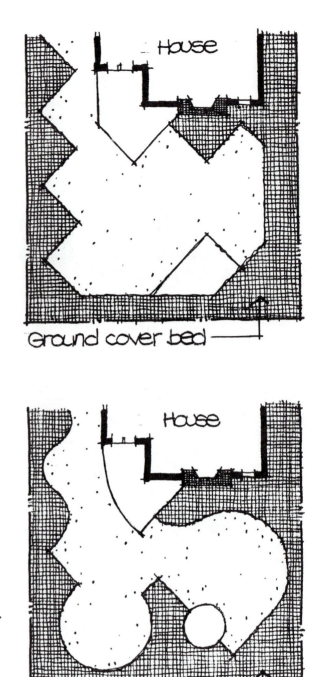

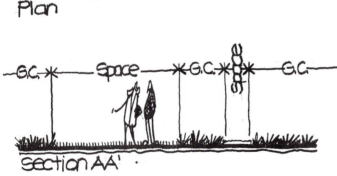

FIGURE 11–36
Ground cover can imply the edges of outdoor space.

FIGURE 11–37
The edge of ground cover beds should be coordinated with the overall design theme.

or recreational lawn area (Figure 11–39). Evergreen plant materials are usually more desirable for screening views than deciduous plants because they furnish year-around screening, though a mixture of evergreen and deciduous plants provides the most visual balance and interest.

Both foliage mass and tree trunks can be used to enframe views (Figure 11–40). Again, they should be coordinated with other elements to enhance their ability to direct views to selected areas or points of the landscape.

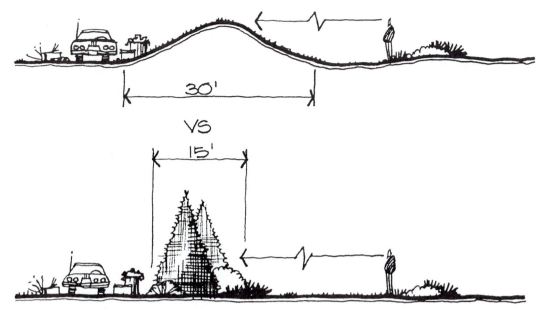

30'

VS

15'

FIGURE 11–38
Plant materials take up less space than earth mounds in screening views.

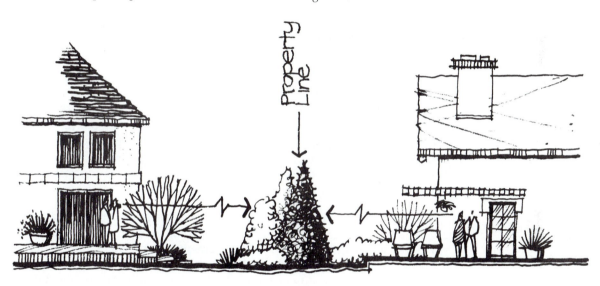

FIGURE 11–39
Plant materials can provide privacy between adjoining neighbors' living and entertaining spaces.

FIGURE 11–40
Tree trunks and foliage mass can enframe a view to a selected point in the landscape.

313

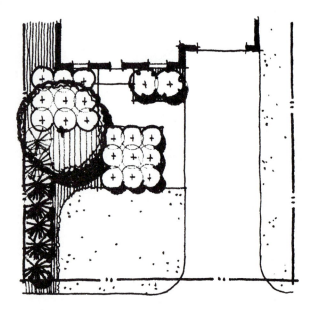 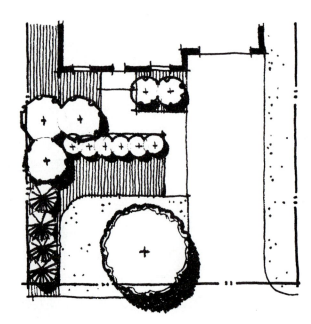

FIGURE 11–41
Examples of trees used as dominant elements based on size.

Aesthetic Uses

Plant materials can be used to provide several aesthetic functions on the residential site, including providing visual accents and complementing the architectural style of the house.

Providing Accents. The residential site designer should have established the location of focal points or accents of the design composition while preparing the functional diagrams. During preliminary design, many of these focal points can be established with plant materials that stand out in contrast to their surroundings due to size and form.

1. *Size.* Plant materials that are larger and especially taller in size than surrounding plants act as visual accents. Trees can act as dominant plants when they are the largest element among other plants (left side of Figure 11–41), or when they are placed by themselves in an open lawn area, (right side of Figure 11–41). Tall shrubs or ornamental trees can also serve as accents when they are larger than surrounding plants in a group (Figure 11–42). In all these situations, care must be exercised not to use plants that are too large for their context. Plants that overpower their setting can make all the other elements of a design seem too small.

2. *Form.* Plant forms that differ from a neutral rounded form are commonly seen as accents in a design. Focal points are most easily created by plants that are columnar/fastigiate, pyramidal, or picturesque in form (Figure 11–43).

Ornamental trees work especially well as accents based on their size and form. Ornamental trees are small- to medium-sized trees (10- to 15-feet height and spread) that have appealing form, color, and texture throughout the year, like crab apples (*Malus* sp.), dogwoods (*Cornus* sp.), hawthorns (*Crateagus* sp.), or olives (*Olea* sp.). Ornamental trees can be located at strategic points such as near the entrance walk, outdoor living and entertaining space, or at a distant point in the yard (Figure 11–44).

Often, accent plants are best placed at prominent points of planting beds, corners, areas that will be seen from many different vantage points, or at the end of an

FIGURE 11-42
Plants that are larger than surrounding ones in a mass serve as accents.

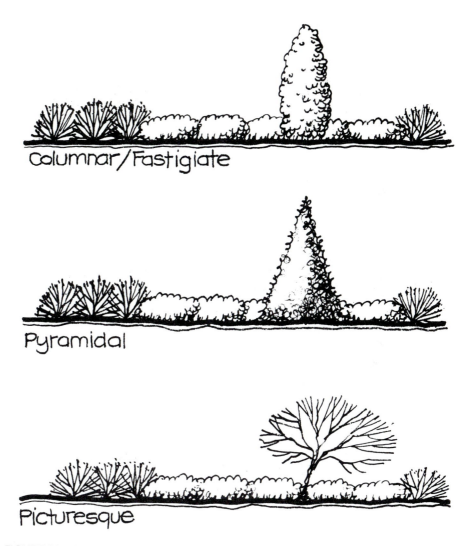

Columnar/Fastigiate

Pyramidal

Picturesque

FIGURE 11-43
Columnar/fastigiate, pyramidal, and picturesque plant forms can be used as accents in a planting composition.

axis (Figure 11–45). The shape of these areas (form composition) and the placement of accent plants within them (spatial composition) need to be carefully coordinated during preliminary design. The organization and shape of outdoor spaces must allow the accent plant to be fully expressed.

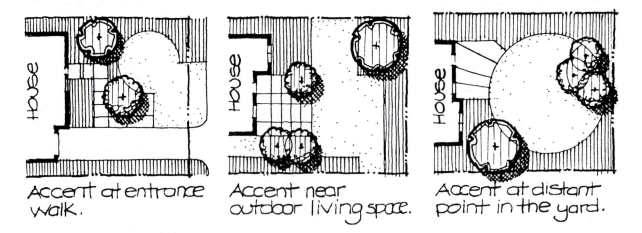

Accent at entrance walk.

Accent near outdoor living space.

Accent at distant point in the yard.

FIGURE 11–44
Examples of ornamental trees used as accents at strategic points of the site.

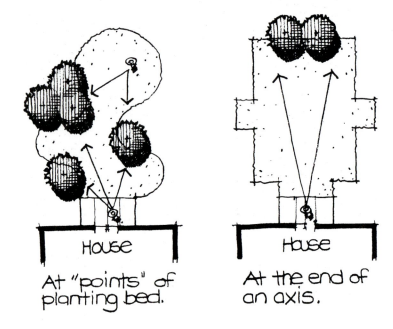

At "points" of planting bed.

At the end of an axis.

FIGURE 11–45
Accent plants should be placed at prominent points within the design.

Complementing the House. Another aesthetic use of plant materials is to complement the architectural style of the house. Forms, lines, and colors of the house can be echoed or repeated in the site with plants. For example, the horizontal mass and lines of a one-story house can be carried into the adjoining site with a mass of plants that continues the horizontal line (top of Figure 11–46). Or a house with numerous peaks and gables can be complemented with a grouping of fastigiate and pyramidal plant forms (middle of Figure 11–46). Sometimes, it is desirable to contrast the architecture with plants of opposite forms (bottom of Figure 11–46).

Engineering Uses

Engineering uses of plant materials on a residential site include controlling erosion, directing pedestrian and vehicular circulation, and screening glare from reflective surfaces.

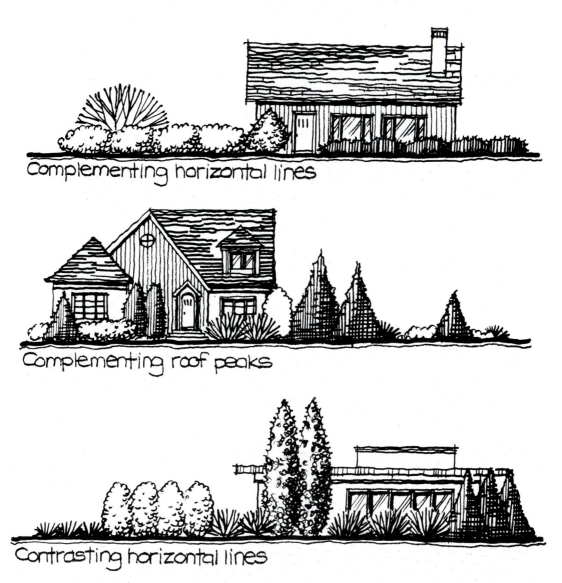

Complementing horizontal lines

Complementing roof peaks

Contrasting horizontal lines

FIGURE 11-46
Plant materials can complement or contrast the architectural style of the house.

Controlling Erosion. Plant materials can be used on steep slopes or areas of loose soil to minimize erosion. Ground covers and plants with dense root systems are especially valuable because their roots hold the soil in place. The vegetative cover of plant leaves also protects slopes from the potential damage of precipitation striking the ground and from the eroding effect of blowing wind. Plant materials can be used on loose soil or slopes up to 2:1 or 50 percent in steepness. Even plant materials have limited usefulness in preventing erosion on slopes that are steeper than this.

Directing Circulation. Plant materials can be used as walls to direct how and where people and vehicles move on a residential site. One good application of this use is along the front entrance walk leading from the driveway to the outdoor entry foyer. A mass of low plants can contain people on the walk as well as reinforce the direction of movement (Figure 11-47). A similar use of plants is along the driveway to keep vehicles on the driveway surface (Figure 11-48). However, plants should not crowd the driveway in such a way as to hinder the opening of car doors, or the removal and piling of snow in northern climates.

Spatial Composition

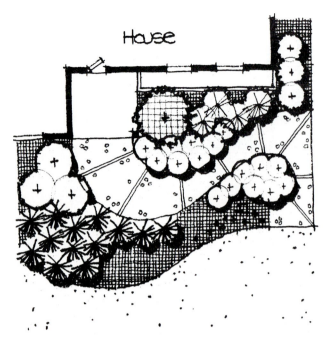

FIGURE 11–47
Plant materials can direct pedestrian movement along the entrance walk.

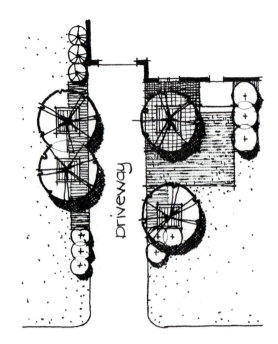

FIGURE 11–48
Plant materials can direct vehicular movement along the driveway without limiting pedestrian circulation.

Screening Glare.   Plants can also minimize and screen glare from reflective surfaces. One way is to shade reflective surfaces such as cars or water. Glare is eliminated when the sun cannot strike the reflective surface directly. Glare can also be screened when plant materials are placed between the reflective surface and the viewer (Figure 11–49). One possible application of this is the placement of a low- to medium-height hedge between a swimming pool or large panel of glass windows and an outdoor sitting space.

Planting Design Guidelines and Process

There are a number of guidelines the residential site designer should consider while designing with plant materials in preliminary design. Some of these were covered in the section on design principles in Chapter 9. Perhaps the most important guideline of planting design is that plants should be massed together (Figure 11–50). Plants that are grouped together are more unified (the principle of mass collection) than those that are scattered about as individual elements.

There are several other suggestions about massing plants together. First, all plant materials should be used and drawn in plan as mature or near mature plants. This is especially true of shrubs and small trees. Large trees can be drawn at 50 percent to 100 percent mature size because they take many years to reach full growth. This requires the designer to be familiar with plants and their sizes. If this guideline is followed, the installation of immature nursery-stock plant materials will at first appear sparse or spotty because there will be gaps between individual plants in a mass. However, with time and growth, the plants will fill in to create a mass (right side of Figure 11–50). When presenting plans to clients, it is important to tell them that the effect portrayed in the plans may take several years or more to achieve.

On preliminary designs, it is typical to represent shrubs as masses without distinguishing the individual plants within these masses. The drawing of individual plants within a mass is usually reserved for the master plan. Figure 11–51 shows the graphic differences for showing plant materials in a functional diagram, preliminary design, and master plan of a selected portion of a site. The functional

318   Chapter 11   Spatial Composition

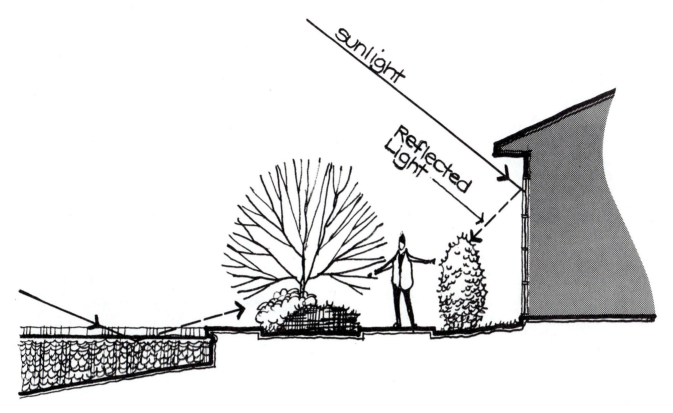

FIGURE 11–49
Plant materials can screen the reflection from glass, water surfaces, and so on.

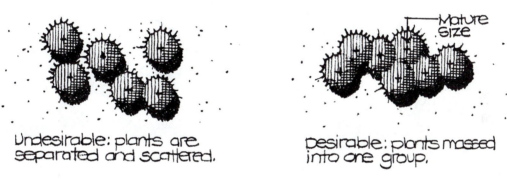

Undesirable: plants are separated and scattered.

Desirable: plants massed into one group.

Mature size

FIGURE 11–50
Plants should be organized in masses.

diagram is the most generalized while the master plan is the most detailed. The detail in the preliminary design is between these other two types of drawings.

Another guideline for planting design is to use a variety of plant species without making the design too complicated or busy. Unfortunately, there is no rule of thumb for defining when too few or too many different types of plant materials have been used in a design (Figure 11–52). This judgment is based on "feel," an eye for good design, and experience. An inexperienced designer is apt to use too many different types of plants so that an arboretum of plants results. Be careful to avoid this.

In selecting plant materials, a balanced mix between deciduous, coniferous evergreens, and broad-leaved evergreens should be the goal. This is especially needed in those climatic zones where deciduous plants lose their foliage in the winter. A winter landscape with too many deciduous plants will lack weight and be too transparent because of the lack of evergreens (top of Figure 11–53). On the other

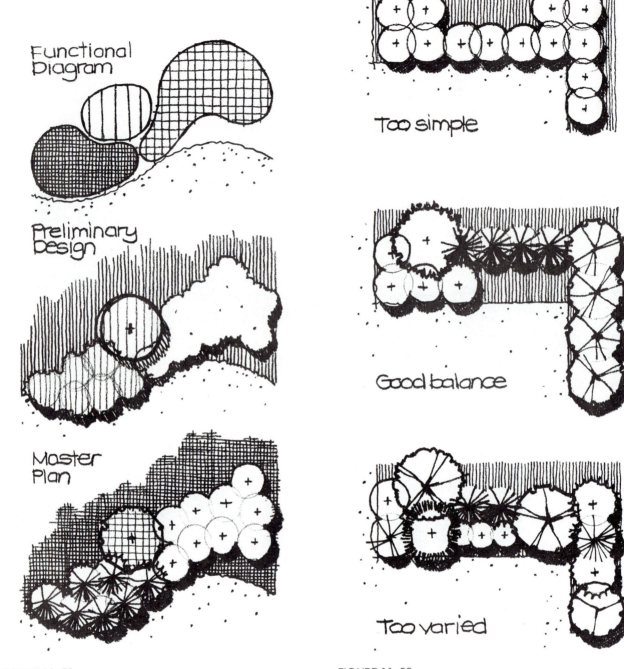

FIGURE 11–51
An example of the graphic differences among the functional diagram, preliminary design, and master plan.

FIGURE 11–52
There should be a balance between simplicity and variety in a planting composition.

hand, a winter landscape with too many evergreen plants (middle of Figure 11–53) will look too dark and gloomy, not a pleasant sight when the general climate conditions are similar. Ideally a proper balance among the various plant types will make the winter landscape a visual success (bottom of Figure 11–53).

To organize and select the plants in a design, the designer is encouraged to follow a process similar to that used to develop the overall plan of the site. That is, the designer should start with general concepts and then add detail through a series of refinements. The first step should be to establish the structure of the planting design (Figure 11–54). At this stage, the main concern is to decide on the location of the pri-

Undesirable: too many deciduous plants lack visible structure in the winter.

Undesirable: too many coniferous evergreens create a dark, somber feeling.

Desirable: balance between deciduous and coniferous evergreen plants.

FIGURE 11–53
There should be a balance between deciduous and coniferous evergreen plants in a composition.

mary plants such as shade trees, mass screens, and accents. These elements define the principal walls and ceilings of the outdoor spaces as well as points of attraction.

The second step builds on the first by studying and drawing the size of the plants. The size of the primary plants is first considered by converting the diagrammatic symbols to actual plant sizes (Figure 11–55). Next, smaller scale shrubs are proposed as bubbles representing generalized masses. The height of these plants is also studied and proposed at this stage. The general intent is to visually link (interconnect) the primary plants and to provide a composition of varied heights. Additionally, the designer often places taller plants toward the background and shorter plants near the foreground. The designer has now established the skeletal framework of the planting design.

The next step should be to study the relative foliage color and texture of the plants. This can be done by adding graphic value with lines or color to the previous

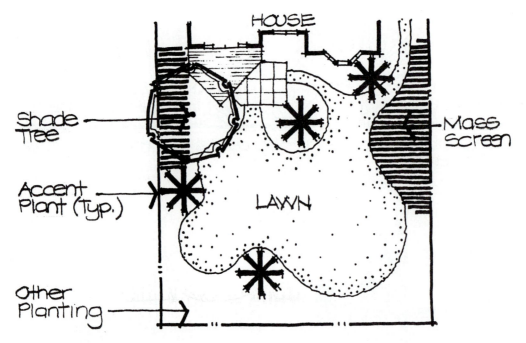

FIGURE 11–54
First, establish the major structure of the planting scheme.

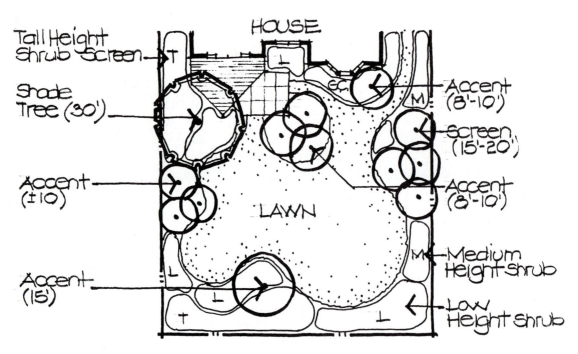

FIGURE 11–55
Second, draw the specific sizes of plant material within each major area.

drawing (Figure 11–56). The objective is to create a tapestry of varied colors of green along with a range of textures. Plants with dark green foliage are typically used as backgrounds or as visual "anchors" below the canopy of lighter or more open deciduous trees. Plants with light green foliage are best used as foreground plants or as contrasting elements in relation to darker ones. Coarse textured plants are commonly located to serve as accents while fine textures are used for contrast. After

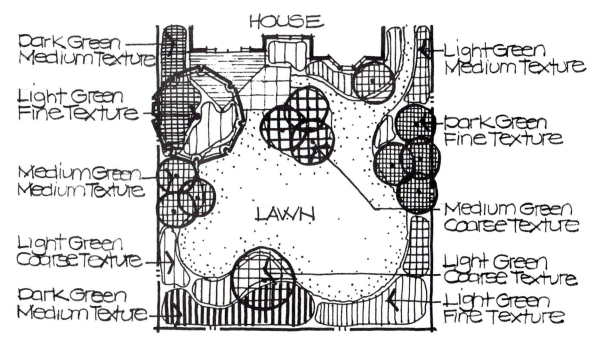

FIGURE 11–56
Third, select the foliage color and plant textures.

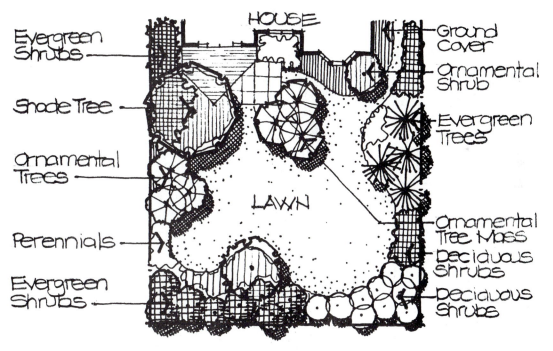

FIGURE 11–57
Fourth, draw the plants in a semirealistic fashion.

completing this step, the designer has defined the visual characteristics (size, color, and texture) of all the plants in the design and has coordinated them to fit appropriately into the overall scheme. It should be pointed out that specific plant names have not been considered; only plant characteristics.

The final step in the planting design process is to complete the drawing of the plants on the preliminary design (Figure 11–57). All the primary plants such as

FIGURE 11–58
An example of a retaining wall.

trees are drawn as single plants or masses of single plants while shrubs are shown as large undifferentiated masses. An attempt should also be made to use graphic symbols which represent the visual character of the plants. For example, dark foliated plants should ideally be drawn with a darker value while coarse textured plants can be given a rougher outline. Nevertheless, good graphic techniques should prevail, making it likely that not all characteristics can be illustrated. As is typical of preliminary design, plant names are not identified or included. This occurs during the development of the master plan.

WALLS AND FENCES

Walls and fences comprise still another set of elements the landscape designer can use to define the third dimension during spatial composition. As with plant materials, the designer is typically most concerned with the location and function of walls and fences as well as with their general materials during preliminary design. For example, the designer may decide that a wall near the outdoor entry foyer should be stone while a fence along the east property line should be constructed of rough-sawn cedar. The designer usually does not determine the actual appearance of walls or fences or the specific pattern that the materials will have on these vertical planes. Again, this study of details occurs in a later step (see Chapter 12).

There are two general categories of walls and fences that can be used on the residential site: (1) retaining walls and (2) free-standing walls or fences. Retaining walls hold back a slope or upper level of ground from a lower area of ground (Figure 11–58). As indicated in the earlier section on grading, retaining walls can be considered as a visual and functional part of the ground plane. Their location and function is directly tied to the grading of the ground's surface. Retaining walls are usually constructed with a masonry material, such as stone, brick, or masonry block, or with a pressure-treated wood that can withstand constant contact with the ground.

Free-standing walls or fences are elements that stand in the landscape without the support of other structural elements (Figure 11–59). Free-standing walls are most often constructed of a masonry material, while fences are usually built with wood or one of the many types of metals.

Both retaining walls and free-standing walls can be used for a number of functions on the residential site. Walls and fences can fulfill the same functions as

FIGURE 11-59
An example of a free-standing fence and wall.

FIGURE 11-60
Walls and fences can repeat the material of the house facade in the site.

plant materials do in the vertical plane by serving as spatial edges, screening views, creating privacy, directing views, modifying exposure to sun and wind, and directing movement through the landscape. As stated before, the advantages that walls and fences have in fulfilling these functions in comparison to plant materials are that walls and fences do not take time to mature and they do not require specific environmental conditions for location. Walls and fences also do not take up much area on the site and are very practical where space is limited.

In addition, walls and fences can be used for several other purposes: (1) architectural extension of the house, (2) background to other elements, (3) unifier, and (4) visual interest of form and pattern.

Architectural Extension.   Walls and fences can be used to visually and functionally connect a house or other building to its surrounding site in several distinct ways. First, walls and fences can repeat the materials that are on the house's facade in the landscape, thus providing a visual link between the house and the site (Figure 11–60). This repetition of materials creates a strong sense of unity between house and site. The second way walls and fences can connect a house to its surroundings is by serving as extensions of the house that stretch out into the site from the house (Figure 11–61). Such architectural extensions act like "arms" that reach out to "embrace the site." Both these techniques make the house and site appear as a totally integrated environment.

FIGURE 11–61
Walls and fences can extend out from the house
into the site like arms.

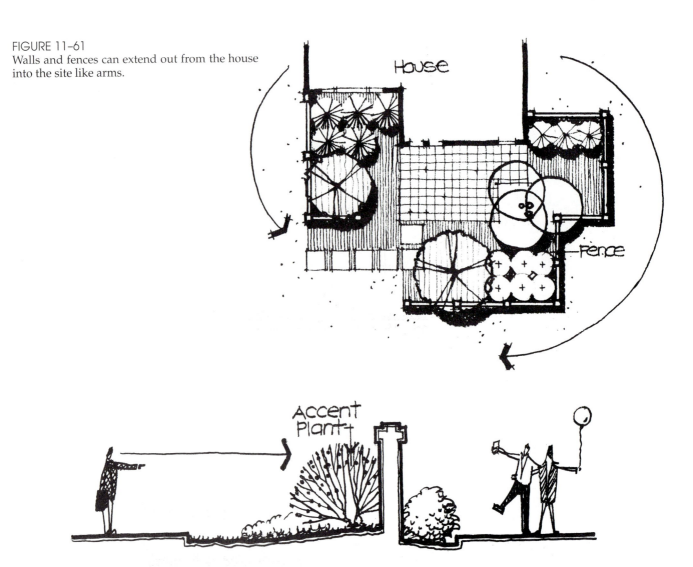

FIGURE 11–62
Walls and fences can serve as a neutral background to accent features while also screening out distracting sights.

Background. Walls and fences can serve as neutral backgrounds to other foreground elements if the color and material patterns of the walls or fences are subdued. In this use, walls and fences can screen out distracting views so the eye can rest comfortably on the intended focal point in the foreground (Figure 11–62). Walls and fences used for this purpose are often best placed at the edge of a space or along the site boundary.

Unifier. A similar use of walls and fences is to visually connect or link otherwise unrelated elements (Figure 11–63). A fence or wall can unify separate elements and make them all seem like they are a part of a cohesive composition.

Visual Interest. Walls and fences can be designed and detailed with attractive patterns of materials and textures that delight the eye (Figure 11–64). Walls and fences can also be designed so that protrusions or indentations cast attractive light and shadow patterns that change throughout the day and year. While the designer might not detail these ideas during preliminary design, they can still be considered as part of the concept and intent at this point.

The layout of walls and fences can also furnish visual interest. Walls and fences do not always have to be placed in absolutely straight lines. Instead, walls and fences

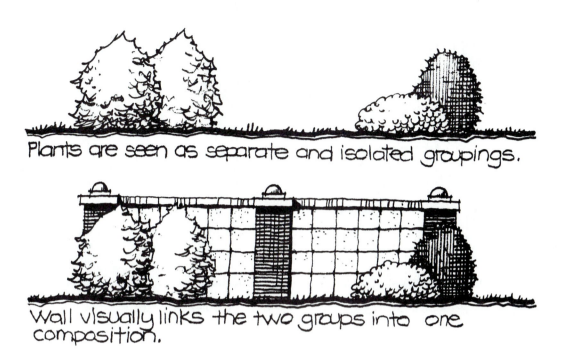

Plants are seen as separate and isolated groupings.

Wall visually links the two groups into one composition.

FIGURE 11–63
Walls and fences can visually unify elements that are otherwise seen as separate elements.

FIGURE 11–64
Examples of walls and fences detailed with decorative material patterns.

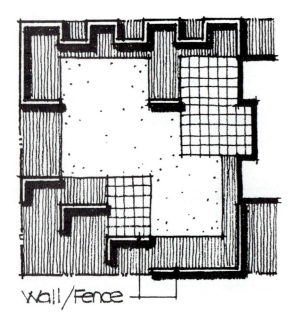
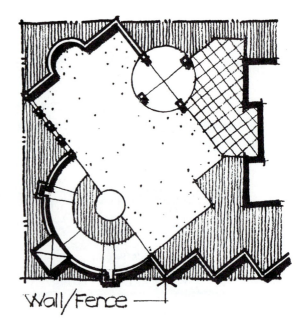

FIGURE 11–65
The plan layout of walls and fences can provide visual interest while complementing the design theme.

can create attractive lines and patterns in their plan alignment (Figure 11–65). The layout of walls and fences can accentuate the overall design theme architecturally. Here again, the design of walls and fences needs to be closely coordinated with form composition so that it is reinforced in the third dimension.

The material presented here on walls and fences has shown the basic and typical ways these two design elements are used in landscape design. But, it is important for the landscape designer to go beyond the norm to realize the variety and opportunities that these vertical planes offer in the spatial development of quality residential design. To do this, walls and fences should be designed with as much concern, attention, and sensitivity as interior walls.

The illustration in Figure 11–66 shows an interior and exterior setting in which walls and fences (1) help create a variety of spaces, (2) vary in height to provide different degrees of privacy, (3) include openings (windows) for defining special areas and views, and (4) support a number of furnishings (potted plants, sculpture, pictures, etc.) that provide additional character to each of the spaces.

These four aspects of designing with walls and fences need to be explored so that these design elements can be as spatially valuable as interior walls.

Height Variation and Spatial Separation

Walls are commonly thought of as (1) separations between other rooms and (2) background settings for furnishings. While true, exterior walls can be incorporated to serve other uses. Figure 11–67 illustrates nine (9) different heights and uses.

When designing walls or fences for outdoors, it is strongly suggested that the designer incorporate them in a variety of heights to provide similar heights that are used each day indoors. This will make walls more usable, and thus more appreciated.

Transparency and Degree of Privacy

Walls and fences, regardless of height, can also be designed to provide varying degrees of openness. By allowing vertical planes to have openings in them, walls and fences provide opportunities for viewing beyond, as well as for adding

Indoors

Outdoors

FIGURE 11–66
Varied heights and character of outdoor walls can be as spatially valuable as indoor walls.

additional character to the space. Windows are very important parts of interior walls and should also be so for outside walls.

A solid fence is best for cases where complete privacy is needed (top of Figure 11–68). It is recommended that changing patterns be explored to create special places along the fence to serve as focal areas to display a special plant or sculpture. The center of Figure 11–68 shows a privacy wall with some open pattern in it. This area, because of its design, provides an accent area where vines can grow, as well as a place to have a partial view into the distance.

The bottom portion of Figure 11–68 shows a wall with varied heights and patterned openings. These small open areas can provide places for small pots or outdoor knickknacks.

The degree of transparency will vary depending upon how much open area is planned for the wall or fence. Some localities, like those adjacent to large bodies of water, may specify the minimum amount of openings for fences or walls. Some codes require at least 50% openness in a vertical screen to allow breezes to travel throughout the neighborhood. Figure 11–69 illustrates several examples of varying percentages of openness in fences that are constructed of 2 × 2 wood. The smaller the open pattern, the lower the percentage of openness in the fence.

- 8'-0"
- Interior wall ht.
- Very private
- Often needs zoning variance

- 7'-0"
- Good exterior wall ht.
- Very private
- Might need zoning variance

- 6'-0"
- Common fence ht.
- Adequate privacy (except tall people)

- 5'-0"
- Chin ht. of average adult
- Semi-private
- Good privacy seated

- 4'-0"
- Chest ht. of average adult
- Separation; no privacy
- Ledge to rest elbows; converse with neighbors

- 3'-0"
- Kitchen counter ht.
- Separation; no privacy
- Wide cap serves as counter or ledge for pots.

- 2'-6"
- Table height separation; no privacy
- Potential counter or high seat

- 2'-0"
- Too low for table top
- Slight separation
- Good seat height

- 1'-6"
- Common bench ht.
- Minimal separation
- Ledge for pots or cushions.

FIGURE 11–67
Different wall heights have different functions.

Support for Furnishings

Exterior walls and fences can support many different elements like interior walls. One such use for exterior walls is to serve as a background surface on which to display various wall decorations (Figure 11–70). Strong privacy is provided at the left side of the space, while an open feeling is kept to the right side of the space.

A similar concept is to use walls to support shelves on which potted plants, sculptures, or other objects can be placed (Figure 11–71). This example shows a stucco wall built to reflect an arc and tangent landscape design theme.

FIGURE 11-68
Outdoor walls can be solid, partially open, or mixed.

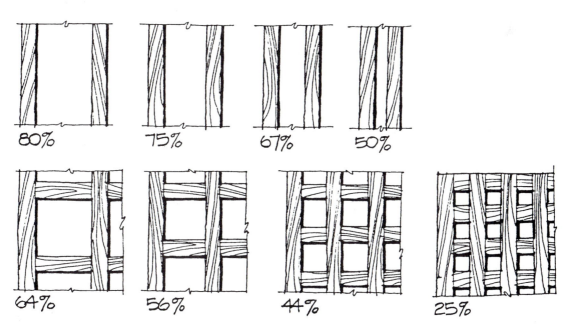

FIGURE 11-69
Percentage of openness depends on the amount of solid area versus open area.

FIGURE 11–70
Walls can be used as background for wall hangings.

FIGURE 11–71
Shelves can be incorporated in a wall to provide places for potted plants.

FIGURE 11–72
Walls can be decorated with hanging baskets to add spatial character.

FIGURE 11–73
Lights can be incorporated into walls to provide for night use.

A fence or wall can likewise be used to support hanging plants (Figure 11–72). Here, a fence is built with vertical panels on the sides of a special pattern. The location of this pattern is adjacent to an outdoor eating area. It accents the area, especially with a higher arched area in the center of the panel.

Just as interior spaces can be used in the nighttime hours, so can outdoor spaces. Lights can be positioned across the top of a fence (Figure 11–73) to light the vertical panels. The reflected light of the fence would then provide enough light to use the adjacent space.

Windows are an integral part of indoor rooms. Without them we would feel too enclosed. They provide for views and for light to enter into a space. They are made in many sizes and shapes and are often complemented with drapery or blinds for varying the degree of privacy or darkness. Windows may be used similarly for exterior walls and fences (Figure 11–74). The left side of the illustration shows an opening that can be adjusted with an exterior blind. It can be closed when privacy is needed and opened when one wants to talk with neighbors or provide a view. The right side shows a stained glass wall light, built into the wall, with the same size and trim as the opening on the left.

When privacy is not needed, but containment for pets is critical, lower fences and walls can be incorporated into a design. Just as in the taller walls, patterns can be used to provide additional character to the wall, as well as places for pets to view into the adjoining spaces (Figure 11–75).

FIGURE 11–74
Openings can be used as windows or wall lights.

FIGURE 11–75
Patterned openings can be incorporated in low walls to allow pets to look out of the space.

OVERHEAD STRUCTURES

The last element that should be considered during spatial composition is overhead structures such as gazebos, arbors, and pergolas. All these provide outdoor ceilings that provide scale and protection from the elements in spaces where people will congregate.

Outdoor ceilings are very important design elements. Their heights, patterns, and character can be as varied as the walls and fences used in the design. Overhead structures should be given as much attention as and used in similar ways as ceilings inside homes are used. It is important for designers to realize the potential of overhead planes as they relate to: (1) height, (2) degree of openness, and (3) support of other furnishings.

Figure 11–76 shows an interior and exterior section through several different spaces. Changes in height and openness coupled with elevational change on the ground plane make for a variety of spaces. The far left spaces in both sections are closed and intimate in scale. As one moves through the other spaces to the right, they open up and become larger in scale. The important thing to note is that outdoor ceilings are as spatially valuable to outdoor use as indoor ceilings are to indoor use.

Not only can ceilings be altered to provide for different senses of scale, they can also be designed with varying degrees of openness for functional and aesthetic purposes. Figure 11–77 shows an outdoor structure that primarily serves as a shelter from the elements. Yet, portions of the structure hover over other parts of the space to create a patterned overhead plane, as well as places for hanging plants.

Figure 11–78 shows a structure that is supported partially by the fence. This overhead structure provides shelter from the elements over the table space and identifies a subspace beneath the lower patterned overhead to the right.

Depending on the situation, there may be times when there is no need to create a sheltered area, especially where houses have screened-in porches. In cases like these, clients may wish to have some partial protection from the hot afternoon sun. Figure 11–79 demonstrates how a patterned overhead arbor can be used to provide protection from the sun. The fence in the background, with a partially open central panel, was designed to accent this area beneath the arbor.

Arbors can also cast interesting shadow patterns on the ground and vertical planes. These shadow patterns provide texture and depth to an outdoor space while also changing throughout the day to give it a dynamic, evolving quality.

In addition to ceilings being varied in height and in openness, it is important to use them to support other spatial furnishings. Figure 11–80 shows three examples of how overheads can be varied in height, character, and pattern and provide places for hanging potted plants, swings, and lights.

Indoors

outdoors

FIGURE 11-76
Outdoor ceilings can be just as spatially valuable as indoor ceilings.

FIGURE 11-77
Overhead structures can provide protection from
sun and rain.

FIGURE 11-78
Overhead structures can be partially solid and
partially open for varied use.

FIGURE 11-79
Arbors can provide partial protection from the
sun and create interesting shadow patterns.

FIGURE 11-80
Overhead structures can support hanging plants, swings, and
lights to help furnish the space.

FIGURE 11–81
The patio, wall, and arbor are modeled after the character of the house. Design #N3452 (top) © Home Planners, LLC Wholly owned by Hanley-Wood, LLC. Blueprints available, 800-322-6797.

ARCHITECTURALLY RESPONSIVE LANDSCAPE STRUCTURES

Four examples will be presented to illustrate how architectural character of the house can be incorporated into a designer's thought process and design studies. Each figure depicts how: (1) a patio, (2) a fence/wall, and (3) an overhead structure could be designed to reflect the architectural character of the house. It is assumed at this point in the process that the major design theme and forms have been selected. So, it is the designer's next step to create the vertical and overhead structures in an architecturally sensitive manner and be reflective of the form composition.

In Figure 11–81, the patio was generally modeled after the major front window. The arch is the key accent of the patio layout. The majority of material could be concrete or stone to match the patterns of the windowpanes.

The wall is made of brick and changes direction and elevation to reflect the angles of the roofs of the house. This allows for some strong privacy to the right

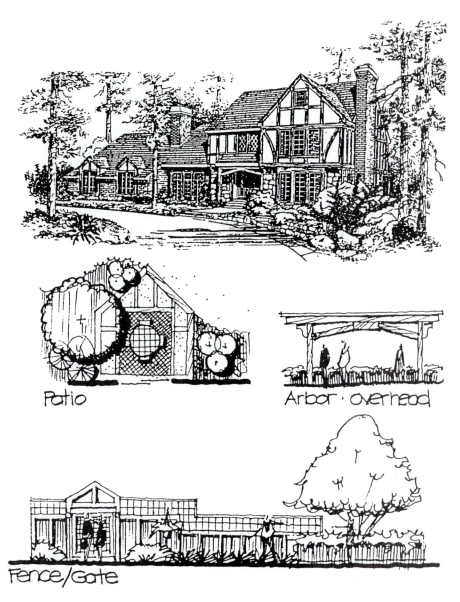

FIGURE 11–82
The patio, wall, and arbor are modeled after the character of the house. Design #N3452 (top) © Home Planners, LLC Wholly owned by Hanley-Wood, LLC. Blueprints available, 800-322-6797.

side of the yard, where it might be needed, and more open to the left where views are important. An arched entryway provides an accent to the low wall. The circular opening in the high wall provides a view into a pleasing area beyond. It mimics the character of the decorative vent above the garage door.

The overhead arbor was designed to have simple repetitive arches, similar to the main entry arch. It would be supported by columns that would have some detail taken from some of the interior or exterior trim work.

A much different house is pictured in Figure 11–82, so it is likely that the three hardscape structures would look much different than the previous ones. Due to its height and contrasting colors, the large gable on the second floor is a strong architectural feature. As you can see, the patio was designed to resemble this gable pattern. The edges of the patio could be landscape timbers that are stained to match the wood trim on the house. The light-colored material could be concrete to match the stucco in color and texture, or concrete pavers with a light color. The central

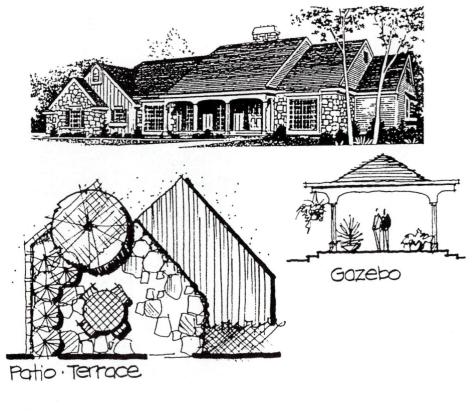

Gazebo

Patio · Terrace

Fence / Gate

FIGURE 11–83
The patio, fence and gazebo are modeled after the character of the house. Design #N2791 (top) © Home Planners, LLC Wholly owned by Hanley-Wood, LLC. Blueprints available, 800-322-6797.

portion of the patio is an accented area reflecting the window area. In this example, a basket weave brick pattern at a 45-degree angle was selected.

The fence is modeled after three elements. The lower portion is a paneled system that reflects the panels of wood and stucco on the house. The wooden open grillwork above the fence is meant to be similar to the windows of the house. This type of grillwork can serve as an excellent structure for growing vines. The gated area is reflective of the window patterns and the peaked roof.

The design for the overhead structure was related specifically to the entryway detail at the front of the house. The small curved brackets reflect the same brackets seen as detail just beneath the large second-story gable.

Figure 11–83 shows another example. The major patio spaces were designed to reflect the double gable to the left side of the house. The top level is a stone terrace, which steps down to a wood deck, which then steps down to the lawn area. The stone and wood patterns are used in a very similar fashion as they are on the front of the house.

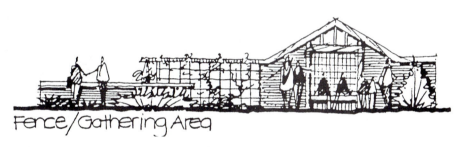

Patio   Arbor · Overhead

Fence/Gathering Area

FIGURE 11–84
The patio, wall, and arbor are modeled after the character of the house. Design #N3351 (top)
© Home Planners, LLC Wholly owned by Hanley-Wood, LLC. Blueprints available, 800-322-6797.

The privacy fence extends from one end to the other. It is constructed of material and color similar to the horizontal wood siding on the house. A window box with plants was placed on it to resemble the window box on the front window of the house. The fence was also designed to have an accent area, in this case a place to grow some vines. This area was accented by using the arch from the front porch and a grillwork to match the windowpane pattern.

The overhead gazebo was developed from the design of the arches on the front porch, including the columns. The roof was made into a hip roof to reflect both angles of the roof.

The last example to illustrate architectural attention in the spatial composition phase is shown in Figure 11–84. Here the patio was designed to reflect the major window designs in the front of the house. The patio might be made of concrete, while the banding and borders could be brick to match the brick on the house. Even though the major windows have large wood members as borders to the window, that doesn't mean the patio has to be done in the same way. Again, landscape structures can be modeled after a feature to whatever degree the designer feels it could be or in whatever way that seems appropriate to the materials being used.

Brick is used to create a low wall to lean or sit on, as well as for the higher wall to the right. An open, wood grillwork is also used here to provide a place for vines. This will eventually provide a partial view into the space beyond. The wall is angled to a peak to match the peak and pattern of the roofs.

The overhead arbor is a simple structure that uses the exact pattern of the wood eaves and trim work at the major peaks of the house. The arbor is shown to rest on a lower brick wall that could provide for partial enclosure. This, too, is seen at the base of the major windows in front of the house.

Developing the character of the hardscape structures can be an exciting design adventure during the spatial composition phase. Creating floors, walls, and ceilings to have architectural detail that is responsive to the house is something that should be done for all landscape designs, since these are highly visible three-dimensional objects in the landscape. What better way to design these structures than to blend them into the landscape with the same character as the house.

PRELIMINARY DESIGNS FOR THE DUNCAN RESIDENCE

After reviewing the three form composition studies prepared earlier in Chapter 10, the designer decided to develop two preliminary designs. The preliminary design shown in Figure 11–85 was prepared on the basis of the form composition study of Figure 10–79, while the preliminary design in Figure 11–86 was prepared based on the form composition study of Figure 10–80. It is suggested that the reader take a moment at this point to compare the preliminary designs with the form composition studies. As can be seen, the preliminary designs have essentially completed the spatial composition with the addition of plant materials, fences, and pavement.

In Figure 11–85, plant materials and other elements reinforce the organization of the form composition in a number of locations. In the front yard, low evergreen shrubs and ground cover along the entry walk help to define this space and separate it from the lawn area, while ornamental shrubs have been placed next to the sitting area as accents. All the new planting has been organized around the existing sugar maple. Additional shade trees have been located along the west side of the house to screen hot afternoon summer sun. The planting on the east side of the driveway provides balance to the front yard while also incorporating the existing trees and screening views of the work/storage area. In the back yard, the largest plants have been placed along the property lines for screening and spatial enclosure. Evergreen trees on the west side screen views from the neighbor's second-story deck and block cold northwest winter winds. The ornamental trees on the north property line provide focal points to view from the house and the outside eating and living areas. Fences immediately adjacent to these outside living spaces provide additional enclosure and privacy.

The thoughts for the preliminary design shown in Figure 11–86 are similar. In the front yard, low shrubs, ornamental trees, and medium-sized trees have all been used to accent the curve of the arc on the ground plane. The planting immediately adjacent to the entrance walk is more limited, thus allowing the existing sugar maple to stand out in the lawn as a prominent focal point. Again, an ornamental shrub is used near the sitting area as an accent. In the back yard, the planting concept is very much like that depicted in Figure 11–85 except here it has been molded to the curve of the arc. The ornamental trees again serve as accents and are strategically placed at the apex of the curve where they are most visible.

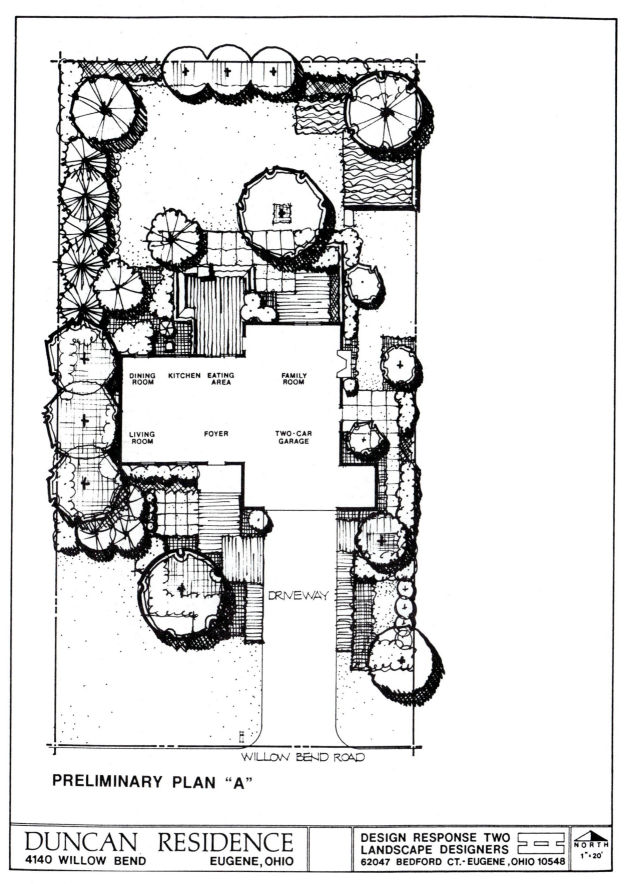

Inside the plan:

DINING ROOM   KITCHEN   EATING AREA   FAMILY ROOM

LIVING ROOM   FOYER   TWO-CAR GARAGE

DRIVEWAY

WILLOW BEND ROAD

PRELIMINARY PLAN "A"

DUNCAN RESIDENCE
4140 WILLOW BEND   EUGENE, OHIO

DESIGN RESPONSE TWO
LANDSCAPE DESIGNERS
62047 BEDFORD CT.· EUGENE, OHIO 10548

NORTH
1"= 20'

FIGURE 11–85
Preliminary Plan A for the Duncan residence.

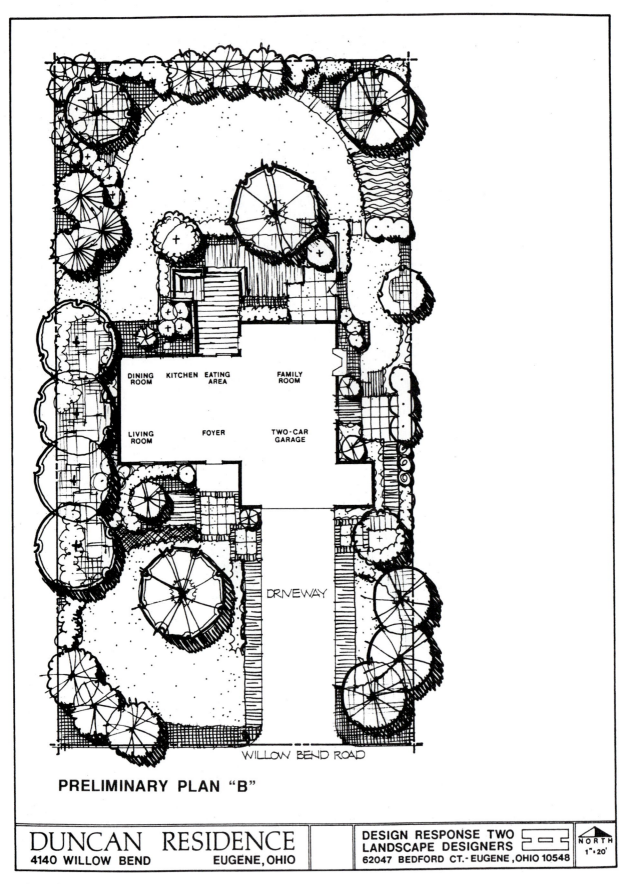

Within the illustration:

DINING ROOM KITCHEN EATING AREA FAMILY ROOM

LIVING ROOM FOYER TWO-CAR GARAGE

DRIVEWAY

WILLOW BEND ROAD

PRELIMINARY PLAN "B"

DUNCAN RESIDENCE
4140 WILLOW BEND   EUGENE, OHIO

DESIGN RESPONSE TWO
LANDSCAPE DESIGNERS
62047 BEDFORD CT.- EUGENE, OHIO 10548

NORTH
1" = 20'

FIGURE 11–86
Preliminary Plan B for the Duncan residence.

SUMMARY

Spatial composition addresses the third dimension of a residential site and creates the spatial shell of the design's outdoor rooms. The designer should first study the relief of the base plane in terms of both necessity and aesthetics. Next, the location of vertical and overhead planes is considered along with the types of elements that will define these planes. Plant materials, walls, fences, and overhead structures are all possible elements the designer may use to create walls and ceilings in the design. Each of these elements has its own unique characteristics and potential functions in a residential site design.

Spatial composition should build on and reinforce the form composition. Again, form composition and spatial composition, though separated in this book for explanation, typically go hand in hand during the design process. More often than not, these two steps are undertaken simultaneously. When these two interrelated steps are finished, the designer should have at least one and hopefully several completed alternative preliminary design solutions.

As suggested previously, several attempts and refinements on tracing paper may be required before the designer is satisfied with the results. Once again, the development of alternatives is highly encouraged. The first and obvious solution may not be the best, a fact the designer may not see until the solution is compared and tested with alternatives. Having selected the best alternative or combinations of alternatives, the designer is now ready to present the preliminary plans to the clients for review.

The designer should present the preliminary design solutions to the clients and give them time to fully comprehend the alternatives. Then the designer should seek feedback from the clients so that their reactions can be incorporated into preparing the master plan.

12

Material Composition and Master Plan

INTRODUCTION

As discussed in the previous three chapters, preliminary design addresses and studies two key issues. First, it establishes the two- and three-dimensional spatial frameworks of the outdoor environment through form composition and spatial composition. Two-dimensional forms on the ground plane and three-dimensional elements such as earth, plant materials, walls, fences, and overhead structures are carefully coordinated to create the outdoor rooms. Second, preliminary design studies the general appearance and the style of the design. The design theme, selection and organization of the various design elements, and preliminary selection of materials collectively establish the mood or personality of the proposed design.

But as the name itself suggests, the decisions made about these key issues are preliminary. Ideas and designs should not be considered final until they are reviewed by the clients. Clients' feedback is necessary. The designer often uses the preliminary design phase as an exploratory step where different ideas are examined. This is especially true when the designer ideally prepares alternative design solutions. Detailed decisions are not considered during preliminary design. The designer makes only a general selection of materials (brick versus wood, evergreen versus deciduous, and so on), but not the exact color or pattern of the materials.

The more complete and detailed decisions about the design are made during the preparation of the master plan as the last step of the design phase. The master plan builds on all the previous steps of the design process to formulate a proposed design that the clients will use to guide the development of their residential site. The master plan is the culmination of all the designer's efforts and is sometimes the end of the designer's involvement with the clients. Other times, the designer carries the project on to subsequent phases as discussed in Chapter 4.

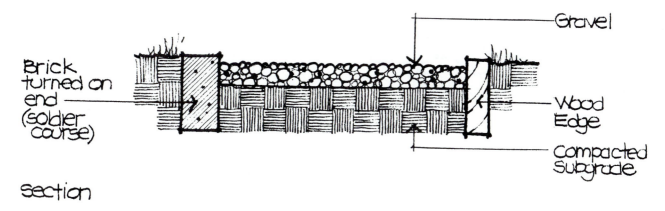

Brick turned on end (soldier course)

Gravel

Wood Edge

Compacted Subgrade

Section

FIGURE 12-1
Loose materials such as gravel need containment along their edges.

MATERIAL COMPOSITION

Material composition is the process of refining the selection of materials and developing material patterns for the two- and three-dimensional elements of the design. Only general consideration for the selection of materials takes place during preliminary design. Attention is now given to the actual appearance of the design as established by the composition of materials.

Material Selection

The general selection of materials during preliminary design and the refined selection during the preparation of the master plan should be based on four key factors including: (1) function, (2) form, (3) style/character, and (4) budget. Additional consideration should also be given to the clients' preference, compatibility with the architecture of the house, material availability, and regional appropriateness. The selection of materials should not be based solely on the designer's personal preference or on what is immediately available from a local supplier. Appropriate material for any given element or area of the design results from careful study and knowledge of materials.

The following paragraphs provide a brief outline of the different categories of materials generally available for use on a residential site. A short description of each type of material is given along with suggestions for the appropriateness of the material to function, form, style/character, and budget. The description of materials focuses on the appearance and design character, but does not discuss the technical or construction techniques. The reader should consult other sources for this information.

Pavement Materials.   Pavement materials used in the landscape can be placed in the following categories according to their physical characteristics: (1) loose materials, (2) unit materials, and (3) adhesive or fluid materials.

1.   Loose materials such as gravel or crushed stone are those not fixed in place or physically held together by adhesive. These types of materials are usually some of the least expensive to install and can be used in any design theme or form on the ground plane to provide an appealing texture. Loose materials have the advantage of allowing surface water to drain through them to the subgrade below and thus help the process of natural drainage. Loose materials have to be contained along the sides of the area in which they are placed (Figure 12–1). Sometimes loose

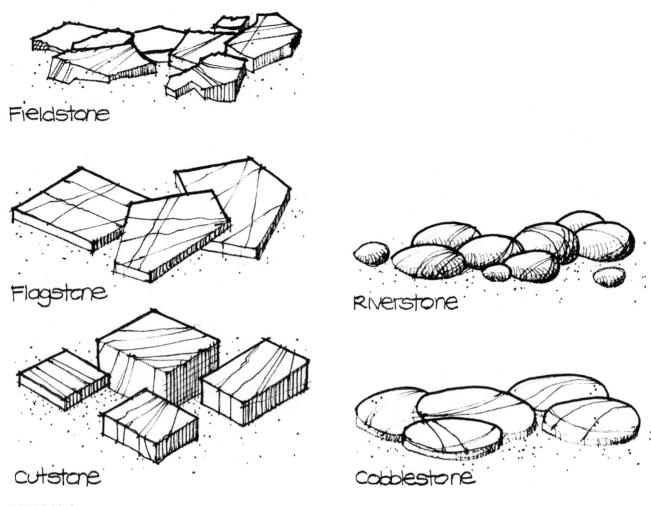

FIGURE 12-2
General categories of stone.

materials are a maintenance problem when they scatter out of their intended location. On the residential site, loose materials can be used for driveways (in areas where snow removal is not a problem) or secondary pedestrian circulation paths. They can also be used as a ground cover in arid regions or in areas of a site where vegetative ground cover is difficult to grow.

2. Unit materials are those that are found or manufactured in fixed sizes and shapes such as stone, brick, tile, concrete pavers, or wood. Generally, unit materials are more expensive to use than either loose materials or adhesive materials because they require more labor to quarry, manufacture, and install. The following paragraphs discuss some of the characteristics of commonly used unit materials.

Stone is one type of unit material that is both found naturally or quarried. Figure 12–2 illustrates the different general categories of stone which include fieldstone, flagstone, cutstone, riverstone, and cobblestone. Fieldstone is any irregularly sized and shaped stone randomly found at or near the earth's surface without quarrying. Fieldstone is usually used in the form in which it is found and is best used in settings where a naturalistic character is desired.

Flagstone is stone that is split into relatively thin slabs or "flags." Unlike fieldstone, flagstone is quarried and can be cut into many shapes, though the shapes shown in Figure 12–3 are most common. Because of its relatively smooth surface, flagstone has a wide application for pavement on the residential site. It is a good surface to walk on or to put furniture on though it is usually not good for a driving

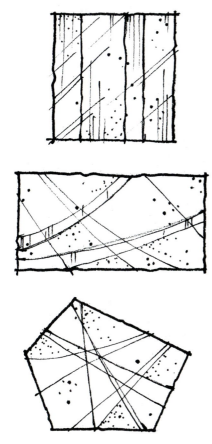

FIGURE 12–3
Examples of commonly used flagstone.

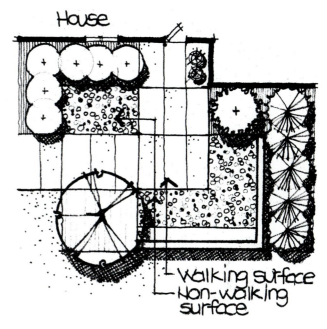

FIGURE 12–4
Riverstone and cobblestone can be used for nonwalking surfaces or decorative edges.

surface unless thick flags are used with proper base support. Flagstone is much more expensive than fieldstone.

Cutstone is stone of any type that is cut to a dimensioned shape. It may be cut into relatively thin pieces for pavement or thicker blocks for walls. Because this type of stone is cut either during quarrying or during installation, it can be shaped to conform to almost any need.

Riverstone and cobblestone are two other unit materials that can be used for pavement. Riverstone is stone that has been rounded over a long period of time by the force of running or falling water. Sizes generally range from 1 inch to 2 inches. Cobblestone is similar because it, too, is rather rounded. By comparison, cobblestone is flatter and a little larger (3 inches or more across) than riverstone. Both types of stone are best used to furnish strikingly textured surfaces that are more for decoration than for pedestrian circulation. Consequently, both are commonly used where the intention is to slow the rate of movement or suggest a nonwalking surface (Figure 12–4).

Brick is a manufactured unit material that is available in a standard rectangular size of 2-1/4″ × 4″ × 8″ for dry-laid brick and 2-1/4″ × 3-5/8″ × 7-5/8″ for mortared brick. Because of its shape, brick is easiest to install when used in rectangular and diagonal design themes where less cutting and fitting are required (right side of Figure 12–5). Brick can be used for curvilinear and angular design themes, but bricks must be cut to conform to these shapes (left side of Figure 12–5). Brick's attractive color and texture make it a good choice in places where a warm, friendly atmosphere is desired. Similarly, brick is very good to use in contrast with colder materials such as concrete or certain stones. Brick can be used both on the

Material Composition and Master Plan

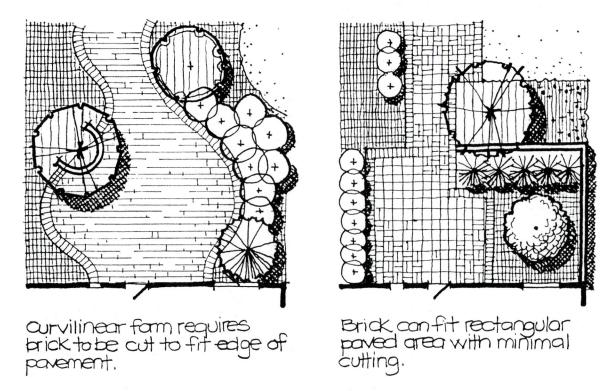

Curvilinear form requires brick to be cut to fit edge of pavement.

Brick can fit rectangular paved area with minimal cutting.

FIGURE 12–5
Brick is best used in areas that require little cutting of individual bricks.

FIGURE 12–6
Examples of concrete pavers.

ground plane or vertical planes and is often used in the landscape to repeat brick on the house's facade. Brick may be used in virtually any space on the residential site though it does need a stable base. Brick pavement also requires containment if it is placed on a sand or crushed limestone base.

Unit pavers and tile are two other materials that can be used on the ground plane in a manner similar to brick. Unit pavers are usually precast concrete units that are available in a variety of shapes and earth colors (Figure 12–6). They function like brick and work equally well as a pavement. Tile is available in a variety of shapes, sizes, and colors. In addition, decorative tile can be created with any color or pattern painted on its surface. Since tile is a relatively thin material, it is set on a concrete slab where decorative trim or surfaces are desired.

Wood is one other commonly used unit material in the landscape. Wood is both modular and yet somewhat flexible in its potential uses. Wood is modular be-

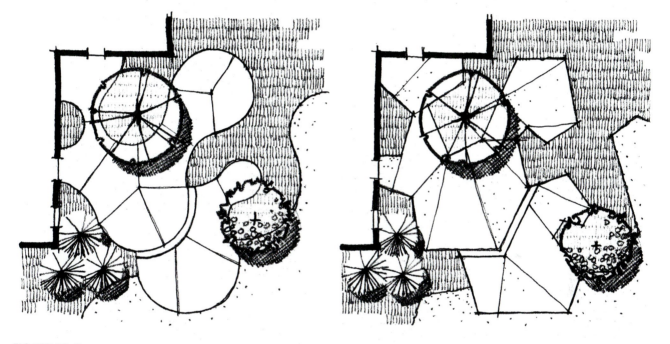

FIGURE 12–7
Wood can be used in standard lengths to minimize cutting and leftover material.

FIGURE 12–8
Concrete is an appropriate material for curvilinear or irregularly shaped areas.

cause it is milled and cut to standard sizes. Yet wood is flexible because it can be
cut to almost any size or shape. However, as more labor is required to cut and
shape wood, it is more costly to use. Thus, wood is most practical when it is used
in rectangular or diagonal design themes where less cutting is required. Also, an
attempt should be made to use standard sizes of wood to reduce the amount of cutting and leftover material (Figure 12–7). Wood has an appealing natural color and
texture though it can be stained or painted to any color, thus adding to its versatil-
ity. Wood may be used on any plane in outdoor spaces.

3.   Adhesive or fluid materials are those that are pliable when they are first
installed, such as concrete or asphalt. Concrete must be poured into forms which
define its shape before it cures and hardens. This initial plastic state allows concrete
to adapt to any shape or form in which it is initially placed. Owing to this, both concrete and asphalt are well suited for areas that are curvilinear or irregular in shape
(Figure 12–8). Unlike unit materials that must be cut to conform to these shapes,

Material Composition and Master Plan

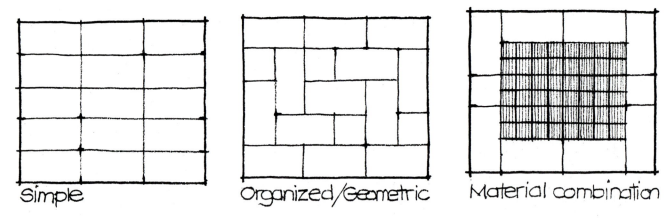

FIGURE 12-9
Examples of three general types of material patterns.

concrete and asphalt can be used rather inexpensively for irregular forms. While asphalt has the disadvantage of being unappealing to the eye, concrete can be colored in the mix or by treating its surface directly. Exposed aggregate concrete in which the aggregates within the concrete are exposed at the surface to give a gravel-like appearance is one alternative treatment of concrete. Concrete can be used on any ground or vertical surface within a residential site. Asphalt is usually restricted to areas of vehicular circulation.

Material Patterns

The second aspect of material composition is the determination of material patterns of pavements, walls, fences, and overhead structures. This level of design is sometimes called detailed design or design development because it addresses the actual appearance of the design elements.

There are three general types of material patterns (Figure 12–9). The first and most simple is a uniform pattern created when one material is used to cover an area. In this situation, the material is placed uniformly throughout the area without any attempt to vary the size, color, or direction of the material. The second type of pattern is created when a material is placed within an area in a more organized and geometric basis. The size, color, texture, and direction of the material can be used to vary the pattern within the area. The third type of material pattern is created by combining two or more different materials. Here, the varying size, color, and texture of each of the materials is used to form clearly defined patterns, often geometric in nature.

In designing material patterns, there are a number of factors that should be considered including: (1) context, (2) material characteristics, and (3) visual qualities. Each of these factors should be considered simultaneously while designing material patterns. For explanation's sake, each factor is discussed separately in the following sections.

Context. Like any good design, material patterns should fit their surrounding context on the residential site. Material patterns should complement and add to the overall appearance and feeling of their surroundings. To make sure this happens, the designer should study material patterns in relation to (1) form, (2) architecture of the house or other nearby structures, and (3) character.

A material pattern should be compatible with the form of the area in which it is placed. Recall from Chapter 10 that a variety of design themes can be employed to create outdoor spaces. For each design theme, there are some material patterns that are more suitable than others. The following paragraphs outline potential pavement patterns for the design themes discussed previously (Chapter 10).

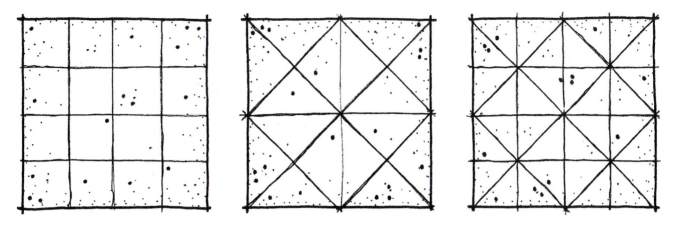

FIGURE 12–10
Potential grid systems for subdividing a square pavement area.

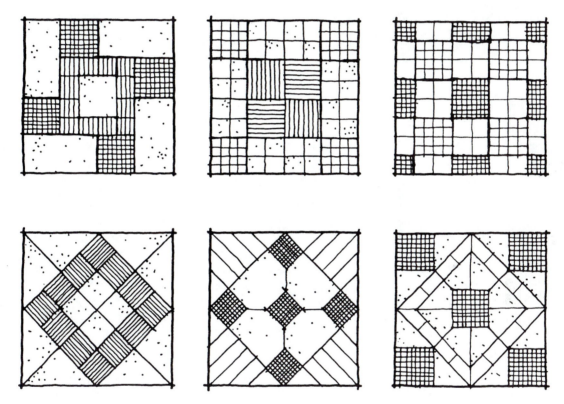

FIGURE 12–11
Examples of possible pavement patterns based on the grid systems within the square.

1. *Rectangular theme.* Material patterns for a rectangular design theme can be based on the geometry of the square or rectangle. A good way to create a pattern in a square or rectangular area is to first subdivide the area into a grid pattern (Figure 12–10). Once the grid lines are established, they can be used to generate an almost infinite number of possible patterns (Figure 12–11). A similar approach to creating patterns for two rectangular terrace pavement areas is shown in Figure 12–12. Note how the grid system extends the edges of the house into the pavement pattern.

2. *Diagonal theme.* The material pattern for a diagonal theme can be created the same way as it is for the rectangular theme. The only difference is that the grid system can be turned on an angle to fit the diagonal direction of the area (Figure 12–13).

Material Composition and Master Plan

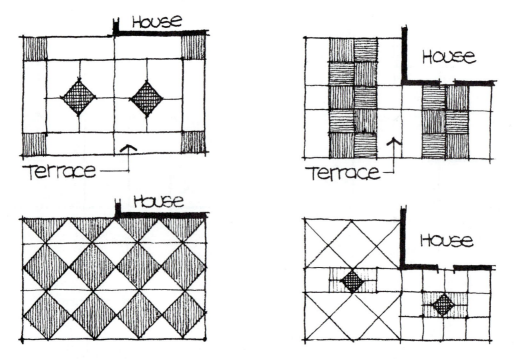

FIGURE 12–12
Examples of possible pavement patterns within two rectangular terrace areas.

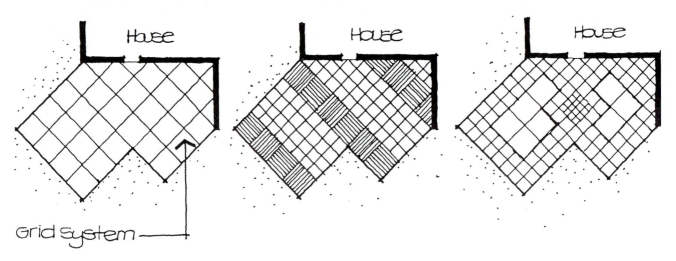

FIGURE 12–13
Examples of possible pavement patterns for a diagonal terrace.

3. *Angular theme.* There are three possible ways to create a material pattern for an angular theme. They each involve subdividing the overall area into smaller segments (Figure 12–14). The first method, shown in the left example, is to extend the line of those edges which cut into the area. The second method is to repeat the overall form at a smaller scale within the original form and connect the corners of the small forms to those of the original form respectively. The third method is to create smaller areas of patterns inside the pavement area that echo the overall form.

4. *Circular theme.* Patterns inside circular pavement areas should be based on the internal geometry of the circle. There are three fundamental concepts for doing this. The first (Figure 12–15) uses the circle's radii to subdivide the circle to define a pattern. As with the rectangular patterns, it is best to first draw guidelines with the circle's radii at some regular interval and then use these guidelines to gen-

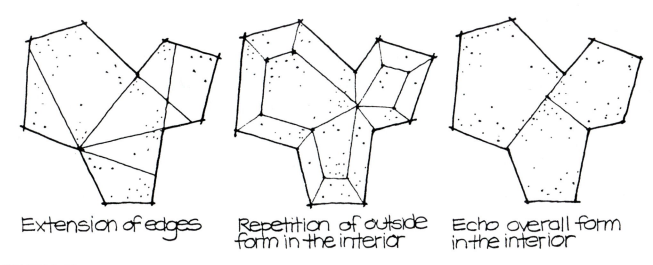

Extension of edges Repetition of outside form in the interior Echo overall form in the interior

FIGURE 12–14
Three possible methods for creating pavement patterns within an angular form.

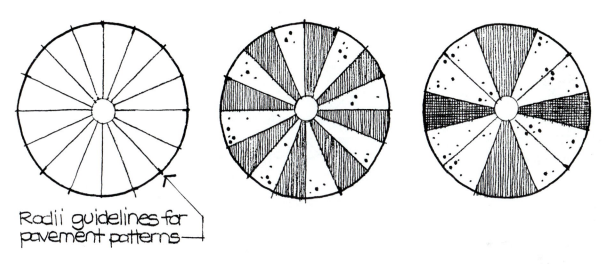

Radii guidelines for pavement patterns

FIGURE 12–15
Pavement patterns in circular areas can be based on radii guidelines.

erate different alternative patterns. In order to avoid acute angles at the center, it is suggested that a small circular form be used. The second method is to use concentric circles of different diameters to form patterns within the circular pavement area (Figure 12–16). The last method uses both radii and concentric circles to formulate patterns (Figure 12–17).

5. *Arc and tangent theme.* It is frequently difficult to create a material pattern with the arc and tangent theme because it is a combination of two different geometric forms. However, material patterns can be developed if the basic component parts of both the square and circle are kept in mind. When this is done, there are two general ways to create material patterns with the arc and tangent theme. The first is based on extending edges and diameters of the outside forms into the internal area (left side of Figure 12–18). The second method isolates and accentuates selected circular portions of the overall form. These circular segments are then treated like other circular patterns, while the remainder of the pavement area is treated in a gridlike fashion (right side of Figure 12–18).

6. *Curvilinear theme.* The curvilinear theme, often the most difficult for lending itself to material patterns, has three fundamental approaches for establishing material patterns (Figure 12–19). The first is based on the geometry of the

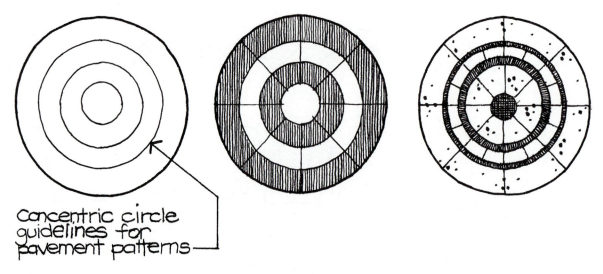

FIGURE 12–16
Pavement patterns in circular areas can be based on concentric circle guidelines.

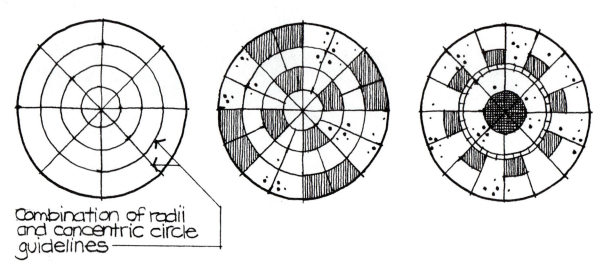

FIGURE 12–17
Pavement patterns in circular areas can be based on a combination of radii and concentric circle guidelines.

circles found within the curvilinear form. Here, radii are extended to meet the outside of the curvilinear form at a right angle, while other radii are extended inward to meet at a common point within the pavement area. The second technique is somewhat similar. With this approach, circles are positioned inside the curvilinear area. Then radii are extended away from these circles to the outside edge of the curvilinear pavement area or to the edges of other nearby circles. The last method uses additional curvilinear lines and forms to subdivide the pavement area. To do this successfully, these additional curvilinear lines must meet the outer edge of the pavement area or each other at about a 90-degree angle. Acute angles should be avoided with this method.

As can be seen from the preceding paragraphs, each design theme suggests different material patterns. What is compatible with one design theme is not necessarily suitable for other design themes. Regardless of the theme, the geometry of form composition discussed in Chapter 10 is the basis for creating all material patterns.

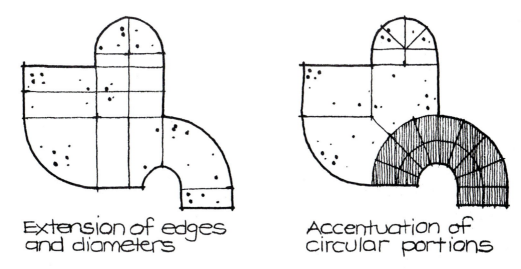

Extension of edges
and diameters

Accentuation of
circular portions

FIGURE 12–18
Two possible methods for creating pavement patterns within an arc and tangent form.

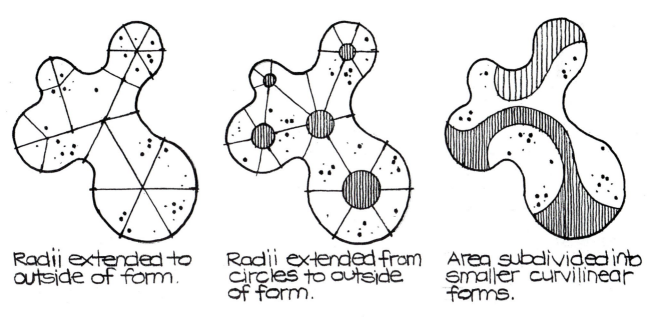

Radii extended to
outside of form.

Radii extended from
circles to outside
of form.

Area subdivided into
smaller curvilinear
forms.

FIGURE 12–19
Three possible methods for creating pavement patterns within curvilinear forms.

Thus, the designer should allow each design theme and an understanding of form composition to suggest what material patterns are appropriate for any given form of the design.

Another factor, as it relates to the context, that should influence the design of material patterns on the residential site is the relation to adjoining structures such as the house, gazebo, walls, fences, overhead structures, and so on. Material patterns should visually fit both the architectural forms and style of these adjoining structures. There are several ways this can be accomplished. First, prominent corners, edge of doors, windows, and posts of the structure that are adjoining a pavement area can be used to align material patterns so the structure and the adjoining material pattern appear as a unified composition. Figure 12–20 shows examples of material patterns that have been aligned with the corners and edges of the house.

Material Composition and Master Plan

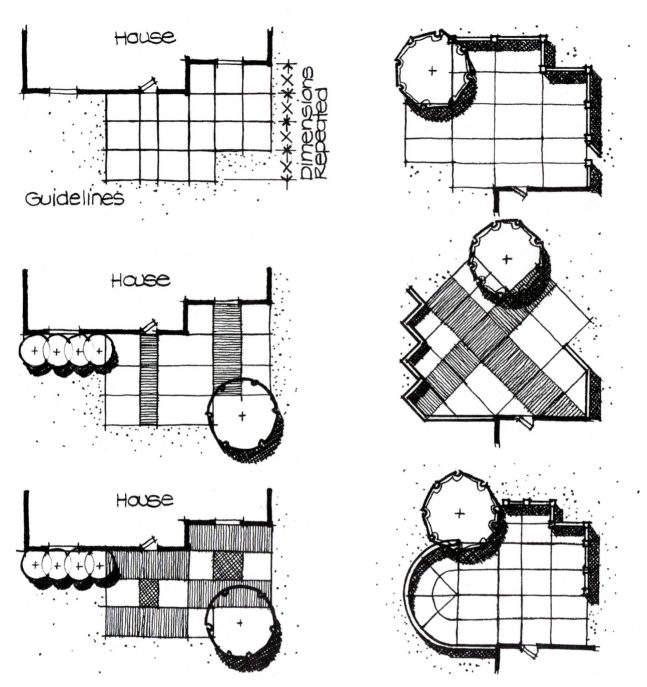

FIGURE 12–20
Pavement patterns can be coordinated with the house by relating to prominent corners, edges, and so forth on the house.

FIGURE 12–21
Pavement patterns can be coordinated with walls and fences
by relating to corners, edges, posts, and so on.

Figure 12–21 shows similar examples of how material patterns have been coordinated with a wall and fence. Note how the corners and post of the wall and fence
relate to the pavement patterns. Figure 12–22 shows how material patterns on
walls and fences have been related to the adjoining house and pavement. The material patterns on both vertical and ground planes should visually link together so
that each "goes hand in hand with each other."

A second way the architecture of the house or other structures can be related to
material patterns is by repeating or echoing a particular form or feature of the architecture in the material pattern itself. Figure 12–23 shows a few examples where arches
and circular windows have been repeated in nearby fences and pavement areas.

FIGURE 12-22
Material patterns on walls and fences should relate to the adjoining house and pavement.

FIGURE 12-23
Material patterns of walls and fences can be related to a nearby house by repetition of a form or feature of the house.

Material Composition and Master Plan

FIGURE 12–24
Material patterns can be coordinated with significant historical patterns of an adjoining house.

A third technique for relating material patterns to context is to make sure material patterns are suitable to the character of the spaces. Material patterns should reinforce the character or feeling of outdoor spaces, not add or provide a contrasting personality that will seem out of place. For example, geometric patterns suggest order and structure, angular patterns suggest dynamic action, and curvilinear patterns suggest relaxation or casual movement. Care must also be taken to make sure that material patterns are appropriate to the style of nearby structures. For example, material patterns with an historical house may echo the style of the house by using patterns that were found in that era (Figure 12–24).

Material Characteristics. Every material has its own quality of structure, size, color, and texture, which should influence the selection of material patterns. Due to these qualities, not all patterns work equally well with every material. This section suggests guidelines for using material patterns appropriate to the different categories of materials identified in the previous section.

As indicated before, loose materials are best used to create a uniform surface. They do not lend themselves to geometric patterns unless they are held in place by

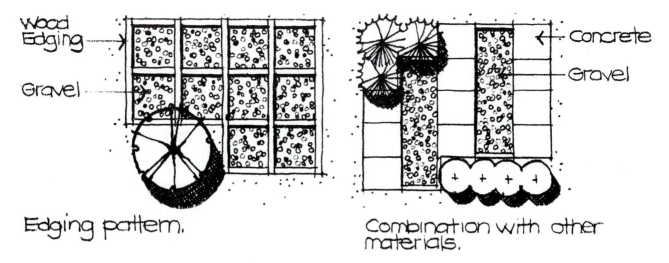

Wood Edging

Gravel

Concrete

Gravel

Edging pattern.

Combination with other materials.

FIGURE 12-25
Patterns with a loose material can be established by an edging pattern and/or combining it with another material.

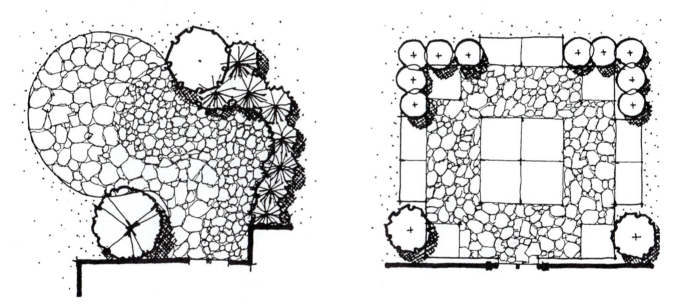

FIGURE 12-26
Two possible ways of creating a pavement pattern with fieldstone.

some binding or "cement" within a specified area of the pattern. One other method for creating a pattern with a loose material, such as gravel, is to place it in adjoining areas that are contained by edging (left example of Figure 12–25). A pattern can also be created by varying the size, color, and/or texture of the loose material by combining it with other materials (right side of Figure 12–25).

Patterns created with stone are extremely varied because of the many types of available stone. Nevertheless, there are some patterns that are more common than others.

Fieldstone is usually used to create a pattern that is based on its texture and color throughout an entire surface area. In some instances, a pattern with fieldstone can be created by organizing different sizes of fieldstone into geometric shapes (left side of Figure 12–26). A pattern can also be created by combining fieldstone with another material, especially if it is smoother and more geometric (right side of Figure 12–26).

Flagstone can be cut into a variety of sizes and shapes, each of which suggests different possibilities for material patterns (Figure 12–27). As with other materials,

FIGURE 12–27
Examples of different pavement patterns using flagstone.

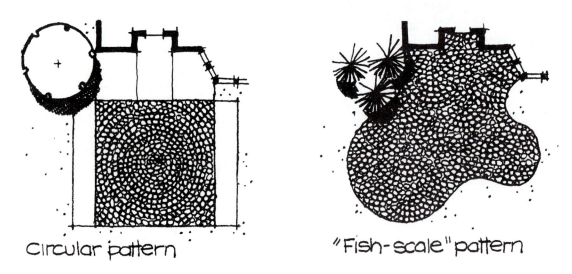

Circular pattern   "Fish-scale" pattern

FIGURE 12–28
Examples of possible pavement patterns with riverstone or cobblestone.

rectangular flagstone is best used to create rectangular patterns. Some of these patterns use one standard size repeated throughout the pattern while other patterns use a variety of sizes. With the latter, an attempt is usually made to minimize the distance that any particular joint extends. Angular or irregularly shaped flagstone can be used very much like fieldstone to create an irregular pattern with the material itself. Flagstone has a much smoother surface than fieldstone.

Owing to their size, riverstone and cobblestone can easily be used to create patterns for an area of any size or shape. Most often, these types of stone are used like gravel to give a uniform cover over the entire area in which they are used. Unlike gravel, however, riverstone and cobblestone are often held in place by mortar. Riverstone and cobblestone can also be used in more geometric or defined patterns (Figure 12–28).

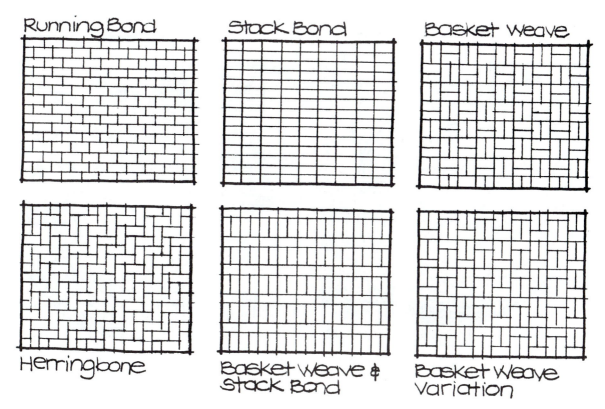

FIGURE 12–29
Common brick patterns for pavement.

FIGURE 12–30
Common brick patterns for walls.

Brick is a widely used material in many residential projects, although there is additional cost for cutting and fitting individual bricks. Thus, it is advisable to use patterns which require little or no special labor. Owing to this quality, brick is easily used in rectangular patterns that build on its modular shape. Common brick patterns for pavement areas that are based on its inherent modular quality are shown and identified in Figure 12–29. Typical brick patterns for walls are shown in Figure 12–30.

Brick can also be used in concentric circular patterns or patterns that use extended radii from a central point (Figure 12–31). The limitation with these patterns is that the radius of the circle must be large enough to minimize the size of the joint space between individual bricks. A radius that is too small creates unsightly and unsafe joints. One suggestion for minimizing joint size is to place the long direction of

Material Composition and Master Plan

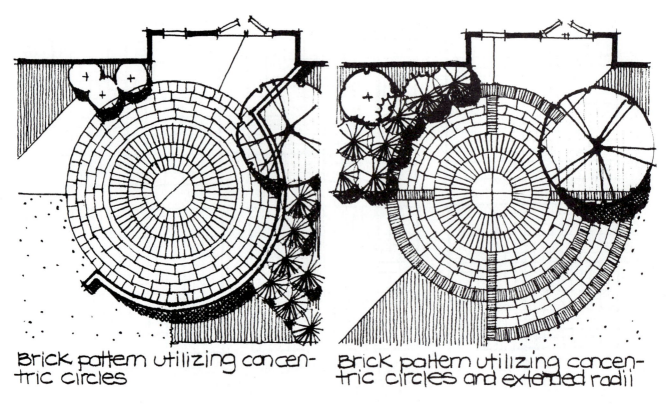

Brick pattern utilizing concentric circles

Brick pattern utilizing concentric circles and extended radii

FIGURE 12–31
Examples of brick pavement patterns for circular areas.

bricks parallel to the radius closer to the inside of the circle, while either the short or long dimensions can be parallel to the radius farther away from the circle's center.

Similar thoughts apply to the use of tile, unit pavers, and concrete block for patterns in pavement and on walls. Again, an attempt should be made to use as much of these materials with minimal labor for cutting and shaping individual pieces.

Wood has some of the same restrictions that other unit materials do for material patterns. But as stated before, wood can also be cut making its potential use more varied. A number of potential wood patterns for a square deck surface are shown in Figure 12–32. As with other materials, the more elaborate patterns illustrated are the most time consuming and costly to use. Where possible, the designer should use standard sizes to minimize the need for cutting and for the waste of material that usually results.

Wood also has numerous possible patterns for fences (Figure 12–33).

Visual Qualities. In addition to considering the context and material characteristics, the landscape designer also needs to think about a number of visual qualities when creating material patterns. As the landscape designer studies material patterns, thought should be given to borders, emphasis, and contrast within the surface area of the material pattern.

Many successful patterns use borders around the outside perimeter of a surface area. This acts like a frame to visually contain the pattern. Borders can be created by using either the same or different material. If the same material is used, its size, color, or orientation can be changed to set it off from the rest of the area (Figure 12–34). If a different material is used, it automatically establishes a border due to its difference in size, color, or texture. Borders can be rather simple or elaborate (Figure 12–35). For walls and fences, edges on the top and bottom can and should be distinct. Again, the designer can use either the same or different materials to define the cap and base to a wall or fence (Figure 12–36).

FIGURE 12-32
Potential wood patterns for a square deck.

FIGURE 12-33
Potential patterns for a wood fence.

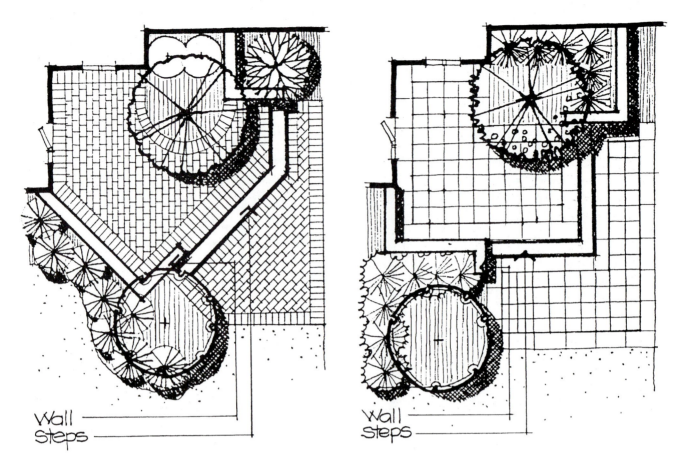

FIGURE 12–34
Examples of pavement edges created by altering the size and/or orientation of the pavement material.

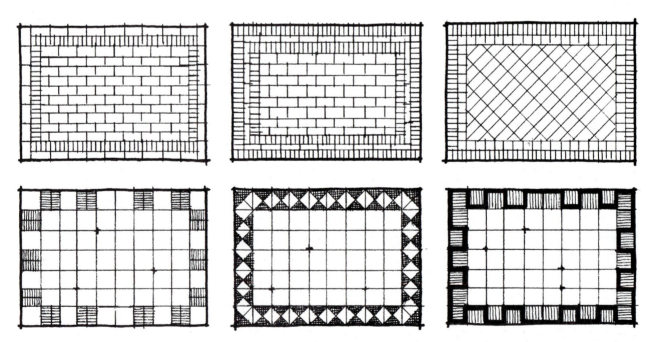

FIGURE 12–35
Examples of simple and elaborate pavement edges.

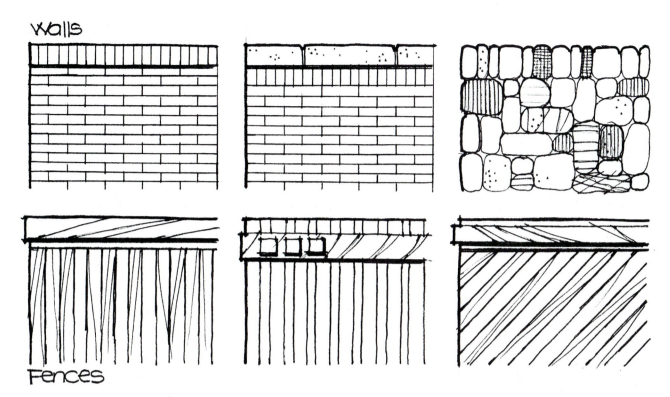

FIGURE 12–36
Examples of potential caps for walls and fences.

Some material patterns can have areas of emphasis within them to attract the eye to important places. An accent can be created by using a different size, color, texture, and/or orientation of material in comparison to other areas of the pattern. A dissimilar material can also be used to create emphasis (Figure 12–37). Varying the shape of the pattern is particularly effective in attracting attention to key areas.

The design of material patterns should also consider contrast. Contrast can be created in a material pattern by doing something that is noticeably different or the opposite (the principle of inversion) than the rest of the pattern or surface area (Figure 12–38). Changing the material or color of material is very effective for achieving contrast. Contrast can be used for emphasis or simply for visual interest. Often, a material pattern can become monotonous to the eye if it is used too much or over too large an area. Contrast provides variety and visual stimulation.

SPECIAL ATTENTION TO ARCHITECTURE AND DETAIL

Design detail is so important to the success of the visual character of the final design solution. Design detail, not construction detail, is something that so often is neglected and left to the discretion of the client or contractor. There are many examples of quality designs that went sour due to the lack of coordination between the overall design forms and the internal patterns within those forms. Structures on the ground plane, vertical plane, and overhead plane need to be fitted with pattern. Just calling out a material for a structure is not good enough.

Three examples will be dealt with as they relate to material composition: a two-tiered patio, a wall, and an overhead structure.

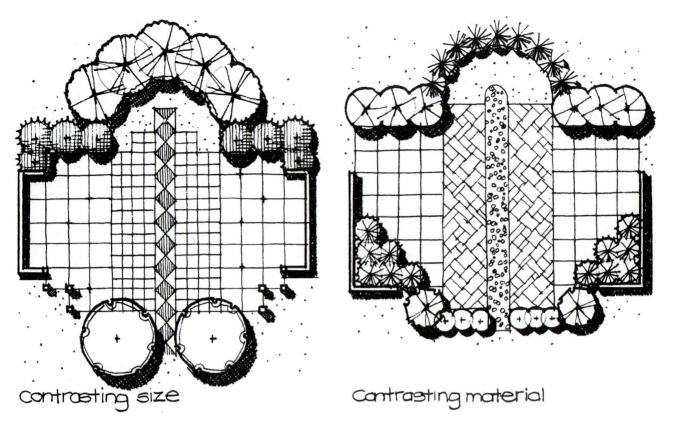

contrasting size   Contrasting material

FIGURE 12-37
Emphasis can be created in a pavement area by using contrasting materials and/or patterns.

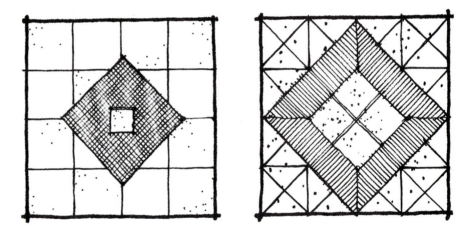

FIGURE 12-38
Contrast can be achieved by using a pattern that is noticeably different from the rest of the pattern.

Ground Plane Pattern

The first structure is a two-level patio with a low wall adjacent to a family room. It is accessed by means of a sliding glass door. A rectangular design theme was selected. Materials for these examples have been established as brick and stone or brick and concrete. As you can see in Figure 12–39, the house borders the patio on the top and left sides. The upper level is a square shape, with two sets of steps connecting it to lower rectangular patios. All three patio alternatives have the

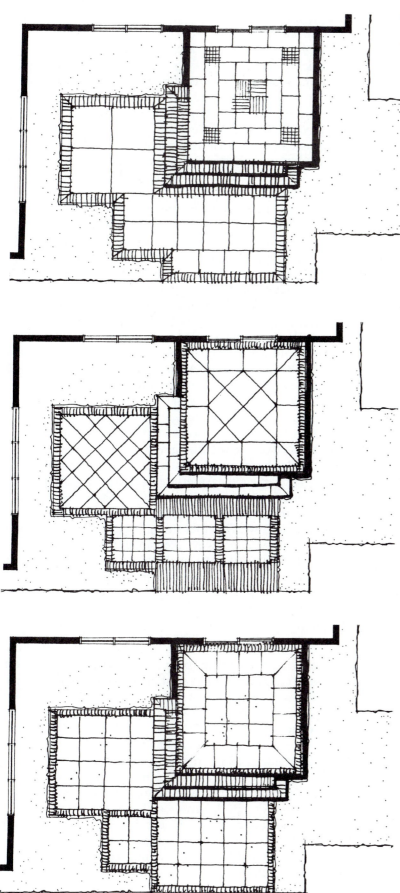

FIGURE 12-39
Three alternatives for the internal pattern of a
rectangular patio design.

exact same outlines and planting bed lines. The differences are in the ways that the internal patterns were established.

Each of the upper-level square terraces has been segmented and subdivided in different ways that reflect the geometry of the square. Each provides a unique look to the terrace, much the same way as three different area rugs do inside the house. Likewise, the lower-level areas have been divided: (1) to relate to the rectangular forms, (2) to reflect the lines of force on the house; and (3) to resemble some of the patterns established in the upper level.

And these are only three of many ideas that could be developed. While it is not suggested that you develop an exhaustive set of alternatives, it is helpful to explore the internal pattern so it can reflect more detail of the architectural character of some feature on or in the house.

Figure 12–40 uses the same house as in the previous example. But this time the design theme is a modified diagonal. This offers some different types of internal patterns, other than the rectangular theme, and also offers the opportunity to emphasize two different places upon exiting the sliding glass doors.

The example at the top of Figure 12–40 uses angled lines to lead people either into the upper-level space or down the steps into the lower level. In the other two examples, one emphasized a strong angular pattern while the other defined a more rectangular relationship to the house. As you look carefully at each of the lower areas, you will notice that the patterns relate: (1) to the diagonal and rectangular forms of the outlines, (2) to the lines of force on the house and walls, and (3) to some of the patterns established in the upper level. Again, exploration, even at this detailed level will enhance and enrich your design abilities.

The last example (Figure 12–41) shows the same house with an arc and tangent design theme. In this theme, it is critical to pay attention to the center of the circle as an option for pattern. While it is not necessary to design a pattern that focuses on the center of the circle, it can be an exciting design. The lower-level design patterns relate: (1) to the circular forms and the outlines, (2) to the lines of force on the house and walls, and (3) to some of the patterns established in the upper level.

There will be times while you are exploring a specific pattern, when you realize it would be better to enlarge or reduce an area to make the pattern fit better. In situations where the designer discovers that fitting a pattern necessitates the shifting of a line developed earlier, it is always recommended to investigate the possibility of shifting an edge for the sake of a final internal design pattern. More often than not, the pattern within a structure is more important than the specific dimension of the structure.

Vertical Plane Pattern

The patterns of the walls and fences can be just as important to the success of an outdoor space as interior walls are to an indoor space. As was noted earlier in spatial composition, fences and walls can be much more exciting design elements if they are conceived and developed in a way similar to that in the interior. In addition, it is critical that specific size or scale of materials, as well as the colors of materials, be consistent with those features used to develop ideas earlier in the design. If 4″ wide siding is used on the house, and a fence is proposed to be a similar design, then strongly consider the use of the same size of siding. This is true for most of the design detail taken from the house. It is not necessary to change the sizes of materials when applying them to another structure; in many cases, it is more appropriate to replicate architectural detail because it ties separate design elements together in a visual fashion.

Figure 12–42 illustrates the development of material patterns of several walls. Each design is different, though each was based on the same functional diagram. In addition, the existing plant material along the wall needed to be considered as part of the scene. The diagram at the top shows four different functions to be satisfied along the length of the wall.

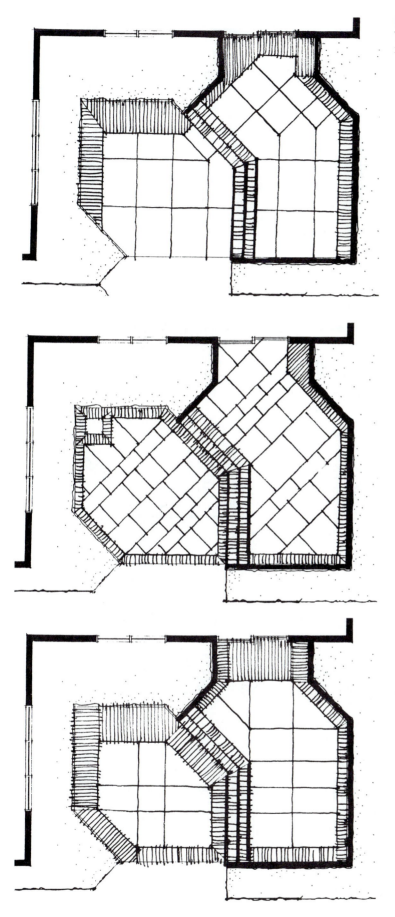

Material Composition and Master Plan

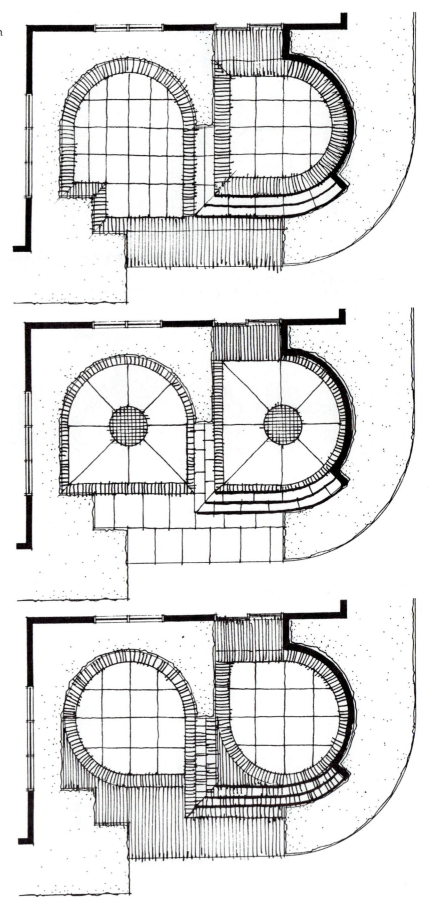

FIGURE 12–41
Three alternatives for the internal pattern of an arc and tangent patio design.

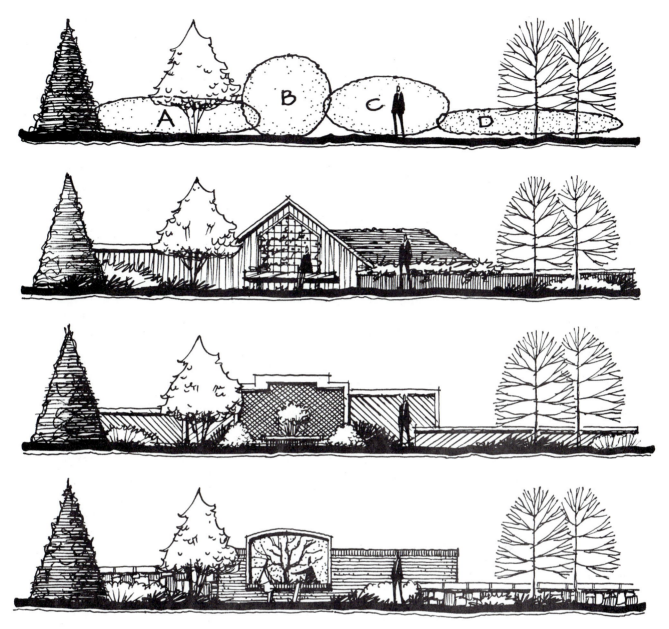

FIGURE 12–42
Three alternative fence/wall designs based on the same functional diagram.

Section "A" was to be high enough to serve as a background for some 2' to 4' shrubs, but low enough that one can see a pleasant view beyond.

Section "B" was meant to serve as a very private section that also serves as a focal area.

Section "C" was to provide for privacy similar to "B."

Section "D" was established as a low seat wall that could be viewed over for a nice view beyond.

Each of the three final wall designs was based upon a completely different house design, but all three satisfy the functions as required. In each of these designs, decisions were made regarding the size of material to use for the final design of the wall. For instance, the width and color of vertical wood and the grillwork size would be needed for the first wall example. Similarly, the size of the lathe work and the width of wood for the second wall would have to be decided. Likewise, the size and color of brick and the stone color, along with the background material and color for the espaliered plant, would need to be defined.

Overhead Plane Pattern

Last, but not least, is the overhead plane. This is the enclosure that provides a sense of intimacy to a space. Overhead planes are wonderful elements to use in the landscape for they can also provide varying degrees of protection from the elements and they cast interesting shadow patterns on the walls and floors of outdoor space. In developing specific overhead patterns, hints should be taken from the architecture. Just as some architectural elements of a house were used to develop ideas for patios and walls, those same elements might be explored as potential patterns for overhead structures.

In addition to the variety of forms that can be borrowed from the architecture, there are some basic forms that can be examined to offer potential patterns. These basic forms are: (1) the square, (2) the circle, (3) the hexagon, and (4) the octagon. Each of these forms is used in many designs throughout the landscape design profession.

Figure 12–43 illustrates four rows of potential overhead patterns, all assuming that partial sun/shade is required. The top row depicts how a square can be segmented to create two types of patterns for the overhead. Each of them relies on the internal geometry of the square. Exploring with the square will undoubtedly provide many more options.

The second row also deals with the square, but focuses on its diagonal qualities. Thus, different patterns are created by focusing on these aspects of the square. The first one consists of a series of diminishing sizes of squares that shift direction. It is a strong pattern to emphasize the diagonal patterns with a square. The second pattern is an asymmetrical design, including an L-shaped overhead with an open portion at the corner. The third pattern bisects the square into two triangular pieces with wood patterns perpendicular to each other.

The next row deals with the circle. Each of these are two-layered overhead planes. One of them, the lower one, is a square in each of the three examples. This lower system serves for supporting the upper pattern which creates the circular character. The first example is a parallel pattern spaced equally across the circle. The second one is a radiating pattern coupled with a connecting outer ring. The third one explores changing the wood members to create alternating patterns in different directions.

The last row shows examples of two hexagonal and one octagonal pattern. The first consists of a series of smaller hexagons within the original. The radiating members are used to connect the smaller hexagons to the larger ones. The second example originated by connecting each of the six corners to each of the other corners. What occurs is a series of overlapping triangles which form a six-pointed star. The third example is similar to the layout of the first example in row two. They both deal with the angled square in alternating patterns. The square and octagon are very much related, for the square has four sides and the octagon has twice as many sides as the square. Each of these fit within each other in many different ways. Exploration of these two forms will provide other alternative patterns.

Again, these are just some of the overhead pattern opportunities that exist from dealing with simple forms. Imagine the number of other possibilities that will arise as different architectural forms are explored.

MASTER PLAN PROCESS

The master plan starts with the preliminary design and goes beyond it to study the design in a more detailed manner. If the preliminary design consists of only one al-

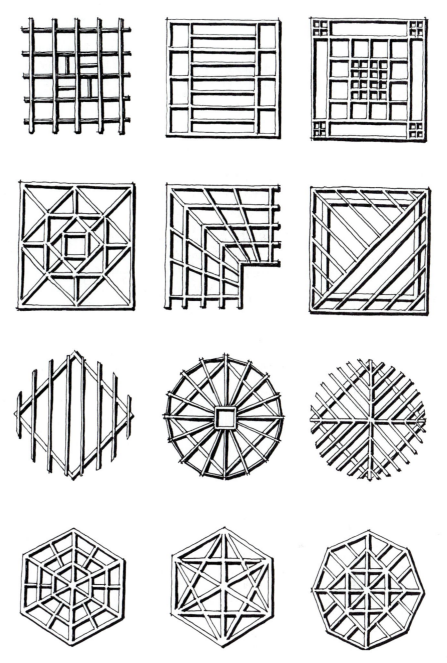

FIGURE 12–43
Possible overhead arbor patterns based on the square, circle, hexagon, and octagon.

ternative, then the master plan proceeds to add more refinement and detail to it. If the preliminary design is comprised of two or more alternative plans, then the master plan is based on the best alternative or combination of alternatives.

One of the first steps in preparing the master plan is to seek the clients' feedback about the preliminary designs. Typically, the clients will offer some reactions and opinions while the designer is presenting the preliminary design to them. If they don't, the designer should ask for their thoughts after the presentation has been completed. The feedback at this point is "a first impression" and can help the designer to judge the general acceptance of the alternative. The designer should be able to assess where and how the clients generally agree or disagree with what was presented to them.

However, the designer should also give the clients some additional time to absorb the preliminary design(s). The clients are apt to need time to think about important ideas or to make decisions about key aspects of the design. The designer should not expect the clients to make hasty judgments that both parties may regret later. The time required for this extended thought about the preliminary design may vary from several days to a week. On the other hand, it is best not to give clients too much more time than this because they may begin to forget many of the points that were made during the presentation.

To facilitate the process of getting feedback, the designer should leave an extra copy or two of the preliminary design(s) with the clients. Remember, never leave the original drawing with the clients; the designer should keep that in the office. The clients should be encouraged to study the drawings thoroughly and to write comments directly on the copies. After the clients have been given adequate time to comment on the preliminary designs, the designer should have a clear direction for proceeding with the master plan.

In addition to seeking the clients' feedback, the designer should also take time alone to review the preliminary design. More often than not, the designer will identify certain areas of the preliminary design that need additional study. In some cases, the designer may discover some areas of the design that simply do not work. These areas of the plan will have to be reworked. In other places, the design may work, but doesn't yet "feel right" to the designer. These areas may need some "massaging" and adjustment to improve their quality. And in still other places, the designer may find a better solution than was originally developed.

After receiving the clients' feedback and reviewing the preliminary design(s), the designer can "return to the drawing board" to revise the design. As the designer revises the plan in preparation of the master plan, there may be three related and simultaneous activities that take place: (1) redesign, (2) refinement, and (3) more detail. The following paragraphs describe how a preliminary plan for a pool area was revised in terms of the three master plan activities (Figure 12–44).

1. *Redesign.* First, the designer may have to change certain areas of the design so that a new solution is created. This is the most radical type of revision that is made and often involves completely altering some forms and/or elements of the design (Figure 12–45). In this example, the shape of the pool and location of the pool house have been changed while still maintaining an overall axial design.

2. *Refinement.* Second, the designer may revise or improve certain areas of the design. This often involves selective repositioning and modifying of certain forms and/or elements of the design (Figure 12–46). In this example, the shape of the pavement, design of the steps, and organization of the plant materials have been refined in relation to the preliminary design.

3. *More detail.* And finally, the designer may study and show some areas or elements of the design in greater detail in comparison to the preliminary design (Figure 12–47). Here, the pavement pattern and plant materials are shown in greater detail than in the preliminary design.

It should be noted that the combination of refinement and more detail will be the most typical activities if the designer was thorough during the preliminary design phase.

After the master plan has been completed along with other drawings, such as sections and perspectives, the designer once again meets with the clients for a final presentation. During this presentation, the designer should review all the changes, refinements, and additions made to the design after the preliminary design presentation.

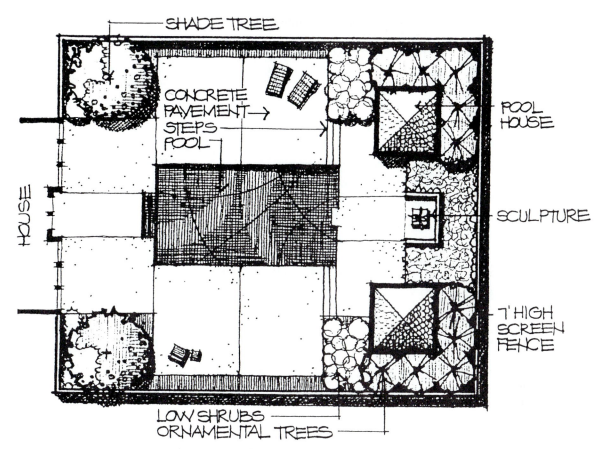

FIGURE 12-44
An example of a preliminary design.

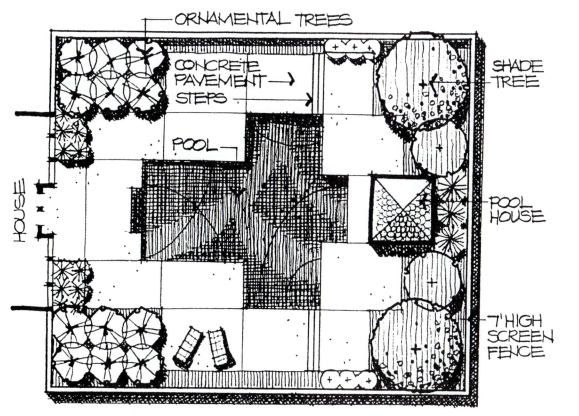

FIGURE 12-45
An example of a master plan that has been redesigned in comparison to the preliminary design.

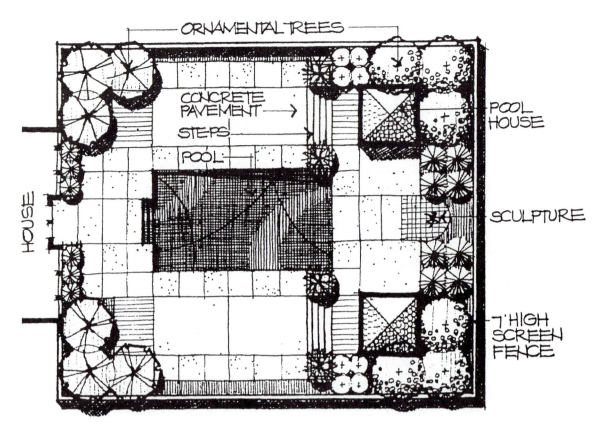

FIGURE 12–46
An example of a master plan that has been refined in comparison to the preliminary design.

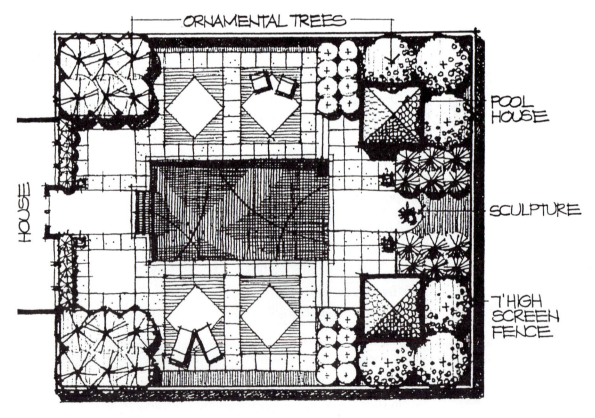

FIGURE 12–47
An example of a master plan that has greater detail in comparison to the preliminary design.

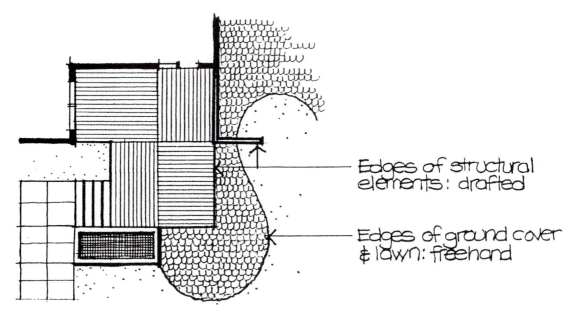

Edges of structural elements: drafted

Edges of ground cover & lawn: freehand

FIGURE 12-48
The edges of structural elements in the master plan can be drafted.

In many instances, this final presentation of the master plan is the end of the project for the designer. However, the designer should make it clear to the clients that there are many critical steps that must be undertaken before the master plan can become reality. The designer should offer (with proper compensation) to stay involved with the installation and implementation of the design so that the intended quality is fulfilled. Depending on the nature of the situation, this involvement may vary from occasional supervision or review of the implementation to direct and complete control. Whatever the role the designer plays, some involvement is better than none.

MASTER PLAN GRAPHIC STYLE AND CONTENT

The master plan is drawn in a more exact and controlled graphic manner in comparison to the preliminary design. There are several ways this is achieved. First, the master plan is usually drawn on higher-quality paper than the preliminary design. If a base sheet was drawn earlier in the design process, as described in Chapter 6, then the easiest approach at this point is to obtain a copy made of this base. The original base sheet should be returned to the file drawer while the master plan is drawn directly on the copy. This procedure eliminates the necessity for redrawing the house, property line, and existing features that are to remain on the site.

A second means for achieving a controlled graphic style is to partially draft the master plan. All edges of structural elements (*hardscape*) such as the house walls, free-standing walls/fences, pavement, steps, pools, and so on, can be hand drafted or laid out with a computer CAD program (Figure 12–48).

Lighter lines should be drawn first and darker lines last to reduce smudging. It should be noted that some designers may nevertheless prefer to draw structural elements in the master plan freehand. This is perfectly acceptable as long as the drawing is neat and legible.

Plant materials and other natural elements (*softscape*) should be drawn freehand in the master plan. For plant materials, it is best to first use a circle template to lightly draw the outlines of plant masses as well as the individual plants within them (left side of Figure 12–49). When the light outlines or guidelines have been

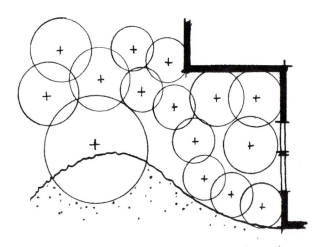

Step 1: Circle-template guidelines.

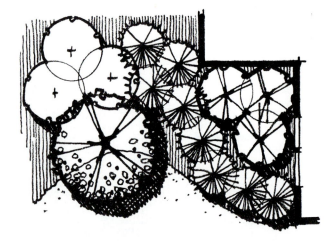

Step 2: Freehand plant symbols.

FIGURE 12–49
A process for drawing plant materials in the master plan.

completed, the designer can go back over them with a pen or soft pencil to draw darker outlines around plant materials (right side of Figure 12–49). This technique gives plant materials a somewhat natural appearance in comparison to the structural elements in the drawing. Plant materials and other natural elements should not be drafted in the master plan because this gives these elements a stiff, engineered look.

The master plan should graphically show essentially the same information as the preliminary plan that preceded it. The master plan should show the following to scale:

A. Property line and adjoining street
B. Outside walls of the house including doors and windows
C. Existing site elements or features that are to remain part of the design solution (should be on the base sheet)
  1. utilities such as air conditioner, heat pump, gas meter, telephone poles, and so on
  2. existing areas of pavement such as driveway, walks, and so on
  3. existing vegetation that is to remain
D. All elements of the design drawn and illustrated with the proper symbols and textures including the following:
  1. pavement materials and patterns
  2. walls, fences, steps, and other structures. Overhead structures may need to be shown on a separate drawing so they do not become confused with pavement, plant materials, and so on
  3. woody plant materials shown as individual elements (though still in masses) so exact quantity and location can be determined
  4. perennials, annuals, herbs, and so on, shown as generalized masses
  5. water fountains, pools, streams, and so on
  6. outdoor lighting locations
  7. rocks, boulders, and so on
  8. furniture, planter boxes, sculpture, and so on

In addition, the master plan should identify the following with notes and/or a legend on the drawing:

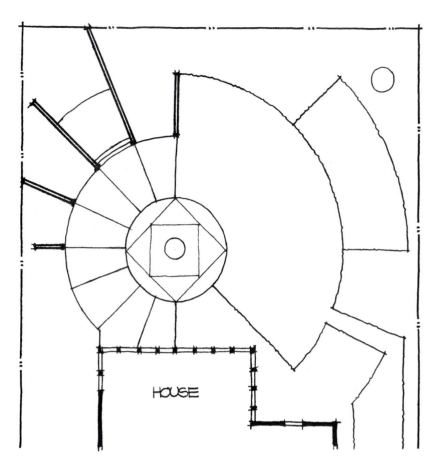

FIGURE 12–50
An example of a partially completed master plan used as a base for other drawings.

1. Major use areas such as outside entry foyer, living and entertaining area, terrace, pool, lawn, garden, and so on
2. Materials and patterns of pavement, walls, fences, overhead structures, and so on
3. Plant materials by quantity and scientific name (unless a separate planting plan is to be drawn)
4. Ground elevations defined with spot grades and/or contour lines
5. Heights of walls, fences, steps, benches, and so on
6. Other notes that help explain the design to the clients
7. North arrow and scale (graphic and written)

If the landscape designer anticipates that additional plan drawings of the design such as a planting plan, layout plan, and/or grading plan will also have to be completed, then the master plan should be drawn so that copies can be used for bases of these additional drawings. To do this, the master plan is at first only partially completed. The house, property lines, and all elements and edges of spaces that are common to all these drawings should be drawn first (Figure 12–50). The title block information, north arrow, scale, and borders should also be completed at this time. However, no plant materials, textures, shadows, or labels should be drawn.

When the master plan is in this partially completed state, as many reproducible copies as necessary for the additional drawings should be obtained. After this has been accomplished, the master plan drawing can be completed by adding plant materials, textures, shadows, labels, and so on (Figure 12–51). Each of the copies is then used as a base for the additional plan drawings

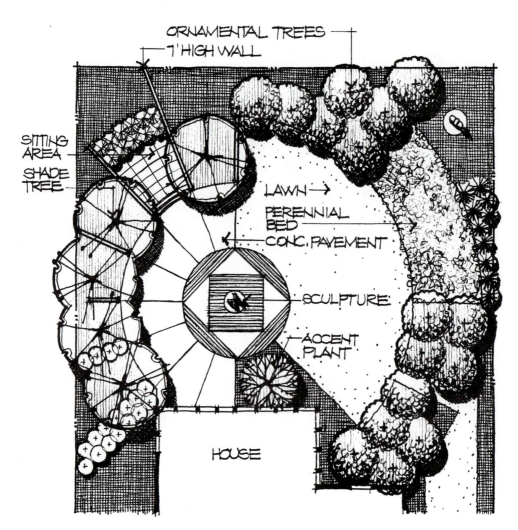

ORNAMENTAL TREES

7' HIGH WALL

SITTING AREA

SHADE TREE

LAWN →

PERENNIAL BED

CONC. PAVEMENT

SCULPTURE

ACCENT PLANT

HOUSE

FIGURE 12–51
An example of a master plan.

(Figures 12–52 and 12–53). This procedure will save the time needed to redraw all the lines and symbols that are common to the master plan and additional drawings.

MASTER PLAN FOR THE DUNCAN RESIDENCE

After reviewing the two preliminary plans (Figures 11–85 and 11–86), the Duncans decided on Preliminary Plan "B" (Figure 11–86). After further discussions about this particular preliminary design, Mr. Kent, the landscape designer, undertook another study of the design to incorporate a few revisions and refinements. The result is the master plan shown in Figure 12–54.

As can be seen, this master plan is very similar to the preliminary design that preceded it. However, a close inspection will also reveal a number of subtle changes. In the front yard, the shape of the sitting area has been revised and the planting has been refined. For example, the massing of low taxus and the group of hawthorns in the southwest corner more clearly define and strengthen the arc of the lawn area. The western side of the house has been treated in a manner very much like the preliminary design. The area along the eastern side of the house has been revised slightly. The shape of the work/storage area and lawn has been made

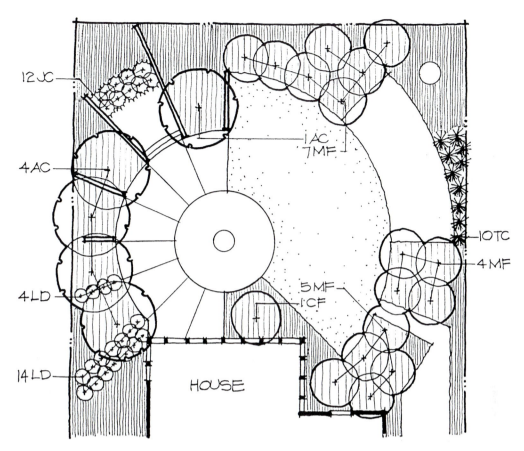

FIGURE 12–52
An example of a planting plan.

more rectangular so they fit the narrow yard area more comfortably. In addition, the shrub planting near the weeping cherry has been eliminated to make this ornamental tree more prominent. In the back yard, the planting has been refined in a number of locations. The existing Norway maple has been incorporated with the planting bed adjacent to the brick terrace. The planting near the air conditioner has also been altered. Along the northern edge of the lawn area, a ground cover bed is used to define the edge between the lawn and planting bed. A perennial bed is placed behind the ground cover to provide height and a splash of color during the summer. All of this is backed by a massing of shrubs which has been refined.

Figure 12–55 shows the proposed designs for the 1) fence on the east side of the brick terrace and 2) an arbor over the deck. The terrace fence serves as a screen to separate the terrace from the side yard. It provides an extra layer of privacy from the east. The arbor is partially open for filtered sun and to support vines. The patterns and character of these structures are reflective of the rectangular design theme.

SUMMARY

The master plan is the end of the design phase of the design process. It is the culmination of all the hard work and long hours that have preceded it. The master plan shows the clients what their site will eventually look like in graphic form if everything in the plan is implemented. While the reality of most master plans is not realized immediately, master plans do provide a long-term goal for coordinated development of the residential site. They give direction and ensure the outdoor residential environment will be treated as a complete environment tailored to the specific conditions of the site and special needs of the clients.

Material Composition and Master Plan

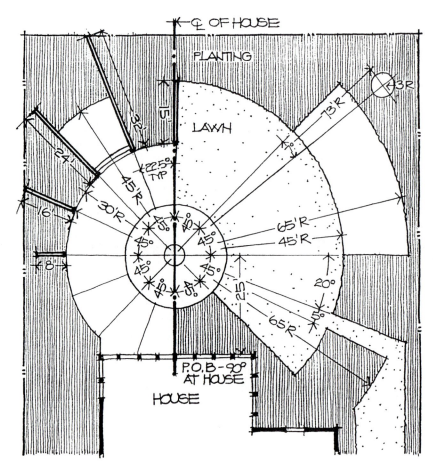

FIGURE 12–53
An example of a layout plan.

While the master plan ends the design phase, it is by no means the end of the design process. Additional drawings such as planting plans, layout plans, grading plans, and construction details may have to be prepared before some or all parts of the master plan can be installed and implemented. Furthermore, the implementation of the master plan should be occasionally supervised by the landscape designer to make sure the ideas and quality that were envisioned are in fact realized.

The master plan is not the end in other ways as well. The master plan itself may need to be revised from time to time as the needs and circumstances of the clients change. In a way, there never is a final master plan, and the designer should never completely leave a project after the master plan. Even after the project is built, the designer should periodically review the results to observe the effects of time and to analyze strong and weak points. The designer should consider each project to be a learning experience that can be applied to the next project. If approached this way, residential site design will be a never-ending joyful experience for the designer and clients.

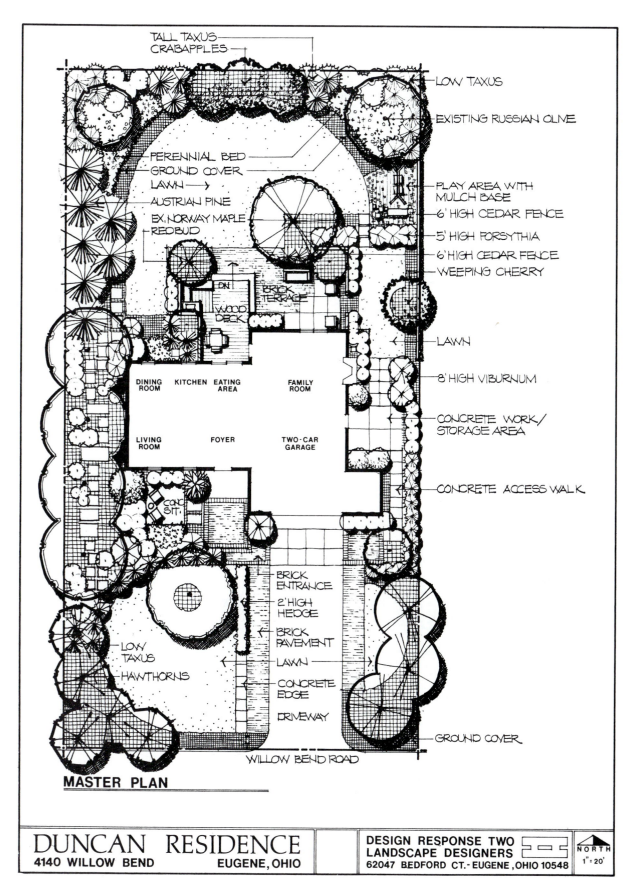

TALL TAXUS
CRABAPPLES

LOW TAXUS

EXISTING RUSSIAN OLIVE

PERENNIAL BED
GROUND COVER
LAWN →
AUSTRIAN PINE
EX. NORWAY MAPLE
REDBUD

PLAY AREA WITH
MULCH BASE
6' HIGH CEDAR FENCE
5' HIGH FORSYTHIA
6' HIGH CEDAR FENCE
WEEPING CHERRY

DN

BRICK
TERRACE

WOOD
DECK

LAWN

8' HIGH VIBURNUM

DINING
ROOM

KITCHEN

EATING
AREA

FAMILY
ROOM

CONCRETE WORK/
STORAGE AREA

LIVING
ROOM

FOYER

TWO-CAR
GARAGE

CONCRETE ACCESS WALK

CONC.
SIT.

BRICK
ENTRANCE

2' HIGH
HEDGE

BRICK
PAVEMENT

LOW
TAXUS

HAWTHORNS

LAWN

CONCRETE
EDGE

DRIVEWAY

GROUND COVER

WILLOW BEND ROAD

MASTER PLAN

DUNCAN RESIDENCE
4140 WILLOW BEND   **EUGENE, OHIO**

DESIGN RESPONSE TWO
LANDSCAPE DESIGNERS
62047 BEDFORD CT.- EUGENE, OHIO 10548

NORTH
1" = 20'

FIGURE 12–54
Master Plan for the Duncan residence.

Material Composition and Master Plan

FIGURE 12-55
Arbor, railing and fence patterns for the Duncan residence.

13

Special Project Sites

INTRODUCTION

The previous chapters discussed the ideal process and guidelines for designing the site around a private single-family residence. From this, it is hoped the reader understands that there is much to consider in creating a master plan that meets the requirements of the client, fits the existing site conditions, and is something that is enjoyable to look at and be in. Designing a master plan for a single-family residential site is a complex undertaking that also requires the best effort from a talented individual or firm. Ultimately, the success of the project depends not only on following a process or adhering to a set of principles, but also on the inherent abilities of gifted designers who can creatively solve problems and sensitively assemble elements and materials into an attractive spatial composition.

The Duncan residence was used in the previous chapters as a way to illustrate how the different steps of the design process can be applied to an actual project site. The Duncan residence is similar to many single-family residential properties found in suburbs throughout the United States and Canada. The two-story house is located in the middle of a rectangular lot that is about a quarter of an acre in size. The level site is clearly divided into a front yard facing the street and a back yard behind the house. Like many residential sites, the house was originally built on a cleared site and so was essentially a blank canvas for the original homeowners. The relatively flat, open qualities of the Duncan residence provided few restraints and easily permitted the designer to create a series of well articulated outdoor rooms with plant materials, structures, and pavement.

Though prototypical, the Duncan residence does not represent all potential site conditions that one encounters as a residential landscape designer. Some sites are smaller while others are larger. Other sites have distinct topographic change in some or all areas of the property. Still other residential sites have large areas covered with trees or other types of native vegetation. Some residential projects are

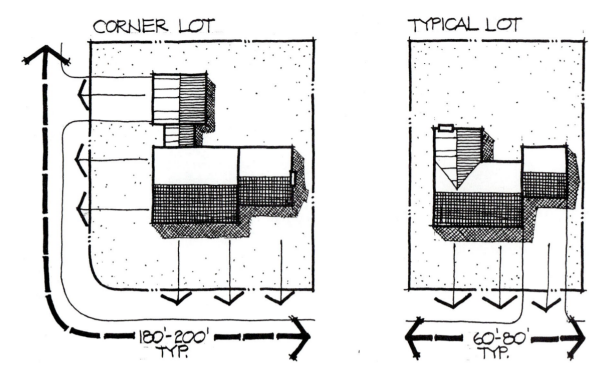

FIGURE 13-1
The street frontage is two to three times greater on a corner lot in comparison to a typical lot.

limited to an enclosed space adjacent to a townhouse while other projects are surrounded by and open to a rural wilderness. All in all, the landscape designer is apt to discover a wide variety of site conditions, each requiring a slightly different application of the design process to create a master plan. The purpose of this chapter is to demonstrate how the design process and guidelines presented in the previous chapters can be modified and adapted to sites that have special conditions.

THE CORNER SITE

Most suburban subdivisions are planned so that the majority of lots are similar to the Duncan residence with a public street on one side and other single-family properties on the remaining adjoining sides. However, a small portion of the lots in most subdivisions are located at the corners of intersecting streets. Corner lots are typically rather square-like in area with two sides that face the public right-of-way. This lot configuration creates a number of distinct site conditions that require special attention.

Special Site Conditions

Double Front Yard. One of the most unique qualities of the corner lot is that it faces two intersecting streets and therefore has two "front yards." The corner lot may have as much as two to three times the length of adjoining street and curb as a typical lot (Figure 13–1). Thus, all the attention that is commonly afforded the front yard in a typical property must be doubled on the corner lot. The site areas that directly face the streets must establish "curb appeal" and provide the proper "public image." This requires extra effort and sometimes twice the expense. Even the tax or charge for public services such as sidewalk installation, lighting, sewer

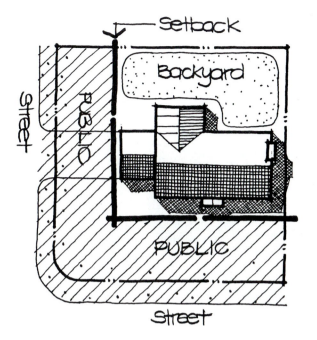
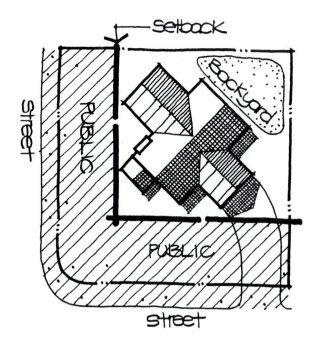

FIGURE 13-2
The majority of a corner lot's area is located in the public realm with little space available for the backyard.

or water line replacement, etc., is frequently more expensive for a corner lot because of the double frontage.

Majority of Site in the "Public Realm."   Directly associated with the double front yards of a corner lot is the fact that the majority of a site area is located in the "public realm" (Figure 13–2). That is, the largest area of the site is located between the house and the two intersecting streets. This situation results from both the double street frontage and the setback requirements that locate the house toward the back of the site. The house placement increases public surveillance of the site and simultaneously reduces privacy. It may force activities like lawn recreation or outdoor sitting that are normally reserved for the back yard to take place in the more public area of the site.

Limited Back Yard Space.   While the majority of a corner lot's area is located in the public realm, the private domain or back yard is simultaneously reduced to a relatively small area (Figure 13–2). In fact, some houses are located on corner properties in such a way that the back yard is reduced to the size of a standard side yard, leaving little room for outdoor activities. Common outdoor features such as decks, terraces, recreational lawns, vegetable gardens, etc., must be drastically reduced in size, moved to the "public" street sides, or eliminated altogether.

Front Entry Confusion.   The double frontage sometimes creates puzzlement about where the front of the house is and where the appropriate location is for entering the house from the street or driveway. This occurs for several reasons. One cause is that the front door of houses on some corner lots faces one street while the driveway connects to other. A second reason for confusion is that some corner lot houses have several doors, one facing one street and another facing the other street. Which one is THE front door? Unless there is a clear distinction about entry, the first-time visitor may well end up entering the site from the wrong street or arriving at the improper door.

FIGURE 13-3
Views from the adjoining streets may extend into both the front yard and back yard, thus reducing privacy.

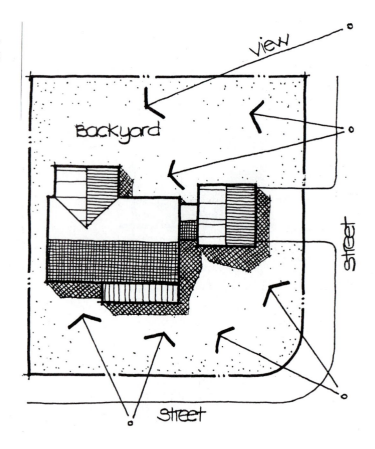

Lack of Privacy. Privacy on the corner lot is reduced because of the increased public surveillance from the two adjoining streets and from the close proximity of the house to the back and side property lines. On some corner lots, views from the streets not only extend into the front yard, but also directly into the back yard (Figure 13–3). In this situation, the house and yard are seen from almost three different sides of the property. Furthermore, the reduced back yard area easily allows views, sound, and smells to extend back and forth to the neighbor's yard. Limited area also means there is less space for screen planting. The house location on other corner lots reduces privacy by orientating the back of the house directly toward the back yard of the adjoining property (Figure 13–4). The result is that the neighbor's back yard is directly seen from windows and spaces located at the back of the house.

Design Guidelines

The designs of a corner site possess a number of challenges. The following design guidelines are offered as a means to address these special site conditions associated with a corner residential property.

Unify Street Frontage. The site design for a corner lot should unify the two street frontages through a common set of design forms and palette of materials (Figures 13–5 and 13–7). It is important for the designer to treat the two sides as one so the house and property appear as one site, not two competing or unrelated areas. This should be done even if there is a clear "front" and "side" to the orientation of the house toward the streets. A unified composition for the areas facing both streets will provide a consistent public identity to the site and house from all vantage points.

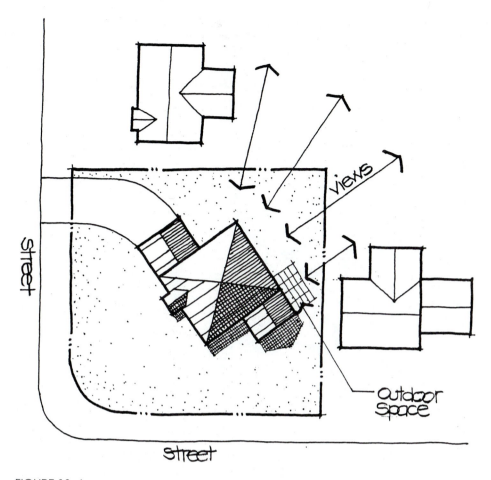

FIGURE 13–4
The lack of privacy in some corner sites is exaggerated by the house's orientation toward the back yards of the neighbors.

Establish a Hierarchy of Emphasis. There should also be relative importance placed on a selected area or areas within the framework of a unified public frontage. One area, usually the front of the house and its associated entry, should be emphasized to visually lead the eye and visitors to the front door (Figure 13–5). This concept will likewise avoid the possibility of a monotonous appearance along the street frontage.

Identify Entry Walks. A directly related need is to clearly identify where and how one gets to the front door of the house, especially when it cannot be immediately seen from all site entry points. In addition to visually emphasizing the front door itself, it is important to locate and design entry walks so guests and service people can easily find their way to the door. Two different walks are often required on a corner site. One walk should extend directly from one of the streets to the front door and be emphasized with showy planting, accent lighting, address sign, etc., to acknowledge its prominence (Figure 13–5). A second walk is frequently necessary from the driveway. It, too, should be clearly visible and lead directly to the front entry area. The two walks should meet at one common outdoor entry foyer giving everyone the same experience of entering the house (Figure 13–6).

Locate Selected Uses in Front. Because space is often limited in the back yard, the designer should consider locating appropriate uses in the more public areas facing the streets. Small sitting or eating areas may be located adjacent to the public side

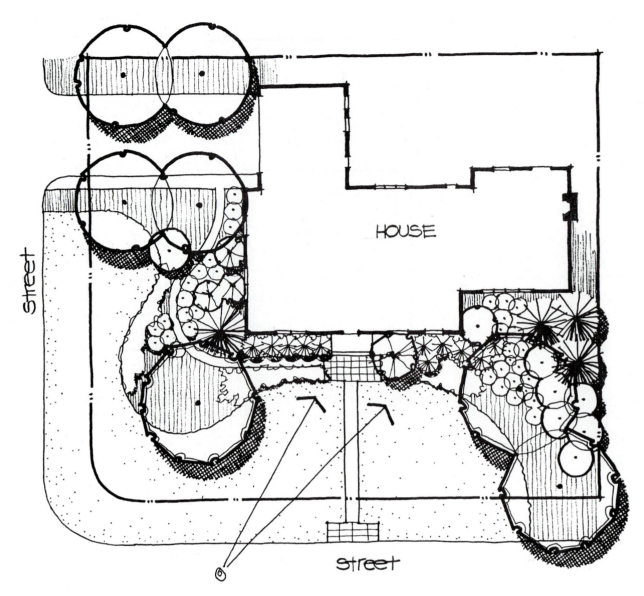

FIGURE 13-5
The front door should be emphasized to attract the eye and visitor.

of the house if proper separation and screening from the street is established. The ideal situation is to create a space that is partially enclosed from the street, but allows for some view out. Plants, walls, and/or fences that are about 3'–4' high can provide a low partition while sitting, but still allow homeowners to view other areas of the front yard and the street. This locality gives homeowners a direct connection to the activity of the street without jeopardizing privacy. Lawn areas along one of the streets might also be used for recreation. Again, separation from the street might be provided with plants or structures if local zoning codes permit.

Establish Privacy. It is critical to establish privacy in a corner lot because it is so often jeopardized due to the location of the house on the site. Screening should be provided from both the adjoining streets and from neighboring properties. To separate the site from the streets, walls, fences, or hedges may be placed along the street or sidewalk edge in selected locations if local zoning permits this (Figure 13–7). Even a low vertical plane that is between 2'–3' in height can provide a sense of partition and help separate the public street from the yard area of the home.

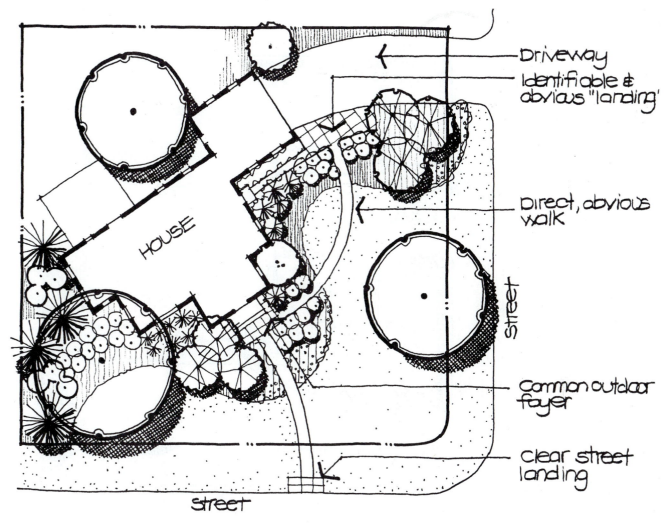

FIGURE 13-6
Two entry walks are often necessary and should meet at a common outdoor entry foyer near the front door.

Screening along the property lines is most critical in the back yard because of the close proximity of the house to the property line and the lack of outdoor area. Here walls and fences are usually the best solution because they can provide a solid structural separation from neighbors without taking up much space. In addition, it may be necessary to provide overhead planes to screen views from the upper stories of nearby houses (Figure 13–8).

Urbanize Back Yard. Because it is usually small in size, it is recommended that the back yard of the corner lot be treated like a small urban space rather than a typical suburban back yard (Figure 13–9). Thus, lawn should be minimized or eliminated altogether with a series of paved outdoor sitting, entertaining, and/or eating spaces established in its place. These should be carefully detailed to provide spatial enclosure in both the vertical and overhead planes. Walls, fences, and overhead trellises may be used with plants to create space and separation from neighbors. Attractive pavement should dominate the ground plane and be balanced by carefully located planting beds. If treated appropriately, the back yard of a corner lot can be viewed as an architectural extension of the house with a room or series of rooms that visually and functionally carry the indoors into the exterior (also see "The Townhouse Garden," the last section of this chapter).

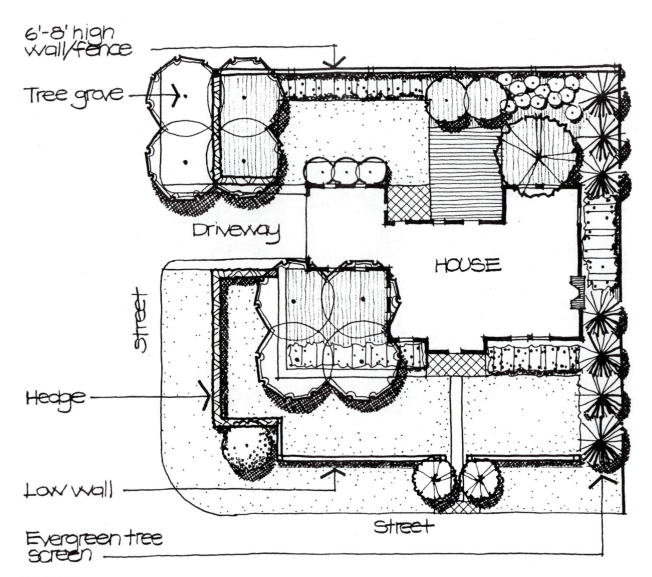

Labels on figure:
6'-8' high wall/fence
Tree grove
Driveway
HOUSE
Street
Hedge
Low wall
Evergreen tree screen
Street

FIGURE 13–7
Walls and hedges can be used to separate yard areas from the adjoining streets.

THE WOODED SITE

Many suburban lots, like the Duncan residence, are laid out on an existing site that is either devoid of trees before development or is cleared in the process of development. In either case, new suburban single-family sites oftentimes have few or no existing trees to consider when creating a master plan. Still, some residential properties are placed in wooded locations where they are partially or even completely covered by existing trees. The presence of trees on a residential site establishes a unique environment that must be understood and respected if the trees are to be preserved as an integral part of the site over a number of years.

Special Site Conditions

Microclimate.   A stand of deciduous trees creates a distinct microclimate that varies over the course of a year (Figure 13–10). In the summer season, the leaves in the tree canopies block a significant amount of sunlight along with some precipitation. This creates a relatively dark, cool, and dry environment below. Air temperatures may

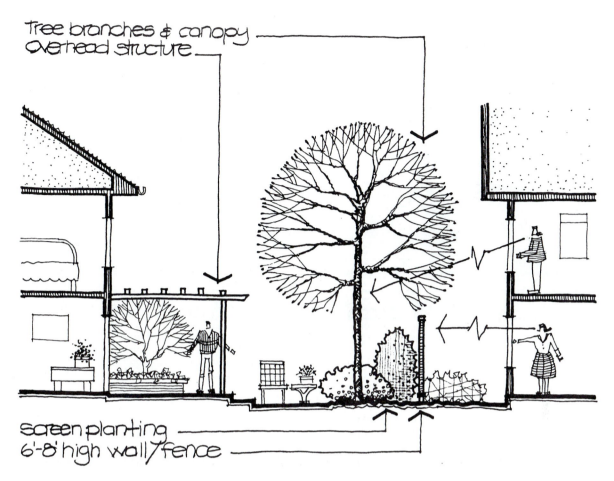

Tree branches & canopy
Overhead structure

screen planting
6'-8' high wall/fence

FIGURE 13-8
Overhead planes and fences/walls should be used in the back yard to establish privacy from nearby neighbors.

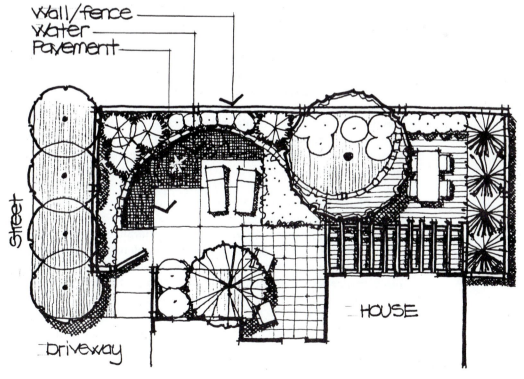

Wall/fence
Water
Pavement

Street

Driveway

HOUSE

FIGURE 13-9
The back yard of a corner site should be treated as an urban garden with a series of well defined outdoor rooms.

Special Project Sites

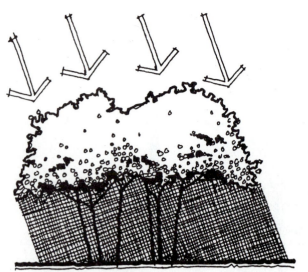

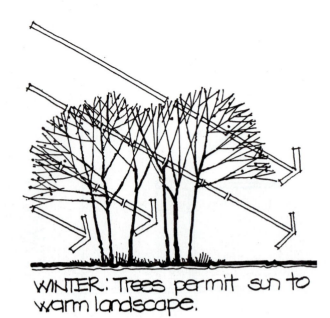

SUMMER: Trees block sun to create a shaded, cool landscape.

WINTER: Trees permit sun to warm landscape.

FIGURE 13–10
The presence of deciduous trees will create distinctly different seasonal microclimates on a residential site.

be as much as 10 to 15 degrees Fahrenheit cooler in the shaded area below trees than in an open area exposed to direct sunlight. This microclimate is generally more comfortable and can produce substantial savings in air conditioning costs for houses in wooded areas (also see "Designing with Sun" in Chapter 3). During the winter season, deciduous trees lose their leaves thus allowing considerably more sunlight to penetrate through. This sun exposure creates a warming effect during the season when it is needed. Thus, the presence of trees can work favorably with the cooling and heating needs of both indoor and outdoor spaces.

Tree Roots. Tree trunks are obvious physical elements that must be worked around in a wooded site. Numerous tree roots are woven in a complex network below the ground surface and are usually located within the top several feet of soil directly below the tree canopy, though some roots extend well beyond the tree canopy (Figure 13–11). Tree roots are the source of food, water, and air for trees in addition to providing structural support. Tree roots are healthiest in a naturalized condition where a layer of leaf debris and rich, porous humus soil exist. Tree roots also need adequate moisture and air in the soil. Tree roots, and the related trees they support, are susceptible to soil compaction or change in drainage across the ground's surface.

Visual Separation. A grove of trees can create visual separation to nearby residential sites and the adjoining street. A cluster of tree trunks function like a group of columns that help to define and separate one space from another. While tree trunks may not be dense enough to completely screen views, they nevertheless do imply a partition of one area from another. Thus, a wooded site frequently has a greater sense of seclusion and privacy even though it may not be completely screened from its surroundings (Figure 13–12).

Design Guidelines

Wooded sites require special design consideration in order to preserve and enhance existing trees. A number of design guidelines should be considered to accomplish this.

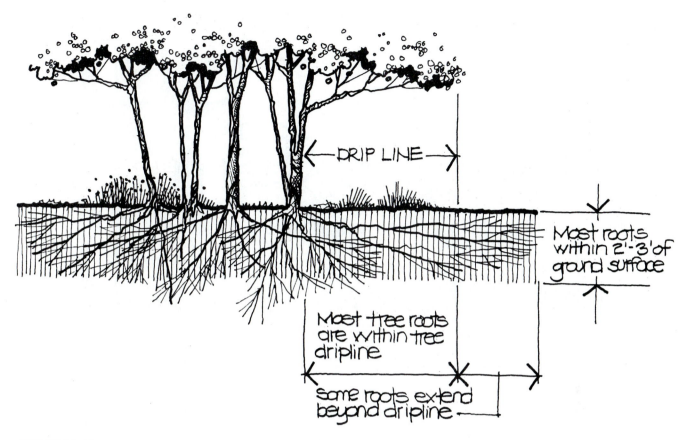

FIGURE 13-11
Most tree roots are in the top two to three feet of soil directly below the tree's canopy; however, some roots extend well beyond the canopy.

FIGURE 13-12
A clump of tree trunks can provide a feeling of visual separation from nearby properties.

Special Project Sites

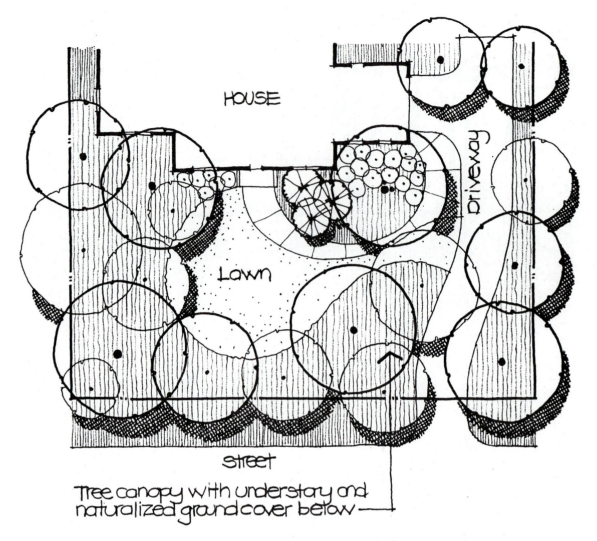

HOUSE

driveway

Lawn

street

Tree canopy with understory and
naturalized ground cover below

FIGURE 13–13
Lawn should be eliminated or minimized in area on a wooded residential site.

Minimize Lawn. The typical suburban lawn should be minimized or even eliminated on a wooded site. There are several reasons for this recommendation. As already identified, a wooded area has noticeably little sunshine and relatively dry soil conditions during the summer season. A lawn frequently struggles under these circumstances, even if it is a variety that will tolerate some shade. A wooded environment is simply not conducive to lawn. In addition, the installation of lawn generally requires that understory plants be removed and that the ground surface be regraded. The loss of understory plants is apt to reduce the overall health of a wooded ecology while also eliminating the ability of the wooded area to regenerate itself. Regrading is apt to harm tree roots and change drainage pattern, both of which can injure or even kill trees.

If a lawn area is deemed necessary, it should be minimized in size and located in an area that receives some sunshine during the course of a summer day. It might be located adjacent to the street where sun probably shines through because of the open street corridor, or the lawn might form a space near the house where it can provide some separation between the house and preserved woods (Figure 13–13). The remaining area of the site should be allowed to remain in its naturalized state with native ground covers and understory trees.

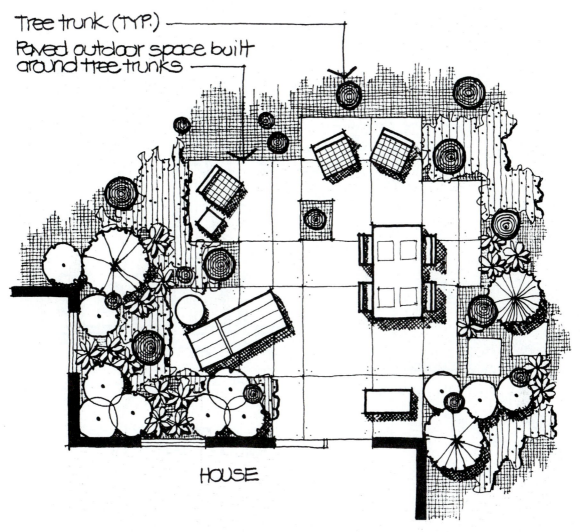

Tree trunk (TYP.)

Paved outdoor space built around tree trunks

HOUSE

FIGURE 13–14
Outdoor use areas must be designed in and around the trunks of existing trees on a wooded site.

Design Around Trees. Every effort should be made to design outdoor spaces and functions around existing trees. This requires extra effort because the exact location of trees must first be mapped. Then, spaces must be carefully woven among tree trunks so that few, if any, trees are removed to accommodate exterior functions. This is especially necessary for structured outdoor spaces like sitting, entertaining, or eating spaces that have paved or wood deck ground planes. Existing trees may need to be allowed to extend up through these surfaces and will probably result in spaces that are more divided and complex than if the trees were not present (Figure 13–14). This approach is also likely to require field adjustment during construction.

Maintain Existing Grade. There should be minimal grading or alteration of the existing ground elevation on a wooded site in order to minimize disturbance of tree roots. If the site is a newly built house, it is likely the ground will have been altered most around the house. Beyond this construction zone, every effort should be made to retain the existing ground level. Again, this is most significant in locating paved walks, structured outdoor spaces, walls, or even lawn areas if they are part of the design. These uses should, as much as possible, be molded to the existing ground while also maintaining proper standards of construction. If significant regrading is necessary, then retaining walls or tree wells should be used to maintain

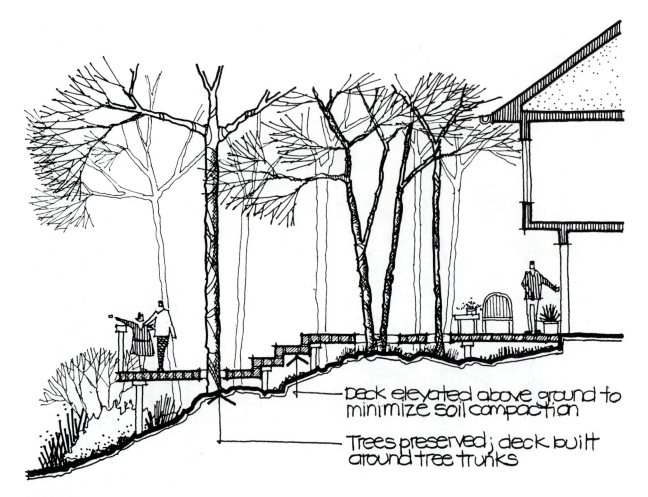

Deck elevated above ground to minimize soil compaction

Trees preserved; deck built around tree trunks

FIGURE 13–15
Outdoor use areas and walks should be elevated on decks above the ground to minimize soil compaction in a wooded site.

the existing grade around the base of existing trees. At a minimum, the existing grade should be preserved within the entire drip line of a tree or grove of trees. Never place fill (soil that is added to the existing ground surface) below the drip line of a tree because this will change the ability of existing tree roots to obtain air and moisture from the soil.

Minimize Soil Compaction.   The existing soil on a wooded site should not be compacted because this too reduces the amount of both air and water in the soil. Compacted soil is also more difficult for roots to grow through. Soil compaction results from the constant use or movement, including foot traffic, across the ground. While occasional walking through a wooded area will probably do little harm, repeated movement over the same ground will compact and damage the underlying soil. One way to avoid soil compaction is to elevate walks and outdoor use areas on decks above the existing ground level (Figure 13–15). The initial installation of posts to support a deck system will cause some disturbance, but in the long term the ground soil will be preserved. This concept also minimizes regrading and allows precipitation to still reach the ground.

Use Shade Tolerant Plants.   Plant materials introduced to a wooded site should be carefully selected for shade tolerance. Some zones on wooded sites may receive no direct sunlight during the course of a summer day, while other areas may receive sun during only a portion of the day. Plants must be chosen to fit each of these conditions. Thus, the palette of plants should be different than that used

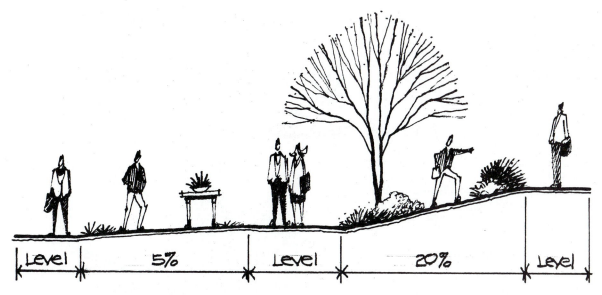

FIGURE 13–16
Sloped ground creates unstable footing for people and structures.

on a more typical residential site. One approach to planting in a wooded site is to use native plants that are already found on or near the site. Native wooded plants not only tolerate the special wooded conditions, but also look like they belong to the wooded environment.

THE SLOPED SITE

A sloped site is one that has some portion of the ground surface located on an inclined plane. Commonly, the ground has to be steeper than 3% (3 feet vertical change in 100 horizontal feet) to be perceived as being sloped. At 5%, the ground does indeed have a distinct slope to it. Ground surfaces greater than 5% are perceived as being more sloped and become increasingly difficult to work with as their degree of slope increases. However steep, all sloped sites possess a number of special circumstances that should be thought about in designing a single-family residential site. The steeper the site, the more pronounced these conditions are.

Special Site Conditions

Instability.   All sloped ground has an unsteady feeling to it for several reasons. First, it is difficult to get stable footing on sloped ground. A person must exert continual energy to stay put in any given location because there is a constant feeling of being pulled downhill. While standing on sloped ground, one foot is invariably higher than the other (Figure 13–16). This is also true for buildings and other structures placed on a sloped site. They, too, must be designed to get "stable footing" by creating level terraces for their location or by special structural systems that connect them to the sloped ground. In either situation, extra time and money must often be spent to overcome the inherent instability of a sloped site.

The instability of a sloped site is also a visual one. When compared to a level or horizontal plane, a sloped plane visually implies potential movement, action, or change. The eye is invited to move along a sloped plane rather than resting as it is able to do in a level surface. This potentiality can be exciting in some cases, but also disconcerting in others.

FIGURE 13–17
The natural orientation on sloped ground is downhill toward a lower elevation.

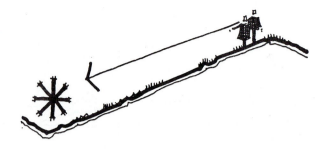

FIGURE 13–18
Some areas of a sloped site may drain toward the house, thus creating potential wet conditions and damage in the house and basement.

Downhill Orientation. Both objects and views on a sloped site have a tendency to move downhill. It is obvious that any mobile object that is placed on sloped ground will likely move downhill. Water, soil, stones, debris etc., all gravitate down the slope over time. Even people usually find it easier to walk down a slope than up one. In addition, the visual orientation for people on a slope is also toward the lower slope. People readily see objects or areas of the landscape located at the bottom of a slope very much like what occurs in an outdoor amphitheater (Figure 13–17). On steep sites, the orientation is very likely to be away from the site toward some distant area of the landscape. Steeply sloped sites located in areas of distinct topography are frequently valued for the views they afford.

Drainage. Surface drainage is a constant issue on a sloped site. Unless the house is located on the crest of a hill, it is quite likely that some portion of a sloped site will drain toward the house (Figure 13–18). As discussed in Chapter 11, it is necessary to regrade the uphill area of the site to divert the surface drainage around the house. If not handled correctly, some walls and floor areas of the house may get wet causing visual and structural damage. Drainage becomes more problematic as the degree of steepness increases. Steeper slopes have a greater amount of surface water moving across them at faster velocities than more gentle slopes or level ground. Thus, there is more water to drain away on steeper slopes. The likelihood of erosion increases as well on steeper slopes because exposed soil is easily washed downhill by a greater volume of surface water draining at a faster velocity.

Design Guidelines

The design of sloped sites should be undertaken with care and understanding for the unique conditions that exist. The design guidelines that follow will help to accomplish this objective.

Fit Uses to Slope. Extra study is typically needed to mold proposed site uses to a sloped site. This should start by preparing a slope analysis, a map depicting the different categories of slope on the site. A slope analysis will show which areas of the site are steepest and which are the most gentle (Figure 13–19).

Then, the designer should attempt to match the proposed uses to slope conditions where they will fit the site with minimal grading (Figure 13–20). For example, a recreational lawn area should ideally be placed in a location that has a slope between 2% and 4%. A lawn that is not for recreation can be placed on an area that is up to 25% slope. Above this, it is too steep to safely mow. An outdoor entertaining space, on the other hand, could be placed on a slope that is between 5% and 15% by terracing it on different levels. The reader is referred to Chapter 11 where slope standards for other uses are outlined.

Outdoor use areas can also be properly tailored to a sloped site by orienting them on the site to minimize grading. This is frequently accomplished by placing the long dimension of outdoor spaces parallel to the contours (Figure 13–21). This stretches the space out along the slope rather than into the slope. Cut (soil that is excavated) and fill (soil that is added to existing ground) and costs are reduced by the approach.

On steeper site areas, outdoor uses may need to be molded to the site by creating terraces that are cut into the slope at different elevations. This creates a series of large "stair-steps" on which outdoor uses are placed (Figure 13–22). Planted slopes that do not exceed a 50% or 2:1 grade can serve as a transition between the elevation of the individual spaces. This approach gives a soft appearance to the landscape and separates spaces by the horizontal distance across the slopes. Retaining walls, sometimes located on both the uphill and downhill sides of spaces, can also be employed as a means of accommodating the different elevation between spaces. Retaining walls give a landscape a more architectural appearance and allow spaces to be placed closer together (Figure 13–23). They likewise can be designed as visual extensions of the house by extending materials and edges of the

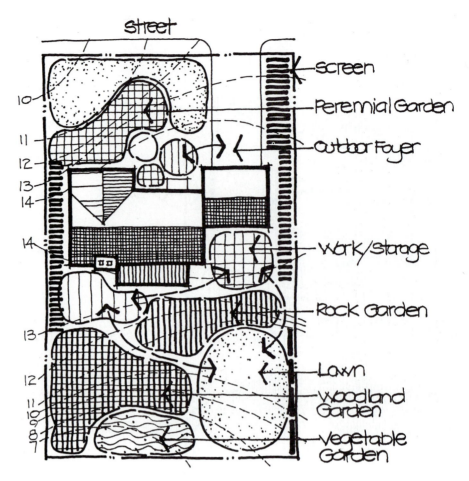

FIGURE 13-20
Outdoor use areas should be carefully matched to the different slope conditions of the site.

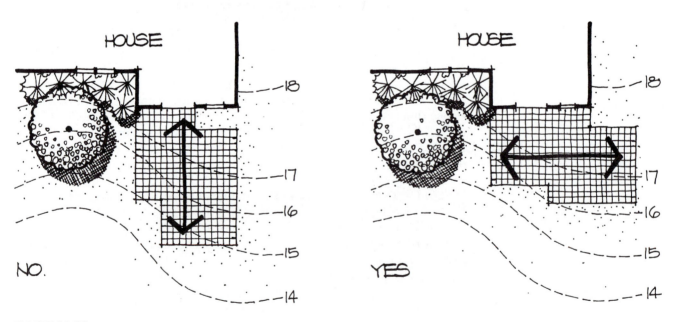

FIGURE 13-21
Outdoor use areas should be oriented parallel to the contours to minimize grading on a sloped site.

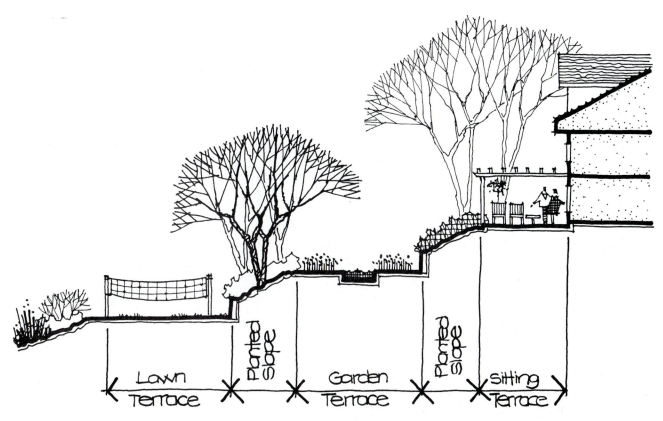

FIGURE 13-22
A series of terraces can be established to fit outdoor use areas into a sloped site.

FIGURE 13-23
A series of terraces separated by walls can establish an architectural character on a sloped site.

FIGURE 13-24
A deck preserves the existing steep slope of a site while affording outward views.

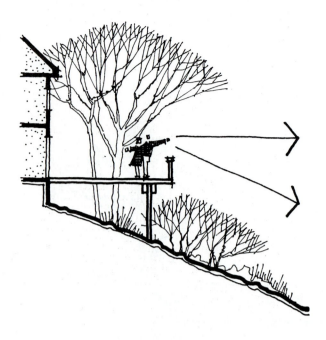

house into the adjacent landscape. Retaining walls should not exceed three or four feet in height without requiring special engineering and cost.

To locate outdoor use areas on sloped areas in excess of 15% most often requires a deck. A deck is simply built above a slope, allowing the existing grade underneath to remain essentially as is (Figure 13–24). Decks work well for spaces of limited size such as outdoor sitting, entertaining, eating, etc. and many times can serve as architectural extensions of the house (also see following section, Take Advantage of Views).

Some outdoor uses may not be able to be placed on steeply sloped sites. Outdoor areas that are large in size and/or require a gentle ground surface may need to be eliminated from a design program for a steep site. There is a point where it is simply best not to force a use onto a site if it does not easily fit. The steepest areas of a site are often best left alone. This is especially so where existing trees or other forms of natural vegetation cover the site. The designer might reserve the steepest areas for revegetation on disturbed or regraded lots as well.

Accommodate Movement. Special attention should be given to accommodating movement on a steep site. This is required because movement, particularly foot traffic, is frequently difficult and restricted on a sloped site. Walks or paths, as suggested in Chapter 11, should not exceed a 5% grade. Walks that are between 5% and 8.33% are considered to be ramps and must adhere to ADA (American with Disabilities Act) standards. To maintain this standard, walks may need to take a more indirect route between two points. In other words, the elevation difference between the top and bottom of the walk should be spread out over a greater distance in order to reduce the walk gradient. In extreme situations, walks or paths may need to "switch back" to avoid being too steep.

Steps are also a common necessity on sloped sites to provide access between nearby spaces. Where possible, extreme elevation differences between adjoining spaces should be avoided to minimize the number of steps that are required. Steps should follow the guidelines provided in Chapter 11 when they are incorporated into a design. In addition, they should visually fit into the site context in terms of form and materials. Steps between adjoining spaces might also be wider than necessary so that the spaces feel more connected. Wide steps allow adjoining spaces to visually flow together.

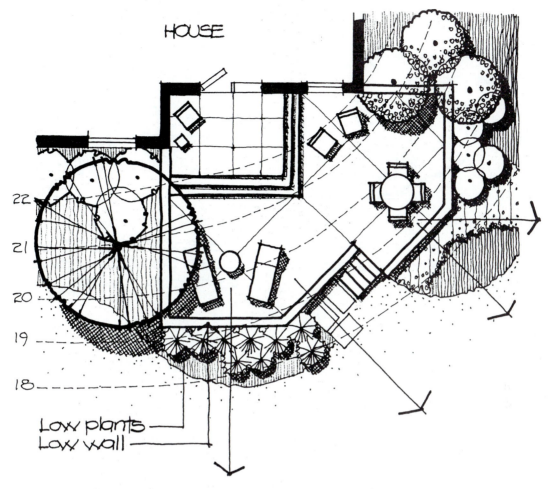

HOUSE

22
21
20
19
18

Low plants
Low wall

FIGURE 13-25
Outdoor use areas should be located and designed to take advantage of views downhill or off the site.

The one disadvantage of steps is that they form barriers to universal accessibility. Therefore, it may also be necessary to incorporate ramps, especially in the public areas such as the approach to the front of the house.

Take Advantage of Views.   Everything possible should be done to take advantage of the inherent views from a sloped site, assuming they are worth capturing. During site analysis, the designer should determine what locations on the site have the best views, both toward other areas of the site as well as to the landscape beyond. Then, selected uses should be consciously placed in these locations to utilize the views (Figure 13–25). Some sitting or gathering spaces might even be located on the front or public side of the house if the views there are worth savoring. Portions of the site that lie downhill from the remainder of site should likewise be studied and enhanced if necessary. Remember, these low areas will definitely be looked at and so they should be worthy of the attention they will receive.

The spaces themselves should also be designed to take advantage of the views. Reducing the height of the vertical plane on the side with the best view can accomplish this (left side, Figure 13–26). Vertical planes that must extend above eye level should be as transparent as possible. Even glass or Plexiglas might be used for vertical enclosure along the downhill side of space (right side, Figure 13–26). In some instances, it may be desirable to frame views by locating vertical objects on either side of the view as well as placing an overhead plane above. Again, decks should be used to take advantage of views on especially steep ground. On dramatically sloped sites,

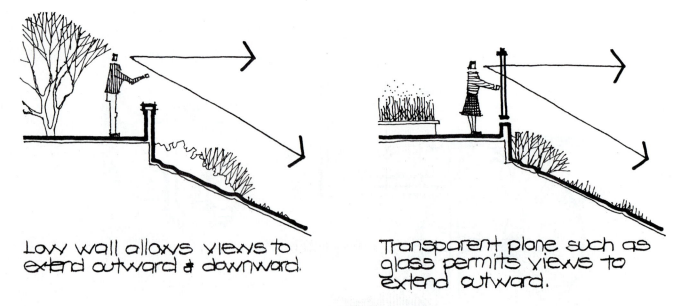

Low wall allows views to extend outward & downward.

Transparent plane such as glass permits views to extend outward.

FIGURE 13–26
The vertical planes should be low or transparent to allow views to extend outward from a space.

decks may be at or higher than surrounding trees, thus providing a panoramic view into the distance.

Control Runoff and Erosion. As indicated previously, care must be taken to drain surface runoff around the house and outdoor use from site areas that are located uphill from them. This is necessary on all sloped sites, but becomes more difficult on steeper sites because of the potential for erosion. Swales, valley-like excavations into the earth, that are cut into the site to catch and direct water should be designed so they visually fit into the topography of the site. Swales that look like gashes due to overly steep side slopes should be avoided. The low side of the site, on the otherhand, may be wetter because of the water that drains to it. This location is usually not good for many outdoor uses and may be best set aside as a planted area or place where native vegetation is allowed to grow. Finally, all slopes that are over 50% also should be left untouched to minimize erosion on a slope site.

THE TOWNHOUSE GARDEN

The townhouse garden is uniquely different from the typical suburban single-family lot. It is normally a relatively small walled or fenced space that is located immediately adjacent to an urban townhouse. Similar outdoor spaces are also associated with many one and two-story condominiums, some first floor apartments, duplexes, and even diminutive back yards of some single-family lots. This small architecturally defined garden requires special consideration.

Special Site Conditions

Space in a Box. For all intents and purposes, the typical townhouse garden site is a rectangular box with an open-top. Walls or fences commonly enclose the "box" on three sides while the residence forms the fourth side (Figure 13–27). The top of the "box" is ordinarily open to the sky and the ground is often a simple, level plane. The wall-like vertical planes and relatively flat ground surface establish a precise, architectural quality that is very much like the interior room of a house. From inside the house, the townhouse garden site appears to be just another room with the same inherent characteristics as other rooms throughout the dwelling.

FIGURE 13-27
The townhouse garden site is like an open-topped box.

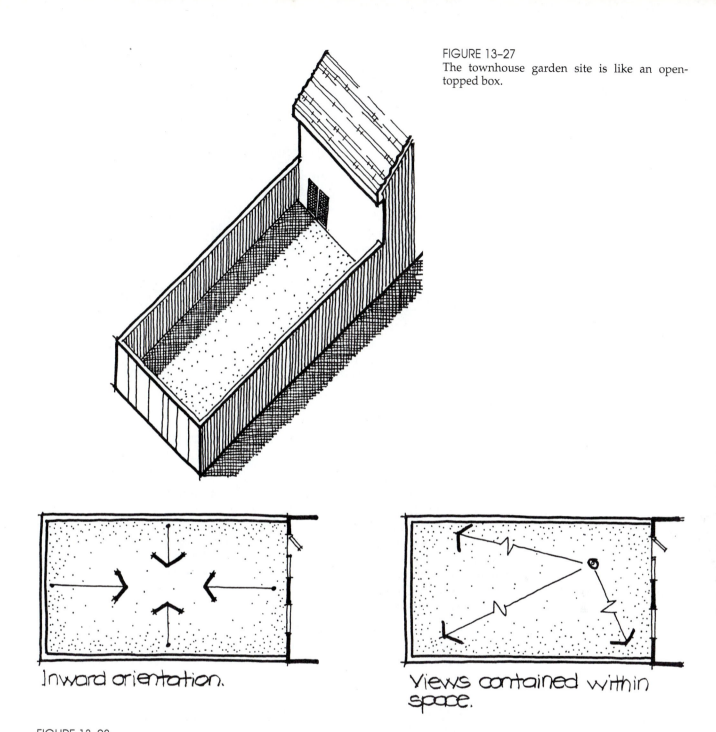

Inward orientation.

Views contained within space.

FIGURE 13-28
The townhouse garden site has an inward orientation with few views extending to areas outside the site.

Limited Views and Interest. The surrounding walls and/or fences of a townhouse site create a space that is inward and self-focused (Figure 13-28). Views and contact with the nearby environment are limited at best because of the separation created by the walls. Thus, views tend to be contained internally on the townhouse site.

Simultaneously, the townhouse garden site has little spatial interest in and of itself. The singular spatial quality is frequently stark and completely without intrigue or appeal. Everything within the space is seen from all vantage points. This is true when standing in space and viewing it from inside the house. One look reveals all.

FIGURE 13–29
Views from inside the house tend to be focused on the back wall of the townhouse garden site.

FIGURE 13–30
Access into and circulation through the townhouse garden site tend to be fixed by door and gate locations.

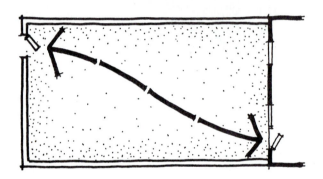

Furthermore, most views into or through the townhouse garden site tend to be directed to the back or outside wall. This is particularly true for views from inside the house (Figure 13–29). Anything placed on or in front of this end wall is readily seen and typically functions as a focal point.

Limited Area. The townhouse garden is relatively modest in size. It may be as small as 100 SF, and usually not any larger than 500 SF. This diminutive size accentuates the qualities already discussed and limits the uses or elements that can be placed within the space. The little townhouse garden site creates a rather intimate and personal setting that often fits the relative scale of the human being. However for some people, this kind of space can also feel claustrophobic. The petite size additionally makes all decisions about its design critical. There is little room to make mistakes or adjust to special site issues.

Fixed Access Points. Fixed entry and exit points frequently determine access into and through the townhouse garden site (Figure 13–30). One point of access is from the house itself. This may be through a standard door or sliding glass doors, which are included on most houses built in the last 40 years. Another point of entry is often from a gate or door in the end wall. This may lead to a street, parking area, garage, or public green space. Access points are located less frequently on

FIGURE 13–31
Views from upper story neighboring windows reduce the privacy in a townhouse garden.

the side walls. The points of entry and exit normally cannot be altered because of the fixed position of existing doors, gates, windows, or off-site conditions.

Lack of Privacy.   Even though solid walls or fences enclose the townhouse garden site, it commonly lacks privacy because nearby neighbors can see into the garden space from upper story windows (Figure 13–31). This creates a "fish-bowl" like experience for people in a townhouse garden site. Whatever happens in this space feels like being on a theater stage to nearby upper-story windows. The limited size of the townhouse garden site makes this experience a difficult one to escape. Some townhouse garden owners simply choose not to use their outdoor space because of this quality. They give up what little outdoor space they have because they do not wish to be "on display."

Design Guidelines

Designing a townhouse garden is like no other residential design project. It requires the designer to think more like an interior designer or architect, but with

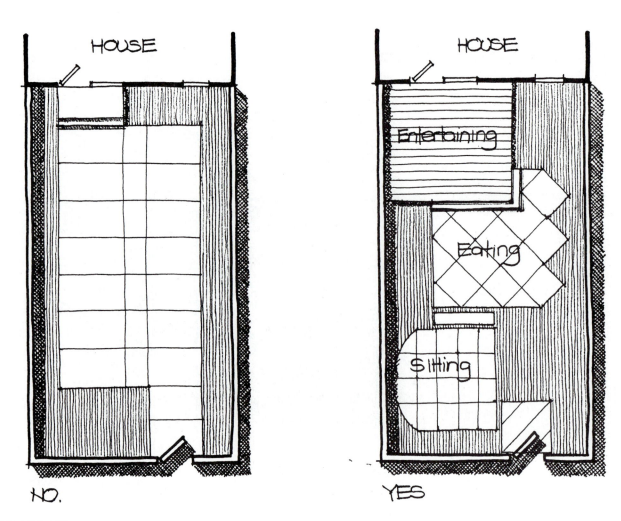

FIGURE 13–32
The townhouse garden should be divided into subspaces for visual interest and to create an illusion of a larger site area.

a different palette of materials. As with the other sites that have special conditions, there are a number of suggestions to guide the designer of a townhouse garden.

Divide into Subspaces. A townhouse garden site should be divided into subspaces to provide spatial and visual interest. This is typically a necessity to relieve the monotony created by the existing simplicity of the box-like space. Spatial subdivision can be created by a combination of techniques. Like other residential design projects, the designer should start by organizing the site into different outdoor uses (Figure 13–32). Functions like entertaining, sitting, eating, reading, potting, etc., that meet the clients' wishes and fit within the garden area should each be given their own space. The individual subspaces may be allowed to overlap or might be separated by a short distance depending on functional and spatial considerations.

At a more detailed scale, individual spaces can be given definition and identity by a number of means. Plant materials, walls/fences, or even low-earth mounding can be used to enclose the spaces in the vertical plane while simultaneously letting the spaces flow from one to another (Figures 13–33 and 13–34). On the ground plane, different pavement materials can be employed to give each space its own character and identity. Grade changes between individual spaces also help to subtly separate spaces. Collectively, these techniques create multiple subspaces within the framework of the perimeter garden walls, just like furniture, room dividers, house plants, rugs, etc., do in interior rooms.

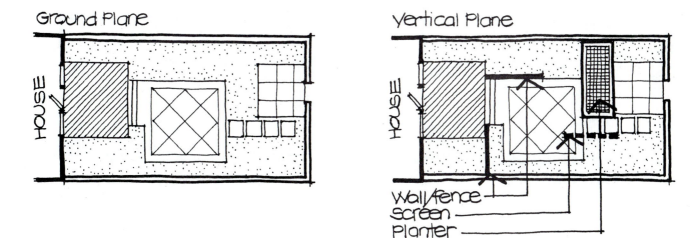

FIGURE 13–33
Different pavement materials and wall/fences can be used to subdivide the spaces in a townhouse garden.

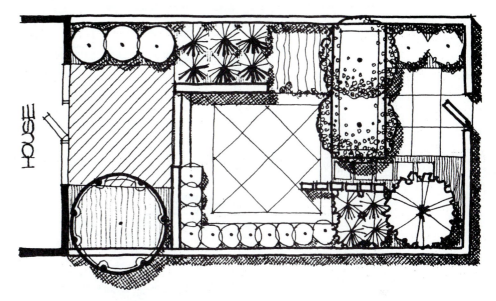

FIGURE 13–34
Plant materials can be coordinated with other vertical planes to define subspaces within the garden.

Increase Perception of Spatial Size. Every effort should be made to increase the perceived size of the townhouse garden site. Subdividing the site into different spaces with overall organization, different pavement patterns, and the careful placement of internal vertical planes as previously suggested is one way to accomplish this. Another technique for giving the illusion that the townhouse garden is larger than its actual dimensions is through forced perspective. One way this can be done is by converging the edges of spaces as they extend farther away from the house (left side of Figure 13–35). This will give a greater sense of depth and distance to the spaces as viewed from inside or near the house. A similar approach is to make the spaces located near the house comparatively large while making other spaces progressively smaller in size the farther away they are located from the house (right side of Figure 13–35). This, too, gives the illusion of greater distance through the garden. Material colors and textures can likewise establish forced perspective by contrasting materials that are coarse textured and/or bright colored near the house with materials that are fine textured and/or light hued at the back end of the garden area (Figure 13–36).

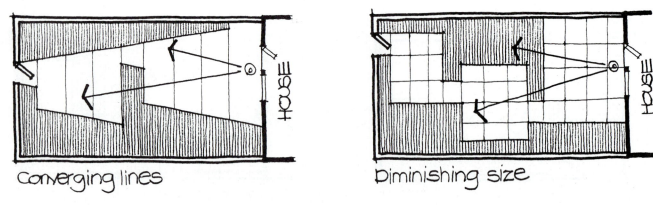

Converging lines

Diminishing size

FIGURE 13–35
Different techniques of forced perspective can give the illusion of a greater distance through a townhouse garden.

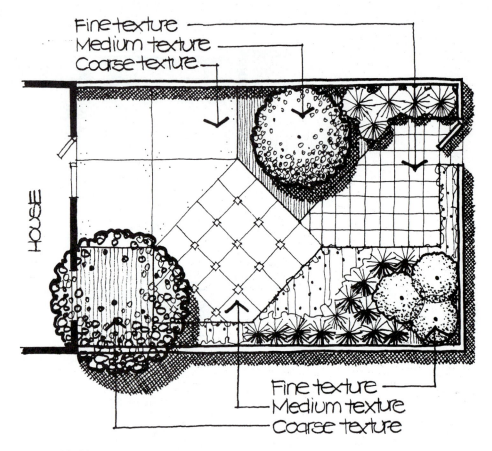

Fine texture
Medium texture
Coarse texture

HOUSE

Fine texture
Medium texture
Coarse texture

FIGURE 13–36
Locating coarse textured materials near the house and fine textured materials away from it can give the townhouse garden a greater sense of depth.

    One other way to increase the overall feeling of size is to force views through and/or around various elements like trees, walls/fences, water features, and sculpture. When a person looks around an object or through a semi-transparent plane like a multi-stemmed tree, the background on the other side appears to be farther away (Figure 13–37). Thus, the designer might carefully place an open-canopied tree or similar architectural element in a location where views from the house pass through the tree. This will make the remainder of the garden area behind the tree look farther away. Additionally, vertical planes can be located to hide selected areas of the

FIGURE 13–37
Forcing views through or around tree trunks or other vertical objects can increase spatial depth.

garden as well. The feeling that a space is larger than it actually is occurs when not everything can be seen at once and when a space is seen disappearing behind an object or vertical plane (Figure 13–38). Concealing the terminus of space or view is a technique common to small gardens in China and Japan.

Provide Overhead Planes. Overhead planes should be strategically located throughout a townhouse garden in coordination with the other elements of the design. This is a desirable objective for all residential sites, but is more critical in a townhouse garden where small size and upper story views from neighbors are frequently a notable problem. A tree canopy, pergola, canvas awning, etc., should be located over frequently used spaces in a townhouse garden to screen upper-story views and provide a ceiling (Figure 13–39). Various types of overhead planes might be used for different subspaces in the garden to reinforce spatial identity as discussed in the previous paragraphs. Overhead planes will also create shade, a factor that is a necessity for townhouse gardens located on the south or west side of a dwelling. Overhead planes should be more open in garden areas on the north or east sides of a house to allow more light into these potentially dark areas. Architectural overhead planes like a pergola should be carefully detailed because of the small scale of the spaces they help to define.

Use Existing Perimeter Walls/Fences. The existing walls or fences that surround a townhouse garden should be utilized for various purposes. Like interior walls, these vertical planes should be taken advantage of to enhance the quality of the different garden spaces (Figure 13–40). One use of perimeter walls/fences is to hang plants. Given the limited size of the townhouse garden, the surrounding walls are good locations for shelves of plants, hanging plants, or even vines that can grow up the wall surface. These techniques are sometimes referred to as "vertical gardens" and are an excellent means of incorporating vegetation in a narrow area. These approaches also soften the surrounding vertical planes and make their presence less obvious.

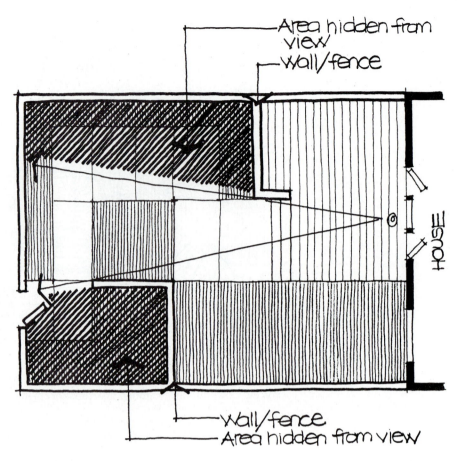

FIGURE 13-38
The perceived size of a townhouse garden can be increased when some areas of the site are hidden from view.

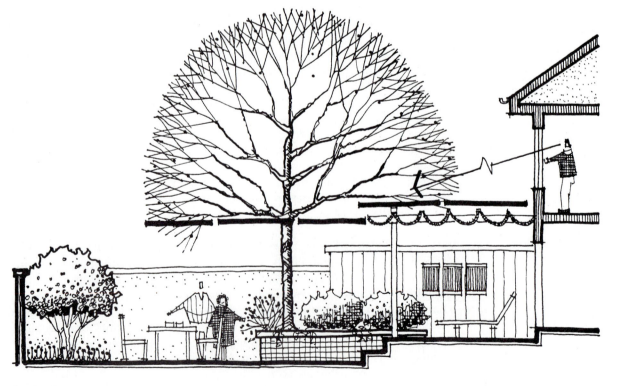

FIGURE 13-39
Overhead planes created by trees or structures should be used to screen views from upper-story windows.

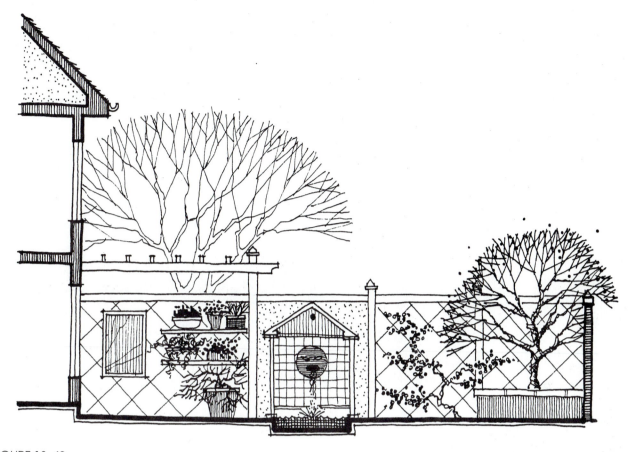

FIGURE 13-40
The visual interest of the surrounding walls in a townhouse garden can be enhanced with shelves of potted plants, mirrors, murals, niches, vines, etc.

Art and sculpture can also be hung on the perimeter walls, again just like in indoor rooms. This provides visual interest and can give relief to an otherwise monotonous wall surface. A similar concept is to place mirrors in selected locations of the exterior walls. Mirrors act very much like windows in interior rooms and reflect a space back onto itself. This too helps to give the illusion of a greater spatial volume.

Index